El Lenguaje de los Chicanos

Regional and Social Characteristics
Used by Mexican Americans

edited by

Eduardo Hernández-Chavez
Andrew D. Cohen
Anthony F. Beltramo

Center for Applied Linguistics

Library of Congress Catalog Card Number: 75-18946
International Standard Book Number: 87281-033-X

Copyright © 1975
by the Center for Applied Linguistics
1611 North Kent Street
Arlington, Virginia 22209

Printed in the U.S.A.

Table of Contents

Introduction

The Chicanos

Speakers of Spanish have inhabited what is now the Southwestern United States since the end of the sixteenth century, following the first explorations of Francisco Coronado in 1540 and Juan de Oñate who, in 1598, established the settlement of San Juan de Nuevo México. Within a few years, further settlements had been established in present day New Mexico, Southern Colorado, Arizona and Texas, and in the latter half of the eighteenth century several presidios and missions were founded in California. By the middle of the nineteenth century there were perhaps 100,000 Spanish speakers in these northern territories. Thus, for 250 years Hispano-Mexican culture and language grew and flourished, and wherever speakers of English, in their inexorable westward movement, came into contact with the Hispanos, they found a rich source of linguistic and cultural innovation.

But after the military conquest of Mexico by the United States, the Mexicans of the Southwest suddenly became a subjugated people, foreigners in their own homeland. Now they and those who were to follow them were relegated to the status of immigrants, even though for the Mexicans who went back and forth across the newly established political border, it was nothing more than an artificial barrier at best, for in the Southwest they encountered a people like themselves and a culture hardly distinguishable from their own.

Thus, with the social, political, and economic dominance of the Anglo, Spanish was no longer the respected language of a proud and independent people, but the despised tongue of a stubborn foreign minority who refused to accept English graciously and the full-fledged Americanism that presumably came with it. Ignoring the long history of Spanish in the Southwest, the Anglo-Americans systematically pursued English-only policies. Only in New Mexico, with the relatively greater proportion of Spanish speakers, were official bilingual policies carried out for a time, but even there as elsewhere in the Southwest, there were strong institutional pressures, especially through the schools, to conform to the English-speaking norm.

Today, there are upwards of six million Spanish speakers in the southwestern states along with millions more attracted to the agricultural and industrial centers of the Midwest and East. Depending upon the region in which they live, the history of their settlement in the United States, local custom and other factors, they call themselves variously *hispanos, mexicanos, latinos, Mexican-Americans,* or *chicanos.* They are a diverse people, for in the past they were isolated from each other by great geographical distances, yet they are unified by language and by a common cultural background. Because of rapid communication and with distance of little import, they have today developed an even stronger bond of unity, recognizing not only their common background, but also the shared conditions of economic exploitation and social and political discrimination. This unity has given favor to the term *chicano,* a hypocoristic form of *mexicano* formerly used solely as an in-group name for their own ethnic group among lower class Mexican and Mexican-American youths. Still shunned by some because of its lower class origins, the term nevertheless symbolizes for increasing numbers of Mexican-Americans the struggle of their people for equality in the United States.

Among other things, equality means for Chicanos the right to keep their language, to develop it, and to use it freely for all forms of communication. One purpose of this book is to stimulate an interest in the serious study of the language used by Spanish speaking people in the United States. In order to develop its use through the institutions which most closely touch the Chicano—the home, the school, the church, the government—and thereby to encourage its maintenance as a living, functioning mode of communication, we need very much to understand what that language is, its characteristics and its varieties, and how it is used by the people in their everyday interaction. Thus it is appropriate that the term *chicano* should be used in our title, for it expresses the striving for linguistic equality and the role that language plays as a unifying force among Chicanos.

Despite their numerical importance and the profound influence that Chicanos have had on cultural, economic, and political life in the Southwest, research on their language is relatively scant. It has frequently taken the form of master's theses or doctoral dissertations (usually by Anglos) whose results are seen by few scholars and by even fewer of the people that the studies are about. Articles on the subject often appear in obscure or not easily accessible publications. This situation has been one of our primary motives for compiling this anthology—to bring to the attention of Chicanos who have an interest in their language as well as to that of linguists, a representative sample of the work already done in the various areas relating to Chicano speech and to encourage additional work in these and other areas.

Spanish in the Southwest

By the mid-nineteenth century, significant differences had developed in the Spanish spoken in the various regions of the Southwest. There were vast distances, measured in weeks and months of travel, between California, New Mexico, and Texas or between these areas and the political and cultural capitals of Mexico. Even in the Spanish and Mexican period, the Spanish speakers of the north were isolated from each other and from the Mexican cultural centers. Especially in northern New Mexico, which has the longest history of continuous settlement, the language shows important differences from surrounding dialects of the Southwest and of northern Mexico. Daniel Cárdenas, in his brief but informative survey of Spanish in the Southwest ("Mexican Spanish"), notes close links to the Spanish of Mexico and singles out grammatical and lexical features which define four dialect zones. Conforming roughly to state boundaries, these are Texas, New Mexico-Southern Colorado, Arizona, and California. The greatest amount of homogeneity among these dialects is in the regions adjacent to the border because of the constant contact with the speech of northern Mexico.

But even in the areas that diverge the most from the Mexican norms, it is found that few of the dialectal features are unique. Most are also encountered in other Spanish speaking regions throughout the hemisphere and in Spain. What serves to distinguish the dialects are the proportions and combinations in which these features are found.

This point is easily demonstrated in the phonology of southwestern Spanish. Most of the variations from the *standard* encountered here are also found in other Spanish speaking areas.[1] Thus Anita Post ("Some Aspects of Arizona Spanish") cites several general differences from the standard language such as the collapsing of two adjacent vowels into a single syllable, accompanied in certain cases by a shift in stress, e.g. *maiz* and *cuete* for standard *maíz* and *cohete;* the pronunciation of *f* as *j* as in *jué;* and the retention of an 'archaic' *j* as in *jalar* or the nearly universal shift of *ll* to *y* and *z* to *s*.[2] All of these phonological divergencies are to be found in other areas though perhaps not all together. Donald M. Lance ("Dialectal and Nonstandard Forms in Texas Spanish") mentions some of these same features and in addition observes the loss of *ll* that is next to an *i* or an *e* and the aspiration or weakening of *s* to *h* not only in syllable final position but also between vowels as in *nohotroh*. In California, Yolanda Lastra ("El habla y la educación de los niños de origen mexicano en Los Angeles") noticed a phenomenon similar to Lance's "loss of *ll*." But her data show a loss of consonant quality in the *ll* rather than a complete loss. She also finds that *ch* is pronounced like English *sh* and *b* and *v* like English *v*.[3] She interprets this, properly in our view, as a dialectal feature and not as a result of English interference. Robert N. Phillips, Jr. ("Variation in Los Angeles Spanish Phonology") also studies the question of *b* and *v,* finding a complex and not entirely predictable variation among [b], the bilabial fricative [β], and [v]. Unlike Lastra, however, he attributes the variation to the influence of English *v* and to interference from the spelling conventions (see note 1). Phillips also notes a great deal of variation in the *r* sounds, observing besides standard *r* and *rr,* an English-like *r,* a fricative *r,* and several voiceless varieties.[4]

As with phonology, the grammatical characteristics which set the Southwestern dialects off from other dialects of Spanish are not unique to the region. It is in the verb forms that most differences are noted. Thus Jacob Ornstein ("The Archaic and the Modern in the Spanish of New Mexico") reports the use of *-ates* for *-aste,* the replacement of *-mos* by *-nos* in forms with antepenultimate stress such as *habláranos,* and the regularized stress placement in the present subjunctive, giving *véanos* instead of standard *veamos*. Ornstein offers no explanation for these, but Lance, who reports the same forms in Texas, cites authorities who have traced their development in earlier stages in the language. An important syntactic difference from the modern standard is also noted by Lance. This is the use of the imperfect verb forms in certain constructions in which the standard uses either the past subjunctive or the conditional inflections, resulting in sentences like *Yo les daba (daría) el dinero pa' ver si iban (se irían)* (I would give them the money to see if they'd go). Lance also encountered a number of other differences, but an important conclusion that we can draw is that the grammatical divergencies of Texas Spanish from standard Spanish are few indeed and are not "corruptions" of the language but have their roots in the normal development of earlier periods.

The large number of non-standard lexical items is perhaps the most noticeable feature which distinguishes the Southwestern dialects. Because of the geographical, social, and cultural isolation of those regions, we might expect that many of the forms used would be words imported by the early settlers but no longer in current use in the standard language.

Aurelio M. Espinosa, Jr. ("Problemas lexicográficos del español del sudoeste") shows this to be the case, and divides these words into archaisms, i.e., Castilian words which have fallen into disuse elsewhere, and regionalisms, words with a probable origin in non-Castilian Spanish dialects brought by the *conquistadores*. Several researchers have reported the strongly archaic character of the Spanish of the entire Southwest but especially of the New Mexico-Colorado region. Ornstein, too, notes considerable differences between northern and southern New Mexico, especially in vocabulary, and for this reason believes that the southern part of the State should be considered a dialect area apart, belonging more properly to "border Spanish."

Another important source of lexical difference in the Southwestern dialects is innovation internal to Spanish. In his contribution to this volume, Juan B. Rael ("Associative Interference in New Mexican Spanish") discusses these developments, which he labels "associative interference" and explains how they have operated in various ways to bring profound changes to the vocabulary of New Mexico. His treatment distinguishes two main processes: BLENDING (a new word arising from a fusion of two words formally similar, e.g. *plázamo* 'congratulations,' from *pláceme* plus *pésamo*) and ANALOGY (an existing word changes under the influence of an existing morphological pattern, e.g. *impedimiento* < *impedimento* by analogy with words ending in *-miento*). The author abundantly illustrates these and other phenomena with over 150 words in current use.

The English Influence

Perhaps the most important factor of all that distinguishes the Southwest from Spanish speaking regions outside the United States and Puerto Rico is the influence of English, especially on the lexicon. While the other lexical divergencies from the standard—archaisms, regionalisms, analogical formations, and the like—find their counterparts in other areas within the Spanish speaking world, most of the anglicisms in the Southwest are unique to this region. For, while anglicisms have entered Spanish wherever it is spoken, outside the United States these usually enter via the printed word. But here, through constant and intense interaction between the two language groups and, probably more importantly, through the mediation of bilingual Chicanos, English words are taken over into Spanish largely through the spoken medium. Thus, their form and their flavor is distinctively *pocho*. (This term, originally applied disdainfully by Mexicans to the speech, and by extension to the speakers, of a "cut-off" or mutilated Spanish, presumably because of the very noticeable anglicisms which characterized it, is now used unapologetically by Chicanos themselves to refer to their own dialects of Spanish and sometimes to the rapid alternation of English and Spanish known as code switching.)

The importance of the influence of English on the Spanish of Chicanos and on their speech in general is underscored by the fact that scarcely any of the articles in this collection fails to make mention of this phenomenon in one way or another. It is in the lexicon especially that far-reaching changes have taken place. In his pioneering and still unsurpassed *Studies in New Mexican Spanish*,[5] Aurelio M. Espinosa (Sr.) devotes a large part of his analysis to the English elements. His article entitled "Speech Mixture in New Mexico: The Influence of the English Language on New Mexican Spanish," which we reproduce in this collection, summarizes a very small part of his work. In it he explains how important are the effects of American commercial and political institutions, pointing out that the compulsory introduction of English into the schools has caused the importation of great numbers of English words into the Spanish lexicon. Janet Sawyer ("Spanish-English Bilingualism in San Antonio, Texas") sees the heavy influx of anglicisms into Spanish without a corresponding use of Spanish loans in English as the result of the relative prestige of the two languages in the eyes of Chicanos. Espinosa, on the other hand, views the situation as a necessary consequence of the political and economic dominance of the Anglos and of the imposition of their institutions upon the Hispanos. He notes a racial and cultural pride which holds tenaciously to the highly valued ancestral tongue in spite of the immense counter pressures. As Ornstein points out, New Mexicans use anglicisms purely and simply because of their "more forceful presence," though he deplores what he considers the wholesale incursion of English influence which, he says, rather than enriching the language, impoverishes it.

He is joined in his concern by the Spanish language media, teachers, and the clergy who, along with Jerónimo Mallo, perceive the influence of English as a barbaric invasion on the Spanish language.[6] There is no evidence, however, that these puristic attitudes prevail among the great majority of Chicanos. To the contrary, the regular use of anglicized forms in Spanish in a wide variety of speech situations would appear to indicate a fairly general acceptance of them.

To be sure, Chicanos are amply aware of the influence of English in their Spanish, but how this awareness is reflected in their actual use of language is very much an open question. Anthony F. Beltramo and Antonio de Porcel in their article "Awareness of English Borrowing in San Jose Spanish" look at this aspect of attitudes toward language and find consistent agreement among Chicanos on the kinds of forms that are considered to have English influence. Remarkably, differences among Chicanos relating to such factors as age, sex, length of residence in San Jose, or even relative usage of the two languages produced almost no variation in their level of awareness of borrowing from English. Yet different types of loans, e.g. words imported merely by the substitution of Spanish sounds for English sounds or words which add Spanish grammatical elements to English words, etc., are seen as being either closer to English or closer to Spanish depending upon the manner of their adaptation into Spanish.

By what processes are words from English incorporated into Spanish? Espinosa, Jr., in his brief discussion of the question, identifies four different types of loans: translation, phonetic adaptation, adaptation with the addition of native morphological elements, and loans which are imported intact. In the first type he includes forms like *abanico eléctrico* 'electric fan' and *escuela alta* 'high school'; *suera* 'sweater' and *lonchi* 'lunch' are adapted phonetically while *baquiada* 'a backing up' and *tofudo* 'tough guy' add morphological elements;

intact importations are *balún* 'balloon,' *champión* 'champion' and *shain* 'shine.'
It is not clear how these latter words differ from forms like *suera* or even *lonchi*
since they all involve adaptation of English sounds to the phonetics of Spanish.
J. Donald Bowen, in a section of his dissertation which is published here as
"Adaptation of English Borrowing," provides several examples of these processes
and adds a category of partially adapted forms which he divides into two types:
those which form new syllable structure patterns such as *scul* 'school' with an
initial *sc* which is not permitted in the standard and those which introduce
non-Spanish sounds as when *armi* is pronounced with an English *r*. Besides the
entry of English loans, Bowen also notes the influence of English on words of
Spanish origin. Words which are both formally and semantically similar to
English forms but which were obsolescent in Spanish have gained new life due to
the existence of the English counterparts. Thus *acre* and *tanque* are common
terms in New Mexico but have a limited extension in the standard language.
Further, semantically similar words may be extended or shifted in meaning to
conform to the English usage, e.g. *atender* 'attend' (std. 'pay attention to') or
cámara 'camera' (std. 'chamber'). In this regard, Lance cautions that it is not
easy to distinguish between a semantic loan and the natural semantic
generalization internal to a language due to cultural or technological developments.

The phonological adaptation of loans requires that speakers identify sounds
and sound sequences in the source language with analogous ones in the recipient
language. These interlingual correspondences are highly regular, and the phonetic
units, once transferred, are integrated into the phonology of the receiving
system. Thus, for example, English *r* is adapted in Spanish either to *rr* or to *r*
according to the position in which it occurs within the word. English *b*, *d*, and *g*
when they are adapted to Spanish show the same phonetic variation and
distribution as the corresponding sounds in native words.[7]

Problems arise with certain vocalic sounds which appear to show irregular
modes of adaptation such as English *-er* in final position which sometimes appears
as *-or* and sometimes as *-a* in Spanish. But *-or* can usually be explained on the
basis of the identification of meaningful elements rather than as phonetic
transfer. Both English *-er* and Spanish *-or* have the meaning 'one who performs
an action.' Similarly the transfer of English *sh* sometimes to Spanish *ch* and
sometimes to *s* is explained by the identification of an English suffix with its
Spanish counterpart, e.g., *-tion: -ción* or *-tial: -cial*.

Occasionally, however, English *sh* appears in Spanish as *sh* in words where *ch*
would be expected. Such forms illustrate a tendency in some speakers toward
incomplete adaptation of English loans, i.e. the retention, in borrowings, of
certain non-Spanish sounds or sound sequences.[8] English *sh, j, z, th,* r, among
the consonants and the *a* vowels of *sofa* and *hat* ([ə] and [æ]) are particularly
susceptible to retention in this way when borrowed into Spanish. Both Bowen
and Phillips cite several words of this kind which either retain non-Spanish
combinations of consonants, e.g. *futol, escarf,* or which use unadapted English
sounds as in [fəɹlo] (furlough), [dæði] (daddy). Examples such as these raise a
question as to whether occurrences of these forms are indeed "borrowings" into
Spanish which are incompletely adapted or whether they are imperfect attempts
to reproduce an English word which is still felt by the speaker to be English. The

distinction is not trivial. This phenomenon – the switching over momentarily to another language – is quite common among bilinguals and a nearly monolingual Spanish speaker with an unperfected knowledge of English, in attempting to perform a switch, may very well approximate the pronunciation of some sounds better than that of others. In such a case the interference would be due to the speaker's knowledge of Spanish rather than the other way around. Much depends on the relative bilinguality of the speaker and his intention with regard to the item in question as well as to factors of performance.

Of course, this is not to say that none of such words are examples of incompletely adapted loans. Rather, we merely wish to insert a cautionary note that their interpretation is not at all a straightforward matter. Putative borrowings cannot be categorized *in vacuo*. Not only must we take into account the linguistic characteristics of the speaker, but also the psychological and social conditions under which the forms are produced. Thus, a form such as *shaine* (pronounced [šáine] from English *shine*) may be produced as an English loan in Spanish by an English-dominant speaker, in which case we should consider the *sh* as resulting from his knowledge of English, i.e. as interference–the transfer of elements from one language to another as a result of the speaker's knowledge of the first language. The *sh* cannot be considered interference resulting from knowledge of English, but rather as a diffused form, the product of the learning of a new distinction in Spanish, at least in English loans. But if in producing *shaine*, the Spanish speaker thinks he is pronouncing an English word, i.e. if he attempts a switch, the *sh* needs to be interpreted as learning of a different sort. Now, the *sh* has been learned as an English distinction and has no necessary impact on Spanish whereas in the previous instance the influence was direct.

The difficulties occasioned by the concept of interference are just as great in the area of syntax. The interpretation of even such obvious calques as *fueron puestos libres*, 'they were set free' or *consiste de*, 'it consists of' listed by Espinosa (Sr.) is not entirely a simple matter. The notion that the bilingual who uses constructions such as these is "thinking in English" but using Spanish words, a notion expressed both by Espinosa and Lance, implies that the English grammatical structure comes actively into play. There is no doubt that the constructions ultimately owe their form to the rules of English. The question is how much knowledge of English syntax is needed to produce them. A case could certainly be made for the interpretation of these constructions, or even of ones like *trabajo de pinturas*, 'paint job' or *murió en comite*, 'it died in committee,' reported by Ornstein, as lexical borrowings, i.e. complex lexico-semantic units imported *in toto* with no necessary knowledge of English grammar and without repercussions on the receiving grammatical system. As Lance points out, "English has served mainly as the source for lexical borrowing. In only a few instances . . . was clear evidence found of English [syntactic] interference."

Nonetheless, several examples are provided by Espinosa, Lance, and Yolanda Lastra which do suggest grammatical transfer. Lastra reports forms like *mi chiquito hermano* and *mi tío's cama* in the speech of Chicano children. Presumably these are sporadic errors of performance due to the imposition of the set of rules from one language upon the production of the other. Clearly, this is a case of interference. In constructions like *fue para atrás* 'he went back,' a motion verb plus an adverbial phrase is modeled on a standard Spanish

xii   *Introduction*

construction as in *corrió para (hacia) atrás* 'he ran toward the rear.' But influenced by the meaning 'to the point of origin' of English *back,* the Spanish construction extends its meaning to overlap with the directional verb *volvió.* The regular correspondence between English modifier-plus-head and Spanish noun-plus-prepositional phrase in a pair like *número de teléfono: telephone number* is generalized to constructions like *leche de bote* 'canned milk' (standard *leche embotada*) or *máquina de lavar* 'washing machine' (standard *lavadora*). Thus one Spanish construction comes to replace a variety of other constructions under the influence of English. But as distinct from *mi chiquito hermano,* these do not involve performance errors. For the speaker they represent part of the rule structure of Spanish. They are not produced by English rules nor even as a direct result of knowledge of the English rules. Monolingual children learn these from preceding generations of speakers directly as Spanish constructions, and not as foreign forms. Therefore, it would be inaccurate to characterize these constructions as involving interference except in a historical sense. The English influence has left its mark, but it no longer operates. Thus we can say that it has been *integrated* into the speech of the user. The fact, obviously of great importance, that these constructions have been generalized by virtually the entire Chicano community has little bearing on these definitions.

The English of Chicanos

The influence of Spanish upon the English that Chicanos speak poses similar conceptual problems. For the most part, divergencies from standard English are the result of incomplete learning even in the case of those speakers whose English is no longer changing. For such speakers, their English grammars share many rules with their Spanish, especially as regards phonology and the semantics of the lexicon, but also to some extent in syntax. Janet Sawyer points out in her article that the linguistic model is the Anglo community, and succeeding generations of Chicanos approximate that norm in proportion to their level of acculturation. However, she also notes that there are "social isoglosses" between the two communities and that, in the lexicon at least, there are dialectal differences in the English of the two groups. This would indicate that, while some social assimilation does occur, it is not necessarily a fully accepted goal. If this is so, we might reasonably expect that differences in phonology and syntax could become relatively stabilized. This would result in a Spanish-influenced dialect of English which children learn directly and which is passed on to succeeding generations. Aside from Sawyer's work, little has been done in this important area. Lastra notes some phonetic interference and also provides some interesting examples of syntactic divergencies. Some of these may be attributable to Spanish influence, but others, as Lastra notes, coincide with the non-standard speech of monolinguals. Still others may be due to normal language development.

Code Switching

As mentioned earlier, a very common phenomenon among Spanish-English bilinguals is what has come to be known as code switching. There have been few clear statements about the nature of this phenomenon and its relationship to interference. Uriel Weinrich believed that the ideal bilingual controlled his choice of language rigidly, switching according to interlocutor and topic but "certainly not within a single sentence."[9] Alternating rapidly between the languages is seen as a lack of ability to hold close to the ideal pattern. Haugen excludes switching from his definition of interference and sees it as the first stage in linguistic diffusion (the second stage being interference and the third stage, integration).[10] The senior Espinosa also considers switching to be an important factor in the introduction of words into Spanish. He calls the phenomenon speech mixture and views it as a random intermingling of Spanish and English words and phrases. Lance's second article ("Spanigh-English Code Switching") demonstrates that it is not entirely random, but that perhaps certain kinds of lexical items are more susceptible to switching than others. Nor is the lack of knowledge of words in one of the languages the principal reason for switching. Lance found that the speakers knew the appropriate words in both languages. Their use on different occasions, he says, may have stylistic implications. John Gumperz and Eduardo Hernández ("Cognitive Aspects of Bilingual Communication") expand on this notion, seeing a very direct functional similarity between code switching on the one hand and style switching within a single language on the other. Their work indicates that very subtle social and psychological factors operate in code switching where the interlocutor and situation are held constant.

Lance suggests that, because of the variety of possible phrasal switches, there may be no syntatic restriction on switching. But Gumperz and Hernández found that in fact certain grammatical constraints do operate. For example, adverbial constructions may be switched: *Vamos ('We will go') next week,* but not as interrogatives: **When vamos?* Similarly, a switch may occur at a noun phrase but only after a determiner. Thus, *Se lo di a mi ('I gave it to my') grandfather* is grammatical but **Se lo di a my grandfather* is not. In addition, switching may be occasioned by grammatical structure. In *Me torcieron por una modida ('They busted me for an action') that I didn't know anything about,* the Spanish *de la cual* 'about which' is an unusual construction in Chicano Spanish and much too formal a structure for colloquial usage. The English construction neatly fills the gap, but this requires a switch since there is no possibility in Spanish grammar of shifting a preposition to final position in the sentence.[11] The extent of these kinds of constraints is not known, but this is certainly a promising area for investigation. If there is a sociolinguistic grammar of switching, as some of the work in this area appears to indicate, then switching is not a breakdown in the ability to maintain the languages apart but rather a complex ability commanded by some bilinguals which reflects the intricate socio-cultural situation of language contact.

The Use of Language

That the sociolinguistic situation is not a simple one is evidenced by George C. Barker's goundbreaking study on the Spanish and English of Tucson, Arizona ("Social Functions of Language in a Mexican-American Community"). Long before sociolinguistics was considered a worthy discipline, Barker demonstrated the intimate interplay between the linguistic and non-linguistic behavior of a speech community. While Barker was certainly not the first to write in this area, his work provided new and valuable insights into the functioning of language in

Mexican-American communities. He identified four fields of personal relations which were correlated with language use. These were family, informal, formal, and Anglo-Mexican relations, with Spanish used at one end of the scale and English at the other. The Mexican-American community itself is not homogeneous, and the varieties that each individual speaks take on different values according to the varying social experience of the individual. Some bilinguals, who are marginal to both the Chicano and Anglo groups, may favor standard Spanish; others, whose activities and interests center around barrio life, prefer the Arizona dialect and disdain the use of English in their intra-group contacts. Still others, seeking mobility Anglo contacts, give a greater importance to English.

In another Tucson study, a part of which is also included in this volume ("Pachuco: An American-Spanish Argot and Its Social Functions in Tucson, Arizona") Barker studies the social functions of *caló*, the argot of lower class Chicano youths. He describes the argot and its speakers and concludes that its basic function is to serve as a secret language of a youthful segment of the population that is disaffected from both Mexican-American and Anglo societies. It also functions as a symbol of sophistication among these youths.

No study of the language of Chicanos can be complete without taking *caló* into account, for its influence has reached to all levels of the language. Most studies of this speech form look at the language of the Pachucos as a curiosity and as the speech of delinquents and criminals (even Barker speaks about delinquents). *Caló* is frequently seen as a form of speech that represents a disaffection from "law-abiding society" and which is used as a secret code whose function it is to express distance from other groups. But *caló* is much more than that. Used by young people throughout the Southwest as an in-group variety, it represents the values of intimacy, comradeship and ethnicity, expressing the *carnalismo* of its users. In modern times it also symbolizes *chicanismo*, the struggle for social justice of the Chicano movement.

As can be seen from the foregoing, the language situation in Chicano speech communities is not a simple one. A popular conception is that Chicanos are all bilingual; their Spanish is that of Mexicans and they speak English with an accent. But the studies that have been done on Spanish-English bilingualism in the Southwest, some of the most important of which we present in this volume, show not only a considerable regional diversity in the use of Spanish but also a range of variation in the use of both languages that mirrors the multidimensional social dynamics of Chicano communities. Fernando Peñalosa's paper ("Chicano Multilingualism and Multiglossia") explains how Chicanos have access to a number of different codes and searches through current sociolinguistic theory for approaches to studying the extent and nature of Chicano bilingualism. It suggests that for research as well as for schooling purposes, *pocho*, which the author terms "pochismos," ought to be recognized as an important language variety.

Language and Education

In the same vein as Peñalosa, Ernest García ("Chicano Spanish Dialects and Education") is concerned by the attitudes toward the Spanish of Chicanos on the part of educators who often consider *pocho* as "so substandard that they sometimes refer to children who speak it as alingual." His concern motivates him to show that this variety differs only in unimportant respects from other dialects of Spanish and to appeal for the acceptance of the Chicano child's home dialect. The concern with the effects of schooling and the attitudes of educators is voiced by several of the contributors to this volume. The educational systems in the Southwest, in their zeal to Americanize what they consider an alien population, have done irreparable harm to generations of schoolchildren. The failure to utilize Spanish as the language of instruction, not to mention the punishment meted out for the use of Spanish in school, ignores a valuable resource for the education of children. It is ironic that the educational establishment expends immense effort and amounts of money to teach monolingual Americans a second language "in the national interest" yet at the same time attempts to eradicate the mother tongue of non-English speaking schoolchildren. Such policies are based in part on the notions that bilingualism has deleterious effects upon verbal intelligence, emotional adjustment and even upon patriotism, and the misconception that knowledge and continued use of Spanish inhibit the learning of English, unmindful of the fact that stable and fully functioning bilingualism exists in the Southwest and is widespread throughout the world. Even in some of the more enlightened school districts which use Spanish-medium teaching in the early grades (usually, however, as a bridge to English), the instruction is either at much too elementary a level or uses a form of the language unfamiliar to the children. The former, because the teachers consider their pupils linguistically deprived; the latter, because they lack knowledge of the local form of the language. Practically no work has been done on the acquisition of Spanish in children which would yield information about the normal linguistic development for different ages. Such information would be a boon to curriculum writers and educators of Spanish speaking children. While it was not meant primarily as a guide for teachers, Gustavo González' study of the acquisition of Spanish grammar in young children begins to provide this kind of information. In the portion presented here ("The Acquisition of Grammatical Structures by Mexican-American Children") which is a summary of his doctoral dissertation, González describes the development of some of the more important syntactic rules and morphological patterns of children between the ages of two and five years. Future investigation of this sort as well as lexical and phonological studies are necessary to obtain a fuller picture of the level of Spanish achieved by children of varying ages.

Language Maintenance

One of the important effects of school policies negative to Spanish has been the rapid anglicization of Chicano schoolchildren, with a concomitant draining away of ability to use their mother tongue for all but very restricted purposes. Though Spanish is not in imminent danger of being lost in the Southwest, its use is nevertheless being eroded, and one of the agents of this erosion is the educational system. As Andrew D. Cohen notes ("Assessing Language Maintenance in Spanish Speaking Communities in the Southwest"), "until recently, the schools could claim little or no role in Spanish language maintenance." He goes on to say that bilingual education programs have the potential, as yet unrealized, of contributing positively to the maintenance of Spanish as a viable and functioning language alongside English. Cohen reviews major concerns currently being researched, many of which have broader meaning for the understanding of cultural change and bilingual schooling.

Research Needs

By its very size and rate of growth, the Chicano population in the United States draws attention to itself from many fields, among them linguistics which therein finds a great need for investigation in many areas relating to language. Even in the area of descriptions of Southwest Spanish, in which some of the most important of existing studies have been made, additional investigation is needed. For instance, what features of New Mexican, Texan or Californian Spanish are held in common and which of these features are innovations or have antecedents in Mexican or Peninsular Spanish? The same questions must be asked about the English of Chicanos. The one or two studies of this aspect of Chicano speech suggest that it does not differ from Anglo English except for the problem of direct Spanish interference which will automatically disappear as succeeding generations learn English natively. But if there exist discernible Chicano speech communities, it would be but a reasonable expectation to find that they maintain speech varieties that are also distinctive.

Thus, in the crucial yet virtually uncharted area of language use among Chicanos, we need to know much more about where and when the different varieties of Spanish and English are used and about the social determinants of code selection. What are the relationships between the local dialects of English and Spanish and the standard languages? Is *caló* the primary variety of any group of people or is its use superimposed upon that of the local dialect? Barker's studies opened the door to investigation of these questions, but there exists a very serious need to bring up to date, expand, and elaborate his work. Tucson of the 1940's is not Tucson of the 1970's, and much less is it modern day California or Texas.

Currently in linguistics there is great interest in child language research and in the insights that this study provides for understanding how human beings organize language. But the development of Spanish in children is practically unexplored as is the acquisition of bilingualism. The latter study especially has great potential for casting new light on language learning processes and for understanding the psychological mechanisms involved in the separation and/or merger of two linguistic systems. In a more practical way, such studies can help us to understand the effects of early bilingual acquisition which is important information for those who are engaged in the planning of language education programs of various sorts. Also important in this regard is information about the effects of different kinds of bilingual learning conditions.

Some hispanophiles are now beginning to sound the death knell for Spanish in the Southwest. Though we are confident that fears of the imminent disappearance of the language are premature, there is nevertheless room for concern. The maintenance of a language as a viable and vital form of communication ultimately rests on cultural factors and the social dynamics of the given speech community, but intelligent and informed planning efforts can have important effects. So we not only need to know about the linguistic and sociolinguistic characteristics of the Chicano speech community, we need also to know about the language policies of the institutions which most affect that community – the schools, the church, the media, government, commercial institutions. What are their policies and how do they affect the use of language by Chicanos? What are the attitudes of Chicanos themselves toward their various speech varieties? The answers to these and other questions will give Chicanos a strong base from which to formulate meaningful and effective language policies.

A final note. Most of the research about Chicanos in sociology, anthropology, linguistics, education, etc. has been done by Anglos. There are many reasons for this, not the least of which is the fact that the educational system has historically taken Chicanos little into account. Consequently, there have been few Chicano scholars, though this appears to be changing. There is the strong feeling among Chicanos, not entirely unjustified, that much of the research in their communities has not been for the benefit of the communities themselves. It has benefited scholars who have used the results of studies in their publications or, less unkindly, it has been of general benefit to human knowledge. Even so, a flaw in much of the work is a profound lack of understanding on the part of researchers of the people and of their culture. Not all studies suffer these defects, to be sure, and it is our hope that this book will contribute to such an understanding. We also hope that more Chicano scholars will be stimulated to work in areas relating to Chicano speech, thus adding to our knowledge of this field and, inevitably, benefitting the Chicano community itself.

E.H-Ch.
A.D.C.
A.F.B.
June 1975

Notes

[1] For convenience, *standard* is used here in the traditional sense, i.e. accepted by the Real Academia. However, it must be pointed out that there is no monolithic, universally recognized Standard Spanish. Educated speakers in every Spanish-speaking country use forms peculiar to their region, and the importation of Anglicisms into Spanish is very widespread despite the denunciations of purists. Thus, by "variations" or "divergencies" we in no way imply that a particular form is substandard or unacceptable but merely that it differs from the rigid norms of the Academia.

[2] We use the Spanish orthographic conventions for these examples. Stress is unmarked on the penultimate syllable if the word ends in a vowel or *n* or *s*, and on a final syllable if the word ends in a consonant. An unstressed high vowel adjacent to another vowel is phonetically a semivowel; so, *cuete* is [kwéte]. $z = [\emptyset]$, $ll = [\lambda]$, $j = [x]$.

The [x] in *jalar* is archaic in the sense that it derives from an earlier [h] (*halar* < Fr. *haler*, probably < Germanic *halôn*) which was lost during the XVI century in the standard language but was retained in several regional dialects. This [h] fell together with the modern [x] < [š]. Certain words with [h] from a Latin *F* developed in the same way: [xumo] < [humo] < FUMU [xondo] < [hondo] < FUNDU.

[3] The distinction between *b* and *v* in the standard is purely orthographic. [b] occurs as an utterance initially and after a nasal, otherwise only [β] occurs; [v] does not occur.

[4] The assibilated *r* is widespread throughout Spanish America and Spain in colloquial speech. Phillips describes the sound as a voiced alveolar groove fricative, akin to English [ž], but perhaps "some slight retroflexion of the dorsum." Tomás Navarro (Manual de Pronunciación Española, Madrid, 1950), a keen observer of Spanish pronunciation, likens it to a retracted [ð], a slit fricative. Our own observations show that it is indeed an alveolar slit fricative with the constriction produced forward of the tongue blade and just back of the apex. For the English speaker it produces the impression of an *r*-colored [z] or [s].

[5] *Revue de dialectologie romane*, Part 1: Phonology, 57-239; 269-300. Part 2: Morphology, 241-256; 257-286; 142-172. Part 3: The English Elements, 241-317, 1909-1915.

[6] Mallo, Jerónimo, "La invasion de anglicismos en la lengua española de América," Cuadernos Americanos 18:4.115-23, 1959.

[7] See footnote 2. However, both [b] and [β] vary with [v] under conditions not entirely understood. See Phillips' discussion on p. (1) ff.

[8] The interpretation of [č] and [š] in Chicano speech is a particularly thorny problem. /č/ is realized in some dialects of Spanish as [š], especially in front vowel environments. In the case of a speaker from such a dialect, English /č/ reproduced in a loan as Spanish [š] would represent an adaptation to the Spanish sound. For the same person speaking English, the substitution of [š] for [č] would need to be considered interference from Spanish. Among many speakers of Mexican and U.S. Spanish, [š] is used in some Náhuatl loans and has come to represent at least a marginal phoneme in Spanish, thus facilitating the borrowing of the English distinction. Another source of potential difficulty is the phonetic difference between the Spanish palatal affricate and the English alveo-palatal aspirated affricate. The perception of these is quite different and may help to account for the apparently random or even contrary production of [č] and [š] in the English of many Chicanos. In any given instance of presumed interference, any or several of these factors may be operating.

[9] Weinreich, Uriel. *Languages in contact, findings and problems*, Mouton, The Hague, 1953, p. 73.

[10] Haugen, Einar. Bilingualism in the Americas: a bibliography and research guide, American Dialect Society, 1956, p. 40.

[11] These examples are not drawn from Gumperz and Hernández, but are from unpublished data collected by the authors.

Mexican Spanish

Daniel N. Cardenas

Since the Spanish of speakers of Mexican extraction is the most widely spoken of these four varieties of Spanish [Mexican, Puerto Rican, Cuban and peninsular Spanish], and its largest concentration is in the Southwest, it would seem easy to describe that variety based on Mexican-Spanish influence. The problem is not simple, in that within Mexico, itself, there are several varieties of Spanish. As early as 1938, Henríquez-Ureña (BDH, IV, p. xx) divided Mexico into five dialectal zones. One could more easily determine what dialectal differences exist in the Southwest if we knew the migration patterns from Mexico to the United States Southwest. It is safe to suggest that the great majority came from two of the dialectal zones described by Henríquez-Ureña: the North and the Central High Plains.

Even with this information one cannot posit one brand of Mexican-Spanish influence. We would like to divide the Spanish Southwest into four dialectal zones though there are overlappings: I. Texas, II. New Mexico and Southern Colorado, III. Arizona, and IV. California, with the greatest overlapping occurring along the border state areas from the mouth of the Rio Grande all the way to Baja California. In short, constant contact with the northern zones of Mexico infuses daily linguistic life so these areas maintain a certain amount of homogeneity. In addition, recent concern for languages and bilingual education will have its impact on standardizing Spanish to some extent.

At the other extreme, the Spanish of New Mexico has the least overlap with the rest, due in part to its long period of isolation, its bi-cameral laws written in both Spanish and English, and the right to be tried or to defend oneself in either Spanish or English. These unique characteristics have given pride, both cultural and linguistic, to its citizens, many of whom claim to descend directly from the Spanish settlers. Here too, however, bilingual education is becoming the leveler.

Texan Spanish

In general terms, the Spanish of Texas, a state which has been overwhelmed by Mexican migration, would be represented by the phonological and morphological description given for an academic standard. The principal differences which are found in all styles of this Spanish are: the absence of two phonemes /Θ, λ/ which have merged with /s, y/ respectively; the complete absence of the second person plural pronoun (vosotros) and the corresponding verb form (habláis) in all tenses. This is normally replaced by *ustedes* plus the corresponding verb forms whether it be polite discourse or not. There is also almost complete absence of the possessive *nuestro, -a, -os, -as* which is replaced by *de nosotros.*

From *Dominant Spanish Dialects Spoken in the United States* (Washington, D.C., ERIC Clearinghouse for Linguistics/Center for Applied Linguistics, 1970, [ED 042 137]).

The phonology perhaps shows more variance than the morphology and syntax from one level of discourse to the other. In all three levels of discourse one can find the phoneme /ř/ being produced as a fricative sibilant [ř] by some and as a trill [r̄] by others. The phoneme /x/ is frequently weakened into an aspiration [h] very much like the English /h/. This is true of the whole Southwest.

As stated, except for these minor adjustments, the formal level of discourse would be well represented by the academic standard. The normal level vacillates and the colloquial permits certain simplifications of phonological sequences: Four-consonant clusters are reduced to three (transcripción> trascripción); three-consonant clusters are reduced to two (transportar > transportar, trans-bordar > trasbordar); two-consonant clusters are reduced to one consonant (lección > [lesjón, leịsjón, lisjón], septiembre > setiembre, también > tamién). Even the Spanish Academy has recognized some of these reductions by including them in their dictionary. On the colloquial level this simplification is more the rule than the exception.

The single voiced intervocalic consonants /b d g y/ are fricatives on the formal discourse level with some weakening on the normal discourse level, but on the colloquial level in addition to the weakening, /d/ and sometimes /g/ and /y/ tend to disappear completely. Thus we can posit these possible occurrences:

formal	normal	colloquial
[náða]	[náða]	[naða~náa]
[akostáðo]	[akostáðo]	[akoṣtáo]
[elàðoðeré]	[elàðoðeréĉo]	[elàoeréĉo]
[lealtáð]	[lealtá]	[ljaltá]
[áɣwa]	[aw̌a]	[áwa]
[síya]	[síya]	[sía]
[amaríyo]	[amaríʸo]	[amarío]

In the morphology one finds some lack of contrast in the first person plural of the *-er* and *-ir* verbs (e.g., decimos> dicemos, vivimos> vivemos), on both the normal and colloquial levels of discourse.

With syntax, there is definite preference for the paraphrastic *ir a* plus infinitive (vamos a comer) in place of the future (comeremos) on both normal and colloquial levels of discourse. The form *de nosotros* has displaced *nuestro* on all levels of discourse.

All these variances are to be found elsewhere in the Hispanic World and are therefore not unique to Texas. Like any soup, it is the proportion of each ingredient that gives it its peculiar flavor. This peculiar flavor, however, can be sensed, felt, and even observed, but not easily defined.

Vocabulary plays an important part in the make-up of each variety of Spanish, but it will be dealt with in a later chapter. An effort will also be made to throw some light on intonation, which may well be the main distinguishing feature of all these varieties of Spanish, yet the one next to impossible to define.

New Mexican and Southern Coloradan Spanish

The Spanish of New Mexico and Southern Colorado is known for its archaic flavor. This does not mean that it is so different that it is incomprehensible to the other varieties. In fact, every single peculiarity attributable to New Mexico and Southern Colorado is found somewhere in the Hispanic World. What makes this dialectal variety unique is the concentration of so many linguistic peculiarities in one given area.

Isolation may have been responsible for this archaic flavoring. (However, the language may be in the process of leveling or modernization with the current emphasis on bilingual education.) The linguistic pecularities are too many to itemize so we will concentrate on the most obvious. First, we must state that for the individuals capable of the three styles of discourse, the academic standard serves as a base, within the limitations described for Texan Spanish. All of these linguistic peculiarities are found, however, in the speech of those individuals who use the two-in-one formal-normal level of discourse or the colloquial level. Second, all the peculiarities attributed to Texan Spanish exist in the New Mexican-Southern Coloradan Spanish, some perhaps carried to an extreme, giving it an archaic flavor. Most of these linguistic forms were known in the sixteenth century. Most notorious is the simplification of many vocalic clusters, making a diphthong or single vowel the rule (e.g., *maestro*/maéstro/>/máistro/>/ méstro/ or *golpear*/golpeár/>/golpiár/). The simplification of consonant clusters is also the rule. The process is much the same as described above (e.g., *absoluto*/absolúto/>/ausolúto/>/asolúto/).

Another very common phonological feature that smacks of archaism is the retention of a strongly aspirated unvoiced velar fricative /x/, which was a step in the evolution of many words that started with /f/ in Latin and now have /Ø/ in Spanish (e.g., *huir* / xuíre [∼] xuyíre /, *hallar* / xayáre /, *hervir* / xerbíre /, *ahumar* /axumáre /, etc.).

This phenomenon crossed into another phonemic area, perhaps through combined influence of this /x/ and aspiration of syllable-final /s/ becoming /-h/. In any case, one hears *nosotros* /noxótroh/, *los otros* /loxótroh/, *los zapatos* /loxapátoh/. (This does not mean, however, that /x/ always replaces intervocalic /s/.) Syllable final /-s/ is found in two stages: *esta* [ésta] and [éhta].

An assibilated [řَ] is the rule after stop consonants /pr, tr, kr, fr, br, dr, gr/ somewhat close to the English /r/ in *pry, try, cry.*

The /f/ has two allophones [φ] and [f]. There is a replacement of /-l/ by /-r/: *alquilar>arquilar, alfalfa>alfarfa, colmillo>cormío.*

The intervocalic *-ll-* /y/ becomes [Ø] with greater regularity than in Texas, to the extent that it reaches *ella* [éa] and all verb forms that have *-llear* endings.

Nasalization of vowels is most common, to the extent that frequently, but not always, the nasal consonant disappears, leaving a nasal vowel.

An opposite tendency also occurs, since often unstressed vowels weaken and sometimes disappear, with the result that the contiguous consonants [n̥, m̥, l̥] acquire vocalic or syllabic quality: (ex. *una bebida* [n̥naβeβiða], *mi mamá* [m̥mãmá], *con mi papá* [cõmpapá] and *clueca* [kl̥éka or kuléka].

Other phonological peculiarities can best be described within the morphology since they are the result of analogy in most cases.

Some verbal forms reflect the state of sixteenth century Spanish. The preterite of *traer* is an example: (*traje, trajiste, trajo,* etc.>*truje, trujites, trujo,* etc.). In the present subjunctive, by analogy with *caiga,* one finds (*vaya>vaiga, haya>haiga, crea>creiga, vea>veiga*). In the future, by analogy with *pondrá,* one finds an epenthetic *-d-* in (*traerá>traidrá, caerá>caidrá, querrá>quedrá*). The imperfect indicative presents some old forms such as *veía>vía, reía>ría,* and the preterite gives: *vi>vide, vites, vido,* not uncommon in Mexico

The historical process of simplification of thematic vowels in verb conjugations continued in New Mexico more than elsewhere. Latin had four different verb conjugations which were reduced to three in Standard Spanish: *-ar, -er, ir.* New Mexican Spanish has practically reduced them to two: *-ar,* and a decided preference for *-ir.* Some of the analogical formations, however, present some vacillation. *Caer>cáir* and *creer>crer* both follow the *-ir* conjugation except in the imperfect indicative tense where they borrow from the *-ar* conjugation: (*caiba, caibas, caiba, cáibanos, caiban; creiba, creibas, creiba, créibanos, creiban*). In addition, the infinitive endings retain the final vowel /e/, a remnant of the Latin form which persisted through the sixteenth century in Spain: *hablare, comere,* etc.

The verb endings with pronominal function are the same as for academic standard with the usual absence of [*-is*] of the second person plural. However, this set of morphemes is characterized by the regularization of the second person singular [*-s*] of the preterite form: *fuiste>juites;* and the change in position or reduplication of the third person plural [*-n*] of the imperative, thus *denme> demen* or *denmen, díganme>digamen* or *diganmen.* For the first person plural, two allomorphs exist: *-mos* occurs in every tense except the two imperfects and the present subjunctive, whereby analogy with the object pronoun *nos* when it follows a verb form, one finds *-nos* as a verb ending *caiamos>cáibanos, cayeramos>cayéranos, caigamos>cáiganos.* In these cases, the stress on the antepenult is followed by *-nos* and the stress on the penult is followed by *-mos.*

One more factor that gives New Mexican Spanish an archaic flavor is its basic vocabulary. Many words appear as seen in the sixteenth century. Some show diphthongs long since simplified in standard Spanish. A few examples follow taken from Espinosa (BDH,I, p. 49):

agora, ansí, ansina, naidien, traidrá, lamber, ivierno, trujo, escrebir, adrede, cuasi, entención, comigo, pus, anque, dende, mesmo, quese (que es de), escuro, dijieron, vide, vía, (veía), etc.

Let us repeat again that all these linguistic changes also occur elsewhere in the Hispanic World, but nowhere else are they all concentrated in one linguistic area. This unique concentration, nevertheless, does not make this dialect of Spanish incomprehensible to speakers of the other varieties in question.

Arizonan Spanish

The Spanish of Arizona has many points in common with New Mexican Spanish, but leans more heavily toward a Mexican variety of the northern type due to the proximity of the State of Sonora in Mexico. In part this similarity to north Mexico Spanish may be due to the migration from Mexico that took place during the latter half of the first decade and the second decade of this century.

The concentration of archaic features in New Mexico is greatly reduced in Arizona. In general, Arizonan Spanish does not regularly share such phonological features as the unvoiced velar fricative /x/ in place of /Ø/ (*huir* [uir]), and the replacement of /-l/ by /-r/ (*colmillo* [kolmíyo ~ kolmío]); the assibilated /řr/ is rare after stops; syllable final [-s] is hardly ever aspirated; vowels are seldom nasalized to any great extent; and the vocalization of consonants such as [n̥ m̥ l̥] is a rarity.

Many of the verbal archaisms are to be found side by side with the standard forms; however, the analogical form *caiba, creiba,* etc., is rarely heard. Like Texan Spanish, it still retains three verbal conjugation endings to a certain extent, but confusion does exist as in *decimos ~ dicemos.* In all these dialects of Spanish, the *tú* verb form is more frequently used than the *usted* form and is gaining greater use with the younger generation.

Added to all this, one finds two features that flavor all these varieties of Spanish: borrowed words and phrases from English, and intonation. We will discuss these features at more length when we devote a section to intonation to conclude these descriptions.

Californian Spanish

Californian Spanish may be described as an extension of Arizonan Spanish, greatly influenced by or loaded with borrowed words and phrases from English, and perhaps a greater variety of intonation patterns.

The "Pachuco" jargon of the late 30's and early 40's left an imprint. Language change and acceptance seems to be on the upsurge under a different but dignified guise: bilingualism.

Other United States Urban Area Mexican Spanish

The Mexican variety of Spanish in all the other urban areas of the United States contains most of the linguistic peculiarities thus far described. It is never as extreme as New Mexican Spanish and perhaps leans more toward a standard Mexican Spanish of the Central High plains. This difference we could attribute to migration cycles and patterns. The Mexican migration to the northern and eastern United States is of a recent vintage, both from Mexico and from the Southwest, due to the mobility within the United States since 1940. The Mexican colony of Detroit, for example, came principally from the northern and central states of Mexico, while many of the Mexican-Americans came from Texas (Tsuzaki, p. 28).

Notes

[1] Espinosa, Aurelio M., *Estudios sobre el español de Nuevo Méjico,* Parte I, fonética, 1930, tr. and notes of Angel Rosenblat and Amado Alonso; Parte II, morfología, 1946, tr. and notes of Angel Rosenblat, (BDH, I and BDH, II respectively) Buenos Aires.

[2] Henríquez-Ureña, Pedro, *El español en Mejico los Estados Unidos y la América Central.* (Biblioteca de Dialectología Hispanoamericana, vol. IV) Buenos Aires, 1938.

[3] Tsuzaki, Stanley Mamoru, *"English Influence in the Phonology and Morphology of the Spanish Spoken in the Mexican Colony in Detroit, Michigan.* Ph.D. dissertation, University of Michigan, 1963.

The Archaic and the Modern in the Spanish of New Mexico

Jacob Ornstein

In the field of dialectology, New Mexican Spanish has for some years attracted the attention of scholars and linguists. Representing to a large extent the language of the sixteenth-century *conquistadores,* it has developed under peculiar conditions, isolated from both Spain and Mexico, on one hand, and since 1846, subject to strong North American influence, on the other. The feature which has especially interested philologists is the strongly archaic tendency of the language, and the high percentage, in popular speech, of archaisms such as *truje, vide, mesmo, muncho, cuasi,* and *anque.*

The characteristics of New Mexico Spanish have been described, in considerable detail, by competent scholars. The key work on the subject is the two-volume study by Professor Aurelio M. Espinosa, translated and reelaborated by Amado Alonso and Angel Rosenblat, entitled *Estudios sobre el español de Nuevo Méjico.*[1] In this monumental work Dr. Espinosa defines the New Mexican speech area as including all of New Mexico, the valley of San Luis in Colorado, and a small strip of eastern Arizona. In his *prefacio,* however, he specifically states that the study is limited to Colorado's San Luis Valley and to all of New Mexico north of the city of Socorro, with Santa Fe as center. This means that a part of the New Mexico speech area, namely the two hundred miles south of Socorro and including such cities as Hot Springs, Silver City, Deming, Carlsbad, Lordsburg, and Las Cruces, has not been investigated. Espinosa himself, in a personal letter dated May 22, 1950, recommends that research be done on Southern New Mexican Spanish, especially on the vowels, for the purpose of comparing them with their counterparts in the North, described by him, as well as with the closed and open vowels described by Navarro Tomás.

The region south of Socorro, New Mexico, therefore, offers possibilities of various types of research, phonetic and otherwise.[2] The present paper will touch upon various aspects of the speech in this area and will also make certain observations on present-day New Mexican Spanish in general.

Structurally the language spoken in the South follows quite closely the main features of all New Mexican Spanish. The conjugations are virtually reduced to two: *ar* and *er* verbs. The second person familiar preterite commonly ends in *ates* and *ites: tú hablates, tú vendites* (the forms *hablastes* and *vendistes* are also heard). Practically all words ending in *a* (except for a few like *día*) are treated as feminine: *la idioma, la tranvía, la planeta.* The present subjunctive is accented throughout on the first syllable, and peculiarly ends in *nos* rather than *mos* in the first person singular. Thus *hablar* is conjugated as follows: *hable, hables, hable, háblenos, hablen.* In the imperfect subjunctive, as well, *nos* is employed,

Reprinted by permission from *Hispania* 34:1.137-142 (February 1951). This paper was originally read at the 32nd Annual Meeting of the American Association of Teachers of Spanish and Portuguese, New Orleans, December 20-21, 1950.

so that the first person plural would be *habláranos* and not *habláramos*.

From the standpoint of vocabulary, the differences between North and South are often considerable, and it would be interesting to represent them on isogloss maps. In the north *puela* is often used for *frying pan*, in the south it is *sartén*. Instead of *alverjones* the south uses *chícharos* to mean *peas*. The term *barbacoa* (storage room for food or grain) is not generally understood south of Socorro. To the northern New Mexican an apricot is an *albaricoque;* to his southern cousin it is a *chabacán*. South of Socorro *dandruff* is not *salvado* but *caspa, chair* is not *silleta* but *silla, ruco* does not mean *silly* but *very old*. Many northern New Mexicans would not understand *banqueta* as *sidewalk* or the verb *tatemar* as meaning *to burn too crisply*.

At the same time there is no dearth of New Mexicanisms readily understood in both areas, such as *averiguar* (to argue), *ganso* (turkey), *ánzara* (goose), *abrigo* (heavy underwear), *vestido* (man's suit), *túnico* (woman's dress), *miel* (syrup), and *alquilar* (to pawn).

A complete study of the vocabulary of the southern speech area is a desideratum. The following words and expressions are taken from a longer list compiled in the Las Cruces area, and are intended merely to be illustrative. It should be emphasized that not all Spanish speakers use them, for their employment is in inverse proportion to the education of the individual.

aigre, air; *alguacil mayor*, sheriff; *arbolera*, orchard; *atrincar, atrancar*, to lock; *aveno*, oats; *baratío*, bargain, bargain sale; *barbecho*, plowed field; *broche*, safety pin; *cajete*, bathtub; *camear*, to work; *Casa Corte*, Courthouse; *celebro*, brain; *cimbra*, bed spring; *cociñar*, to cook; *común*, outdoor toilet; *correa*, shoe-string; *cubeta*, bucket; *chulo*, puppy; *dejar*, to make a profit, to pay: *Este negocio de deja; dendenantes*, a while ago; *dientista*, dentist; *echar*, to be lying down; *embone*, fertilizer; *empeloto*, naked; *empeño*, ambition; *encajarse*, to mount (an animal); *equívoco: estar –*, to be mistaken; *escarpines*, men's stockings; *estafeta*, post-office; *faja*, belt; *feria*, change (money); *fierros*, tools; *finca*, building; *fincar*, to build; *galera*, farm implement shed; *globo*, light-bulb; *guajolote*, turkey, water-dog; *guisantes*, meats for frying; *guisar*, to fry; *hepoteca*, mortgage; *hortaliza*, vegetable garden; *huerta*, vineyard; *hule*, inner tube, linoleum, rubber band; *saco de hule*, raincoat; *imponer*, to accustom; *ingüento*, ointment; *jalar* to pull, work; *ladino*, shrill, loud; *lavamanos*, wash-basin; *llevarse*, to get along (in mutual harmony); *marro*, sledge-hammer; *marqueta*, butcher-shop, market; *mestro*, teacher, professor; *monte*, desert, wasteland; *naguas*, skirt; *narices*, nose (generally used only in plural); *nodriza*, any kind of nurse; *pader*, wall; *paño*, handkerchief; *parquete, paquete*, paper bag; *peluche*, fur; *saco de peluche*, fur coat; *pisado*, type of wine made by treading upon grapes in a large vat; *plan*, bottom; *quejumbr(i)arse*, complain; *¿quése?*, where is?; *raspada*, type of confection made by scraping ice and adding flavor; *resurarse*, to shave oneself; *resfrío: tener –*, to have a cold; *salarate, salarata*, baking soda; *sombrilla*, umbrella, windshield; *sosprender*, to surprise; *suterrano, soterrano*, basement, cellar; *tasaciones*, taxes; *tela, telón*, screen; *tomate del ojo*, eyeball; *vaqueta*, any type of leather.

The researcher will necessarily be impressed, when studying the southern speech area, by the strong similarities, not only in vocabulary, but also in phonology and syntax, to the Spanish of the neighboring republic to the south. This is scarcely accidental when one considers the proximity of Mexico, and the frequent contacts of both Spanish-speaking groups on either side of the border. Trips to the twin cities of El Paso and Juárez, Chihuahua, are a regular part of the life of the inhabitants in the southern zone. The El Paso and Juárez radio stations are listened to much more than those of Albuquerque and Santa Fe, especially since the reception of the former is better. El Paso's newspaper *El Continental* is generally read far more than the Spanish-language newspapers of the north.

The location of the southern New Mexico speech area, lying close to the Mexican frontier, is of importance for another reason. It places the region squarely in the Border Spanish belt, stretching roughly from Corpus Christi, Texas, in the east to San Diego, California, in the west. Here, too, is a decidedly neglected linguistic field, for aside from Professor Anita Post's study, published in 1934, of the language of southern Arizona, southern California, and the northern part of the Mexican state of Sonora, very little attention has been paid to the topic.[3] John Sharp, Associate Professor of Spanish at Texas Western College, El Paso, who is at present investigating the nonstandard vocabulary elements in West Texas Spanish, refers to Border Spanish as a "linguistic no man's land."

So much for differences and similarities as regards the two speech zones of New Mexico. The remainder of our remarks will relate to New Mexican Spanish in general, and to some influences modifying it at present. Language is never static and unchanging and despite its archaisms the Spanish of New Mexico must be viewed in the light of constant evolution.

One of the strongest influences during the past ten years upon the spoken language of New Mexico and indeed the whole Southwest has been that of the *Pachucos*. A product of semi-assimilation, the *Pachucos* in southwestern cities are a fairly recent group distinguished by an aversion to steady work, outlandish grooming and dress, as well as the use of a special and picturesque vocabulary, meant to serve as a secret language. Although beyond the pale of both polite *anglo* and *hispano* society, the phraseology of the *Pachucos* has appealed to the imagination of Spanish-speaking Southwesterners, who often make humorous use of it in their conversations. However, just as the *germanía* of Spain, the argot of the Parisian Apaches, and the racy idiom of the North American underworld have contributed to the standard languages in their respective countries, much of *Pachuco* speech can be expected to make its way ultimately to respectability.

It ought to be pointed out, in this connection, that the southern New Mexican speech area, due to its nearness to El Paso, the city where the *Pachuco* class and its mannerisms supposedly originated and which has an unusually high proportion of individuals so identified, is particularly rich in *pachuquismos*. The following sample list of slang terms in use in the Las Cruces area contains a high percentage of such words. While some speakers never knowingly employ *Pachuco* terminology, a large share, if not the majority, of the terms below would be understandable to Spanish-speakers in the younger age brackets in virtually any Southwestern city.[4]

agüitarse, to be afraid, to "go to pieces"; *alba: al* —, "swell," excellent; *alfiler*, knife; *alfileriar*, to knife; *apestar*, to do well; *Le apesta para bailar*, He dances well; *arranarse*, to sit down, to get married; *atacarse*, to stuff oneself; *bacil* (or *vacil*), date, fun; *bato, -a*, fellow, guy; girl, "gal"; *birria*, beer; *bola*, American dollar; *borlo, borlote*, dance; *borlotear*, to dance; *buti* much, many; *cachar*, to steal; *calco*, shoe; *camear*, to work; *canicarse*, to fall in love; *estar canicas,* to be in love; *carnal, -a,* brother; sister; pal; *carrucha,* old automobile; *catos,* fisticuffs; *darse –,* to have a fight; *¡ chale!,* No ! By no means!; *chancla,* slipper; *tirar –,* to dance; *chante,* house; *enchantarse,* to get married; *chicano,* Mexican; *chícharo: ponerse ojo de –,* to become alert; *chota,* cop; *chupar,* to smoke; *entacucharse,* to dress up in one's best; *entraña,* ill will; *Me tiene –,* He has it in for me; *escame,* fear; *tener – ,* to be afraid; *¡ésele!* Hi, there!; *frajo,* cigarette; *gabacho,* anglo, non-Spanish speaker; *garras,* clothes; *hacerle a algo,* to excel in something; *Le hace a la máquina de escribir,* She's good at typing; *huachar,* to watch, see, look out for; *Ai te huacho,* I'll be seeing you!; *huevón,* idler, loafer; *huisa,* girl, "gal," girl-friend; *jaino, -a,* boy-friend, girl-friend; *jambar,* to steal; *jambo,* dishonest; *jando,* money; *jaspia,* hunger; *tener –,* to be hungry; *jefe, jefa,* father, "old man"; mother, "old lady"; *león: tirar a –,* to "cold shoulder"; *lira,* guitar; *lurio,* crazy; *llevar,* used idiomatically in such an expression as *¿A onde la llevas?* Where are you going?; *manito,* Northern New Mexican; *manoplia,* hand, catcher's mitt; *tirar manoplia,* to be handy with one's fists; *mono,* movies; *moras: agarrar en las –* to catch red-handed: *nel,* no; *Pachuco,* El Paso, Texas; *penco,* individual who attempts to steal another's sweetheart; *perra: hacer la –,* to loaf; *pisto,* drunk, intoxicated; *plancha: tirarse –,* to be rebuffed, disappointed; *refín,* meal; *refinar,* to eat; *relaje,* joke, farce; *rol,* automobile; *sardo,* soldier; *simón,* yes; *sirol,* yes; *suave,* "swell," wonderful; *sura: caerle a uno –,* to dislike; *tacuche,* suit; *talonear,* to walk; *tartana,* dilapidated auto; *tarzán,* "zoot-suiter"; *tecolote,* policeman, guard; *trola,* match; *vacilar,* to have a good time, "fool around," flirt, flatter.

Thus the philologist in New Mexico can observe the forging, and gradual acceptance, of a whole new vocabulary. He must, however, at the same time witness another process which, rather than enriching it, impoverishes the language. It is a fact that in our only officially bilingual state Spanish comes off a poor second in its competition with English and in its struggle to meet the demands of a society growing politically and technologically more complicated by the day.

An advertisement in the Santa Fe newspaper *El Nuevo Mejicano* reads as follows: *1949 Mercury 4 puertas Sedan, desescarchador, calefactor, overdrive, azul. Un robo en $2,095.* This example reveals three tendencies common in New Mexico Spanish today. The first, exemplified by *overdrive,* is that of relying upon English in referring to new technological processes or socio-political institutions and developments. The term for *overdrive* given by the Ford Motor Company's Spanish handbook for dealers is *sobremarcha,* but this would be unintelligible to most auto mechanics here.[5] The second, represented by the words *calefactor* and *desescarchador,* is the puristic tendency, in which some sort of Spanish equivalent is sought. The third, reflected by *cautro puertas Sedan* and *un robo en $2,095,* reveals the tremendous impact of English syntax and phraseology upon the language.

Little new can be added here concerning the wholesale use of English vocabulary and phraseology in the Spanish of today in New Mexico or the Southwest in general. Examples can be culled at random from conversations or newspapers. A new "paint job" is *un nuevo trabajo de pintura.* Reading the political columns one learns that a certain bill *murió en comité.* A wholesale basement sale is announced as *venta de bodega al mayoreo.* The social column announces that: *La señorita X fué obsequiada con una llovizna baile.* And so on *ad infinitum* and probably *ad nauseam.*

It is not because Spanish equivalents do not exist that the New Mexican, in speaking of his car, refers to *las brecas* and *el cloche.* Nor does one need to seek the explanation in Bloomfield's highly controversial analysis of what he terms *intimate borrowing, cultural borrowing* and *dialect borrowing.*[6] It is purely and simply, as Professor Einar Haugen puts it: "the more forceful presence" of the foreign term.[7]

As for the puristic tendency, it fights an unequal battle, supported mostly by teachers of Spanish, the clergy, and Spanish-language newspapers. The efforts of teachers in their courses to teach Spanish equivalents of Anglicisms are not crowned by conspicuous success, as far as the actual use of the correct terms is concerned. The influence of the newspapers is difficult to measure, and often these organs are themselves hardly desirable models of Spanish prose.

It is probably the newspaper *El Nuevo Mejicano* that is most interested in the purity of the language and it often repeats its intention to *Seguir adelante manteniendo vivo el idioma español y las tradiciones de los habitantes hispano parlantes.* A reading of this and other newspapers will give insight into the struggles of the purists to defend Spanish from the devastating attacks of English. It is interesting to note that, to insure understanding, English equivalents are often written in parentheses after the Spanish words: *bombas* (pumps), *casa de remolque* (house trailer), *vigilantes* (pickets), *cabildeo* (lobbying), *equipos* (appliances).

The efforts to find some sort of Spanish equivalents are not always felicitous, but one might say of this process precisely what Dr. Sturtevant remarks of the coining of new words: that it is a "function of artists."[8] Here are some typical examples. A headline announces a war against one-armed bandits: *Hacen guerra contra máquinas ladronas.* A certain department store tells of its easy lay-away or lay-by plan using the words *plan fácil de apartar.* The Future Farmers become the *Agricultores Progresistas,* while the home demonstration agent is the *agente de demonstración en general.* Whitewall tires are either *llantas "caras blancas"* or *llantas blancas al lado.* Modern household terms provide thorny problems. Mold- and drip-proof jars become *cubetas garantizadas a prueba de moho y goteo;* pressure cookers, *ollas de presión;* an aluminum cold-pack canner, *envasadora de aluminio para envase frío,* breakfast nook set, *ajuar nook para el almuerzo;* and electric heating pad, *almohadilla eléctrica.* Tourist court is neatly converted into *campo turista.* Finally, terms like "on-the-job training program" tax the abilities of even the most ardent purists, as can be seen from the following rendering, which appeared in the *Nuevo Mexicano: comisión que está encargada de la dirección de adiestrar en el oficio a los veteranos que se preparan para aprender algún arte u oficio.*

In conclusion, it might be said that New Mexican Spanish, while clinging tenaciously to many sixteenth-century archaisms, nevertheless displays considerable receptivity to the new, and a fair measure of adaptability to the linguistic exigencies of the modern world. In 1936 H. L. Mencken, reviewing the status of the various foreign languages spoken in the United States, remarked: "This Southwestern Spanish, like Pennsylvania-German, Yankee-Dutch and Vestur-Islanska, seems doomed to vanish sooner or later."[9] Despite this dire prediction, however, New Mexico Spanish continues to maintain itself and to evolve.

Notes

[1]Aurelio M. Espinosa: *Estudios sobre el español de Nuevo Méjico*, (*traducción y reelaboración con notas por A. Alonso y A. Rosenblat*), Buenos Aires, vol. 1, 1930, vol. 2, 1946. A highly useful volume is also: F. M. Kercheville and George E. McSpadden, *Preliminary Glossary of New Mexican Spanish*, University of New Mexico Bulletin, vol. 5, No. 3, July 15, 1934.

[2]Professor R. M. Duncan of the University of New Mexico is at present making phonetic studies in the middle Rio Grande Valley of New Mexico.

[3]See Rex Robert Kelly, "Vocabulary as Used on the Mexican Border," unpublished Master's thesis, Baylor University, Waco, Texas, 1938. Also consult George C. Storz, *Mexican Spanish*, 2nd ed., San Diego: Publicationes Fronterizas, 1946.

[4]Cf. Alfred Bruce Gaarder, "Notes on Some Spanish Terms in the Southwest," *Hispania*, XXVII (1944), pp. 330-334; Renato Rosaldo, "A List of Slang and Colloquial Expressions of Mexico City," *Hispania*, XXXI (1948), pp. 437-445.

[5]*Rasgos Sobresalientes Comprobados acerca de los Automóviles Ford*, Dearborn, Mich.: Ford Motor Co., 1949.

[6]Leonard Bloomfield: *Language*, New York: Holt, 1933, pp. 444-495.

[7]Einar Haugen, in his review of Leo Pap's *Portuguese-English Speech*, in *Language*, XXVI, 438-9 (1950). Prof. Haugen's views on loan-words, expressed in this review, are extremely interesting.

[8]E. H. Sturtevant, *An Introduction to Linguistic Science*, New Haven: Yale University Press, 1947, p. 22.

[9]H. L. Mencken, *The American Language*, 4th ed., New York: Knopf, 1936, p. 649.

Discussion by Daniel Wogan, Tulane University

Professor Ornstein's admirably concise and extremely informative essay on New Mexican Spanish suggests three topics which I should like to bring up for discussion.

First of all, I think we can agree that the most important point Professor Ornstein makes is that there are enough differences between the Spanish spoken in northern and in southern New Mexico to justify the division of the New Mexican region into two linguistic zones. However, the evidence he presents in support of this theory is entirely lexical and perhaps for that reason not altogether convincing. As Professor Ornstein himself says, the Spanish folk speech south of Socorro has yet to be investigated from the standpoint of phonetics, morphology and syntax. The validity of the two-zone theory would therefore appear to hinge on the results of such investigations as well as, of course, on more comprehensive studies of the regional vocabularies, north and south.

Secondly, I am not quite clear as to what Professor Ornstein means by "New Mexicanism." Word geography involves difficult problems; but in drawing up lists of non-standard Spanish terms in New Mexico it would seem desirable to group such expressions into three classes: New Mexicanisms, Mexicanisms, and

Hispanoamericanisms. In the absence of any classification, one is puzzled by discovering that Professor Ornstein accepts as New Mexicanisms a number of words in current use far beyond the limits of the State of New Mexico. Among the "New Mexicanisms readily understood" in both areas of the state he mentions *averiguar* (to argue), a verb widely employed in Mexico and Central America; *vestido* (man's suit), a noun current in virtually all Spanish America; and *túnico* (woman's dress), a term well known to Cubans, Central Americans, and also to many Mexicans. Moreover, his two lists of words and idioms gathered in the Las Cruces vicinity include such words as *fierro, jalar, hule, llevarse, agüitarse, catos, chota, jambarse, lurio, tacuche, talonear,* and *tecolote* (policeman), none of which are New Mexicanisms either in the sense that they originated in New Mexico or reflect exclusively regional usage. As for one of the idioms in Professor Ornstein's list, *tener (mala) entraña,* I doubt whether it is an Americanism at all.

Finally, I wish to emphasize the great value and interest of Professor Ornstein's remarks on *pachuco* speech. He is the first, as far as I know, to draw attention to the important part this picturesque argot is likely to play in the development of vernacular Spanish in the Southwest. Professor Ornstein predicts that a goodly number of *pachuquismos* will eventually work their way up to levels of respectability. He is on firm ground here. In the dynamics of language there are always movements from the bottom upward. It is instructive, in this respect, to draw a comparison between *pachuco* speech and *lunfardo,* the *caló* of the *compadrito* that has exerted a steady influence on Argentine Spanish for over a century. For what is the *pachuco,* after all, if not the twin brother, linguistically and sociologically, of the *compadrito* of Buenos Aires? Even their characteristic terminologies, to judge from Professor Ornstein's list of *pachuquismos,* have obvious common elements: *sardo* (soldier) and *cachar* (to steal) are as familiar to the *compadrito* of the River Plate as to the *pachuco* of the Rio Grande. As yet, however, the *pachuco,* less fortunate than the *compadrito,* has inspired no writer of genius to dramatize his restless existence and immortalize his colorful idiom. But the day when the *pachuco* will find *his* Florencio Sánchez may not be far off.

Problemas Lexicográficos del Español del Sudoeste

Aurelio M. Espinosa, Jr.

Uno de los aspectos más intersantes del español del Sudoeste de los Estados Unidos, el vocabulario, no ha sido aún suficientemente estudiado. Existen estudios valiosos sobre la fonología y la morfología del español de Nuevo Méjico y de Arizona, por ejemplo,[1] pero falta todavía un estudio del vocabulario que dé una idea cabal del léxico como reflejo auténtico del estado social y cultural de la región.[2]

Las siguientes palabras tienen por objeto describir algunos de los rasgos importantes del vocabulario de esta región, indicando las materias y problemas que merecen atención especial.

En un tema tan amplio sólo podremos fijarnos en unos cuantos puntos interesantes. En general, el léxico americano consta de tres grandes grupos de palabras: 1°, las de origen español, incluyendo los neologismos que proceden de elementos de la misma lengua; 2°, los préstamos a las lenguas indígenas, y, 3°, los extranjerismos, es decir, los préstamos al inglés, al francés, al italiano y a otras lenguas, así como los neologismos formados sobre ellos.

Vocabulario de Origen Español

Fijándonos primero en las voces de origen español, es conveniente repartir la discusión en varias partes. Discutiremos primero los arcaísmos y los regionalismos, luego los cambios semánticos, y después la formación de palabras nuevas.

La lengua española del Sudoeste representa una evolución algo arcaizante del castellano del siglo clásico, y no es de extrañar que formas y pronunciaciones de aquella época se encuentren todavía en el lenguaje común. Perduran, como en otras partes de Hispanoamérica, arcaísmos *com ansí, añidir, dende, de contino, endenantes, escurana, mesmo, ivierno, saludes* (por *saludos*), *troja* (por *troj*), *trompezar* y muchos otros.

Lugar aparte merecen los arcaísmos fonéticos y morfológicos. Como en el siglo XVI, por ejemplo, subsisten las vacilaciones de timbre en las vocales no acentuadas, y se emplean formas como *recebir, sospirar, melicia, ciénega.*

Los grupos cultos de consonantes se simplificaron en los siglos XVI y XVII, sin que se llegara a una solución general. Esta situación se conserva en Nuevo Méjico, donde se dice *efeto, dino, perfeto* (al lado de *perfeuto*), *imperfición, ilesia, duce, leción—lición.* Por influencia de la escuela se restauraron muchas de las formas cultas, si bien la pronunciación se transformase luego, dándose formas como *aición, aución* (por *acción*), *esauto, nuncias* (por *nupcias*), etc.

Otro arcaísmo es la abundante prefijación de *a* (tan frecuente en los dialectos

Reprinted by permission from *Hispania* 40:1.139-143 (February 1957). This paper was originally read at the 38th Annual Meeting of the American Association of Teachers of Spanish and Portuguese, Washington, December 28-30, 1956.

13

judeo-españoles): *acual, ahoy, alevantar, aoler, aprobar* (por 'probar un manjar'), *ameado* (*mellado*), *alesna, ataimau* (*taimado*), *aprevenirse,* etc.

En la morfología del Sudoeste hay arcaísmos como los pretéritos *vide, truje,* y abundantes formaciones analógicas que en otras épocas tuvieron acceso al habla normal.

No existe aún un estudio detallado de los regionalismos en el español de América. Algunas palabras han sido señaladas como posibles regionalismos del Occidente de España. Hay leonesismos seguros, como *fierro, lamber* (con sus multiples derivados: *lambiache, lambeta, lambuzco, lambuzquear*), pesquisia (*pesquisa*), *urnia* (*urna*).

Muy probables occidentalismos son *abostadero* (de *bosta*), *botar* (*botarse* se emplea por 'irse' en Tejas), *pararse* 'ponerse de pie', y *voltiar* (*voltear*).

La influencia de extremeños y andaluces se observa en el gran número de voces que conservan la *h* aspirada: *jayar* (*hallar*), *jeder, jiel, jongo, jociar—jocicar* (*hozar*), *juir, retajila, jarrumbre, jurgunear, jumadera,* etc. Son casi los mismos ejemplos que aparecen en las zonas limítrofes entre Castilla y los dialectos del Sur de España.[3]

Si es cierto que el vocabulario que trajeron los conquistadores se ha ido empobreciendo, se remedia el desgaste, en parte, por la operación de dos tendencias poderosas: la de la evolución semántica y la de la creación de palabras nuevas.

Desde fecha muy antigua se observan cambios semánticos que muestran la adaptación del vocabulario españól a las nuevas condiciones de la vida americana. Es sobre todo en los nombres de plantas y animales donde se manifesta la originalidad del nuevo ambiente. Pero aun en este terreno ha sido frecuente que los objetos nuevos recibieran nombres viejos. A veces la denominación antigua generaliza su significado: en Nuevo Méjico se emplea la palabra *lince* por cualquier animal del tipo de la comadreja, y *almendra* por cualquier fruto del tipo de la nuez. El pavo tiene nombres indígenas, como *guajolote* (que se emplea también en sentido metafórico, como *pavo,* para indicar al bobo) y *huíjalo;* pero el nombre más frecuente es *gaína de la tierra.*

Hay multitud de nombres asignados a base de alguna característica del objeto. Nombres de plantas son: *hierba de víbora, mala mujer, manca de caballo, lengua de vaca.* Nombres de animales son: *venau alazán* 'anta,' *berrendo* 'antílope,' *ratón volador* 'murciélago.' Nombres de aves: *paisano, pechero—pecho amarío* 'petirrojo,' *picolargo* 'agachadiza,' *pinonero* 'especie de azulejo,' *chuparrosa* 'colibrí.'

Cambios especiales han tenido muchas voces, como *entremés* 'figura fea y extravagante,' 'adefesio'; *colmena* 'abeja' (en Tejas), *carátula* 'esfera del reloj'; *célebre* 'agraciado,' 'gracioso'; *vivienda* 'piso superior'; *laberinto* 'tumulto'; *caravana* 'saludo,' 'cortesía,' y otras muchas.

La formación de palabras nuevas es muy intensa y pone en juego todos los recursos de la derivación. América ha recibido el idioma español como un sistema vivo y coherente, y el hispano-hablante satisface sus necesidades expresivas dentro de este sistema.

Para los sustantivos postverbales el Sudoeste prefiere la terminación *-e: arranque, desenraice, relaje* (al lado de *relajo*).

Hay sufijos fecundísimos, como *-ada,* para indicar la acción del verbo:

cuereada, hablada 'palabra ofensiva.'

Para indicar el agente, el sufijo *-ón* es más frecuente que *-dor: abusón, molón* 'persona molesta,' *quejón, rogón, roncón, rezongón.* El mismo sufijo indica también la acción del verbo: *arañón* (por *arañazo*), *raspón* (por *raspadura*), *rozón* (por *rozadura*).

Para la formación de adjetivos, sufijos muy activos son: *-iento: caspiento* 'casposo,' *garriento* 'haraposo,' *bulliciento, anguliento* 'goloso,' etc.; *-ero: amiguero, cuchillero* 'pendenciero,' *mujerero, parrandero, tracalero; -oso: claridoso, encimoso, labioso, terroso* 'polvoriento,' *paquetoso, zoquetoso;* y *-udo: cachudo* 'de semblante adusto,' *mechudo* 'de pelos desordenados,' *talludo, trompudo, patudo* 'rico,' 'orgulloso.'

Cada región ha desarrollado también su propio sistema de aumentativos y, sobre todo, de diminutivos, poniendo en ellos distintos matices afectivos.

En el Sudoeste el sufijo de aumentativo más común es -ón: lenguón 'deslenguado'; *naranjón, timbón* 'de barriga grande'; *vaquetón* 'descarado.' El sufijo *-azo* se emplea más bien para indicar movimiento o golpe: *fregazo* 'golpe'; *riatazo, chirrionazo* (el sufijo *-iza* expresa lo mismo: *cueriza* 'azotaina'; *cuartiza* 'golpe con látigo o cuarta').

Uno de los rasgos más extendidos es el empleo de diminutivos: *ahorita-horita, despuesito, endenantitos.*

En Nuevo Méjico el sufijo de diminutivo más común es *-ito: agrito* es el árbol llamado *agrillo* en Méjico; *cariñito, antojitos, cepíito.* Otros sufijos de diminutivo se emplean también, pero parecen limitarse a grupos determinados del léxico, y a menudo han perdido su valor de diminutivo. El sufijo *-ete* es frecuente para objetos de la casa: *sïeta* 'silla' (por *sillita* se dice *sietita*), *chapeta* 'arete,' *cajete* 'tina de lavar.' Pero obsérvense *petaquía* 'baúl,' *harinia* 'harina para tortía,' *rondanía* 'roldana,' *sopaipía, postemía* grano.' En juegos de niños predomina *-ito: ahogadito, los angelitos, el coyotito, Santiaguito de Palo,* etc.

Para la formación de verbos la terminación más típica en toda América es *-iar* (*-ear*): *cueriar* 'azotar,' *chifletiar, chiquiarse* 'hacerse rogar.' Este sufijo ha atraído a muchos verbos en *-ar: salpiquiar* (por *salpicar*), *socapiar* (por *socapar*), *valsiar* (por *valsar*).

Voces Indígenas

La abundancia de voces indígenas da fisonomía especial al léxico americano. Tres idiomas son las fuentes principales de las palabras indígenas en el español: el taíno (de las Antillas), el náhuatl (de Méjico), y el quechua (del Perú).

El más antiguo y principal núcleo de americanismos procede del taíno y de las lenguas vecinas emparentadas con él, de la familia arahuaca. Del taíno proceden *batata, cacique, maíz, naguas, tabaco* y muchas palabras más, que, aprendidas por los españoles en las Antillas, se extendieron después a otras regiones americanas.

A partir de 1519, el náhuatl proporcionó numerosas voces al español americano. Se emplean en el Sudoeste palabras como *aguacate, atole, cacahuate, camote, coyote, chicle, chile, chocolate* y *hule,* que han entrado en el idioma general, y otras de uso más localizado, como *pinole, chinchonte* (*sinsontle* en Tejas), *tepalcates* 'trastes,' *mecate* 'cuerda,' *cuate, jumate* y *zacate.*

En 1527 llegan los españoles al imperio de los Incas. Palabras de origen quechua que se difundieron por el mundo hispánico y se emplean en el Sudoeste son: *china* 'mujer indígena,' *guano, papa, yapa* (o *ñapa*).

Del aimará, araucano, guaraní y otros idiomas indígenas no conozco vocablos que hayan pasado al habla popular del Sudoeste con excepción de alguna en época reciente, como *maraca* o *maracá*, de origen guaraní.

De los indios de los pueblos hay posibles préstamos, como *tegua* 'mocasín,' 'abarca de piel de gamo.'

No es raro formar palabras nuevas a base de los préstamos a las lenguas indígenas: *mecatiarlas* 'marcharse corriendo'; *petaquía* 'baúl; *petatiarse* 'morirse.'

Aunque muchos de los americanismos citados se encuentran en casi todas las lenguas occidentales, no puede decirse que el español de América esté inundado de indigenismos. Abundan éstos sobre todo en los países donde el indio aún constituye una parte fundamental de la población, como en Méjico. En cuanto al español del Sudoeste puede afirmarse que los indigenismos no pasan del centenar.[4]

Los Extranjerismos

La aportación de lenguas extrajeras completa el léxico del español de las zonas estudiadas. En el Sudoeste, a causa de la situación desfavorable del español en competencia con el inglés, el influjo de este idioma ha sido arrollador. La influencia de otras lenguas, aun del francés, que dominó en la cultura hispanoamericana durante el siglo XIX, ha sido menor.

En el Sudoeste el anglicismo ha penetrado profundamente en el habla de todas las clases sociales. Centenares de palabras inglesas son de uso común, y el español se halla en pleno retroceso. Las palabras inglesas entran en el español de tres formas. Algunas entran sin variar de forma; otras se disfrazan, adaptándose a la fonética hispana, o agregando terminaciones o sufijos españoles. Otras, en fin, se traducen al español. Los ejemplos son tan numerosos que me limitaré a las formaciones más típicas.

Entran sin variar de forma: *overol* (*overalls*), *balún, champión, ricés* (*recess*), *shain* (*shine*), etc.

Se adaptan a la fonética hispana, o se agregan terminaciones o sufijos españoles: *suera* (*sweater*), *bogue* (*buggy*), *espichi* (*speech*), *pompa* (*pump*), *jaitún* (*high-toned*), *lonchi* (*lunch*), *rinque* (*drink*), etc. Pueden formarse neologismos mediante los sufijos citados anteriormente: *-ada: baquiada* 'la acción de echar a andar un coche hacia atrás, *shainiada, shequiada* (del inglés *to shake*); *-azo: trilazo* (de *thrill*) 'alegría grande'; *-udo: tofudo* (de *tough*) 'fuerte.' El neologismo más frecuente es en la formación de verbos, mediante el sufijo *-ar: abordar* (*to board*) 'hospedarse,' *deservar, lonchar, chachar* (*to charge*), y, sobre todo, mediante *-iar: blofiar, sainiar* (*to sign*), *chitiar* (*to cheat*), *tritiar* (*to treat*), *fuliar, loviar* (*to love*), *shainiar, requiar* (*to rake*), *suaipiar* (*to swipe*), *trostiar* (*to trust*).

Traducción del inglés: *abanico eléctrico, cuerda de leña* (del inglés *cord of wood*), *gabinete de cocina* (*kitchen cabinet*), *seguro* (*safety-pin*) 'imperdible'; *rueda* (*wheel*) 'bicicleta.; *escuela alta, ropa de abajo, tener sucesito*, etc.

La mayoría de los galicismos de América son voces que se han consolidado en la lengua general: *favorito, interesante, control, controlar,* y otras muchas censuradas en el siglo XIX. Se trata de voces impuestas en casi todas las lenguas occidentales, incluyendo el inglés, que habrá servido de vía de transmisión en muchos casos.

En el léxico del Sudoeste la influencia francesa se manifiesta en la vida social: *buqué* 'ramillete de flores,' *coqueta* 'arete,' 'pendiente,' *matiné, velís–valís* 'maleta' (tal vez a través del inglés *valise*), en la moda: *canesú* 'encaje,' *garsolé* 'gorra con ala para guardar del sol,' *crepé, crinolina, chapero* 'sombrero'; y en la vivienda: *sofá, sopanda* 'muelle,' *tren* 'aparato,' *buró* 'cómoda,' *canapé, garaje.*

El número de neologismos tomados de otros idiomas es mucho más limitado, no sólo en el Sudoeste, sino en el idioma general. La contribución del italiano, por ejemplo, se reduce casi a términos de arte y música, aunque hay italianismos de otra índole, como *póliza.* Ejemplo de interés histórico es *chirinola* 'disputa,' 'riña' en Nuevo Méjico (del cual deriva *chirinolero* 'pendenciero').

Del húngaro o del alemán sólo conozco *chotis* y *valse.*

Los veintitantos arabismos documentados pertenecen igualmente al fondo patrimonial del idioma. Se relacionan con la vivienda: *almuada (almohada), lacena (alacena), zotea (*azotea)*, alfiler, adobe;* con los alimentos: *ad-, al-, armóndiga (albóndiga), aceite, aceituna, azúcara (azúcar), cemita (acemita),* y con el comercio: *almur (almud), arquilar (alquilar), duanero (aduanero), fanega.* Otros ejemplos son *abricias–albricias, cequia (acequia), jabalín (jabalí),* y la interjección *ójali (ojalá y).*

Por último hay que mencionar la posible aportación de las lenguas afro-negristas. Es posible que la voz *ñango* 'flaco,' 'delgado', 'anémico', en Tejas y Méjico, sea de este origen. El aporte afro-negrista parece ser escaso, aun en las Antillas, donde es más perceptible.

Para resumir esta breve discusión, cinco conclusiones me parecen las más indicadas.

1ª. La lengua española del Sudoeste representa una evolución algo arcaizante del castellano de la época clásica, empobrecida en cuanto al vocabulario, y con abundantes popularismos comunes a la mayoría de los dialectos españoles y americanos.

2ª. El desgaste léxico ha sido remediado, en parte, por dos tendencias: la evolución semántica y la intensa creación de palabras nuevas.

3ª. El vocabulario ha sido enriquecido con centenares de palabras de origen inglés, muchas de ellas completamente hispanizadas. La influencia del inglés es arrolladora en estas regiones, si bien ha sido contrastada durante los últimos años por fuertes corrientes inmigratorias que suben desde Méjico.

4ª. La relativa abundancia de voces indígenas es una de las notas características del español de América. Además de los indigenismos que han pasado a enriquecer el vocabulario de todas las lenguas del mundo, numerosas palabras de origen náhuatl han sido incorporadas a la lengua español del Sudoeste.

5ª. El número de neologismos tomados de otros idiomas es mucho más limitado.

Notas

[1] La obra básica es la de Aurelio M. Espinosa, *Estudios sobre el español de Nuevo Méjico,* Parte I. Fonética, Buenos Aires, 1930, y Parte II. Morfología, Buenos Aires, 1946. Otros estudios son: E.C. Hills, "El español de Nuevo Méjico," en *Biblioteca de Dialectología Hispanoamericana,* IV, Buenos Aires, 1937 (pp. 1-73); Anita C. Post, "Southern Arizona Spanish Phonology," *Univ. of Arizona Bulletin,* V (1934), No. 1; y Juan B. Rael, "A Study of the Phonology and Morphology of New Mexican Spanish Based on a Collection of 410 Folk-Tales" (tesis doctoral inédita), Stanford Univ., 1937.

[2] El estudio más extenso publicado hasta ahora versa sobre el vocabulario español de Tejas: Gilberto Cerda, Berta Cabaza y Julieta Farias, *Vocabulario español de Texas,* Univ. of Texas Hispanic Studies, Vol. V, Austin: Univ. of Texas Press, 1953. Obras más limitadas son Stuart M. Gross, "A Vocabulary of New Mexican Spanish" (tesis inédita), Stanford Univ., 1935, y Francis M. Kercheville, *A Preliminary Glossary of New Mexican Spanish,* Albuquerque, New Mexico, 1934. Hay estudios sobre puntos particulares: Aurelio M. Espinosa, "The Spanish Language in New Mexico and Southern Colorado," *Historical Society of New Mexico,* No. 16 (May, 1911), Santa Fe, New Mexico; "Speech Mixture in New Mexico," en *The Pacific Ocean in History,* by H. Morse Stephens and Herbert E. Bolton, New York: The Macmillan Co., 1917; y "Studies in New Mexican Spanish," Part III. The English Elements, *Revue de Dialectologie Romane,* VI (1914), pp. 241-317; George E. McSpadden, "Some Semantic and Philological Facts of the Spanish Spoken in Chili, New Mexico," *Univ. of New Mexico Bulletin,* V (1934), iii, 71-102.

[3] Pueden verse ejemplos en A. M. Espinosa (hijo) y L. Rodríguez Castellano, "La aspiración de la *h* en el Sur y Oeste de España,"*Revista de Filología Española,* XXIII (1936), 225-254, 337-378.

[4] El profesor J. B. Rael, en la obra citada arriba, en Nota 1, no encuentra más que una veintena de voces de origen indígena en el texto de más de cuatrocientos cuentos populares recogidos de la tradición oral en los estados de Colorado y Nuevo Méjico.

Associative Interference in New Mexican Spanish

Juan B. Rael

This phenomenon, present in all languages, has been a very important factor in the development of New Mexican Spanish.[1] It accounts for a very large number of the differences between this dialect and the literary language. Analogy alone, one of the phases of associative interference, is responsible for hundreds of new forms. Indeed, it is to analogy that one must ascribe the reduction of the number of the regular conjugations from three to two (the endings of the third conjugation being exactly the same as those of the second conjugation),[2] the change of the accent from the ending to the stem in the first person plural of the present subjunctive (*ténganos* or *téngamos* for *tengamos*),[3] and the occurence of *n* in place of *m* in the first person plural endings of the imperfect and conditional indicative and throughout the subjunctive (*hablábanos, hablaríanos,* etc., for *hablábamos, hablaríamos,* etc.).[4] Associative interference, of paramount importance in the morphology, as the few examples above indicate, has also been strongly felt in the syntax, as it will be shown in a separate article which is now in preparation.

Most of the linguistic material that forms the basis of this article falls either under the heading of *Blending* or under that of *Analogy.* However, before attempting a classification and a discussion of the material, the terms *blending* and *analogy* should be defined, since there are various interpretations of these two terms.[5] *Blending,* as the writer understands it, is a fusion of two or more words belonging to the same sphere of discourse, as a result of which there arises a new form containing some element of each of the words fused. The blending forms are ordinarily synonyms or words closely related in meaning but may also be opposites.[6] *Analogy,* on the other hand, is the alteration of a word due to the association of that word with a certain group of morphologically related words to which the affected form does not correctly belong.

Blending

The following forms appear to be cases of blending:

Achachurrado (24),[7] 'wrinkled, shrunk,'[8] <*achicharrado,* 'fried or roasted too much, hence dried up and shrunk,' + apachurrado[9] (*despachurrado*), 'smashed, crushed.'

*Arrentar[10] (26) <*arrendar* + *rentar.* It is hard to determine whether *arrentar* is the result of the changing of *d* to *t* in *arrendar* under the influence of *rentar,* in which case the new form should be classified as blending, or whether it is the result of the addition of the prefix *a-* to *rentar* under the influence of words that have the same prefix, in which case it would be analogy.

Atolondronado (216), 'hare-brained,' <*atolondrado* + *tolondrón.* All three forms mean the same thing.

Reprinted by permission from *Hispania Review* 7:4.324-336 (October 1939).

*Atrompillar (292) <*atropellar* + *trompillar.* Both *atrompillar* and *atropellar* mean 'to trample upon' and both are very common in New Mexican Spanish. *Trompillar,* meaning 'to stumble,' does not appear to be used in the dialect. Dr. Espinosa explains *atrompillar* as being derived from *atropellar* through a phonetic change, the *m* being considered as epenthetic.[11] The change of *e* to *i* is not explained.

*Capiruza (409) <*caperuza* + *capirote. Capiruza,* just as the parent forms, means 'a pointed cap.'

*Caribajo (183), 'downcast,' < *cariacontecido* + *cabizbajo.*

Carrumaco (222), 'a cart,' <*carromato* + *carruco.*

Conociencia (393), 'consciousness, knowledge' <*conocimiento* + *conciencia.*

*Chamuz (375), 'a shoe made out of chamois' <French or English *chamois* + *gamuza,* 'chamois.'

*Desadisgusto, 'uncomfortable,' < *desagusto* (*des-* + *a gusto*) + *disgusto. Desagusto* and *desadisgusto,* identical in meaning, are very common in New Mexican Spanish.

*Diforme (266) <*deforme* +*disforme.*

*Envicionar, 'to create a greed in some one (ordinarily a child) for something by showing or speaking to him about that thing,' <*aficionar,* 'to inspire a fondness,' + *enviciar,* 'to teach a bad habit.'

*Gorgollones (128), "bubbling, gushing up of water,' < *gorogoritos* + *borbollones.*

Estrillido (262), 'a loud shrill noise,' < *estrépito,* 'a deafening noise,' + *chillido,* 'a shrill noise.'

*Garruñal (24) appears to be a fusion of *garra, uña* and *marañal,* all three of which suggest things that scratch. *Marañal* and *garrunal* are used synonymously and refer to 'a place covered with brambles.'

*Letardo (355), 'lethargy,' <*letargo* + *retardo. Letargo,* 'lethargy,' and *retardo,* 'delay,' are related in the sense that the former connotes slowness or tardiness in returning to consciousness.

*Luvia, 'a flood,' <*aluvión* + *lluvia.* A propos of *aluvión,* the *Pequeño Larousse* says, "Es barbarismo hacer esta palabra femenina o tomarla por *lluvia, diluvio.*" It is quite possible, then, that the close association of terms *un aluvión* and *una lluvia* gave the form *una luvia.* Dr. Espinosa, on the other hand, suggests that *luvia* possibly comes from *lluvia* through a phonetic change of *ll* to *l.*[12]

*Melancón (183), 'melancholy,' <*melancólico* + *tristón.*

*Turra (107), 'a sound beating,' <*tunda* + *zurra.*

*Valumen, 'volume,' <*volumen* + *balumo (balumbo).* Dr. Espinosa explains the occurrence of *a* in place of *o* in *volumen* as due to dissimilation,[13] but since the terms *volumen* and *balumo* are almost identical in meaning, the writer is more inclined to think that it is a case of blending.

*Varaña (145) <*vara* + *maraña. Vara* and *maraña* are closely related in meaning, the former meaning 'twig, stick,' while the latter means 'underbrush, thicket.' *Varaña,* on the other hand, is used as a synonym of *maraña.*

Vergonzao (150) <*avergonzado* + *vergüenza.*

*Plázamo (357), 'congratulations,' < *pláceme* + *pésamo* (*pésame*), 'condolence.' This word appears to have been influenced by an opposite.

Resquisito (316), 'demand, requirement,' <*requisito* + *exquisito*. Though *requisito* and *exquisito* are not synonymous, they are somewhat related in meaning, the former being used to mean 'demand, requirement,' while the latter is often used in referring to a person who is demanding (with regard to food, neatness, etc.).

Analogy

A far more important phase of associative interference than blending is analogy. However, the number of analogical forms contained in this article is far from being complete. None of the numerous forms mentioned by Dr. Espinosa in his "Studies," already cited, has been included here.

The forms contained in this article have been classified into three groups, depending on whether the part of the word affected is the prefix (if the word has a prefix), the ending or the stem.

1) *Analogical Forms that Involve the Addition or Change of a Prefix.*

a) The following are forms to which the prefix *a-* has been added by analogy with verbs that have such a prefix:

Abastimentar (292), 'to provision,' <*bastimentar*. The change has probably been reinforced here by such words as *abastecer, alistar, apercibir,* etc., which are similar in meaning to *bastimentar.*

Amachar (121) <*machar*. *Aferrarse* and other verbs in which the prefix *a-* expresses intensity have probably helped to induce the change. Both *machar* and *aferrarse* mean 'to insist,' but the form *amachar,* in New Mexican Spanish, has taken the meaning of 'to insist on not moving, to balk.'

Aorillarse (5), 'to come near or reach the shore,' <*orillarse*. The influence of such words as *acercarse, arrimarse, alejarse, aproximarse,* all of which belong to the same sphere of discourse, may have helped to bring about the change.

Apachurrar (54), 'to crush,' <*despachurrar*. The change of prefix here is probably by analogy with such words as *aplastar, achatar, abollar,* etc., which have a similar meaning. In *apachurrar,* and for that matter in *despachurrar* also, the idea of intensity, commonly expressed by the prefix *a-,* is much stronger than that of negation, frequently expressed by *des-.* The change is thus quite reasonable.

Apataliar (357), 'to kick violently,' < *patalear*. The association of this verb with *apalear, apedrear* and *aporrear,* which express similar ideas, must have reinforced the change.

Aprevenir[14] (109), 'to prepare,' <*prevenir*. The change may have been induced, at least in part, by the existence of such verbs as *alistar* and *apercibir,* which are synonymous with the form affected.

Arrempujar (271), 'to push,' <*rempujar*. The verbs *arremeter, arrebatar* and *arrastrar* may have helped to reinforce the change.

Asaciarse (216), 'to satiate oneself,' <*saciarse*. The words *asaz,* 'enough,' and *atacarse,* 'to eat too much,' may have had a special influence in effecting the change.

Asaltiador (89), 'assailant,' < *salteador*. The change here has probably been reinforced by the form *asaltador.*

*Asiñalar (338), 'to point out, mark,' < *señalar. Asignar* and *apuntar* may have exercised some influence in bringing about the alteration.

*Atocar (112) <*tocar.* The archaic form *atentar,* 'to touch,' which is used synonymously with *atocar* in New Mexican Spanish, may have helped to induce the change. Incidentally, the forms *atocar* and *atentar,* 'to touch,' exist alongside of their doublets, *tocar,* 'to play (an instrument), to knock,' and *tentar,* 'to attempt.'

b) In the following forms the change is due to analogy with verbs with the prefix *des-:*

Descudriñar (4), 'to scrutinize,' <*escudriñar.* It is possible that *descubrir* and *desentrañar,* which convey ideas related to that expressed by *escudriñar,* had a special influence.

*Destraviarse (203), 'to get lost,' <*extraviarse.* Such verbs as *desviarse, descarrilar* and *descarriar,* which mean almost the same thing as *extraviarse,* must have helped to induce the change.

*Desfender (34) <*defender.*

c) In the following forms the transformation is by analogy with words with the prefix *en-:*

*Encurucarse[15] /**encorucarse,* 'to huddle up,' <*acurrucarse. Encogerse,* a synonym of *acurrucarse,* may have helped to strengthen the change.

*Enjarrar, 'to plaster with mud,' <*jaharrar.* The change was undoubtedly reinforced by *embarrar,* which means exactly the same thing as *jaharrar,* and possibly by *encalar,* 'to whitewash.'

*Enlistar <*alistar.* Its English equivalent, *enlist,* which is rather familiar to New Mexicans, must have reinforced the alteration.

*Enregistrar (211) <*registrar.* The form *enscribir* (*inscribir*) and possibly *enlistar,* discussed above, both of which are similar in meaning to *registrar,* may have exerted a special influence in inducing the change.

*Ensarta[16] (230), 'a string (as of beads, pearls, etc),' <*sarta.* The change may have been reinforced by the forms *ensartar,* 'to string,' and *ensarte,* a synonym of *sarta.*

Ensolver (103), 'to absolve,' <*absolver.*

d) The change in the following is by analogy with verbs with the prefix *re-:*

Recautelar (118), 'to guard against,' < *cautelar.*

Rejuntar (232), 'to gather' <*juntar.* The change was probably reinforced by such verbs as *reunir* and *recoger* which are synonymous with *juntar.*

e) Miscellaneous analogical changes of prefix:

*Emponjarse, 'to swell, to puff up,' < *esponjarse.* This change is very likely by analogy with such verbs as *empaparse, empanzarse, empanturrarse,* etc., which convey a similar idea to that expressed by *esponjarse.*

Incortés (229), 'discourteous,' <*descortés.* The prefix change here is due to the influence of adjectives in *in-* and very likely the special influence of *inculto, indiscreto* and *impolítico,* the latter form being synonymous with and more common than *descortés.*

Risión (184), 'laughing stock, <*irrisión.* This is by analogy with *risa* and all its derivatives.

2) *Analogical Forms Involving a Change in the Ending.*

By analogy with verbs in *-iar* (< *-iar, ear*), the following infinitives have the ending *-iar* instead of *-ar: *bosteciar, *cociniar* (17), *pastiar* (115), *incensiar* (120), *trotiar* (10).

Agileza (337), 'agility,' < *agilidad.* The change is due to analogy with nouns with the ending *-eza,* and, in particular, *destreza,* a synonym.

Cintón (259), 'band, ribbon, string (of pearls)' < *cinta.* This change is by analogy with nouns that have the termination *-ón,* the change probably being reinforced by *listón,* a synonym.

Concursión (101), 'crowd,' < *concurso.* Undoubtedly this change is due to the influence of nouns ending in *-ión,* such as *reunión, congregación,* etc.

Chapero (171) < *chapeo.* By analogy with nouns with the termination *-ero.* *Sombrero,* a synonym of *chapeo,* must have helped considerably to induce the change. *Chapero* is ordinarily used in referring to 'a very old hat.'

Depositú (278) < *disposición.* The change must be due to the influence of nouns ending in *-tud,* and in particular *actitud,* a synonym.

Humellecido (235), 'humbled,' < *humillado.* This form is the result of analogy with past participles ending in *-ecido* (*agradecido, bendecido, humedecido,* etc.).

Lindura (264) < *lindeza.* The influence of nouns ending in *-ura* and, in particular, *hermosura,* a synonym, is responsible for this change.

Mitiguar (216) < *mitigar.* The change here is due to analogy with verbs with the ending *-uar. Menguar,* a synonym, may have reinforced the change.

Posiando (144) < *poseyendo.* Here the influence of the present participle of verbs of the first conjugation is plain.

Destruygas (157) < *destruyas.* This is by analogy with present subjunctive forms ending in *-ga* (*caiga, traiga,* etc.), while *riygo* (321) < *río* is by analogy with first person present indicative forms that end in *-go* (*caigo, traigo,* etc.). Dr. Espinosa gives many other similar examples.[17]

Through the influence of words ending in *-iza* (*cambiadiza, erradiza, postiza,* etc.) which are exceedingly more common than those ending in *-ifa,* one finds *engañiza* (307) < *engañifa.*

Impedimiento (26) < *impedimento,* under the influence of words in *-miento* (*amontonamiento, acercamiento,* etc.) which are more numerous than those in *-mento.*

Horizante (17) < *horizonte.* The change is by analogy with words ending in *-ante.* The existence of such forms as *confinante, levante,* etc., may have helped to reinforce the change.

Pesquisias (100), 'inquiry, investigation,' < *pesquisas.* The alteration in this form is due to the influence of words with the termination *-sias, -cias* (*noticias, albricias,* etc.).

Riumos (171) for *reuma,* a masculine noun, is probably by analogy with masculine plurals in *-os. Reumatismo* may have influenced the vowel change. In Mexico one finds the form *riumas.*[18]

Verruguiado, 'having rough, lumpy scars' < *verrugoso.* The transformation in this word is by analogy with adjectives that have the ending *-iado,* such as *picotiado* (*picoteado*), *golpiado* (*golpeado*), etc.

Verruguiento < *verrugoso.* The change here is by analogy with adjectives with the termination -*iento*, particularly *sarniento*, *mugriento*, which, just as *verruguiento* does, refer to a condition of the skin. *Verruguiento* and *verruguiado* are synonymous.

Redas (93) <*redes*. The alteration is due to the influence of feminine nouns in -*a*. Hence, one also finds the singular form *reda* (93) <*red*.

Tallo (357) <*talle*. This is the result of analogy with masculine nouns ending in -*o*.

Apparently by analogy with such adverbial phrases as *a tientas*, *a oscuras*, *a gatas*, etc., one finds *al cabos* (97) <*al cabo*, *a rapis* (86)<*al rape*.

3) *Analogical Forms Involving a Change in the Stem.*

Plegue (157) <*pliegue*. The change is by analogy with *plegar*, *plegando*, etc.

Esfórzate (9) <*esfuérzate*. This is by analogy with the infinitive and other forms with an atonic stem vowel.

**Nublina* <*neblina*. The alteration is due to the influence of *nube*, *nublar*, etc.

**Podiendo* (261) <*pudiendo*. The influence of *poder* and other forms with an atonic stem vowel is evident here.

All the inflected forms of **helar*, whether they have a strong or weak stem, have *e* as the thematic vowel. The *e* in the forms with the stressed stem is undoubtedly due to analogy with those forms with an unstressed root. Hence, one hears 'yo me helo' instead of 'yo me hielo.' On the other hand, the noun *hielo* remains unaltered.

The forms **quero* (139), **queres* (182) and **quere* (139), for *quiero*, *quieres* and *quiere*, must be by analogy with the forms that have an atonic stem vowel.

Analogical Creation

Unaware of an already existing form, a speaker will often coin a new derivative or reconstruct a primitive by analogy with sets made up of primitive and derivative with which he is quite familiar.

Following the noun pair, *marqués* and *marquesa*, as a model, the masculine forms *duqués* (304) and *princés* (33) are formed to match the feminine forms *duquesa* and *princesa*. The form *príncipa*, on the other hand, is formed from *príncipe* by analogy with nouns whose feminine form is made by changing the vowel ending of the masculine form to *a*.

The forms **andalón*, **enojón*, **espantón*, **platicón*, derived from *andar*, *enojar*, *espantar*, *platicar*, must be by analogy with such nouns as *comilón*, *tragón*, etc., derived from *comer*, *tragar*, etc.

By analogy with object names from which a feminine noun has been derived to designate the vessel that contains the primitive (*azúcar* : *azucarera*, *café* : *cafetera*, *aceite* : *aceitera*), **florera*, for *florero*, has been derived from *flor*.

Under the influence of masculine nouns that have a corresponding feminine form in -*a* (*brujo* : *bruja*, *sabio* : *sabia*, *jugador* : *jugadora*, etc.) we find the following: *genia* (224) from *genio*, *taura* (122) from *taure* (*tahur*).

By analogy with such names of sounds as *aullido*, *bufido*, *chiflido*, *chillido*, etc., which are derived from *aullar*, *bufar*, *chiflar*, *chillar*, etc., the forms **llorido* and *resollido* are derived from *llorar* and *resollar*. As for the form *volido*, derived from *volar*, it is very possible that, since its use is restricted almost entirely to its usage in the phrases, *dar un volido* and *pegar un volido*, it is by analogy with forms ending in *-ido*, such as those that appear in the phrases *dar un estampido, dar un estallido*, all of which connote suddenness. The form *volido*, which has not entirely replaced the form *vuelo*, occurs also in South and Central America and does not appear to be unknown in Spain.[19]

By analogy with nouns whose diminutive form is made by adding the ending *-ito*, one finds the following diminutives in *-ito* instead of *-ecito* : *cuerito*, *piesito*, *tiernito*, *lengüita*, *pueblito*, *piedrita*, etc.

The forms *enfandangado*, *enfiestado* and *ennoviado*, designating a person absorbed in or extremely fond of the thing expressed by the primitive, are derived from *fandango, fiesta* and *novio* by analogy with *enfrascado, enviciado*, etc., derived from *frasco, vicio*, etc.

Apensionado (179) derived from *pensión*, and *asucidiado*, derived from *sucidio*, are probably the result of analogy with *apenado*, from *pena, apesarado* from *pesar, apesadumbrado* from *pesadumbre*, etc. The above five derivatives, just as all five primitives, are synonymous in meaning or nearly so.

In all the forms of *arriesgar* in which the stem vowel is atonic, New Mexican Spanish has *e* in place of *ie* : *arresgar* (144), *arresgara* (181), *arresgado* (233), *arresgó* (227). This must be by analogy with radical changing verbs that have *ie* when the stem is stressed and *e* when not stressed.[20]

Resgoso (124), for *riesgoso*, the only derivative form coming from *riesgo* that exists, has suffered the same fate as forms of *arriesgar* with weak stems.

Deshabilitado, for *inhabilitado*, has been formed apparently by analogy with the English word *disabled*. The newly coined form is probably the result of an attempt to translate the English term, which frequently appears in government literature sent to Spanish-speaking ex-service men in New Mexico and Colorado. This form, of course, could also be the result of analogy with words with the prefix *des-*.

By analogy with verbs that have noun derivatives in *-era* (*cerrar* : *cerradera*, *plañir* : *plañidera*, etc.), we find *agarradera*, derived from *agarrar*, instead of the accepted form, *agarradero*.

Under the influence of *faldero*, derived from *falda*, and applied to 'a man excessively fond of being among women,' one finds *mujerero*, derived from *mujer* and synonymous with *faldero*. By a further analogical formation, one also finds *hombrera*, from *hombre*, meaning 'a woman who is extremely fond of being among men.' The form *mujerero* occurs also in Central and South America.[21]

By analogy with such pairs of noun and verb as *corazón* : *descorazonar*, *cabeza* : *descabezar, nuca* : *desnucar*, according to which a verb expressing negation is formed by adding the prefix *des-* and the ending *-ar* to the noun, the word *descuadrilar*, for *descuadrillar*, is formed from *cuadril*.

Desagusto is formed from *a gusto* by analogy with *desagradable, descontento*, etc., derived from *agradable, contento*, etc.

By analogy with such forms as *desenredar*, derived from *enredar*, one encounters *desenraizar*, derived from *enraizar*.

Allagado, derived from *llaga*, is by analogy with such formations as *agrietado,* from *grieta, alocado,* from *loco,* according with which the prefix *a-* and the ending *-ado* are added to the noun stem in order to form the adjective.

By analogy with *encorajarse, encolerizarse, endiablarse, enfurecerse,* etc., derived from *coraje, cólera, diablo, furia,* etc., one finds *encorajinarse,* derived from *corajina* (also in Southern Spain).

*Entretorcer, derived from *tocer,* has been formed under the influence of such verbs as *entretejer,* from *tejer, entrelazar,* from *lazar,* etc.

*Estrufuniar/*estrujuniar, from *estrujón* and *estrufón (estrujón),* are apparently analogical creations under the influence of such forms as *taconiar (taconear),* from *tacón, taloniar (talonear),* from *talón,* etc. *Estrufuniar* and *estrujuniar* mean in New Mexican Spanish 'to shake someone angrily.' The literary form, *estrujar,* appears to be unknown in New Mexico.

*Sueñoso, for *soñoliento,* derived from *sueño,* is by analogy with such forms as *calenturoso,* from *calentura, deseoso,* from *deseo,* etc.

By analogy with such derivatives with the ending *-ista,* as *maquinista,* from *maquina, violinista,* from *violín,* etc., one encounters **valorista,* for *valiente,* derived from *valor.*

Ultracorrection

The occurrence of *facalito* (143), **fuego* (358), **fuez* (358), for *jacalito* (from Mexican *xa-calli*), *juego,* 'game,' and *juez,* is probably due to ultracorrection. Such must also be the case with *f* in **fuella* (159) for *juella* (*huella,* from *hollar* < Latin *fullare*). *Fuella* can hardly be considered an archaism. This untracorrection, if it is such, must be due to a consciousness, on the part of the speaker, of the incorrect occurrence of *j* in place of *f* in many words (*jué, juerte,* etc.).

Popular Etymology

*Solesía (227) for *celosía,* 'a window blind,' is plainly by the association of the word with *sol.*

*Cuerpo espín, for *puerco espín,* is very likely the result of popular etymology. *Puerco* being rarely used substantively in southern Colorado and northern New Mexico,[22] the form *puerco espín* sounds incorrect to the Spanish-speaking people of the region, so much so that to a certain acquaintance of the writer it seemed preposterous that anyone should consider *puerco espín* more correct than *cuerpo espín.* In view of the lack of familiarity of New Mexicans with *puerco* in the sense of 'pig,' *cuerpo espín* sounds more descriptive to them of the animal in question than *puerco espín.*

Malapropisms

The following are examples of words used with meanings belonging to other words similar in form:

*abrazada for *brazado, alvertido (advertido)* (6) for *vertido, *apercibir* (313) for *percibir, *antes* (336) for *ante, *aprobar* (244) for *probar, *arrapar* (62) for *rapar, *carretilla* for *carrete, cautivo* (236) for *cautiverio, *convenir* (236) for

convencer, encaramar (338) for *encarar, encastillado* (231) for *encasquillado, estrecho* (1) for *trecho, *guajalote*[23] for *ajalote, impensablemente* (35) for *impensadamente, intestable* (177) for *intestado, *machucar* for *machacar, *en pues* (15) for *en pos, *pos* (15) for *pues, pronóstico* (118) for *pronosticador, proposición* (314) for *propósito, rentar* (26) for *arrendar, representar* (93) for *presentar, responder* (27) for *corresponder, *saludes* for *saludos, *sanitario* for *sanatorio, *servicial* (116) for *sirviente, *tanque* (232) for *estanque.*[24]

Cuanta[25] < *cuanto ha,* meaning 'formerly' or 'long ago,' becomes **cuantuay* apparently by a confusion of *ha* and *hay.*

Of all the forms discussed in this article, as far as the writer has been able to ascertain, at least seventy-five percent (those designated with an asterisk) are frequently heard in daily New Mexican Spanish. With regard to those forms not marked with an asterisk, it is possible that they are individual errors rather than forms in common use. While the general acceptance in the dialect of so many analogical forms may not be of any great significance, since analogical forms very often meet popular sanction, it is quite remarkable that so many of the blends and malapropisms given above should have found such a wide-spread acceptance in New Mexican Spanish, in view of the fact that blends and malapropisms are generally considered individual peculiarities which are not repeated by others.[26] In the case of the blends, seventy-five percent of them have become generally accepted in the region where they were recorded, whereas, with respect to the malapropisms listed, at least half of them have become a part of the general vocabulary.

Notes

[1] The term 'New Mexican Spanish' is used here to mean the Spanish spoken in northern New Mexico and southern Colorado, the region studied by the writer.

[2] A. M. Espinosa, "Studies in New Mexican Spanish" (Morphology): *Revue de Dialectologie Romane,* 1912, IV, 241-256, § 105.

[3] *Ibid.,* § 106, B, 1.

[4] *Ibid.,* § 107.

[5] According to Strong, Logeman and Wheeler (*The History of Language,* London, 1891, p. 140), blending occurs "when two synonymous forms or constructions force themselves simultaneously, or at least in very closest succession, into our consciousness, so that one part of the one replaces or, it may be, ousts a corresponding part of the other; the result being that a new form arises in which some elements of the one are confused with some elements of the other." Analogy, on the other hand, "manifests itself as the alteration of one form in compliance with a rule more or less consciously abstracted from a group to which that form does not, strictly speaking, belong." E. H. Sturtevant (*Linguistic Change,* Chicago, 1917, p. 39) defines blending as follows: "When two words interfere with each other in such a way that the resulting word contains about equal parts of both, the process is sometimes called contamination." He does not give a definition for analogy. I. J. S. Taraporewala (*Elements of the Science of Language,* Calcutta, 1932, p. 187, § 64), speaking of blending, states: "It occurs when two ideas or constructions come up in the mind of the speaker simultaneously or following each other so closely that the two get fused into one, each 'contaminating' the other...." Regarding analogy, he says: "It frequently happens that a certain group of words are associated together in the mind of the

speaker. This association may be due to any reason–phonetic or other; and when another word seemingly related to that group comes along, the human mind desires to put the word also in a form such as may make it recognizable as belonging to that group."

[6]Dr. Frederick Anderson, under whom I have done a large share of my work in philology at Stanford University, was the first to call my attention to the blending of opposites, "as in the case of *reddere* + *prendere*." Since then I have found a number of similar cases of fusion in New Mexican Spanish. Dr. Anderson also believes that "the definition of blending should include semantic blending (e.g., *demean* becoming *to act meanly*, by analogy to *mean*)." However, thus far I have not met any forms in New Mexican Spanish in which this type of blending takes place.

[7]The number in parenthesis after a form refers to the number of the folk-tale in which the word occurs in the writer's unpublished doctoral dissertation, *A Study of the Phonology and Morphology of New Mexican Spanish Based on a Collection of 410 Folk-Tales*, Stanford University, 1937, Part III.

[8]Only the meanings of comparatively rare words and of words whose meaning differs from that in the literary language will be given here.

[9]This form is explained under *Analogy*.

[10]Forms indicated with an asterisk, some of which do not occur in the writer's folk-tale collection, are words which the writer has heard time after time.

[11]Aurelio M. Espinosa, *Estudios sobre el español de Nuevo Méjico*. Traducción y reelaboración con notas por Amado Alonso y Angel Rosenblat, Parte I, Fonética (*Biblioteca de Dialectología Hispanoamericana*), Buenos Aires, 1930, § 34, 2.

[12]*Ibid.*, § 160.

[13]*Ibid.*, § 50.

[14]This form has been recorded by Rufino José Cuervo in his *Apuntaciones críticas sobre el lenguaje bogotano, con frecuente referencia al de los países de Hispano-América*, Paris, 1907, § 903.

[15]The form *encurrucarse* is recorded by Cuervo, *op. cit.*, § 916.

[16]According to *Pequeño Larousse*, this form occurs also in Guatemala.

[17]A. M. Espinosa, "Studies in New Mexican Spanish," *Revue de Dialectologie Romane*, 1911, III, 251, § 119.

[18]Federico Gamboa, *La Llaga*, México, 1910, p. 317.

[19]Miguel Luis Amunátegui Reyes, *Observaciones i enmiendas a un Diccionario, aplicables también a otros*, Santiago de Chile, 1927, III, 296.

[20]Cuervo, in *op. cit.*, § 870, records *resgoso*.

[21]Darío Rubio, *La anarquilla del lenguaje en la América Española*, México, 1925, Tomo II, p. 50.

[22]In place of *puerco*, meaning 'pig,' the words *marrano* and *cochino* are used almost exclusively, *cerdo* being heard occasionally.

[23]This word means 'tadpole' in southern Colorado and northern New Mexico. The word never means 'turkey' in that region as it does in Mexico.

[24]It is quite possible that some of these forms (*apercibir, aprobar*, etc.) are analogical forms rather than malapropisms.

[25]This form occurs in Chile. See Manuel Guzmán Maturana, "Cuentos tradicionales en

Chile," *Anales de la Universidad de Chile*, Tercer trimestre, 1934, No. 15, p. 76.

[26]I. J. S. Taraporewala, "Contamination in Language," in the *Sir Asutosh Mookerjee Silver Jubilee Volumes*, Vol. III, Orientalia–Part 2, Calcutta, 1925.

Some Aspects of Arizona Spanish

Anita C. Post

The early Spanish explorers, Vasco Nuñez Cabeza de Vaca (if we accept Carl Sauer's contention that de Vaca and his companions crossed Arizona in 1536),[1] Fray Marcos de Niza, and Francisco Coronado, not to mention others, while they figure in legend and story and lend romance to a glorious past, did not establish any permanent settlements in the state. Not until Father Eusebio Francisco Kino founded San Xavier del Bac near Tucson in 1700, and Guevavi and Tumacacori in 1702, was this accomplished.[2]

The success of Father Kino as ranchman, stockman, and missionary made possible the later expeditions of Captain Juan Bautista de Anza to California—expeditions which led to the founding of San Francisco, and made possible permanent settlements in your state.[3]

In spite of the failure to establish Missions and, therefore, permanent settlements on the Colorado at Yuma, there was some intercourse with California across Pimería Alta (southern Arizona) between 1774, the date of Anza's first expedition, and the discovery of gold. The opening of navigation on the river, the establishment of forts, the movement of troops during the Mexican War, the Gadsden Purchase, all stimulated trade. For this reason, the language of southern Arizona, Sonora, and California is very similar. Colonization was late; many of the colonists and soldiers were from the north of Spain, and the language they brought with them was the Spanish of the sixteenth and seventeenth centuries.[4]

Material for this paper was taken from a study based on the oral tradition of the older communities of the Gadsden Purchase in Arizona. The language has suffered little change, owing to isolation and scanty immigration. Phonetic changes have followed a normal development. There has been no Indian influence upon syntax or pronunciation and little on vocabulary. A large number of words from Nahuatl or Aztec were brought by the settlers from Mexico. At first the Indians learned Spanish; now they are learning English.

English began to make itself felt on both sides of the border about the middle of the nineteenth century. Early settlers and their children had to learn Spanish. Spanish was the language of the playground and the street. With the establishment of schools in the early 'seventies, however, English soon began to dominate, with the result that almost everyone now speaks English, or understands it, at least. As a consequence, there has been a mixing of the two languages, with an impoverished vocabulary in both. Americanization, especially since the World War, tends to lessen the use of Spanish, although many children of Spanish-American parents are studying Spanish in the schools—a language

Reprinted by permission from *Hispania* 16:1.35-42 (February-March 1933). This paper was originally read at the Sixteenth Annual Meeting of the American Association of Teachers of Spanish, San Francisco, December, 1932.

almost foreign to some of them.

It is difficult to predict what the Spanish of the future will be. Many archaic forms are disappearing; new words are coming in from Mexico; many more are being formed from English words. The Spanish of the future may be purer or it may disappear.

As is to be expected, words obsolete or provincial in Spain today are still current in Arizona and the rest of Spanish America: *fierro, platicar, semos, truje, vide, vido, asina, ansí, ansina, áunque, onque, muncho, lamber, onde, cuasi* (rare).

Phonology

In general, articulation is slower, more relaxed than in Madrid or Mexico City. Intonation, however, is not unlike that of Spain, but very different from that of Mexico City.

There is the same tendency to reduce vowels to a single syllable or diphthong, as in Castilian, in New Mexico, Mexico, and Spanish America.[5]

Accent

Following a universal law, accent shifts to the more open of two contiguous vowels:[6] *ái, cáir, cái[r], léido, Helóisa, egóista, incréible, sáuco, máis, páis, ráis, periódo, ociáno, máistro, máistra.*

General changes in accentuation: *méndigo, sélebre, pántano.* Strangely enough, the correct pronunciation is preserved in the geographical name, Pantano Wash.[7]

In the present subjunctive, first person plural, of all verbs of more than two syllables, accent shifts to the first syllable: *váyamos, véngamos, haígamos, siéntemos, siéntamos, muéramos.*

Diphthongization without shift of accent: *almuada, lión, cuete, pueta, antiojos, golpiar.* These changes were regular in Old Spanish.[8]

Vowel Changes

In general, accented vowels remain unchanged. New infinitives are usually formed in *-iar*, a few in *-ear* and *-ar*, but many infinitives in *-ar* become *-iar* verbs: *galopiar, trotiar;* and from English: *espichiar, telefoniar (telefonar* in Mexico City), *tritiar, cranquiar.*

The diphthongs *ie* and *io* from accented *e* and *o* do not change when the accent shifts to another syllable in forming derivatives: *vientesito, casuelita, suelaso, espuelaso, espuelón* but *ventarrón* and *pedrada* do not diphthongize as a rule.[9]

Vocalic Groups

Vocalic groups simplify: *aijado, orrar, orcar, ogarse, estrordinario, tapojo, sanoria, umear, umiar, umar, orita, oritita, p'onde (para donde).*

Two like vowels are reduced to one: *crer, ler.* This single vowel is often lengthened.[10]

Other Vowel Changes

Ei is *i: sonrir, rir, engrir, frir, vía.*
Eo is *io* and sometimes *o : creo que* > *crjoke, croke.*
Leocadia gives *Ljocadja,* but *Teodosia* gives *Tjodosa.*
Ia is *a* in *molesta,* but *saliva* and *lombriz* give *salivia* and *lombrisia.* These two examples may be influenced by analogy to nouns in *-ia* or be confused with some medical term.
Ie is *e : pasensja, consensja, sensja, esperensja*—old forms. *Diferjensja* and *indiferjensja* are common to Spain as well as Spanish America and show the opposite change: *e* to *ie* assimilation.[11]
Ie is *i* in *sintopie*—plural *sintopies* or *-pieses.*
Ue is *u* in *pus* (oftener *pos*), *tútano.* The correct forms alternate with these.
Ue is *e* in *prebo, prebar,* commonest in the speech of children.[12]
Uo, stressed or unstressed, is *o : lengón, individo, respetoso.*[13]

Consonants

Intervocalic *b, v* in any position are pronounced by those who speak Spanish and English as a labiodental.[14] Initial *bue, vue* are sometimes *güe,* especially in the speech of children, but generally *we: weno, welbe, welta.*[15] *B* is generally lost before *ue* except when emphatic. This phenomenon is characteristic of Old and New Castile, Chile, Mexico, New Mexico, etc.[16] *B* is lost, also, when final in a syllable: *oscuro, escuro;* in *sub-: sustansia, sustitusión, suterraneo, suterraño, sumarino, sumiso. Mb* in *lamber* is archaic.[17] Other forms are: *lambrusco, lambida, lambión.*
F is the same as in Castilian. It is often aspirated in words like *fuego, fue, fuerte: xwego, xwe, xwerte.* Same conditions for medial *f: dixunto, axwera.*
Donde is *onde,* an Old Spanish form, everywhere.[18] All final *d*'s are lost: *verdá, libertá, mercé;* intervocalic *d* is pronounced in the past participles, although very softly: *hablaðo, léiðo, viviðo.* It has fallen in two interesting phrases: *en casa de* and *en ca[sa]* become *énkese, enke; con todo y todo* becomes *con toitodo* and not *contwitodo,* as in New Mexico.[19]
Ll is generally *y: cabayo, siya, faldiya.* This *y* is lost sometimes, but is retained in emphatic speech.
Intrusive *m: trompesar, trompesón; lamber* gives *lambrusco. Zambullir* is *sambutir. Se sambutió 'nel awa.*[20]
N as in Castilian. *Nm* are both pronounced in careful speech, but, as in Spain and the Americas, it generally becomes *m.* Final *m* is *n: albún, Abrán.*
Y as in Castilian. Sporadically it becomes *y* in *yo, ya,* especially with a negative: *ya no, yo no.*
All forms of *r* as in Castilian. Sporadically final *r* is trilled: *mujer, morir, salir.* There is a growing tendency to pronounce *r* in *carne* with the value of English *r.* Final *l* is *r* in *delantar, platanar.*
S for *s, z, c* before *e, i.* Both *s* and *z* become sonant [*s*] before *d, b, g,* but not before *m, n,* or *l: mismo, fresno, las manos;* medial *s* becomes *r* in *murlo, irla.* Sporadically *s* is aspirated in *sí, hi.*
The velars as in Spain and New Mexico, but initial *g* is fricative sometimes:

gato, gusto. Initial *g* before *ua* nearly always falls, except after *n*: *un guarda, un guante;* otherwise *warda, wante.* The same is true of intervocalic *g: awa, auwa, iwal. G* frequently replaces initial or medial *k: godornís, garraspera, desgote, desgotado. Haiga* for *haga* is the survival of an old form.[21] *G* drops in the group *gn: Inasio, inorante, persinarse.*

K as in Castilian. It drops in groups: *letor, perfeto, dotor, defeto; ks* (*cc* or *x*) simplifies in *estranjero, sesto, lesión.*

X (*j, ge, gi,* and sometimes *h*) is a voiced pharyngeal spirant, much softer than in Castilian. Aspirated *h* in Arizona is a survival of Old Spanish: *xalar, xalado, xediondo. H* for *f* has been noted: *xwersas, xwi, xwe.* Medial *h: retaxila, moxoso, enmoxesido.* [2]

Vocalization of consonants is rare: *cápsula* gives *káusula.*[23]

Addition of Sounds

Aprobar, arremedar, afigurarse, rempujar, rempujón, destender, destornudar, descarmenar. Cuervo ascribes this to confusion of prefixes.[24]

Groups of Sounds

Alrevesado, emprestar, entengas, endenantes, titiritar, cacaraquiar, dedeveras. Intensive *rede, reteque,* or *requete* plus *bueno, malo,* etc.[25]

La sorra y el coyote

La sorra y el coyote qu' eran muy amigos, eya que tenía muchambre le dijo: "Hermano Coyote, vamos aquí en qui un' amiga. Se casó su hija di un amigo mío." Y entonses le dijo: "ayí vamos porque tienen munchas gayinas en un gayinero detrás de la casa. Cuandu está la bod' andando tu y yo vamos a comer gayina." Y al ruido qu' hisieron las gayinas salió la gente y corrieron al coyote contoi sorra y arrancaron sin comer nada. Y entonses le dijo la sorr' al coyote: "No te vayas, Hermano Coyote. Yo te voy a yevar en un ranchit' onde hay munchos quesos." Lo quiso haser en crer que la luna qu' estab' adentro di un tanque di auwa calient' er' un queso. "Mira, Hermano Coyote," y si asomó y luego le peg' un rempujón y cayó dentro. Y como pudo salió y luego arrancó muy 'nojado con la sorra. Y la sorra sescondió. "Oiga, Señor de las Mangas Coloradas, ¿qué nu ha vistu a mi marido por ái? " Más coraje le daba' al coyote. Voltea y le dise: "Anda, sorra condenada, que ni he de voltiar payá."

El viejo pobre y el Diablo[26]

Habí' una familia muy pobre. " 'Stamos muy pobres," diju el vieju a la vieja, su mujer, "tengo que salir a buscar la vida y voy a ver si encuentru al diablo y le voy a vender mi vida." "Amigo, ven: te necesito, amigo Diablo." Y va saliendo en un cabayo muy generoso, muy bonito. Y le dijo que le vendía la vida por mil pesos. Y dijo que 'staba bueno. Le diu el dinero y se lo yevu el viejo. Y luegu hay muncho tiempo fue a yevarse al hombre. Y luego le dijo: "Dáme tiempo," le diju al Diablo, "teng' un niño chiquito. Y vas [a] haser todo lo qu' el muchachitu hag' en el cuarto." Brincab' en una mesa y él hasía lo mismo. Y luego, catatumbas en el suelo y él hasiendo todo. Y al fin, se bajó y s'embarró la cara con soquete y toda la cochinada que pud' agarrar. Entonses diju el Diablo: "Hast' aquí agarrat' el dinero, que no me debes nada."

*Las prendas nuevas*²⁷

Una ves había cuatro señoritas. Una tenía sapatos nuevos; otra tenía un aniyo; otra, unos aretes y l'última una soguia todos nuevos. Pa yamar l'atensión dijo la del aniyo: " ¡Mir' el animal! " "¿En dond' está? " dijo la de la soguia, alargando el pescueso. "Yo lo mataré," dijo la del sapato, sacando el pie, y la de los aretes dijo, meneando la cabesa: " ¡No, no, no! "

Popular or Traditional Songs

Cápitán di un buque
Mé mand' ún papel
Qué si no quería
Cásarme con él.

Tánt'anduv' ési hombre,
Cón ese papel,
Hásta que mi máma,
Ló yegu á saber.

"Vén acá, muchacha,
Díme la verdá."
"Nó crea, mamá,
Es púra falsedá."

Mé'nserru én un cuarto;
Mé dio de comer
Sémitas calientes,
Y miel de maguey.²⁸

A la rorro, niño lindo
A la rorro, mi creador.
Duérmete niño, adorado,
Duérmete, mi Redentor.

Duérmete, mi chiquitito,
Duérmete, mi corazón,
Duérmete, mi dulce dueño,
En la cuna de mi amor.

Duérmete, niñito hermoso,
Duérmete, mi dulce amor,
Duérmete, niño chiquitito
Haz cuna de mi corazón.²⁹

Dios te salve, María,
Llena eres de gracia,
El Señor es contigo.
Bendita tu eres,
Entre todas las mujeres,
Y Bendito es el Fruto
De tu vientre, Jesús.

Santa María, Madre de Dios,
Ruega por nosotros, pecadores,
Ora, y en l'ora de nuestra muerte,
Y así sea, Jésus, María. ³⁰

Notes

[1]*Ibero-Americana*, No. 3, *The Road to Cíbola*, Carl Sauer (University of California Press, Berkeley, California, 1932).

[2]Hubert H. Bancroft, *The History of the North Mexican States*, Vol. I (1531-1800), chap. iv, pp. 19-20; Herbert Eugene Bolton, *Kino's Historical Memoir of Pimería Alta* (The Arthur H. Clark Company, Cleveland, 1919).

[3]Charles E. Chapman, *The Founding of Spanish California*, (1916), chap. xii, pp. 273-76, 349-56.

[4]Aurelio M. Espinosa, *Estudios sobre el español de Nuevo Méjico, Traducción y re-elaboración con notas por Amado Alonso y Angel Rosenblat*, Parte I, *Fonética* (Biblioteca de Dialectología Hispanoamericana, Buenos Aires, 1930), Sec. 2, and notes.

[5]Amado Alonso, *Problemas de dialectogía hispanoamericana*, I, *C*, pp. 369-70.

[6]Ramón Menéndez Pidal, *Manual de gramática española* (Madrid, 1929), 5th Ed., Sec. 6, subd. 2; Constantino Suárez, *Vocabulario Cubano*, Supplement to 14th Edition of *Diccionario de la Real Academia de la Lengua* (Habana, 1921); Juan Eugenio Hartzenbusch, Letter to Cuervo in *Apéndices al Prólogo, Apuntaciones críticas sobre el lenguaje bogotano, con frecuente referencia al de los países de Hispano-América*, 6th Ed. (Paris, 1914); C. H. Grandgent, *Latín Vulgar*, Trad. Francisco de B. Moll (Madrid, 1928), Sec. 136; Meyer-Lübke, *Lingüística Románica*, Trad. Américo Castro (Madrid, 1926), Sec. 111.

[7]Espinosa, *op. cit.*, Sec. 12, p. 53 and note 3.

[8]Fritz Krüger, *Studien zur Lautgeschichte westspanischen Mundarten* (Hamburg, 1914), Sec. 167; Alonzo, *op. cit.*, I, *A*, p. 339.

[9]Espinosa, *op. cit.*, Sec. 55.

[10]Tomás Navarro Tomás, "La cantidad silábica de unos versos de Rubén Darío," *Revista de Filología Española*, IX, 1 (1922).

[11]Espinosa, *op. cit.*, Sec. 72, note 3.

[12]C. C. Marden, "The Phonology of the Dialect of Mexico City," *Publications of the Modern Language Association of America* (New Series), Vol. IV, No. 1; M. Pidal, *op. cit.*, Sec. 13, subd. 2; Krüger, *op. cit.*, Sec. 73.

[13]Espinosa, *op. cit.*, Sec. 78.

[14]*Ibid.*, Sec. 92, and note; N. Tomás, *op. cit.*, Secs. 75, 81, 91; M. Pidal, *op. cit.*, Sec. 35, subd. 2*a*, labiodental *v*, Valencia and Majorca.

[15]Espinosa, *op. cit.*, Sec. 118, subd. 3; Carlos Gagini, *Diccionario de costarriqueñismos*, 2d Ed. (San José de Costa Rica, 1919); G. Icazbalceta, *Vocabulario de mexicanismos* (Méjico, 1899); Cuervo, *El castellano en América*, Sec. 44; Krüger, *op. cit.*, Sec. 208.

[16]M. Pidal, *op cit.*, Sec. 70; Alonso, *Equivalencia acústica, Apéndice IX*, pp. 466-67, and notes 1 and 2; Cuervo, *Apuntación*, Sec. 769; M. Pidal, *Orígenes del español*, 2d Ed. (Madrid, 1929), Secs. 52, 90, 94.

[17]Espinosa, *op. cit.*, Sec. 100; M. Pidal, *Orígenes*, Sec. 46.

[18]Espinosa, *op. cit.*, Sec. 100; M. Pidal, *Orígenes*, Sec. 46; Marden, *op. cit.*, Sec. 29.

[19]Espinosa, *op. cit.*, Sec. 77.

[20]*Ibid.*, Sec. 178, subd. 4 and note 3; Marden, *op. cit.*, Sec. 52; M. Pidal, *Orígenes*, Sec. 52; M. L. Wagner, *Beiträge zur Kenntnis des Juden-spanisches von Konstantinopel* (Vienna, 1914); Krüger, *op. cit.*, Sec. 299.

[21]Marden, *op. cit.*, Sec. 51, Vizcaya and Aragón.

[22]Espinosa, *op. cit.*, Sec. 139; Cuervo, *Apuntación*, Sec. 905; Bello-Cuervo, *Gramática*, Notes, pp. 21, 25.

[23]Espinosa, *op. cit.*, Secs. 167-77; Marden, *op. cit.*

[24]Cuervo, *op. cit.*, Sec. 917.

[25]Espinosa, *op. cit.*, Secs. 188; 191, and note 2; 192, notes 1, 2.

[26]These two stories were obtained at Yuma.

[27]This is usually acted out. Collected at Yuma.

[28]I have marked the rhythmic accent, which comes, with the exception of one line, on the first syllable. The others come on the accented syllable.

[29]This lullaby is taken from a *Pastorela* that has been given at Yuma a number of times. I believe the music is traditional.

[30]This Spanish version of the *Ave Maria* is sung by the choir, or by the congregation, in the absence of one, during the Rosary in Arizona and Sonora. I think the music is traditional.

Dialectal and Nonstandard Forms
in Texas Spanish

Donald M. Lance

Introductory Note: One often hears comments to the effect that the Spanish of Mexican Americans is grammatically "corrupt" or "deficient" in any number of ways. Having heard a good deal of Chicano Spanish, and having studied Spanish formally, I have long had doubts about the truth of that kind of statement and thus conducted some research in the spring and summer of 1969 to test the truth of that position. Our research team interviewed three generations of a bilingual family in Bryan, Texas, in order to make a study of their English and their Spanish. The Spanish-speaking population of the city comprises less than 10% of that community. This article and the one titled "Spanish-English Code Switching" in a later section of this volume are reprinted, with minor revisions, from the final report on the project.

The informants in the project were the following:

(1) Grandfather, 58; born in South Texas; no formal education; self-employed: carpentry and yard work; minimal command of English
(2) Grandmother, 55; born in South Texas; no formal education; housewife; no speaking knowledge of English
(3) Father, 33, son of (1) and (2); 4 years of education; semi-skilled employee
(4) Mother, 28, wife of (3); 3 years of education; maid
(5) Sister of (3), 16; in the 9th grade
(6-9) Children of (3,4) (fictitious names):
    Rachel, 12; in the 5th grade
    Tom, 11; in the 4th grade
    Richard, 9; in the 2nd grade
    Mollie, 8; in the 2nd grade
(10) Neighbor, 39; native of Bryan; 5 years of education; housewife
(11) Janie, 8, neighbor's daughter; in the 2nd grade

The most interesting point to be made about the Spanish of the informants in this project is that that they used very few forms that are not also used in other parts of the Spanish-speaking world. Many of the "deviant" forms are actually archaic forms that also occur in other areas of the world, and some of the pronunciation features reflect phonological trends found elsewhere in American Spanish. The only feature that might represent a linguistic change unique to Texas Spanish is a seeming confusion of the forms for the imperfect tense, the conditional, and the past subjunctive forms of certain verbs. The children and the neighbor—who spoke only English between the ages of about eight and

Reprinted by permission of Texas A&M University. This article is a section of *A Brief Study of Spanish-English Bilingualism: Final Report, Research Project ORR-Liberal Arts-15504,* Texas A&M University, August 25, 1969; also available as ERIC Document ED 032 529. Financial support was provided by the Research Council of Texas A&M University.

about eighteen—were the only ones who displayed an appreciable amount of English interference in their Spanish. Many of the children's "errors," like their "errors" in English, seem to be largely developmental. On the whole, no justification was found for the common belief—held particularly by monolingual Anglos, but also by many Mexican-Americans—that Texas Spanish is impoverished in its vocabulary and grammar and is generally "corrupt." A more relativistic, less dogmatic, and undoubtedly more useful description of their language is that it is very much like that of other people who have not received the amount and kind of education required to instruct the children of the speech community in the proper use of the King's or Academy's language. Analogous comments might be made about rural Yorkshire versus Oxbridge, Appalachian versus Princetonian, or Andalucian peasant versus Castillian Academy speech, though no true parallels can ever be drawn in language behavior because the history, sociology, and cultural psychology of each section of any country is inevitably different.

In this paper four general areas will be discussed: general pronunciation features, verb forms, regional vocabulary, and interference from English. In order to compare the Spanish of the informants with the Spanish of the rest of the world, it is necessary to make references to earlier studies of a more comprehensive nature. The following books were used:

Cerda, Gilberto, Berta Cabaza, and Julieta Farias. *Vocabulario español de Tejas.* Austin: University of Texas Press, 1953.

González, Gustavo. "A Linguistic Profile of the Spanish-Speaking First-Grader in Corpus Christi." Unpublished Master's Thesis. University of Texas at Austin, August, 1968.

Lapesa, Rafael. *Historia de la lengua española,* sixth edition. Madrid: Escelicer, S. A., 1965.

Menéndez Pidal, R. *Manual de gramática histórica española,* eleventh edition. Madrid: Espasa-Calpe, S.A., 1962.

Real Academia Española. *Diccionario manual e ilustrado de la lengua española,* second edition. Madrid: Espasa-Calpe, S. A., 1950.

Santamaría, Francisco J. *Diccionario de mejicanismos.* Méjico: Editorial Porrúa, S. A., 1959.

An observation that Anglos often make about Texas Spanish is that it is spoken very fast, all run together. Lapesa, in a comment on the influences of Indian linguistic substrata on American Spanish, makes a similar statement about Mexican Spanish in general:

Cabe admitir influjos de igual origen, primitivos o no, en el ritmo del hablar, que altera la regular duración de las sílabas: el mejicano abrevia nerviosamente las no acentuadas. . . , mientras el argentino se detiene con morosidad antes del acento y en la sílaba que lo lleva, y el cubano se mueve con perezosa lentitud. (p. 346)

Some of his wording might raise American eyebrows, and the Cuban Spanish I have heard is hardly *lento,* but the comment of the Mexicans' suppressing unaccented syllables is easily documented by citing just a few of the many examples recorded in our interviews: *'toy, 'stá, tá, 'taba, 'tuve* (forms of *estar*), *'cer (hacer), vo' (voy), mu' (muy), só (sólo), l'igo (le digo), v'ese (ve ese), l' edad (la edad), es' otras (esas otras), qu' él (que él), pa'l (para el), pa' 'rriba (para arriba), pa' 'llá (para allá), pa' 'cá (para acá), pa' que (para que), pa' 'fuera (para afuera).* As well, a single consonant may be lost: *colora'o (colorado), que'an (quedan), a'eces (a veces), me 'ijé (me fijé).* Sometimes the syllable lost is a medial one that ordinarily carries word stress but is lost because it is in an unstressed position in the sentence: *l'o (luego), pa'ce (parece), tra'a (trabaja).* The initial syllable of a few words was always suppressed in the interviews: *'prender (aprender* in all its forms), *'horita (ahorita).* Certain other words were sometimes contracted and sometimes not: *'hora - ahora, 'apá - papá, 'amá, pa' - para.* The children, quite understandably, had many more contractions than the adults, such as *'pués* and even *'pos* for *después, 'roplano, 'vidó (olvidó), mu'chito (muchachito), 'rina (harina), se 'costó (se acostó), l' nijita (la necesita).*

These contractions have not only the effect of increasing the rate of production of phrases but also the side effect of complicating the phonological rules related to synalepha. For example, in *a'eces* the *a* and *e* formed a diphthong, with *a* being the stronger vowel. Similarly, if *vo'* were to occur before *a hacer,* the effect would be [βwasεr], from which the non-native might find it difficult to reconstruct *voy a hacer* when it occurs in a very weakly stressed part of the sentence. As I was transcribing the tapes for typescripts, I often encountered such difficulties, but after Carmen, the bilingual secretary for the project, had corrected my transcriptions, usually with little difficulty, I was very often surprised that I had not been able to reconstruct some of the underlying forms, which then appeared to be quite clear. In this same regard, I have heard foreign students from the Dominican Republic make statements to the effect that they had to get used to the pronunciation of Bryan Spanish or Argentinian Spanish before they could understand all the words; similarly, students from Mexico make similar observations about Dominican Spanish.

A number of other features of the speech of these informants reflect diachronic phonological developments that are common in both American and Andalucían Spanish. Perhaps the most widespread is that in certain environments an /s/ becomes somewhat like the English /h/. Lapesa (pp. 348-349) observes that in eastern Andalucía, Murcia, Puerto Rico, and Uruguay the *-s* of plural nouns and second person singular verbs is realized not as an aspirated segment but simply as a lengthening and lowering of the preceding vowel. He comments (p. 354) that the final [s] is retained in the plains of Mexico, some Andean regions of Colombia and Ecuador, and almost all of Peru and Bolivia. The final [h] has developed through time in Estremadura, La Mancha, Andalucía, Murcia, New Mexico, and Colombia, and among the lower classes in Chile and other countries. He stresses (p. 350) that these phenomena did not descend from the pre-colonial dialects of southern Spain but rather are parallel diachronic developments. I have heard these pronunciations in the Spanish of many foreign students from all parts of Latin America, most noticeably in those from the Caribbean, Central America, and the northern coast of South America. In the present study I found that all but the two youngest informants also produced the [h] variant of /s/ occasionally, the grandparents doing so many times, in such words as *esa, necesita, nosotros, pos, hicimos, parece, más, dicen, sí, clase, es,* *misma, tres, español.* These words were not always pronounced with [h] by these speakers, whereas that pronunciation is the general rule in other dialects. When this pronunciation in medial position is written in eye dialect it is *nojotros, hijimos, nejesita,* etc., though the pronunciation is clearly not [x], the usual pronunciation of *j*. Thus, this feature of Texas Spanish cannot be interpreted as a "corruption" that is unique to the area.

Another interesting pronunciation is the use of [x] instead of [f], as in *juerza (fuerza), ajuera,* and the preterit and past subjunctive form of *ir* and *ser (jui, juites, juimos, juera,* etc.). The mother and her father-in-law usually pronounced these words with [x] but occasionally used [f]; the others always used [x], though there were not enough examples to establish clearly that this pronunciation would always be used. Lapesa (p. 362) lists *juerza* among the "vulgarismos" that are still used in the common and rustic speech of Spain but are used more extensively in America. Cerda cities occurrences of the preterit forms with [x] in Yucatán, Hidalgo, and New Mexico. I have heard them in other parts of Texas, as has Carmen. (On one occasion Rachel produced the hyper-form *frifoles,* from *frijoles.)*

The children produced some phoneme substitutions that appear to be "baby talk" but also reflect a phonological phenomenon that has been observed in Spain and throughout America: *'güelita (abuelita), güeno (bueno).* Lapesa (pp. 300-301) attributes this shift of [β] to [γ] to a tendency for "el hablar vulgar" of Castilla to retract the point of articulation for voiced consonants. Rachel produced the reverse shift in *juevar (jugar).* Menéndez Pidal (pp. 194-195) suggests that the explanation may be an "error de audición" because of acoustic similarity. As it relates to child language, the latter interpretation seems better. Both Tom and Rachel also substituted [ʧ] for [ð] in *adentro (arentro),* which also appear to be acoustically similar in that environment.

Two interesting metatheses occurred. Mollie said *hevrido* for *hervido* and Tom said *quería* for *creía.* This phenomenon, like the one above, should be of interest in studies of children's Spanish.

Lapesa points out (p. 356) that some features of American Spanish are not Andalucian but rather were either imported from northern Spain or have independently evolved in a parallel manner in both places, such as, respectively, the introduction of "vulgarisms" such as *maiz* (instead of *maíz*) and *pior* (instead of *peor*) and the loss of *-ll-* in words such as *gallina, amarillo,* and *botella.* He cites their occurrence in Rioja, Navarra, Vizcaya, Arragón, and Castilla in Spain and in New Mexico, northern México, Guatemala, and the coasts of Ecuador and Perú. The neighbor produced *pior* (the only occurrence of the word in the interviews) and always used *maiz.* The mother and her father-in-law used both *maiz* and *maíz,* but no reason for the alternation was apparent. Examples of the loss of *-ll-* abound in Texas: *ea (ella), semía (semilla), bolío (bolillo), aí (allí), tortía (tortilla).* Cerda lists *maiz* as a common form in Texas, México, and New Mexico. Menéndez Pidal (p. 39) lists *ahi* alongside *maiz,* attributing them to "la preferencia del habla vulgar por el diptongo," and cites its occurrence in Vizcaya and Bogotá. Cerda lists *ahi* as occurring in Argentina as well as in Texas. All of the informants in this group showed a marked preference for *ahi.* The mother and the sister also said *ahí* on several occasions, but since the *-ll-* is consistently lost or weakened in their speech, they may actually have been saying *allí*, though the context did not clarify which was most appropriate to the meaning.

Another rather noticeable feature of Texas Spanish is the incidence of nonstandard verb forms. As with some of the pronunciation features, many are dialectal items that date directly or indirectly back to early developments in Spanish as it evolved from Latin. There is some vacillation, for instance, in the placement of stress on the first person plural forms of the imperfect indicative (mother: *íbamos, llevabamos;* grandfather: *trabajábanos* with the dissimilation /m/→/n/), past subjunctive (neighbor *hiciéramos;* grandfather *trabajaramos*), and present subjunctive. Menéndez Pidal (pp. 276, 300) points out that in Latin the -*a*- of -*amus* and -*atis* was long but that, as Spanish developed, the stress was retracted on the first and second persons plural of the imperfect indicative and the past subjunctive (amābāmus→amábamos, amaverāmus→ amáramos; erātis→érais, fuerātis→fuérais); and in the first and second persons plural of the present subjunctive the stress was also retracted in Andalucía and a large part of America (*véamos, véais; váyamos, váyais*). The second person plural forms are not used in Texas. González notes (p. 63) that -*mos* often changes to -*nos* when the stress is placed on the antepenultimate syllable. Only two first person plural present subjunctive verbs occurred in the interviews, both spoken by the mother (*llevemos, queramos*) and both with standard stress placement; however, I have heard the nonstandard form many times in Texas, as has Carmen. Not enough examples of these forms were recorded to establish a clear pattern for these speakers, though the alternations in the few examples given above suggest that the explanation cannot be a simple one. Lapesa (p. 302) also associates the retraction of the accent on the present subjunctive forms with the existence of -*ábamos, -áramos,* etc. and says that it was used in the nineteenth century by such literary figures as Espronceda, Hartzenbusch, and Castelar and even appeared in a grammar book, but he adds that at present it persists only "como vulgarismo en varias regiones españoles y, con gran difusión, en América." Cerda comments that *háigamos* is used in Texas, Guanajuato, and Durango.

Other nonstandard verb forms found in this study go back to earlier patterns (neighbor: *semos* for *somos;* Rachel: *salemos* for *salimos;* father, mother, and sister: *haiga* for *haya*). Lapesa (p. 302) lists *semos* and *haiga* among analogue forms that date back to medieval times. Menéndez Pidal (p. 302) lists Augustus Caesar's pronunciation *simus* (instead of *sumus*) and the Old Spanish forms *seemos* and *seyemos* as early sources for the neighbor's *semos.* He also (p. 292) says that *haiga* was often used by classical Spanish writers but is now used only by "el vulgo." Cerda cites current usage of the form in Argentina, Mexico, Texas, and New Mexico in the New World and in the Spanish provinces of Asturias and Galicia. Rachel's *salemos,* like other verbs listed by Cerda (*vivemos, siguemos, muremos, pidemos, durmemos*), is undoubtedly related by analogy to *dicemos,* used by her mother. In discussing the vowel dissimilations that took place in early Spanish, Menéndez Pidal (pp. 180, 272) comments that the Latin verb *dīcere* should have become *dicir,* but dissimilation in the vowels produced the standard modern forms *decir, decimos, decía,* etc. In this respect it is interesting that the mother and the neighbor always used -*i*- in the stem of this verb *(dicía, dicir, dicemos),* as well as in *vinir (vinía, vinimos).* The mother's *dicemos* is a common paradigmatically analogous form matching the rest of the present tense: *digo, dices, dice, dicen.*

The standard form for the second person singular of the preterit indicative (*-aste, -iste*) was not produced by any of the informants; instead these forms were produced: grandmother: *hablates;* mother: *cocineates, trajites, curates;* neighbor: *usates, hicites, comites, 'stuvites, quisites.* Cerda lists this form as occurring in Oajaca, Veracruz, and Argentina. Lapesa (p. 358) cites its occurrence in Andalucía also. Menéndez Pidal (pp. 279-280) attributes the development of the form to an analogical *-s* being added to the standard form (*-stes*), because all other second person singular endings have *-s*, and then a subsequent loss of the medial *-s-*. He cites evidence of it in the early eighteenth century but adds that it must be much older because it is also common in Sephardic Spanish, the language of the Jews who were expelled from Spain in the fifteenth century. Lapesa (pp. 302-303, 357-358) gives much the same explanation, with the additional observation that the confusion of *tú* and *vos* (the latter using the *-steis* ending) facilitated the addition of the final *-s* to the singular form.

The preceding discussion on verb forms, as well as much of the discussion on pronunciation, lends considerable support to a fact that seems to be obvious only to linguists: the speech of the uneducated is generally much more conservative than that of the well schooled. The general public, including most educators, tends to think that people who have not had much formal education are grossly guilty of adding all sorts of corrupt forms and pronunciations to the language. I do not intend to imply, of course, that the language of the uneducated is "better" because it has the older, "purer" forms, but that in attempting to understand why people of different regions and social classes speak differently, much more than mere grammar-textbook rules must be considered—that is, assuming the question to be "Why do they speak as they do?" rather than "Why don't they talk right?"

In this research project we recorded a number of non-standard verb forms that were not mentioned in the historical studies and dictionaries referred to in the preceding discussion. The forms are not unique to Bryan, however, for Gustavo González found them to be used extensively by the informants interviewed for a study of the Spanish of first-graders in Corpus Christi, Texas. Also, Carmen Reyna, the project secretary, reports having heard them in Brownsville.

All present perfect constructions recorded for this study used *ha* instead of *he* as the auxiliary verb for the first person singular (neighbor: *yo ha visto;* mother: *me ha fijado,* [*yo*] *ha oído;* sister: [*yo*] *te ha visto;* grandfather: *yo nunca ha ido pa' Houston*). A possible explanation for the use of the same form for the first and third persons is analogy: the other three commonly used perfective-aspect constructions—past perfect indicative and present and past perfect subjunctive constructions—have the same form for both persons (*yo/él + había ido, haya ido, hubiera ido*).

González (pp. 60-65) found widespread "misuse" of the subjunctive, conditional and imperfect tense forms by the informants in his study. The findings of the present study indicate that the matter is probably one of language development. Except in a very limited number of verbs, the adults used standard forms for both present and past subjunctive constructions. Only two of the children produced sentences that called for the subjunctive mood, all of them deviant in some way. Except for one instance (*supongamos*), none of the children seemed to have even the slightest difficulty understanding present and past subjunctive forms when Carmen used them in asking questions or making comments. Five of the sentences were produced by Rachel, who is 12, and one by Tom, who is 11:

(1) Rach: ¿Cómo se *diga* "Monday" en español?
(2) Rach: Y la dejas ahi hasta cuando *es* caliente y la dejas ahi y se tosta sola.
(3) Rach: Y necesita voltearlos también, después cuando (después de que) *están* tostadas.
(4) Rach: En esa . . . 'onde pone las tortillas pa' que se *cozan.*
(5) Rach: Y despúes los osos [le] dijeron que *vinía* pa'tras (que *volviera*).
(6) Tom: . . . si no creía en Jesús que se *juía.*

In (1) Rachel has simply used a subjunctive verb where an indicative form would be appropriate, and in (2) and (3) she has done the opposite. The only mistake in (4) is that she did not change the stem vowel (*cuezan*), an error which also occurs in the indicative verb *tuesta* in (2). All four children had difficulty with verbs that change the stem vowel, as well as with irregular verbs. In (5) and (6) imperfect indicative forms have been used instead of the past subjunctive; the adults also did so occasionally, as will be shown later. González (p. 61) cites *juía* as an analogical form used both for *iba* and *había* by first-graders in Corpus Christi.

The sister, who is 16, had little trouble with either the present or past subjunctive:

(7) (describing how to make flour tortillas) . . . y le echas la agua, hasta que no se *haga* . . . . Pero no muy aguada, no más que *quede* . . . , tú sabes. Pero que no *quede* muy aguada, porque se pega.
(8) Chance que te *haiga* visto.
(9) Mientras que 'tás 'prendiendo, te pagaba eso, pero ya que *sabieras,* él te pagaba más.

In (7) she left two clauses incomplete, but the three subjunctive verbs are grammatical. In (8) the subjunctive verb, though a dialectal form, is appropriate for the complement of the regional form *chance que*. In (9) she simply has treated *saber* as a regular verb rather than saying *supieras*. (In (7) and (9), as Rachel did in (2-4), she is using the stylistic second person form of address commonly used in describing procedures, and not, as it would seem, addressing me in the familiar.)

Quite obviously, there are not enough examples in this small amount of data to justify more than speculative comments, but the contrast between Rachel and her aunt cannot be slighted. At first, both tried to make me believe that they did not have full command of Spanish, but as shown in Carmen's interview with Rachel and mine with her aunt and her parents, they can communicate quite well in the language. The contrast in their mastery of the subjunctive suggests that these formal and semantic distinctions are not fully mastered until after the age of 12, but this mastery may normally take place at an earlier age in speakers who have not experienced the anxieties of living in a bicultural area where the use of their family language stigmatizes them socially. More detailed studies on language development must be made before conclusions can be drawn on questions such as those raised by the findings of this research project. Also, just the tensions inherent in interview situations could have created additional anxieties that resulted in Rachel's feeling much less secure than she ordinarily would have felt in using the more difficult constructions.

The adults used the standard forms for the present and past subjunctive except for a very limited inventory of verbs. The father used only one subjunctive form (*quisiera*) and the grandfather only four (*haga, sea, tenga, esté*). The mother and the neighbor used considerably more, with the relative number of subjunctive forms paralleling the amount of Spanish used by each (mother 4210, neighbor 2970, grandfather 1300, and father 160). The mother used ten in the present tense, including one dialect form (*haigas*), and twelve in the past, all of them in the standard form. The neighbor used two in the present tense and eight in the past, with only one being deviant in form, and it might have resulted simply from a slip of the tongue:

(10) Si uno *entraja* a mi casa dijera, ". . . ."

In a conditional sentence she also used the standard past perfect subjunctive forms:

(11) Yo hubiera querido que no me hubiera enseñado a hacer tortillas.

In answer to a question, however, she used the imperfect form of the verb when the past subjunctive would have been standard:

(12) DL: Si pudiera trabajar en algo . . ., ¿qué preferiría hacer?
    Neighbor: Pos lo que *podía* hacer. (pudiera hacer)

In another of her sentences the conditional or present indicative might have been more appropriate, but the imperfect has a meaning that could be appropriate for the sentence, with a shift in time reference within the sentence:

(13) Yo gasto más gas en ir pa' 'llá a comprar esa cosa barata cuando *podía* comprarla aquí.

Thus, the neighbor's performance with respect to these forms is rather close to the standard, a fact that is particularly noteworthy in view of the fact that she did not speak Spanish during most of her childhood.

The mother produced several nonstandard constructions. González noted that his informants had a strong tendency to use an imperfect tense form for the conditional and the past subjunctive (neighbor's errors in (11) and (12); the mother did so also, but only with forms of *ser*, *ir*, and *dar*. In answer to a question about what she would do if she were confronted by a dangerous robber, she gave the following answer:

(14) Se me hace que yo lo que *haría*, pos, . . . yo creo, me *pondría* muy nerviosa y con muncho miedo. Yo lo primero *iba (sería)* que . . . lo primero que *pensaría era (sería, fuera)* " ¡Ay, Dios! " O le *pidiera* a Dios, yo creo, en ese caso. Y también, yo creo, se me hace, si me *dicían* pos dinero, o lo que me

pidiera, yo creo que es lo que les *daba (daría),* pa' ver si *iban* (se *irían?*) pronto o algo.

This is the only passage in which she uses these imperfect tense forms in this way. On another occasion she used *iban* for *habían:*

(15) Despues, pos pusimos el radio allí y oí que lo *iban (habían)* traído al hospital. She produced two other sentences with some rather complex constructions that use forms generally not covered in traditional grammar books:

(16) Le *jueran dicho* pa' que los dejara que lo agarraran.

(17) Y luego dijo 'amá, *"Fueran yido* . . . que pa' 'cá en Brownsville también.

In (16) and (17) the form of the word itself would indicate that the past subjunctive of either *ser* or *ir* is used as an auxiliary verb to indicate perfective aspect, but that would be an extremely unusual application of either verb. When I discussed these sentences with Carmen, using her as a native—though linguistically sophisticated—informant, one of her first comments was that the construction is very complicated—an understatement indeed. She would use *hubieran* instead of the mother's *jueran* and *fueran* in each sentence. The general meaning of the verb construction is what might be termed "conditional advisability or desirability," as reflected in an alternative way of saying the sentences, given here with the English translations:

(16') Le deberían haber dicho pa' que los dejara que lo agarraran.

You should have told him so that he would let you get it. (referring to a dog that the children wanted)

(17') Y luego dijo 'amá, "Deberían haber ido [allí] . . . que pa' 'cá en Brownsville también [hay cabrito]."

And then my mother said, "You should have gone [here] . . . because over here in Brownsville also [there's cabrito]."

The intended meaning of (17) had to be figured out from the context, because the sentence was spoken rather fast, with an anacoluthon in the middle of it, as indicated by the ellipsis.

These few examples are certainly not a large enough sample to serve as the basis for broad generalizations on the matter, but it is clear at any rate that the problem area is rather limited in scope and, in view of the small number of verbs involved, is very likely dialectal. Thus, in the speech of the adults, of the 15 present subjunctive forms used, only 1 was dialectal and the remainder standard; of the 25 past subjunctive forms used, including the perfective constructions, only 1 was deviant and 2 were dialectal or anomalous; the total number of conditional forms was not counted, but there were 4 imperfect-tense forms used in conditional clauses and one in a subjunctive clause.

The speakers in this survey produced a number of regional and dialectal vocabulary items. Some of them are rather clearly borrowings from English, but most of them occur elsewhere in the Spanish-speaking world. In the following list I have given the approximate English translation for the word as used by the speaker and have made additional comments where they would be of interest; the words have other meanings too, of course. If the word, with this particular meaning, is mentioned by any of the works listed at the beginning of this paper, the geographical distribution and other comments from that source are also given. If only *Cerda* appears below, that means that the term is used widely in Texas but not attested elsewhere; if only *FJS* (Francisco J. Santamaría) is written, the word is widely used in México. As in the preceding discussion, state or province names will be given only for México and Spain, and of course Texas and New Mexico. The abbreviation *Acad* refers to the dictionary of the *Real Academia Española*, and *MP* refers to Menéndez Pidal's work. The label "used by common people" is used here when the source called the term a *vulgarismo*.

agarrar - to acquire, in many extended senses. Acad: figurative and informal. The informants used this word with a wide enough range of senses to justify further research into its use in Texas and México (e.g., example 16).

arrear - to drive a car; usually refers only to animals. Cerda: northern México, Texas, New Mexico.

asina - variant of *así* - to a certain degree, as in *asina grandote* 'this big'; having certain unspecified qualities, as in *algo así* 'something like that.' Both forms were used by all the adults. Cerda: Texas, New Mexico. FJS: common in all of America. MP: an analogical form; archaic and dialectal; used in Old Spanish in the Toledo-Burgos-León region.

atole - a food made of cereal grains, originally corn; may be either thick or liquid-like in consistency; borrowed from Nahuatl. FJS: *una bebida,* used very much in México. Acad: same comment as FJS.

aventón - a hard, rude push. Cerda: Texas, Guadalajara, Perú. FJS: used by common people. Acad: México.

bien - an adverb, meaning 'very,' used as a modifier of adjectives. Acad: may modify a past participle with this meaning.

bísquete - American-style biscuit. Cerda: northern México, Texas, New Mexico.

blanquillo - chicken or bird egg. Cerda: Texas, México, Guatemala. FJS: now used by people in all social classes. This word is often considered nonstandard for *huevo.*

bolillo - equivalent to *gringo,* an Anglo; somewhat pejorative. Cerda: Texas, New Mexico. The first time the neighbor used the word in my presence, she hesitated and laughed, but later she used it without hesitation. The mother used it only in the interview conducted by Carmen. The sister used it as a common term. The neighbor also used the adjective *boliachi* to refer to a Mexican-American who talks and acts like an Anglo.

cocinear - to cook. The women occasionally used the standard *cocinar.* Unlike *arrear,* the phonological hiatus was maintained after the *e*; for example, the mother said *arrias,* but *cocineé* and *cocinea,* the only nonfinite forms of these verbs that were produced. The *-ear* ending is also very common for Mexican coinages based on English words, as in *cuquear* 'to cook.'

contimás - somewhat like the English idiomatic expressions "let alone," "not to mention," etc. Cerda: Texas, Colombia. FJS: a generalized form that has completely replaced the standard *cuánto más;* used in Spain, among the lower classes in Mexico City, and in the interior of the country. Acad: used by common people for *cuánto más; cuantimás,* a contraction of *cuánto más.*

chamaco - child, through the high school age. Cerda: Texas, New Mexico, México, Central America, Colombia. FJS: from the Aztec *chamauac* 'chubby'; in Central America and other parts of America. Acad: México.

chance - borrowing from the English *chance,* also said as *chanza;* indicates possibility, opportunity, probability, and may be used in a variety of expressions. Cerda: lists *chanza* in Texas and New Mexico. FJS: Used by bilinguals in the southwestern U.S.; "a superfluous and unnecessary anglicism."

chango - monkey. Cerda: Texas, México, Colombia; *machango* in Cuba and Venezuela. FJS: "mono pequeño." The standard word *mono* refers to larger animals, such as apes, also. The children seemed to be more familiar with the word *mono* than the grandparents were; by chance, both groups were engaged in discussions about the two words.

Chifonía - dresser, chest of drawers. Cerda: *chifonir;* in Argentina, *chiffonier.*

chueco - twisted, crooked. Cerda: Texas, México. FJS: used very much. The Castilian meaning is 'bow-legged' or 'badly crippled.'

dientista - variant of *dentista.* Cerda: Texas, Guanajuato.

duro - difficult; hard, as in 'to work hard.' Cerda: Texas, Argentina, Chile, Ecuador, Perú, Uruguay. FJS: lists the second meaning. Acad: lists these meanings as figurative or informal usages.

gente - family, as in *mi gente* 'my children, etc.' Acad: informal.

greve - gravy. (I would list this as an English word if it had been produced by anyone except the grandparents; the grandmother does not speak English.) The grandfather also said *grevecito.*

guachonga - rude, nosy. None of the sources listed it, and no one I asked seemed to have heard it before. Perhaps it is a pejorative adjective based on *guachar,* which Cerda lists as 'to look after, take care of,' from the English *watch.*

guapo - hard-working, resourceful. Cerda: Texas, northern México. FJS: used by common people in northern México. The Castillian meaning for the word is 'handsome, pretty.'

hacerse - an impersonal construction equivalent to *parecer;* e.g., *se me hace* 'It seems to me.' Not listed elsewhere. It is so widely used in Texas that it deserves more study.

huerco - a child younger than fifteen or so. Cerda: northern México and southwestern U.S. FJS: used by common people, equivalent to *chamaco;* northern México, southwestern U.S.

huevón - extremely lazy. Cerda: lists other meanings for the word in other parts of America. FJS: a lower class term.

jamaica - a charity sale held by a church or other such organization. Cerda, FJS, and Acad: México.

jiriola - an adjective referring to a person who acts without regard to the appearance he is giving of himself as a result of his action; used primarily with verbs of motion such as *venir* or *andar.* Cerda: said of a person who goes around very satisfied with himself, in spite of the inappropriateness of the circumstances.

mero - used in a number of idiomatic expressions, as in *ya mero* 'almost' and *donde mero* 'exactly where.' FJS: in Central America, equivalent to *exactamente;* also México. Acad: "inappropriately" used in México in the senses given here.

mixteado - from the English word *mixed.* Cerda lists the past participle with this meaning, without comment.

muncho - variant pronunciation of *mucho* 'much.' Cerda, Acad: México. The grandfather did not use this pronunciation, and the sister vacillated between *mucho* and *muncho;* the others consistently used *muncho.*

nadien - variant of *nadie* 'nobody.' Cerda: Campeche, Michoacán, Colombia. MP: all of Spain and America; an analogous form related to *alguien.*

no más - only; no more; no longer. Lapesa: the phrase has extended its meanings considerably in America.

onde - variant of *donde* 'where,' both as an interrogative and an adverbial relative. Cerda: New Mexico, Texas, all of America.

pa' - to, toward, for. Cerda: Texas, New Mexico, México. FJS. MP: lists as a careless pronunciation of *para* but gives no geographical distribution. All of the speakers said it, but occasionally they also said *para* in certain constructions. The grandfather usually used *para.*

parquearse - to park a car. Cerda: U.S., México. FJS. A Spaniard whom I met in 1962 said that the verb is widely used in Spain also, despite lack of Academy acceptance.

pos - variant of *pues,* the interjection 'well.' Cerda: Texas, New Mexico. FJS: very informal usage among country people, principally in central and northern México. The grandfather tended to use *pues,* and the mother used it occasionally; the others always used *pos.*

prebar - variant of *probar* 'to taste.'

queque - American-style cake. Cerda: Texas, New Mexico, México, Central America, Colombia, Venezuela, Perú. FJS: generalized anglicism. The neighbor said *queique,* a variant form listed by FJS.

qué tanto - interrogative form for 'how much.' Not mentioned in any of the sources, not even as a variant of *cuánto,* the standard form, which was never used by these speakers.

ranchero - adj. referring to a person with somewhat unsophisticated manners, pejoratively applied to rural people. Cerda: Texas, Mexico. FJS.

raspa - a snow cone, a refreshment made of fruit-flavored syrup poured over crushed ice. Cerda.

traer - equivalent to *tener* 'to have.'

traste - dish, usually plural. Cerda: Texas, Mexico. FJS: Acad: America, Andalucía.

trinche - fork. FJS: Mexico, Guatemala, Colombia, Ecuador, Chile, La Plata River area.

velís - suitcase. Cerda: *veliz;* Texas and México. FJS: disapproves of the spelling *veliz.*

vesita - variant of *visita* 'guest, visitor.' Not listed anywhere, but I have heard it on numerous occasions.

vez - occasion. The form *a veces* 'sometimes' alternated with *hay veces, hay veces que, en veces,* all of which are commonly used in Texas. Acad: lists only *a veces.*

vista - movie, motion picture. Cerda: Texas, New Mexico.

weldear - to weld, as opposed to soldering. Cerda: *hueldear.*

yarda - lawn; the general meaning of the English *yard.* Cerda: Texas and New Mexico.

zacate - grass. FJS: México, Guatemala, Honduras, Nicaragua, Costa Rica. Acad: México, Central America, Philippines.

A number of words listed above might appear to be English words and thus perhaps should not have been included so as to give the impression that they enjoy the status of fully legitimate Spanish words (e.g., *bísquete, chance, chifonía, greve, guachonga, mixteado, weldear, yarda).* It is not a simple matter to draw precise lines, as the comments in the entries indicate. In the case of *greve* and *yarda,* for instance, there is a good chance that they have been used by some monolingual Spanish-speakers in the southwestern United States for at least three or four generations. Did the grandmother learn *greve* from her mother? How many generations back did her family borrow the word from the Anglo community? Precisely how widely and how long must a new word have to be used by native speakers before it ceases to carry a "foreign" label? Or, how many miles away does the word have to travel before it ceases to be directly associated with its parent language and is no longer deplored as "foreign?"

Another question that is not resolved very easily is how one distinguishes between borrowing a foreign semantic distinction and the semantic generalization or specialization that develops naturally within a language. Such is the case for *arrear* as described above. Since the words *drive* and *arrear* have many similar syntactic and semantic distinctions, it is tempting to say that the Spanish word has been expanded under the pressures of English usage, but it would be more accurate to attribute the expansion to cultural or technological developments that by chance took place first in an English-speaking country. The semantic expansion was borrowed—or developed—along with the technological development. A purist might deplore this semantic development because the history of the expansion contains non-native influences.

Borrowing should not be confused with interference, though it is not always clear which is taking place in a particular construction. For instance, when the neighbor said, in a side comment, "'Tán corriendo el marrano," she seemed to be saying that someone was chasing a pig, in which case the verb *corretear,* not *correr,* should have been used. (The context did not clarify exactly what she meant.) Since she is English-dominant, it is likely that she was thinking about "running after it" or "running it away," with *correr* being the expected translation of the principal word in her thoughts. It is also possible that she has always confused *correr* with *corretear*—that is, that she never produces the word *corretear.* The confusion, whether it occurred earlier when she learned the word or at the time when she produced the sentence, appears to be a clear case of her knowledge of English interfering with her production of Spanish.

Language interference that involves pronunciation is much clearer. By "interference" I am referring to the use of deviant forms, and not simply accent. For instance, the neighbor said *garache* rather than *garaje,* undoubtedly because of her knowledge of English. That pronunciation, of course, would be acceptable had the French word not already been borrowed and adapted to Spanish phonology and spelling. The mother made a similar "error" in treating the verb for *touch* as if it were an English borrowing rather than a native word. She said *tochar* instead of *tocar*. This sort of nonstandard production (alteration) of certain words is very common in Texas. The neighbor produced two other interesting forms. When we were naming household items, she said *redio*, translating the sound of the English vowel into an approximate Spanish vowel; after the mother and I said the word in the standard form, of course, she also said it the way we did. In naming a vaporizer that was nearby, she produced *vepadora* and did not know *vaporizadora*. In the present discussion I am perhaps using the term "interference" in a unique way, but it seems to be that a distinction should be made between deviant forms such as these and mere accent.

The children, as one would expect, had more difficulty in selecting standard Spanish words and constructions to express their thoughts and produced more interference-induced deviant forms. Rachel used *cucamos* as well as *cocinar* and *guisar*. In saying that her grandmother had moved, she first said *movió*, the standard form, but a few sentences later said *muvió*. Both Rachel and Richard used the verb *naquear* in saying that Goldilocks knocked on the bear's door, with the same vowel sound as the English verb, whereas the standard practice would be to change the vowel to conform to the borrowed spelling, as in the boxing term *noquear* 'to knock out.' In another sentence Rachel went through a rather complicated translation process in selecting the verb:

(18) Le quitaron al dungeon.

Quitar means 'to take away *from*' and not what she means, *llevar* 'to take away *to.*' Rachel also produced an interesting noun, *saquetín*. The word appears to be a combination of *sock* and *calcetín*, an instance of possible English interference. Gustavo González, however, claims (personal communication) that a better explanation is that it results from two processes common to Spanish "baby talk." The form occurs rather often in the speech of very young children who have never heard the word *sock*. Since /l/ is one of the last phonemes for children to master, a child tends to say *cacetín* [kasetín]; then metathesis of the first two consonants would produce [saketín].

Several errors were made in applying the pluralization rules. Rachel said *los leóns*, following English morphology (but with /s/ rather than the standard English /z/), whereas Spanish pluralization rules call for a syllable for the plural of words ending with *-n*: *los leones*. Three times Mollie said *una veces*, failing to add the *-s* to *una*. Tom also said *una veces* on one occasion. Rachel said *su camas* once, the same error. In these last phrases the children followed the English practice of adding the *-s* only to the noun, but Spanish also adds an *-s* to all modifiers of a plural noun.

In other phrases the children followed English word order and translated word for word from English to Spanish. Rachel, Tom, and Richard used *pa' 'trás* 'toward the rear, backward' with a verb of motion, as in *nunca vino pa' 'trás* for "She never came back," instead of using *volvió*. Tom produced *la metió pa' 'trás* to indicate that someone put his hand back into his pocket, rather than using the standard verb construction *la volvió a meter* or the phrase *la metió otra vez*. Rachel and Richard produced some interesting possessive constructions:

(19) Rach: la chiquito oso cama (the little bear's bed)

(20) Rich: el baby bear 'taba buena (the baby bear's was good)
(21) Rich: the bear sopera (the bear's soup bowl)
(22) Rich: su 'apá estaba (his father's was)

The word order in these phrases suggests that the children were thinking in English but speaking with Spanish words. In (19) there is double evidence of English interference: the word order in *chiquito oso* as well as the placement of the genitive before the head noun. The children did not make the phrases conform to English completely, for *la* and *cama* and *chiquito* and *oso* properly show gender, and none of the possessives used the final -*'s*, which is uniquely English.

As can be seen from the data presented throughout this paper, the informants for this project do indeed speak Spanish, that is, a dialect of Spanish, and that dialect fits into the overall historical development of all dialects throughout the Spanish-speaking world. It is particularly interesting that most of the nonstandard forms found in these interviews also occur in Mexico, and many of them also occur in Spain. English has obviously had an effect on the dialect, but has served mainly as the source for lexical borrowing. In only a few instances, principally among the children and the one English-dominant adult interviewed, was clear evidence found of English interference. Their accent—that is, the actual pronunciation and intonation—was not treated in this paper, but only the children seem to experience the kind of systematic influence that might eventually produce an English-like accent.

Of particular interest is the fact that such a small number of "corruptions" have crept into the language of these informants, whereas popular notions about the relationship of formal education to the preservation of the "grammar" of a language would lead one to expect a much higher number of them. None of these informants has had any formal instruction in Spanish, and the grandparents never attended school, though the grandfather indicated that on his own he had learned to read "poquito español y escribir poquito español." This last fact might help explain why he did not use certain of the obviously "bad" forms such as *muncho, pos,* and *pa'.* If one reflects upon the matter, one notices that the deviant forms that are common—and are deplored as corrupted—occur primarily in the highly irregular verbs, in certain expressions with a very high rate of incidence in spoken language, and in the semantic areas in which English borrowings would be most likely to occur.

Variations in Los Angeles Spanish Phonology

Robert N. Phillips, Jr.

The Voiced Stop/Fricatives.

These three phonemes, /b d g/, all have both stop and fricative allophones. While the distribution of the allophones of /d/ and /g/ are fairly straightforward, those of the /b/ are more confusing.

/b/. The /b/ is the most confusing of the three phonemes of its type in Los Angeles Spanish. It is commonly stated that in Spanish the [b] allophone, a voiced bilabial stop, is used after juncture and after a nasal; and that the [ƀ], a voiced bilabial fricative, is used elsewhere. This clear-cut case of complementary distribution is not found in Los Angeles, probably because of the existence of the /v/ phoneme in English. In Los Angeles there are three allophones found: the [b], the [ƀ], and the [v], a voiced labiodental fricative. In some cases, we find that [ƀ] and [v] are in free variation with each other but in complementary distribution with [b]; in other cases, all three seem to be in free variation.

An example of this confusion may be found with the noun *vino*. It was elicited preceded by pause, by /i/, by /n/, and by /s/. Preceded by pause, four informants used the [b], six used the [ƀ], and twenty-one used the [v]. Preceded by /i/, three informants used the stop [b], twelve used the fricative [ƀ], and fourteen used the fricative [v]. When preceded by the nasal, twelve used the [b], eight used the [ƀ], and another eight used the [v]. Finally, when preceded by /s/, of the thirteen who responded, one used the [b], seven used the [ƀ], and five used the [v].

I suspect that spelling may play some part in the confusion with the /b/, although my informants were not reading the words. All of them are literate in at least one language; most of them are literate in both, to varying degrees. Many of them have probably been taught, either by teachers or by parental example, that there is a difference between orthographic *b* and *v*. The fact that there is a phonemic difference in English no doubt contributes to the confusion and the rather wide-spread use of the [v].

/b/ in intervocalic position. The words on the checklist which have the /b/ in this position are *llover, clavo, globo, recibo, huevo,* and *automóvil* (with its variant /atomobíl/). The following chart shows the number of informants using each of the allophones in each of the words.

WORD	[b]	[ƀ]	[v]
llover	0	17	11
clavo	0	28	3
globo	4	18	5

Reprinted by permission from "Los Angeles Spanish: A Descriptive Analysis." Ph.D. Dissertation, University of Wisconsin.

WORD	[b]	[ƀ]	[v]
recibo (v.)	5	22	0
huevo	1	27	3
automóvil	1	16	2
/atomobíl/	1	1	4

It is seen that [b] intervocalically is rather rare and may be due to the eliciting situation. [ƀ] is more commonly used than is the [v]. No one informant used the [v] more than three times, as the summary chart presented below will show. There were six opportunities to use the [v]. We may generalize by saying that it is much more common for a fricative to be used intervocalically than the stop; furthermore, the fricative used is more commonly [ƀ] than [v].

Juncture plus /b/. This environment was obtained by eliciting the following words in isolation: *burro, brujo, boda, vaca,* and *vino*. The chart below summarizes the allophonic variation found:

WORD	[b]	[ƀ]	[v]
burro	28	0	3
brujo	27	3	1
boda	13	4	14
vaca	9	5	16
vino (n.)	4	6	21

Here we see probable orthographic influence in *vaca* and *vino*. It is to be noted that all informants who used a fricative allophone did use a stop allophone in at least one word. It is also noted that the fricative is used more frequently by speakers under twenty-five years of age; six out of ten "high-frequency" fricative users are in that class.

Nasal plus /b/. The checklist has the following three words in which the nasal appears followed by a /b/: *hombre, tumba,* and *buen vino*. The allophones were used as follows:

WORD	[b]	[ƀ]	[v]
hombre	31	0	0
tumba	28	0	0
buen vino	12	8	8

Here we see that if the nasal is word-interior, the /b/ following it is always realized as a stop. It is when the word begins with a /b/ that variation in the choice of allophones is possible. In the section dealing with the nasals, it will be shown that the assimilation of the nasal to the point of articulation of the following consonant behaves the same: it is done regularly if the cluster is word-interior, optionally if the cluster crosses word boundaries.

Consonant (non-nasal) plus /b/. In this environment, there is almost no use of the stop allophone:

WORD	[b]	[ƀ]	[v]
tres vacas	1	14	15

WORD	[b]	[b̵]	[v]
el vino	3	12	14
tres vinos	1	7	5
yerba	1	7	25

No informant used the stop allophone more than once; its use in this position is very limited. [v] seems to be favored slightly over [b̵] in this position, and is quite common with the younger speakers.

/b/ plus consonant. The only word in this category on the checklist was *pobre*. Three informants used the [b]; twenty-four used the [b̵] (it was very weakly articulated by seven of them); and four used the [v].

The following chart summarizes what allophone(s) each informant used in each of the given environments. It is to be noted that none of the informants followed the classical distribution for the allophones. The [v] was found used by all informants but four: 1312, 2222, 2311, and 2322. The [v] is found more commonly among those under twenty-five (0100) and those who speak predominantly English (0030).

In summary, it may be said that the /b/ has three allophones in Los Angeles Spanish. The first is [b], which is most commonly used after a pause or after a nasal. It is mandatory that it be used after a word-interior nasal. The other two allophones are [b̵] and [v] which are used anywhere except after a word-interior nasal. However, their use is generally restricted to the intervocalic and pre-consonantal or post-consonantal positions. It is impossible to predict whether [b̵] or [v] will be used in a given environment.

The Vibrants.

There is no dispute that there is a contrast between *pero* and *perro*; there is, however, some question as how best to analyze this contrast. Some linguists say that the vibrant in each word represents a different phoneme: /r/ is the phoneme present in *pero* and /r̄/ is the phoneme in *perro*. Others have stated that there is but one vibrant phoneme: /r/. In *pero* it is simple and in *perro* it is a geminate /rr/. By this analysis, *pero* would be /péro/ and *perro* would be /pérro/.

There are several reasons for my rejecting this analysis. First, there are no other geminate consonants in Spanish, either in word-initial or word-interior position. While patterning is not a major criterion for accepting or rejecting an analysis, it should be taken into account. This analysis would force a change in the no-geminate pattern of Spanish. My second reason is stronger and is based on phonetic data. In Los Angeles, it is quite common to find a voiced fricative [ʐ] used in the intervocalic position of the word *perro*; it would never be found in the word *pero*. If we were to accept the single versus geminate analysis, we would have to say that the /r/ has one allophone while /rr/ has a completely different allophone. I find this impossible to accept. Therefore, my analysis is that there are two vibrant phonemes in Los Angeles Spanish: /r/ and /r̄/.

There are restrictions on the privileges of occurrence of these two phonemes: while they may both appear in syllable-initial position, only the /r̄/ may appear word-initial. When clustered in the same syllable with another consonant, only

TABLE 1
Informant Use of the Allophones of /b/

INF	Intervocalic [b]	[b̵]	[v]	Juncture plus /b/ [b]	[b̵]	[v]	Nasal plus /b/ [b]	[b̵]	[v]	Consonant plus /b/ [b]	[b̵]	[v]	/b/ plus consonant [b]	[b̵]	[v]
1121	0	3	1	2	0	3	2	0	0	0	1	1	0	1	0
1122	0	5	0	2	0	3	1	0	1	0	0	3	0	1	0
1131	0	5	0	3	0	2	1	0	0	0	2	1	0	1	0
1132	2	1	3	1	0	4	2	0	1	0	0	4	0	0	1
1211	0	4	0	2	1	0	2	1	0	0	2	1	0	1	0
1221	0	3	3	2	0	3	2	0	1	0	1	3	0	1	0
1222	0	6	0	4	1	0	2	1	0	1	2	1	0	1	0
1231	0	3	3	1	0	4	2	0	1	0	0	4	0	1	0
1232	0	5	1	3	0	2	2	1	0	0	4	0	0	1	0
1312	0	6	0	4	1	0	3	0	0	1	2	0	0	1	0
1322	1	5	0	4	0	1	3	0	0	1	2	0	0	1	0
1331	1	5	0	2	1	2	3	0	0	0	1	3	0	1	0
1332	2	4	0	3	0	2	3	0	0	0	1	2	0	1	0
2111	0	6	0	2	2	1	2	1	1	0	2	1	0	1	0
2112	0	6	0	3	0	2	3	0	0	0	3	0	0	1	0
2121	0	4	0	1	0	4	2	0	1	0	1	2	0	1	0
2122	1	5	0	3	0	2	3	0	0	0	3	0	0	1	0
2131	0	3	0	2	1	2	1	1	0	0	1	1	0	1	0
2132	1	3	1	1	4	0	2	1	0	0	4	0	0	1	0
2211	0	5	1	3	1	1	2	1	0	0	3	0	0	0	1
2212	0	5	1	3	1	1	3	0	0	0	3	0	0	1	0
2221	0	5	0	2	0	3	2	1	0	0	3	1	0	0	1
2222	2	4	0	5	0	0	3	0	0	0	3	0	0	1	0
2231	0	2	2	2	0	3	2	0	0	0	1	2	0	1	0
2232	0	3	3	2	0	3	2	0	1	0	0	4	0	0	1
2311	0	6	0	2	3	0	2	0	0	0	2	0	0	1	0
2312	0	5	0	4	0	1	3	0	0	1	2	1	1	0	0
2321	0	4	2	2	1	2	2	0	1	0	2	2	0	1	0
2322	2	4	0	4	1	0	3	0	0	1	1	0	1	0	0
2331	1	2	3	3	0	2	3	0	0	1	0	2	0	1	0
2332	0	2	3	3	0	2	3	0	0	0	1	3	1	0	0

The first digit refers to the informant's sex, the second to his age group, the third to his language preference, and the fourth to his social rank, as is shown below:

1——— Male
2——— Female
—1—— Under 25 years of age
—2—— Between 25 and 50 years of age
—3—— Over 50 years of age
——1— Prefers Spanish to English and speaks it at least 70% of the time
——2— Does not prefer one language over the other; speaks both about equally
——3— Prefers English to Spanish and speaks Spanish less than 30% of the time
———1 Lower social rank of the two informants with the same first three digits
———2 Higher social rank of the two informants with the same first three digits

Thus, informant 1231 is a male between 25 and 50 years of age who speaks predominantly English and who is in a lower social rank classification than informant 1232. Informant 1232 has the same characteristics except that his social rank is higher.

the /r/ may be used. Similarly, only the /r/ may be used in syllable-final position. Only the /r̄/ may appear after /l/, /n/, or /s/.

Unfortunately, there is some overlap in the use of the allophones of the two phonemes, especially in emphatic or deliberate speech. This neutralization is true only in the syllable-final position, and is most common before a juncture. One cannot say, as with the nasals, that this is a morphophonemic change which is phonologically conditioned: it happens or not both across morpheme boundaries and within morphemes. I will therefore have to state what is the norm, but say that some personal variation from the norm exists, and that there is some phonemic confusion on this point. However, it remains true that in the prevocalic position, the two vibrant phonemes are in contrast.

/r/. This phoneme is privileged to occur in any position except in word-initial; it is not found to occur after /l, n, s/. The /r/ has several allophones: [r], the most common, is a voiced alveolar single-tap consonant. This is the allophone most common in pre-vocalic position. There are a few cases in which the allophone used is /ɻ/, the English retroflex vocoid, but its use is sporadic and rare. When the /r/ is grouped with a stop, such as in the cluster /pr/, it sometimes sounds as though there is a multiple trill present. I believe that this is merely the effect of the rapid stop followed by the tap. The spectograms seem to show this clearly.

/r/ intervocalically. In the checklist, the following words appear with an intervocalic /r/: *toro, paró, ahora,* and *ahorita* (/orítα/). Informant 1121 used [ɻ] in *toro*; in all other cases, the [r] was the pronunciation noted.

Consonant plus /r/. Words with this cluster on the checklist include *treinta, padre, hombre, grifo, fruta, monstruo, brujo, producto, Cristo, teatro* (or /triáto/), *proteger,* and *pobre.* In the cases of *hombre, grifo, monstruo, brujo,* and *producto,* as well as *pobre,* there were a few instances when the consonant plus /r/ combination presented the sound of more than one tap. I believe that this is due to the influence of the stop consonant and not the /r/. In the word *fruta,* informants 1231, 1331, 1332, and 2221 were found to use the [ɻ], probably under the influence of the English cognate *fruit.* In *monstruo,* informant 2122 used the [ɻ], as was done in *producto* by informants 1232 and 1332. Informants 2122 and 2221 used the [ɻ] in *teatro* and 1232 and 2332 used it in *proteger.* It is noted that informant 1232 used the [ɻ] more than any other informant, but he used the [r] more often than the [ɻ].

/r/ plus consonant. In this environment, it is possible to find examples of some use of the allophones of /r̄/: [r̄], which is a voiced multiple alveolar trill, and [ʎ], which is a voiced alveolar groove fricative. The latter, however, is quite uncommon in this environment. The words on the checklist fitting this category include *tuerto, yerba, burlé, burla, and enferma.* In *tuerto,* one informant used the [r̄], the others preferring [r]. In *yerba,* three informants used the [r̄], all before the [ƀ] allophone of /b/. The other informants used [r], using it in combination with the [b], the [ƀ], and the [v] allophones. In *burlé,* twenty-two informants used the [r], eight used the [r̄], and one pronounced an [ʎ]. In *burla,* where there is a shift in stress, twenty-one informants used [r], including the one who used [ʎ] in burlé. Six informants used the [r̄] allophone. In *enferma,* all informants used the [r]. We thus see that the [r] is by far the most common realization of the /r/ in this position, although the [r̄] is used sporadically. The [ʎ] is very uncommon in this position.

/r/ plus pause. This environment was elicited by means of the following words on the checklist: *llover, caer, proteger, engañar, llegar, parar, hallar, correr,* and *peor* (or /piór/). The words were elicited in isolation. The following chart will summarize the number of times the various allophones were used. No distinction is made here between voiced [ř] and voiceless [ř̥] and between voiced [ʎ] and voiceless [ʎ̥] because, as the sound is before a pause, they all tend to devoice at the end. Trying to distinguish between them only at the beginning of the articulation is too difficult to do with any degree of accuracy.

WORD	[r]	[ř̥,ř̥]	[ʎ,ʎ̥]	[ʰ]
llover	26	0	2	0
caer	22	3	4	0
proteger	24	1	5	0
engañar	23	1	3	0
llegar	21	4	2	1
parar	19	4	4	1
correr	18	5	6	0
hallar	21	3	6	0
peor	19	1	1	0

Thus it is seen that while most of the informants prefer to use the [r] allophone of /r/ in this environment, a number of them do use both the [ř] and the [ʎ] allophones in this position; the latter is slightly more popular then the former. The [ʰ] was found only in two instances, pronounced each time by a different informant. We may conclude that its use is quite rare.

/ř/. As we have seen, the /ř/ may be used only in a prevocalic position. The two allophones encountered are [ř] and [ʎ]. The sound spectrogram shows that the number of taps in the trilled articulation varies from two to five, with three being the most common number. The fricative [ʎ] is slightly different from the English [ž] sound in that there seems to be some slight retroflexion of the dorsum of the tongue, giving a slight "r-color" to the sound. A few sporadic occurrences were noted of the use of [ʰ].

The two allophones [ř] and [ʎ] seem to be in free variation; some informants use both indiscriminately, but most prefer one over the other. The use of [ʰ] is fairly rare.

The words from the checklist with /ř/ are *perro, burro, rooa, raíz, guitarra, guitarrista, rayo, ruta, reír, río, recibo, correr,* and *corre.* A few sporadic phenomena should be mentioned. In the word *burro,* informant 2231 said [bú-ro]. This was found nowhere else; I take it to be an articulatory error. In the word *perro,* it was noted that informants 2121 and 2212 used an articulation which seemed to be a combination of both the trill and the fricative; I have transcribed it here as [ʎ̣]. The same phenomenon was noted in *ruta* (2332) and in *correr* (2131).

Another phenomenon noted twice was a noticeable amount of aspiration before the onset of [ř]; I transcribe it here as [ʰř]. It was noted in *raíz* pronounced by 1131 and in *rayo* as pronounced by 1121. I thought that I heard informant 2232 pronounce *raíz* with a very slight voiced stop: [ᵈřa-ís]. The chart which follows shows how many times each informant used each of the allophones in pronouncing these words. I have included the [ʎ̣] and the [ɾ̌], but have put the [ʰɾ̄] and the [ᵈɾ̄] with plain [ɾ̄].

	MEN					WOMEN			
INF	[ɾ̄]	[ʎ]	[ʎ̣]	[ɾ̌]	INF	[ɾ̄]	[ʎ]	[ʎ̣]	[ɾ̌]
					2111	10	3	0	0
					2112	8	4	0	0
1121	11	1	0	0	2121	10	2	1	0
1122	13	0	0	0	2122	2	11	0	0
1131	10	0	0	0	2131	10	0	1	0
1132	1	12	0	0	2132	12	0	0	0
1211	11	2	0	0	2211	12	0	0	1
					2212	0	11	2	0
1221	11	2	0	0	2221	9	4	0	0
1222	13	0	0	0	2222	11	2	0	0
1231	7	4	0	1	2231	9	1	0	0
1232	10	1	0	2	2232	10	2	0	0
					2311	0	11	0	0
1312	7	4	0	2	2312	10	3	0	0
					2321	5	6	0	0
1322	8	1	0	3	2322	12	1	0	0
1331	6	4	1	2	2331	12	1	0	0
1332	9	3	0	1	2332	4	6	1	0

From this, we see that the [ɾ̄] is the preferred allophone in Los Angeles; there are eighteen informants who use it well over 75% of the time. There are but four informants who use the [ʎ] that much. The remaining nine informants use both allophones, but, again, more of them seem to prefer the [ɾ̄]. There were but six informants who use the [ʎ] more than the [ɾ̄]. The use of [ʎ̣] and of [ɾ̌] is quite limited. Another significant point is that only five of the informants use but one of the two main allophones; the remaining twenty-six used both of them at least one time.

The Use of Non-Spanish Sounds.

Given the great amount of contact between English and Spanish in the Los Angeles area, it is not surprising to find conflicts and borrowings between them. In the common speech of some of the informants, English and Spanish words are intermixed no matter which language (as determined by the grammar) they happened to be speaking. The phenomenon of switching back and forth from one language to the other is also common. The borrowing of words from English into Spanish, with resultant adaptations to Spanish phonology and morphology is an accepted fact. These phenomena of switching and borrowing are discussed in Chapter 4 of the author's dissertation. However, there is a phenomenon which should properly be discussed in this chapter: the sporadic use of English sounds in words which are otherwise within the province of Spanish. That is, for example, a word which is a "good" Spanish word is pronounced with five Spanish sounds and one English sound.

Almost without exception, these words are either loans from English or are cognate in the two languages. This section is divided into two parts: first are discussed the uses of English vowels in Spanish words. Second is a discussion of the use of English consonants.

English Vowels in Spanish Words.

There are two English vowels which are occasionally found used by the informants: /æ/ and /ə/. The /ə/ has been seen above in discussions of some of the vowels. The /æ/ is the one found used more often. In spontaneous conversation, the following examples were found: *diámetro,* pronounced as [dai-ǽ-me-tro] by 1231, *gasolina* as [gæ̀-so-lí-na] by 1231, Ana María (her sister's name) as [ǽ-ña-ma-rí-a] by 2132, *accidente* as [aēk-si-dén-te] by 2132, and *saxotón* as [sæ̀k-so-fón] by informant 1131. In eliciting, this same vowel was found in words such as *mecanico, adicional, accelerador,* and *gasolina* by informants 1221, 1231, 2131, 2121, and 2231.

The other English vowel occasionally found is the /ə/. It is not nearly so common as the /æ/, but three examples of its use, in addition to those few cited above, were found. The one example from spontaneous conversation was in the word *nursi* meaning 'nurse,' which was pronounced as [nár-si] by informant 2321. It is interesting to note that the /r/ was a Spanish [r]. In eliciting, two examples were found of the use of /ə/: †*jódel,* meaning a 'huddle' in football, which was pronounced as [hó-dəl] by informant 1231, and †*mamases,* the plural of mamá, which was realized as [ma-má-sas] by informant 2321.

The Use of Non-Spanish Consonants.

Three consonants were found which were used as in English but not in Spanish: one example each was found of the use of [θ] and [z] and seven examples were found of the use of [š].

The [θ] must be considered to be a non-Spanish sound in Los Angeles. It is true that it is phonemic in some dialects of Spanish, but it is not known, even allophonically, in the Spanish of Los Angeles. The one time it occurred, it was used completely under the influence of English. Informant 1232 three times said [θè̃-rí-as] meaning, 'theories.' The fact that this word is pronounced with /t/ even in those dialects which do have phonemic /θ/ seems to prove that it is completely influenced by English. My own suspicion is that the informant made up the word on the spot and was trying to impress me with its use.

When asked to translate "zipper," informant 1221 responded with [zí-per]. It is true that Spanish does have a [z] sound, but it is not found to be used before a vowel. This, again, seems to be an influence of the English word on the Spanish.

The English consonant found the most was [š]. One informant used it three times in spontaneous conversation: *extracción, nacionalidad,* and *congresional* were all pronounced with [šjon] by informant 1222. It was also found in the words for "sheriff" [še-rí-fe], "to puch" [pu-šár], and "show (movie)" [šo].

All of these came from non-spontaneous speech. The informants involved were 1231, 1331, and 2331.

Finally, there were a few words which have a more complicated use of English phonemes. Informant 2312 spontaneously said [kláps] as the plural of the word which is borrowed from the English word *club*. It shows not only the use of [ə], but also a final cluster which is not permitted in Spanish. On the other hand, this cluster is not the one which would be used in this particular English word.

For the plural of the word *dólar*, two informants did not give the expected response of /dólares/. Informant 1222 said [dó-laⱬs] with an English [ⱬ] and an impossible cluster for Spanish at the end of the word. Informant 2212 said [dó-lɚs], using an English *r*-colored [ɚ], as well as the impossible cluster at the end. It is interesting to note, however, that both of the informants used [s] as the allomorph of plurality, rather than the [z] which would have been expected from English.

Finally, in spontaneous speech, informant 2322 used the plural form [tróks], apparently as the plural either of *trocas* or of *trogues*. The word was used in a sentence said in Spanish, but I believe that the informant felt that she was using an English word. Her accent in English is so strong that [tróks] is probably the closest she can come to the English. Nevertheless, this consonant cluster at the end of the word is impossible in Spanish.

It could well be argued that these English sounds are really allophones of some Spanish phonemes, at least as far as the informants are concerned. That is, the [æ] is really an allophone of /a/, in free variation with the other allophones of the phonema and used only in certain words. I believe that this may well be true. At any rate, I am positive that the phonemic status of [æ] cannot be proven. Some informants will be found to vary from [æ] to [a] and shades in between with the same word. Furthermore, I have the unprovable impression that I have been hearing [æ] more and more in the past few years from native speakers of Spanish who are not from Los Angeles. It may turn out that a new phoneme, or at any rate, a new allophone, is being added to the phonology of Spanish. For the present, I prefer to classify this only as an English influence.

El Habla y la Educación de los Niños de Origen Mexicano en Los Angeles

Yolanda Lastra de Suarez

Este estudio formaba parte del Proyecto Lingua que tenía por objeto desarrollar y evaluar un programa educativo para los niños de habla española en la escuela primaria para lograr que mejoraran en su rendimiento escolar, basándose en la hipótesis de que los niños tranferirían al inglés, en el transcurso de los años, las técnicas y conocimientos adquiridos en español.

Para poder llevar a cabo este plan era necesario saber en qué dialecto deberían prepararse los materiales de enseñanza y si había que darle a los maestros alguna preparación especial en el habla de los alumnos. Es decir, había que saber si los alumnos hablaban, como se decía, una mezcla de español e inglés que se tuviera que considerar como un dialecto aparte, o una variante sub standard del español de México tan alejada de la norma que se presentaran problemas de comunicación entre el alumno y el maestro de habla standard semejantes a los encontrados en los barrios de Washington y Nueva York.

Se eligió para la investigación el Este de Los Angeles en donde la población es predominantemente de origen mexicano y la deserción escolar es la más elevada de la ciudad. Se escogió la Escuela Humphrey's como representativa y allí fueron entrevistados 42 niños.[2]

Los resultados obtenidos se compararon con los de 23 entrevistas semejantes realizadas en otras 5 escuelas primarias del barrio. Además se entrevistaron 9 padres de familia; se le hizo una grabación a una niña de edad pre-escolar y una entrevista a un niño de 4 años; se visitaron clases en Humphrey's y en una escuela hogar de las afueras de Los Angeles; se estudió el habla inglesa de 6 niños de Humphrey's; se preparó un cuestionario para los maestros de la misma escuela; y se examinó un corpus limitado del español local standard.

Las entrevistas con los niños fueron de dos tipos; individuales y colectivas. Las de los niños de kinder, 1° y 2° fueron no estructuradas y duraron entre 5 y 20 minutos cada una; las de los niños de 3° y 4° duraron 20 minutos aproximadamente y se basaron en un cuestionario. Todas las entrevistas con niños y la de un adulto se grabaron en cinta magnetofónica.

Datos culturales. La población de origen mexicano en los Estados Unidos está concentrada en 5 estados del suroeste: Arizona, California, Colorado, Nuevo México y Texas y es de aproximadamente 4 millones. La mayoría de los habitantes de las zonas urbanas son inmigrantes recientes de clase baja.

Es un hecho reconocido por todos que al mexicano americano se le discrimina en aspectos legales, educativos y de salud pública y que por su origen no obtiene los trabajos que pudiera obtener por su preparación. Su nivel económico, por lo tanto, es más bajo que el del *anglo* (el americano blanco, de habla inglesa y

---

Reprinted by permission of the author. This paper was first presented at the V Simposio Del Programa Interamericano De Linguística y Enseñanza De Idiomas, Sao Paulo, January 9-14, 1969.

apellido aceptable) de educación semejante.

Los mexicanos americanos viven segregados dentro de las ciudades y de hecho hay también segregación escolar. El promedio de años cursados por los mexicanos americanos es menor al de los anglos y al de la población de color. En Los Angeles hay un gran número de personas de origen mexicano que vive en la zona este de la ciudad y ahí el porcentaje de los niños que no terminan la secundaria es el más alto de todos los barrios de la ciudad. Además los resultados de pruebas de lectura hechas en todo el estado de California acusan la deficiencia en la educación recibida por estos niños en comparación con la que reciben los niños de otros sectores.

A continuación presentamos un resumen de los resultados de las diferentes fases de la investigación realizada: el cuestionario de los maestros y las entrevistas con los padres para situar el problema en el medio cultural; las entrevistas con los niños; características del español de los niños comparado con el de los adultos y el standard local; y una caracterización del inglés de los niños.

El cuestionario para los maestros. El cuestionario se presentó por escrito y constaba de 20 preguntas. Fue contestado por 23 maestros de todos los grados en la escuela Humphrey's. Su objeto era obtener datos sobre la actitud de los maestros hacia los niños, su habla y su cultura. Los resultados obtenidos se pueden sintetizar así: el maestro típico muestra una actitud positiva hacia el alumno, pero tiene un conocimiento sumamente superficial de la cultura de éste, lo que resulta en mutua incomprensión y en falta de comunicación con los padres. El niño está expuesto alternativamente a dos sistemas de valores, el de su casa y el de su escuela.

Entrevistas con algunos padres de familia. Se entrevistaron 9 padres de familia con hijos pequeños. Las peculiaridades lingüísticas observadas durante las entrevistas, que fueron todas en español, se dan más adelante. En cuanto a los datos no lingüísticos podemos afirmar que todas las familias pertenecen a la clase obrera, que conservan sus costumbres familiares, su religión y, en gran medida, su lengua y que tienen conciencia de que la educación que reciben sus hijos es deficiente y podría ser mejor.

Las entrevistas con los niños. El comportamiento de los niños durante la entrevista fue bastante espontáneo y natural, pero al visitarlos en su clase actuaban en forma diferente. Hablaban menos y el maestro tenía que animarlos. Su timidez no se debía a mi presencia, según los comentarios de los maestros, sino que era habitual y, sin duda, reflejaba la situación cultural. El 54 porciento de los niños era de segunda generación (padre o padres nacidos en México); el 25 porciento de tercera generación (abuelo o abuelos mexicanos) y el 20 porciento de primera generación (nacidos en México). La mayoría de los padres de los niños son obreros, uno era dueño de un puesto de hot dogs; dos no vivían con la madre y dos no tenían trabajo. El 43 porciento de las madres trabajan. Al tratar de relacionar los datos lingüísticos con los no lingüísticos se obtuvieron los siguientes resultados:

Los niños bilingües en cuya habla dominaba el inglés, pero que entendían, sin embargo, las preguntas que se les hacía en español eran de tercera generación o sólo uno de sus padres había nacido en México.

Seis niños hablaban español standard. Todos eran de segunda generación y tanto el padre como la madre habían nacido en México. Fue   imposible determinar el lugar exacto de nacimiento de los padres. Todos los niños que hablaban español standard sabían lo que querían ser cuando - fueran grandes (e.g. maestro, enfermera). El habla standard no se relaciona con la ocupación del padre y no se determinó si se relacionaba con la educación de los padres, lo cual es probable.

El habla de los niños. La mayoría de los niños habla un dialecto del español semejante al de los hablantes de clase baja de México y que naturalmente recuerda el habla sub standard o rural de otras zonas hispanohablantes, pero además está salpicado de interferencias del inglés. Todos entienden el standard aunque en algunos casos el vocabulario pasivo es limitado en ciertas áreas culturales, por ejemplo no conocen los términos que se usan en la escuela: tarea, matemáticas, geografía.

Fonología. Las características fonológicas más importantes que no son atribuibles a la influencia del inglés son las siguientes:

y⟶i La semiconsonante palatal carece totalmente de fricción:
[éios] , [káie] , [iáma] , [gaí:na] .

c⟶s La africada palatal se hace fricativa:
[éše] , [šikíto] , [šokáron] , [ošo] , [mušášo]

f⟶Φ La fricativa labiodental sorda se labializa:
[aΦuéra] .

b⟶v La obstruyente labial sonora se hace labiodental:
[palávras] , [vés] , [vá] , [véses] , [čaválo] .

Las peculiaridades atribuibles a la interferencia y que son menos generalizadas que las arriba citadas son:

[ɼ] retrofleja: [kaɼne] , [ɛmféɼmo] , [ɨɔpa] , [péɼɔ] .
R múltiple demasiado trinada: ultracorrección: [péɼɔ].
La vibrante múltiple se hace vibrante simple: [aríba] .

s⟶z sonorización de la fricativa alveolar sorda: [xozé] , [zúmo] .

x⟶h la fricativa velar se convierte en una fricativa con poca fricción en el punto de articulación de la vocal siguiente: [méhiko] .

Juntura entre dos vocales consecutivas: [mi+ermáno] .
Cierre glotal entre dos vocales consecutivas y en posición inicial ante vocal: [mi?ermáno] , [?ermano] .

esO⟶sO Pérdida de /e/ inicial ante un grupo de /s/ y oclusiva:
/spañól/, /stá/.

g⟶g La fricativa velar sonora se hace oclusiva: [péga] , [amíga] .

Las características sintácticas más importantes son el uso exclusivo del pronombre personal tú (ausencia de usted) y las formas verbales correspondientes:

el empleo de las formas *los* y *losotros* por *nos* y *nosotros;*
el uso del artículo ante los nombres propios: la Cecilia, el James;
el uso de la forma *mi* como objeto directo: mi pegan, mi lo compró;
el morfema verbal *-mos* a veces es *-nos:* dábanos la vuelta, íbanos, vanos.

A continuación se presentan ejemplos de lexemas no standard; interferencias del inglés incluyendo préstamos asimilados, préstamos no asimilados, calcos, otros casos de interferencia y cambio de código lingüístico (*switching*).

He aquí unos cuantos ejemplos de formas verbales no standard:

páremos
caindo, cayí
xuí, xuimos, etc.
siguía
train
traye
ponelo por *ponerlo*
quero

Ejemplos de lexemas no standard en relación con el standard local:

juar
crebar
mirarse   'verse', 'parecerse': *se mira como el otro*
mirar   'ver', 'visitar': *vamos a mirarlas a su casa*
traer   'tener': *traigo 9 años; los amigos de la escuela que aquí traigo*
rayar   'escribir'
garrar   'agarrar'. Este verbo en realidad significa 'get': *Se garraron married* 'They got married'; *garré muchos juetes* 'I got lots of toys'.

dotrina
chavalo
misa   'iglesia': *Vamos a una misa que está cerca del cementerio*
asina
onde
en veces
muncho
lo más   'no más'

Ejemplos de préstamos asimilados:

los kiris	kitty	gatito
postear	post	mandar por correo
tokador	record player	tocadiscos
puchar	push	apretar: *le puchas al botón*

Ejemplos de préstamos no asimilados:

| sainear | shine | embetunar a los zapatos |
| plonj | plunge | piscina |

Ejemplos de calcos:

se lo di pa tras	I gave it back	se lo devolví
mi chiquito hermano		
Dimitri es no más cuatro	Dimitri is only four	Dimitri tiene cuatro años no más.

Ejemplos de otros casos de interferencia:
mi tio's cama
está away far

Ejemplos de cambio de código lingüístico:
Tengo un *brother*
Lo llevó en *jail*
Soy *game leader* para *hop scotch*

  Comparación con el habla de los adultos. El habla de los niños del Este de Los Angeles es muy semejante a la de los adultos. Podríamos alargar las listas de ejemplos, pero es evidente que el sistema es el mismo tanto en lo fonológico como en lo sintáctico y en lo léxico.

  Comparación con el español standard. El español standard de Los Angeles no ha sido estudiado detalladamente para este trabajo. Se tomaron en cuenta para poder describirlo someramente varios programas de radio y televisión, un sermón, conversaciones con tres personas de clase media: un abogado, un estudiante de universidad y una secretaria, y la prensa.

  Nos encontramos ante una situación lingüística en la cual no hay un standard local definido: los inmigrantes o las personas que han viajado consideran standard el habla de la gente culta de México o de otras capitales de América; los directores de las estaciones de radio y televisión consideran standard el habla culta de la Ciudad de México. Los nativos de Los Angeles no tienen modelos de habla culta en las escuelas ni en las iglesias. El radio y la televisión ejercen sin duda la mayor influencia; no así la prensa que sólo leen los inmigrantes pues la mayoría de las personas nacidas en Los Angeles no saben leer en español. Los nativos de Los Angeles no quieren imitar el habla de la Ciudad de México, pues la consideran peculiar y se burlan de la entonación, pero así y todo probablemente el habla culta de México represente en cierto modo el standard a juzgar por lo que se lee y se oye en el periódico, la televisión y el radio. Podemos establecer niveles en el standard local desde lo formal hasta lo no formal:

(1) *formal escrito*   La Opinión, un periódico local.
(2) *formal oral*   Locutores de radio anunciando.
(3) *informal oral*   Locutores hablando con el público; porgramas donde
                        se dan recetas de cocina.
(4) *coloquial*   Conversaciones de personas cultas que han tenido
                        contacto con el extranjero.

  El habla del Este de Los Angeles difiere naturalmente más del primero es decir, formal escrito, que del cuarto, es decir, coloquial, y se caracteriza como hemos visto principalmente por peculiaridades léxicas (préstamos, arcaísmos, vulgarismos), la ausencia de la forma *usted* y las formas verbales correspondientes en el habla de los individuos nacidos en Los Angeles que no han tenido contacto con el extranjero.

  El inglés de los niños del Este de Los Angeles.
  Fonología
Entonación semejante a la del español: /áy wana bĬ a fútbal pleyár↓/ [221 en vez de 321][3];

vocales altas: [hír] ,   [θijk] ,   [tu] 'here', 'think', 'too';
centralización de la vocal anterior baja: [lámp]   'lamp';
b fricativa   [ober] 'over'   [ay libo] 'I live';
africación de la fricativa palatal: [čéydz]   'shades';
alófono intervocálico de la /t/ y /d/ demasiado apical: [léɾas]   'lettuce'
                        ['béɾar]   'better'   [haéɾim]   'had him';
dentalización de la nasal alveolar final: [ríydin]   'reading';
(este fenómeno se da también en el habla urbana sub standard de monolingües)
simplificación de grupos consonánticos: /pic∂rs/   'pictures'.

Sintaxis
Adverbios de tiempo mal colocados:

Sometimes at night we play games 'Sometimes we play games at night'
(Compárese con: *A veces en la noche jugábamos*);

We all the time used to go outside 'We used to go outside all the time'
(Compárese con: *Siempre salíamos*);

Orden del complemento directo y los complementos adverbiales alterado:

I like to play with my friends Jo and my borther Manuel and my friend Robert
and Danny, football.

Repetición del sujeto: My mother, she doesn't have a job.

Repetición del complemento indirecto: I like them big whales.

Negativos dobles: Mrs. E is not teaching no more 'Mrs E is not teaching any
more'.

You don't do nothing por You don't do anything
(compárese con el habla sub standard de monolingües)

Falta de concordancia: Does Bertha and Sandra play with you at home? 'Do. . .'
She stays home and work
It doesn't come out

Pasado en vez de infinitivo: I used to threw the ball
I haven't gave them a name yet.

Verbos usados en forma sub standard:
I also gone with them to Ashbury
I seen them play

Confusión del gerundio con infinitivo:
I like to doing is math   'I like doing math'
                             'I like to do math'

Construcciones extrañas:

I went to go see 'I went to see'

One of my best TV shows are the Jimmy Louis and I dream of Jeannie and the Monkeys.

Interferencias léxicas:

Because they are going to operate her, basado en *Porque la van a operar* por *operate on her.*

My mother works in a fabric, 'fábrica', por *factory;*

sweet bread, 'pan dulce' por *sweet rolls;*

in the night, 'en la noche', por *at night;*

Como puede verse estas peculiaridades son en parte atribuibles a la influencia del español: la mayoría de las fonológicas, todas las léxicas y algunas de las sintácticas. Pero es importante notar que muchas de las peculiaridades sintácticas son frecuentes en el habla sub standard de los hablantes monolingües de inglés. Por lo tanto podemos decir que el inglés no lo aprenden los niños sólo en la escuela, sino también al entrar en contacto con hablantes de inglés de clase baja. Los maestros no tienen éxito con los hablantes bilingües en inculcar los patrones de la lengua standard, de la misma manera que no lo han tenido con los hablantes monolingües de los barrios bajos de la mayor parte de las ciudades norteamericanas.

Conclusiones.

En conclusión podemos decir que los niños del Este de Los Angeles hablan un dialecto del español mexicano que difiere un tanto de la norma pero no lo suficiente como para requerir textos especiales por lo que respecta a la lengua. Comprenden bien el español mexicano standard y se pordría usar esta variante como lengua de instrucción. La mayoría de los niños de segunda generación son monolingües al entrar al kinder por lo que sería muy conveniente impartirles los primeros conocimientos en su lengua nativa; enseñarles a leer y escribir en español y simultaneamente a hablar el inglés y posteriormente ir cambiando la lengua de instrucción hasta que en 4° grado el español no fuera más que una materia.

Habría que preparar textos especiales en cuanto al contenido con temas comprensibles para el niño dentro del ambiente bicultural en el que se desea que participe, incluyendo por ejemplo para niños de 3° narraciones sobre Benito Juárez así como sobre Lincoln, descripciones de las grandes ciudades hispanoamericanas como Caracas que tiene "freeways" como Los Angeles, etc. etc. Así se le daría al niño un panorama de su tradición cultural que lo haría sentirse digno de contribuir positivamente en la amalgama de nacionalidades que forman el pueblo norteamericano. Sería un buen ciudadano conciente de su origen, pero no avergonzado de él.

Los maestros de los cuatro primeros años (kinder al 3°) tendrían que ser bilingües y recibir un entrenamiento especial: (1) conocimiento del dialecto de los alumnos en comparación con el standard local; (2) conocimiento del inglés sub standard con el que pronto entrarían en contacto sus alumnos; (3) conocimiento del medio socio-económico y cultural de los alumnos y de los propósitos de la nueva educación bilingüe. Los maestros de 4° grado en adelante podrían prepararse adecuadamente conociendo los últimos puntos.

Hoy en día la lengua española no sirve como instrumento para adquirir nuevos conocimientos en el ambiente cultural de Los Angeles y del Sur Oeste de los EEUU en general. El inglés que adquieren los niños de origen mexicano no es standard, es insuficiente y no los capacita para adquirir buenos empleos.

De las entrevistas con niños de escuela y padres de familia pudimos formarnos una idea de la realidad socio-lingüística y notar indicios de la no asimilación de la familia al medio norteamericano: la lengua de la casa es el español, se mantienen las costumbres hispánicas, el padre es, sin lugar a duda, el jefe de la familia aun cuando los hijos van creciendo. Los lazos familiares son fuertes y se respeta y obedece a los mayores; la comida es la tradicional; en muchos casos se mantienen relaciones con amigos y parientes en la República Mexicana.

Los padres tienen conciencia de que la educación que reciben sus hijos es deficiente. Los maestros también se dan cuenta, pero (salvo en un caso) no atribuyen su fracaso al sistema educativo sino a la deficiencia de los alumnos. No es que culpen a los niños o que los consideren tontos, pero los consideran incapaces de alcanzar el mismo nivel educativo de sus propios hijos. En cierto modo tienen razón, dentro del sistema actual los niños no pueden mejorar. Pero esa actitud benevolente y conformista del maestro es en gran parte la responsable del fracaso actual. La actitud bien intencionada del maestro típico es de tenerle lástima al niño porque es pobre y sobre todo porque no es como él y porque está, pudiera decirse, casi predestinado al fracaso. Los maestros desconocen los valores culturales de sus alumnos y por eso hay una falta total de comunicación entre padres y profesores.

Los maestros se dan cuenta, sin embargo, de que muchos de los alumnos tienen inteligencia innata que no demuestran en las pruebas a las que se les somete. Dichas pruebas pueden considerarse como una especie de discriminación institucionalizada, pero es de esperarse que ya que los maestros se dan cuenta de su invalidez, pronto sean desechadas por el sistema educativo.

El niño mexicano americano actúa de diferente manera cuando se siente en confianza que cuando tiene que desenvolverse en una situación formal. Si no sabe inglés y hay un maestro en el pasillo prefiere callar. Cuando por fin logra aprender la lengua del país lo hace en forma tan deficiente que no siempre puede elevar su posición social.

Este último punto es de suma importancia pues revela que el problema del mexicano americano no es el de una barrera lingüística en su significado más elemental: no es que el mexicano americano de Los Angeles no sepa inglés, lo aprende desde kinder y hasta se convierte en su lengua dominante; la barrera es más bien cultural: no está adaptado al medio y su falta de adaptación se refleja en una serie de factores sociolingüísticos que aquí hemos empezado a explorar y entre los que evidentemente se encuentran las variantes de inglés y de español que habla.

Por último, sería conveniente indicar que para ampliar el cuadro sociolingüístico que se esboza arriba, habría que estudiar a fondo el problema del standard local; estudiar otras áreas de Los Angeles, observar el habla de los bilingües en otras situaciones para calcular la proporción de inglés en el habla española y vice versa. También sería conveniente profundizar el estudio de la relación entre los hechos lingüísticos y los sociales por medio de cuestionarios más detallados.

Notas

[1]El ante-proyecto estuvo a cargo de Frieda Libaw y James Lugo del Galton Institute. Paul Garvin hubiera actuado como director de las investigaciones lingüísticas de haberse efectuado el proyecto. Le estoy muy agradecida por haberme puesto en contacto con el proyecto Lingua y por sus sugerencias al iniciarse este estudio.

[2]Se agradece la colaboración del Sr. Caldwell, Superintendente de las Escuelas del Este de Los Angeles y la ayuda prestada por los directores de las escuelas, especialmente la del Sr. William Orr de la Escuela Humphrey's.

[3]Según Trager y Smith.

Chicano Spanish Dialects and Education

Ernest Garcia

The description and analysis of Chicano non-standard Spanish and cultural meanings expressed through language has escaped serious investigation. There is very little firm systematic knowledge of Chicano dialects and much less of the cultural meanings expressed through these dialects. We have some solid information about the persistence of Spanish and good evidence that certain patterns of behavior and values do hold up across the variety of Chicano communities in the Southwest.[1] The following will cover two areas of language and culture that have not been critically presented to the public.

Language Characteristics

An assumption often voiced is that "disadvantaged" children are non-verbal or are verbally deprived.[2] These children are said to have an enormous difficulty expressing themselves verbally in many situations. Authors have gone to great lengths to demonstrate and explain the supposed verbal and cognitive deficiencies which resulted from their "deprived culture" and environment. Supposedly, linguistic deprivation becomes evident when these children first enter school. Consequently, there has arisen a rather firm belief that "disadvantaged" children are basically inarticulate, that they lack the verbal ability so important in reading and eventual school success. This assumption cannot be well supported in the case of Chicano Spanish-speaking children, as we see when we analyze Chicano language characteristics and learn to appreciate the exact nature of Chicano verbal functioning.

Recent systematic research in the inner city has successfully disproved the notions of those who characterize the language of low income populations as degenerate and structurally under-developed. There is overwhelming evidence to show that both middle-class and non-middle-class children, no matter what their native language, dialect, or ethnic background, have control of a fully formed grammatical system at the age of five or six. The mere fact that their system is different from that of their teacher does not mean that their speech is not rule governed, nor is it deficient. Further speech features of differences that the teacher notices do not necessarily indicate inability to adjust to some universally accepted English norm; rather, they are the influence of other dialects, which have equally specific and complex syntactic rules.[3] These dialects are different and distinct from the school standard—no better and no worse, in spite of the social connotations often placed on different forms of expression.

The false assumption that non-standard language is inferior is not confined to speakers of Black English. It has also been applied to the Chicano Spanish-speaking child. It is true that many Spanish-speaking children are essentially

---

Reprinted by permission from *Aztlan: Chicano Journal of the Social Sciences and the Arts* 2:1.67-76 (Spring 1971).

non-verbal in English in their early school years. However, they come to school with a considerable knowledge of their native language, and though the language they speak is sometimes limited due to their age and background, it is and continues to be a useful form of communication for them. Also, it must be kept in mind, as Labov points out, that children may be more fluent when speaking among their peers in a more agreeable place than the classroom. Yet, educators have been primarily concerned with children's speech behavior in school. Labov and Peña made a study to ascertain what basic sentence patterns and fundamental transformations "disadvantaged" Spanish-speaking first graders possess in both Spanish and English. The findings suggest that these children's native language is more developed than most educators have been willing to admit.[4]

Educators generally consider Chicano language "Pocho Spanish," so substandard that they sometimes refer to children who speak it as alingual. For example, many language teachers and authors when questioned about "Pocho Spanish" will express the opinion that this vernacular as spoken in the Southwest is substandard. They advise that, when possible, attempts should be made to change it. Typical is a textbook by Pauline Baker, designed for American speakers of Spanish. In its preface she states:

> ... estamos presenciando una decadencia lamentable del español de los Estados Unidos... Cada día se hace sentir más la necesidad de corregir los errores del mal español que se debe evitar y de desarrollar el buen español que se debe emplear. ... El propôsito a que se ha dedicado la presente obra es ayudar a los alumnos norte Americanos de origin español a hablar y escribir tan bien como les sea posible la lengua que aprendieron en su hogar.[5]

Dr. Bowen points out that there is certainly an advantage in speaking a standard version of one's language, where a standard is recognized. He argues that there is a price one must pay if he speaks a non-standard dialect, especially where the means of acquiring the standard are not easily at hand. Miss Baker's book is certainly intended to provide that means, but though seriously conceived, it has limited potential. In part, this is because the Chicano does not have any intention of doing away with his "Pocho Spanish." If the Chicano is to learn the standard dialect, it should not be at the expense of the legitimacy of his home dialect.

Chicano parents are now asking that instead of teaching language, especially the Spanish language, to the primary school children as a subject that is new, teachers might better attempt to lift to the conscious level those understandings which their children already possess in their usage.

> The fact that the disadvantaged child, speaking a social dialect which the teacher may not even understand, possesses a grammar of his own albeit one radically different in some ways from that familiar to the teacher, indicates certain possibilities as well as dangers in introducing him to a second dialect in the classroom.[6]

The first logical step for the teacher is to give, express, or manifest the recognition and acceptance of the child's home dialect. One must agree with Dr. Bowen when he states:

> Children are encouraged not to denigrate or reject the language of their parents, for

this would imply a value judgment unfavorable to those who speak the dialect of the home. There is ample evidence to support the fact that the value of self-respect and identity that accompanies the comfortable acceptance of one's personal linguistic situation is appropriate and normal. The Blacks, like the Hispanos (Chicanos), and indeed like all of (us), the English-speaking Anglos included, need the security of self-assurance and the conviction that we occupy a position of respect in our community, and that our particular sub-community makes a valid and acceptable contribution to the larger social and political units we are associated with. When this self-respect is lost or denied, the result is discouragement, apathy, frustration, or anger.[7]

The teacher should express and demonstrate respect for everything that the Chicano child brings with him and this certainly includes his most prized possession, his language. It is now time that teachers recognized the essential arbitrariness of language forms, that one dialect is just as valid and effective as another, regardless of social judgments. Several authorities state this position.

It is no less unreasonable to expend great efforts to change dialects of speakers of Southwest Spanish than it would be to Briticize the speech of Anglo-Americans. And it would be an effort equally foredoomed to failure.[8]

It is simply true that change is an aspect of human language as regular and relentless as the birth and death of men. It asks no man's permission and waits on no man's approval.[9]

In the case of Southwest Spanish, changes in both standard Spanish and Southwest Spanish have occurred since the two dialects have had a separate existence, and they no longer fully correspond.

Dialect

Spanish-speakers in the Southwest, because of historical circumstance and social factors, have created their own dialect. This dialect is rich in its use of slang and loan words. Nevertheless, the basic grammatical construction of utterances in Southwest Spanish will not diverge significantly from other Spanish dialects. The deviation of this type of dialect from the so-called standard language will stem from the fact that these constructions will be filled with dialect forms from Peninsular and American Spanish (including many contributions from indigenous languages), neologisms, loanwords and old Spanish words, including some that have taken on new meanings. Also, the Southwest dialect should probably be referred to as the Southwest dialects, since there will be differences depending upon the geographical location of Spanish speakers in these areas. Some of the Southwest Chicanos have been able to maintain dialects more closely related to those of Mexico because of the proximity to the border.

Let us now examine Dr. Bowen's data on the verbal behavior of the people from San Antoñito, New Mexico. All of the examples presented in this section are taken from his excellent paper, *Local Standards and Spanish in the Southwest.*

A number of patterns can be cited in the morphology of the verb. New Mexican Spanish, like most other western hemisphere dialects, has abandoned the plural second person familiar form of the verb, which leaves a paradigm of five forms. The singular second person form is retained, but is regularized. The characteristic of this form is a final *-s*, which appears in general Spanish (hereafter GSp) in all forms except the preterite, where a suffix with an internal *-s-* is added. New Mexican Spanish (hereafter NMSp) logically transfers this *s* to final position so that the forms used are: *hablates, comites, vivites, etc.*

Another helpful modification in the preterite tense is the generalization of the present/past contrast in first person plural forms from the second to the third conjugation. Thus, the pattern exemplified in *comemos/comimos* is extended to *vivemos/vivimos* in a simplification that is useful and efficient.

In the present subjective paradigm another regularization is noted. The pattern of stem accentuation is maintained in all forms of the paradigm, which produces the form *háblemos, cómamos, vívamos,* etc. Modifications of the stressed stems are accordingly preserved, so the following items occur: *cuéntemos, vuélvamos, puédamos, ciérremos, quiéramos, póngamos, tráigamos, hágamos, conózcamos,* etc.

Certain radical changing verbs are regularized. *Pidir* conjugates in the present *pido, pides, pide pidemos, piden,* and in the imperfect *pidía,* preterite *pidi, pidites, pidió, pidimos, pidieron. Siguir* yields *sigo, sigues, sigue, siguemos, siguen, siguía, siguites, siguimos, siguieron. Dicir* conjugates *digo, dices, dice, dicemos, dicen, dicía,* etc.

The final *-d* of GSp is regularly dropped (*verdá, virtú, usté, mercé,* etc.) so NMSp occasionally takes measures to protect it when to do so is felt important. The most common example is the word for wall, which is *pader.* A metathesis of *d* and *r* in the GSp from *pared* saves the *d* and avoids a homonym with the first person singular of the preterite form of *parar.*

As part of the tendency toward a relaxed pronunciation of the *y* sound, the *y* (sometimes spelled *ll*) is dropped between a higher and a lower front or mid vowel (specifically between *i* and *e, a, o* and between *e* and *a, o*). Thus, *mía* and *milla* are not distinguished, and *ella* and *aquella* are pronounced *ea* and *aquea, ladrillo* as *ladrío, capilla* as *capía, cabello* as *cabeo,* etc.

A sequence of two front vowels (except *ie*) does not occur in succession in the same word (and rarely across word boundaries) so the forms *creyer* (to believe), *leyer* (to read), *reyir* (to laugh), and *freyir* (to fry) are found. Following a general rule of the phonology, as described in the preceding paragraph, intervocalic *y* regularly drops when a lower vowel following a front vowel plus intervocalic *y* is in the pattern, to produce the sequences *ie, ía, ío, ea, eo,* but is retained elsewhere, as in *creye, creyemos, leye, leyemos,* etc.

The articles *el* and *la* both reduce to *l* before any word beginning with a vowel, to produce *l amigo, l amiga, l otro, l otra.* This makes superfluous the rule in GSp that accounts for the *el* form of the feminine article appearing before words beginning with stressed *á.* In NMSp such forms are *l agua, l águila,* etc., as well as *l azúcara, l hembra, l iglesia, l hombre, l uva,* etc.

Perhaps the area of Southwest Spanish that attracts most attention and the most enthusiastic censure is in the lexicon. Scholars who concern themselves with the "purity" of the language are apt to forget the thousands of loanwords borrowed from many sources in the early development of the language and concentrate their attention on the recognizably recent arrivals, inveighing against anything that *might* be a result of current language contact. This condemnation has several effects: 1) it ignores the reality of language growth and development in a natural environment that responds to the demands and needs of the actual situation; 2) it tends to shake the confidence of speakers of the criticized dialect in their ability to acceptably express their thoughts; 3) it clutters school classes for Chicanos with a lot of trivia at a time when educational efforts can most profitably be expended in other pursuits; and 4) it denies natural and universal sociolinguistic processes of languages in contact.

Under no circumstances should loanwords be condemned. It is no more justifiable to clean the English loanwords out of Spanish than it would be to remove the Spanish loanwords from English. Imagine the misguided effort that would be necessary to replace *vanilla, banana, potato, avocado, lariat, rodeo, corral, canyon, hurricane, chocolate, tobacco, stevedore, cargo, escapade, mosquito* and many thousands of others! What an incredible amount of effort would be necessary to extirpate *any* class of loanwords! And how foolishly such energy would be spent! There are more important things to do, for Anglos, for Chicanos and for Spanish speakers anywhere.

Loanwords from English are numerous in Southwest Spanish. Many have been used and dropped as unnecessary, and undoubtedly this process will continue. Some loanwords, however, are firmly entrenched, such as the word *lonche,* for 'lunch,' which has spawned *lonchar, lonchería,* and *lonchera* (to lunch, lunchroom, lunch pail). A similar set is *troca, troquero, trocade, trocón* (truck, truck driver, dump truck, truck and semi). Comparable words are *bil, bos, renta, jalar, papel, casa de cortes, sitijól, gato, máquina de lavar, mama grande, gaselín, greda, crocha, bomper, trele, búchale, chategón, londre* (bill, boss, rent, haul, newspaper, court house, city hall, caterpillar (tractor), washing machine, grandma, gasoline, (road) grader, (rock) crusher, bumper, trailer, bushel, shotgun, laundry), and many others.

The question that language teachers, administrators, principals, etc., should have is not "How are we going to purify 'Pocho Spanish'?" but rather "Who should do what to whom and why?" Wayne A. O'Neil observes:

> Instead of enriching the lives of urban children by plugging them into a second dialect (if that enterprise is so enriching: Why don't we let everyone in for the fun and games; "enrich" the suburban kid with an urban dialect), we should be working to eradicate the language prejudice, the language mythology, that people grow into holding and believing. For there is clear evidence that the privileged use their false beliefs about language to the disadvantage of the socially deprived. One way to stop this is to change non-standard dialect speakers at least for some of the time, i.e. when the non-standards are in the presence of the standards, currying favor of them, jobs of them, etc. Another response to language differences would be to educate (especially the people in power) for tolerance of differences, for an understanding of differences. This could be naturally done, easily done in elementary schools, but only by teachers who are themselves free of language prejudice. In many ways this is the most important kind of language study that needs to be accomplished in the schools.[10]

There is support for the idea of teaching non-standard dialects to standard speakers. Dr. Bowen states:

> I would, then, suggest that Mexican-American Spanish be accepted, that misguided efforts to change it should be forthwith abandoned, that standard Spanish, when it is taught, should be taught as an additional, supplementary skill, not as a replacive for a

defective vernacular. I am personally inclined to go even further and claim that Southwest Spanish is a valid and appropriate model for the non-Spanish-speaking students who study in the area where Southwest Spanish is spoken.

To teach this dialect I would (1) equip students to communicate most efficiently with the Spanish speakers most likely to be available to them and (2) to recognize the validity of a historically authentic version of Spanish that is an important part of the linguistic patrimony of the Southwest.[11]

Linguists agree that non-standard dialects are highly structured systems. These same linguists do not see these dialects as accumulations of errors caused by the failure of their speakers to master the standard language. When linguists hear Chicano children saying "Tengo mucho lonche en mi lonchera," they do not hear a primitive, bastardized language. Nor do they believe that the speech of working-class people is merely a form of emotional expression, incapable of communicating logical thought. Assuming that educators take seriously their responsibility for educating the "whole child," the following recommendations are in order: 1) Accept the Spanish dialect that a Spanish-speaking Chicano child brings with him to school. This dialect is so precious that it should not be disturbed, corrected, or tampered with in any way by language teachers, especially by those who are responsible for teaching the Spanish language. The child's speech is his home, his comfort, his mother. Schooling must add to the children's repertoire of learned speech behaviors, but any attempt to subtract from the Chicanos' speech repertoire makes the ultimate ends of schooling more difficult and in many cases impossible to attain. 2) Provide the proper natural environment and maintain their active participation in language development. 3) Use the oral efficiency that children bring to school as the means of developing a complementary efficiency in reading and writing. Given a situation where they need to do it, Chicano children, like any other children, are natural polyglots and can learn two or three languages. To extend, refine, and enhance the oral arts and skills children already possess, and this certainly includes the Spanish Southwerst dialect, should be the first obligation of the people responsible for teaching children of any ethnic group.

There is enough evidence to show that the child always enters public schooling with a set of learned (though, of course, not formally taught) language behaviors. Society needs to do away with the narrow attitude of attempting to correct other people's language, English for the Blacks, Spanish for the Chicano. This does not imply that the teaching of the standard dialect, either in English or Spanish, be prohibited. However, the negativism of antiquated pedagogy which attempts to bring most children to a level of language skills that in daily life only a few practice, should be eliminated. Most Chicano children would master the knowledge necessary to function in this complex society if their experience with language development were positive. Schooling should provide Chicanos with the necessary concepts and confidence for success. Furthermore, it should leave them with the feeling that they will be quite capable of mastering anything written or spoken that they want to learn.

Notes

[1]See, for example, Leo Grebler, Joan Moore and Ralph Guzman, *The Mexican-American*

People, The Nation's Second Largest Minority, (New York: The Free Press, 1970).

[2]Cf. Riessman, 1962, pp. 158-160; Hess and Shipman, 1965, pp. 189-194; Jensen, 1967, pp. 182-191.

[3]Louisa Lewis, *Culture and Social Interaction in the Classroom*, working paper No. 38 (Berkeley: Language–Behavior Research Laboratory, University of California, Berkeley, 1970), pg. 4.

[4]Labov, 1970, pg. 28; Peña, 1967, pp. 1-25.

[5]Pauline Baker, *Español para los Hispanos*, (Dallas: Banks Upshaw and Co., 1953), pg. 1.

[6]Roger Shuy, *Urban Dialects and Language Learning*, (Champaign, Ill.: National Council of Teachers of English, 1965), pg. 59.

[7]Donald J. Bowen, *Studies in Language and Linguistics*, to be published by the University of Texas at El Paso, 1971, pg. 4.

[8]*Ibid.*, pg. 5.

[9]Donald Lloyd and Harry Warfel, *American English and Its Cultural Setting*, (New York: Alfred A. Knopf, 1965), pg. 7.

[10]Wayne O'Neill, "Paul Robert's Rules of Order: The Misuses of Linguistics in the Classroom," *The Urban Review*, Vol. 2, No. 7, (1967), pg. 7.

[11]Bowen, op. cit., pg. 4.

Spanish-English Bilingualism in San Antonio, Texas

Janet B. Sawyer

A frequent criticism of dialect studies stresses the fact that the materials collected by such methods do not readily lend themselves to structural description, since insistence upon phonetic accuracy produces data which is difficult to subject to phonemic analysis. Also the multitudinous detail which so fascinates the dialect scholar is suspiciously lacking in neatness and consistency. Yet it should not be forgotten that such data is the very essence of linguistic reality, the dynamic interplay of language and society, and that any linguistic theory which cannot stand up to the evidence gathered from the speakers themselves is surely of limited value.

Although no such testing of linguistic theory was intended at the time that this bilingual study of the English of San Antonio, Texas, was made,[1] the data revealed unexpected patterns of linguistic behavior which were pertinent to several linguistic theories. For example, since San Antonio was a community where two completely different languages were in contact, the effect of the first language in the community, the Spanish colonial language, upon the immigrant language, English, could be observed, with the result that a clearer understanding of the validity of the "substratum" theory could be attained.[2] Secondly, it was possible to study the linguistic behavior of the bilinguals in the community (who were, by the way, generally Spanish speakers learning English as a second language, since none of the native English speakers found it necessary to learn Spanish well in San Antonio). The records of the bilinguals demonstrated the fact that dialect records of even the most conventional type will reveal the social tensions within a community. The data mirrored the struggle of Spanish-speaking citizens to become acculturated in a society which denied them the opportunities afforded members of the English-speaking community. Even the efforts of second- and third-generation bilinguals to master English were partially self-defeating, since they learned the unnatural, regionless, *formal* style of the classroom. The very social isolation which they endeavored to overcome was increased by their stilted, unnatural, formal style, which was not spoken by members of the English-speaking community. A report upon this aspect of the study was published recently;[3] additional information will appear below.

It also seems advisable to mention a third theory which appeared recently in an article discussing various regional and social dialects in the United States, suggesting methods for teaching a standard dialect to speakers of sub-standard English.[4] Stewart includes a brief reference to a so-called "Mexican-American dialect" of English found in the Southwest among native speakers of Spanish. The term *dialect* is curious in this context, for in order to merit the term, a

---

Reprinted by permission from Glenn G. Gilbert (ed.), *Texas Studies in Bilingualism: Spanish, French, German, Czech, Polish, Serbian and Norwegian in the Southwest* (Berlin: Walter de Gruyter & Co., 1970), pp. 18-41.

particular variety of language should be fairly stable in its structure so that it can be learned by succeeding generations in the speech community. Nothing that could be called a Mexican-American *dialect* of English was found in San Antonio, Texas. The English spoken by the bilingual informants was simply an imperfect state in the mastery of English. A set of language habits does not become a dialect even if a particular speaker uses this system until he dies. What does have significance is the fact that the relatively unskilled bilinguals (who will be further classified below) did not pass on their imperfect English to their children. The children of the least able speakers learned English in school and spoke it with their peers. Parents who spoke English well spoke it with their children. Those who did not, spoke to them in Spanish. It was clear that the linguistic norm was not the English of their relatives or neighbors, but rather that of the members of the prestige, English-speaking community. From generation to generation, the second language was in a fluid state, becoming more and more expert. In the community under study for this report, there was no Mexican-American English *dialect*.

The dialect study upon which this report is based had the primary aim of furthering research for a linguistic atlas being conducted under the supervision of E. B. Atwood.[5] However the additional purpose, somewhat neglected in the earlier American dialect studies on the East Coast,[6] was a study of the bilingual aspects of a community where Spanish residents made up a large part of the permanent population. San Antonio was selected because, in addition to being a focal point of Southwestern culture, it is a bilingual community where Spanish and English speakers in almost equal numbers live together in an urban environment. For the purposes of this study, we shall refer to the informants who were native speakers of English as *Anglos* and to those who were native speakers of Spanish as *Latins*. (The term *Anglo* was that commonly used in the English-speaking community. The term *Latin* was the least offensive one for the Spanish speakers.)

I. History of the Community

San Antonio is located in southwestern Texas in Bexar County, which is at the eastern end of the great ranching area. Until approximately 1900 the county was rural, sparsely-settled ranch country, but by 1877 the city of San Antonio itself was already an important shipping point for cattle and farm products. Five railroads entered the city and promoted its growth into an important industrial center. The population of San Antonio grew from 3,488 in 1850 to 408,442 by 1950. The population of the entire county at that time was only 500,460, with over 80 per cent of the inhabitants being classified as urban.

The sources of the Anglo immigration to the community can be stated with a good deal of authority.[7] During the years between 1865 and 1880, states in which the Southern slave culture and economy predominated (Louisiana, Alabama, Mississippi, Georgia) contributed approximately 15.6 per cent of the settlers. The inland states (Arkansas, Tennessee, Missouri, Illinois, Kentucky, Indiana, and Kansas) contributed 17.0 per cent.[8] Another 27 per cent is unclassified as to source. It is obvious that Bexar County (and San Antonio proper) must be classified as a transition area which was influenced linguistically by several different Eastern dialects during the critical settlement years.

During this same period, numerous foreigners—8.4 per cent from Germany and 28.4 per cent from Mexico—made up the remainder of the immigration into Bexar County. However, Mexican immigration did not begin to avalanche in the area until after the passage of the Reclamation Act in 1902. This bill provided Federal funds for the construction of large-scale irrigation and reclamation projects. A vast truck-gardening business in the Rio Grande Valley, which developed to handle the demands of a rapidly growing urban population, had need of a supply of cheap labor. As a result, between 1918 and 1921 alone over 50,000 Mexicans were directly recruited in Mexico to meet the demand. In 1900 the entire state of Texas had only 71,062 Mexican immigrants; in 1930 there were 683,681, with the highest concentration in the Rio Grande Valley.

Not all of the recruits stayed in the Valley; many settled in towns such as San Antonio and became a part of the permanent community. They formed a lower middle class laboring group whose children attended the public schools and began to learn English.

Those who left the Valley are far better off socially and economically than the transient workers, approximately a million of whom still come into the country every year to pick the crops. Most of these seasonal laborers return to Mexico; however, according to *La Prensa,*[9] the leading Spanish-language newspaper of San Antonio, an average of three hundred people request permission to enter the United States at the Texas borders every day, and one-third of them wish to stay. Nobody knows how many more cross the river illegally and remain in Texas without permission. Numerous articles in *La Prensa* emphasize the fact that the government of Mexico is greatly alarmed over the exodus of its laboring and farming population, feeling that such emigration prejudices the future of the country. But no one seems to be able to control this tide "north from Mexico."

The transient workers, who at present are popularly referred to as *wetbacks, peons,* or *braceros,* are probably not very different from the parents of the Latin informants in this survey at the time of their migration to San Antonio from the central plateau of Mexico between the years 1890 and 1920. Belonging to a peasant culture, they were accustomed to being ruled in Mexico by the *hidalgos* and *patrones* and were surely ill-equipped to become part of a new and very different culture.

Actually, acquisition of the new culture was not a necessity for these immigrants. Indeed, their situation then and now is comparable to that of no other minority cultural group in the United States. They cross a border marked by no topographical change from that of the Mexican land they have left. Since the area was originally settled by speakers of Spanish, the imprint of the language and the Mexican-Spanish culture is everywhere. All about them are relatives, *paisanos* who share the same folk customs and speak the same language. They find their religion and their churches, with priests who speak their tongue. Even the towns and the very streets they live on bear Spanish names.

Complete integration with the Anglo cultural community may never come for the Spanish-speaking population as a whole, since many of them do not seek it either for themselves or for their children. Young people who adopt American cultural ways and master the English language, such as the two Latin college students who served as informants for this study, are often called "agringados," that is, "gringo-like," a derogative term. Yet second and third generation Texas Spanish speakers all want equal opportunities as a part of the nation as a whole. *La Prensa,*[10] on its 43rd anniversary, emphasized its determination to guard jealously the rights of its "Spanish-Mexican" readers. The paper advocated desegregated schools, better teachers, and longer school days; it fought discrimination in the public institutions and in the recreational centers; and it urged its readers to take a greater part in the political life of the community, reminding them that "foreigners" say, "As long as there are so many stupid Mexicans, we can live very well and make a lot of money. . ."[11] But the paper never preached acculturation for the Spanish members of the community.

II. Methodology for the Collection of the Data

The short work sheets devised by Hans Kurath and revised by Atwood for the Southwestern speech area were the primary source for the dialect corpus described herein. However, in order to compensate for a preponderance of citation forms which usually results from questions calling for one-word answers, spontaneous conversation was encouraged during the interviews and all interviews were taped. In addition, each informant read aloud several Dagwood comic strips, which proved very helpful in eliciting natural conversational patterns. The Latin informants were also recorded reading Spanish poetry selections in order to secure information about the phonology of their Spanish. Therefore, the language corpus for this survey encompasses direct questions and answers spontaneously transcribed and taped by the interviewer (which produced the most careful, formal style), spontaneous conversation, and informal readings.

Fourteen informants were interviewed for an average of eight hours, arranged in two- and three-hour sessions. Usually the interviews were conducted in the homes of the informants under very informal conditions, which permitted friends and relatives to contribute additional items of interest.

Seven Anglo informants of various socio-economic levels were selected, including a German bilingual speaker and an elderly Negro lady. Since these informants are of minor interest here, they will be described very briefly: *N.*, female, Negro, midwife and missionary, over 70; *A1*, male, Caucasian, retired railroad man, 78 years old; *A2*, male, Caucasian, retired cattleman, 75 years old; *A3*, female, Caucasian, German bilingual, housekeeper, 64 years old; *A4*, female Caucasian, school teacher, 55 years old; *A5*, male, Caucasian, graduate student and teacher, 27 years old; *A6*, female, Caucasian, housewife and college student, 22 years old.

For the purposes of clarifying many problems of the bilingual aspects of this report, greater detail will be given for the seven Latin informants: *L1, female, Methodist, retired seamstress, 74 years old.* L1 was born of Mexican parentage in Laredo, Texas in 1883 and moved to San Antonio in 1893, where she has lived ever since. Her parents were converted to Methodism while still in Mexico. L1 completed fourth grade in the San Antonio schools and married a Mexican, born in San Antonio. L1 had four children, two living. She preferred to speak Spanish to those who spoke it natively, but in her work as an alteration lady in stores and dress-making establishments she spoke English. Her English phonology was very good; she also used correct verb forms and generally good grammar. A grown granddaughter who was present during part of the interview also spoke excellent English, although her speech lacked the characteristic regional features of San Antonio English. L1 was classified as a Latin bilingual after study of her records.[1][2]

L2, female, Catholic, midwife, 53 years old. L2 was a native of San Antonio, born in 1904 of Mexican parents who migrated to San Antonio before 1900. She married a San Antonian of Mexican parentage and had three children. She was employed as ticket seller in the Mexican theater of San Antonio for many years, where knowledge of English was not essential. L2 spoke English to the interviewer only when it was absolutely necessary, and much of the interview was conducted first in English and then in Spanish to be sure that she understood the references. However, she was a very cooperative informant, very much interested in the project and eager to help. L2 was classified as a Latin unilingual.

L3, male, Catholic, gardener, 46 years old. L3 was born in Mexico in 1909 and moved to San Antonio from Monterrey with his parents at the age of five. He attended school for three years in San Antonio. His parents spoke no English and he learned what English he knew, a considerable amount, on various jobs. During the war he was a skilled worker in a print shop and at the time of the interview he was a gardener at the public gardens which surround the Alamo. L3 was married and had four children who all attended school and spoke good English. L3 used Spanish most of the time in his work and always at home and with his friends. But he spoke English to his boss and to the visitors at the Alamo. Although the interview with L3 was conducted mainly in English, the interference between Spanish and English was strong in his English phonology, morphology, and syntax; he was classified as a unilingual after study of his records.

L4, female, Methodist, saleslady and housewife, 45 years old. L4 was a housewife at the time of the interview. She was born in San Antonio of Mexican-born parents who came to Texas in 1901. Her parents were converted to Methodism after moving to San Antonio, and her father used to return to Mexico, a predominantly Catholic country, on missionary trips. He did not speak English. L4's husband, of Mexican parentage, was born in Texas and moved to San Antonio at the age of four. She and her husband and three children were in better economic circumstances than L1, 2, 3, and 5 (though all five informants lived in neat, clean little homes). L4 was very proficient in English although she had only seven years of formal education. She often worked as a saleslady in dress shops patronized by the Anglos of San Antonio. In her home, English was usually spoken; the children were being well educated. A daughter had graduated from the University of Texas and was preparing to teach in the San Antonio schools. In L4's speech, conflict between Spanish and English was noticeable only in the English phonological system. Her morphology and syntax were excellent. L4 was a very frank, natural informant and very quick in her interview responses. She was classified as a Latin bilingual.

L5, female, Catholic, actress, 41 years old. L5 was born in San Antonio after her parents and her brother, L3, moved there from Monterrey, Mexico in 1914. She lived in San Antonio until she married a Cuban actor and became an actress in the touring Spanish theater; she traveled with her husband for about eight years until they separated. L5 then returned to San Antonio. Her wider experience in the Spanish-speaking world made her unique among the Latin informants since she was the only Latin who was well-educated in Spanish literature and culture and therefore, apparently, the only one who knew several levels of Spanish, formal as well as informal, educated as well as uneducated. Since L5 had continued to act in the Mexican theater in San Antonio as a comic actress, she exhibited the normal linguistic confidence of Spanish speakers from Central and South America, an attitude which contrasted sharply with that of the other Latin informants.[13] She was highly critical of the "Tex Mex" that her San Antonian friends spoke, disapproving particularly of the way they "threw English words" into Spanish sentences. However, study of her interview materials revealed little or no difference between her Spanish and that of the other Latins in basic phonological structure and grammar. What did become clear was the fact that the other Latin informants, who knew only informal, oral Spanish, supplemented their communication with English words and, as a result, felt ashamed of their Spanish as well as their English. This linguistic embarrassment was felt by all of the Latin informants with the exception of L5.

The English of L5 showed considerable interference from Spanish patterns in phonology, morphology, and vocabulary. Like L2, she always gave her answers first in Spanish and then in English, and a considerable portion of the interview was conducted in Spanish. L5 understood spoken English well, however, and could speak it when necessary. She was classified as a Latin unilingual.

L6, male, Catholic, apprentice-architect, 32 years old. L6 was born in San Antonio of Mexican parents who came to San Antonio in 1920. His father and mother did not speak much English. L6 finished high school in San Antonio and then served as a soldier in World War II. Upon his return he worked in a store; he rejoined the army for the Korean War. The army life enabled him to learn English; it also awakened his ambition for more education which he was able to obtain through the G.I. Bill. L6 completed a degree in architecture in 1956 and married the following summer.

L6 was slow in his responses during the interview, evidencing insecurity about his ability to speak English correctly, although his English was remarkably good. His Spanish, which he spoke with his parents and relatives, also was a source of embarrassment to him. He was classified as a Latin bilingual.

L7, male, Catholic, university student, 21 years old. L7 was born in San Antonio of parents who came from Mexico in the 1920's. His parents did not speak much English. L7 finished high school and then attended the University of Texas; he was in his second year at the time of the interview, majoring in architectural drafting. L7 had excellent command of the English language; unlike L6, he felt no embarrassment in the interview situation with regard to his use of English. Like L6, however, he confessed some reluctance to speak Spanish to non-Texans, that is, to natives of other Spanish-speaking countries.

III. A Comparison of the Phonology of Anglo English and Latin English

A. *Anglo English Phonology*

A description of the phonology of each of the two languages as they are spoken in San Antonio is a necessary preliminary to a discussion of the speech of the bilingual Latins. For the description of Anglo speech, the symbols used for handling pronunciation data in the dialect studies in the eastern United States[14] were found to be most workable, since the more highly structured Trager-Smith system,[15] with nine simple vowels and three semivowel off-glides, did not adequately handle either the raw phonetic data or the significant contrasts of the dialect corpus. The assignment of many off-glide phenomena to one or another of the three off-glide phonemes of Trager-Smith was particularly difficult, as they did not always appear to be phonemic in the sense of being capable of distinguishing one utterance from another. For example, [æɪ] varied freely with [æ] as did [ɔᵁ] with [ɔ]. To equate these phonetic features with the Trager-Smith /æ, /æy, /ɔw/ and /ɔ/ would be to distort the system of this particular dialect. Also, four monophthongal vowel nuclei occurred in the lower part of the vowel spectrum, although the Trager-Smith analysis provides for only three. The post-vocalic /H/ was not used in the phonemic analysis that follows, since length, although it did occur, was evidently not phonemic in Anglo English. However, because of the recognized values of the Trager-Smith analysis, the symbols used here will be equated with this system whenever possible.

Vowel Phonemes of Anglo English			*Consonant Phonemes of Anglo English*			
i		u	p	t	k	
ɪ		ʊ	b	d	g	
	ə					
e		o			č	
ɛ					ǰ	
		ɔ				
æ	a	ɑ	f θ	s	š	h
			v ð	z	ž	
			m	n	ŋ	
			w	y		
			r			
			l			

In interpreting the features of the speech of any region of the inland United States, dialect geographers rely on the work done in the East by Hans Kurath and other linguists. As outlined in Kurath's *Word Geography*,[16] there are three large dialect areas in the East: Northern, Midland, and Southern—with subdialects within each large area. As mentioned above in the discussion of the settlement history of Bexar County, Midland and South Midland dialect speakers were slightly in the majority in the county during the critical settlement years. Thus it might be expected that their speech type would predominate in San Antonio. An alternate possibility, since the two groups were so nearly equal numerically, would be the blending or leveling of distinctive features in each dialect, producing a new dialect type. But neither of these possibilities was realized. Southern pronunciation features predominate in the speech of all the older San Antonio informants indicating that the Southern dialect enjoyed a superior or "prestige" status in San Antonio during the early settlement years. The further fact that these Southern features are also regular in the speech of the young, well-educated informants indicates that the South enjoys the same prestige position at the present time.[17]

B. *Latin Spanish Vowels*

For the study of bilingual Latin speech, samples of the Spanish dialect of each Latin informant were recorded. These records were compared with those of Spanish students who had come to study at the University of Texas from various parts of Mexico and the rest of the Spanish-speaking world. It was found that the Spanish of the San Antonio Latin informants conformed to that of Mexican Spanish in its segmental phonemes, so that the structure of Mexican Spanish may be legitimately used for comparative purposes in the discussion that follows. Our records for the Latin informants readily justify such a procedure, since all of them are second or third generation members of families that immigrated from Mexico.

The five vowel phonemes of Mexican Spanish with their allophones are:[18]

Phoneme	*Allophones*[19]
/i/	[i], [I]
/e/	[ɛ], [e]
/a/	[a]ʹ, [ɑ]
/o/	[ɔ], [o]
/u/	[ʊ], [u]

The general rule for the occurrence of the allophones is as follows: The open allophones occur in closed syllables, the closed allophones occur in open syllables, *rico* [riko] versus *listo* [lɪsto], or *mesa* [mesa] versus *resto* [rɛsto].

Thus, phones which have only allophonic status in the Spanish vowel system—[I], [ɛ], [ʊ], [a], [ɑ], [ɔ]—are very similar in quality to separate phonemes in English, often with off-glides (such as [ɔ^U] in *dog* in the speech of many San Antonians) which are frequently extremely important in the signaling system of English. Two types of difficulty can be expected in English of speakers whose first language is Spanish: (1) difficulty in attaining the proper quality distinctions in a vowel system which has over twice as many phonemic contrasts, and (2) failure to make off-glides which are part of the distinctive features of certain vowel phonemes in English but which do not occur in the Spanish vowel system.

C. *A Comparison of Anglo and Latin English Vowels*

/i/ (T.S. /iy/)

This tense high-front vowel occurred as in StAE[20] in *evening, clean, feed,* and *three*, etc. in the speech of both Anglos and Latins in the monophthongal variant [i.]. The anglos frequently followed this phoneme with a high off-glide /y/, represented phonetically as [ɨi] or [Ii].

/i/ was followed by /w/ as in StAE in such words as *beautiful, cute* and *music*. But /iw/ also occurred regularly in *new, due, tube* and *Tuesday*. However, only in Anglo speech was the /iw/ preceded by palatalization in *new* [ŋiw] and *tube* [ţiwb]. Such phenomena are characteristic of Southern American English in words where /u/ occurs in other dialects.

/I/ (T.S. /i/)

This high-front lax vowel occurred as in StAE in *six, this, slip, wind*, etc. in Anglo speech. The Latin bilinguals generally achieved the /I/, indicating a partial mastery of the /i/~/I/ contrast. The unilinguals, L2, 3, and 5, usually used the phones [i] and [i.] in such words as the following: *pig, tin, him, chicken, skillet,* and *kitchen.* The same phones also occurred from time to time in the speech of the Latin bilinguals. In the Dagwood reading both L4 and L6 "corrected" themselves in pronouncing *slip.* First the phone [i.] occurred; then it was changed to [I]. [i] also occurred in *kitchen* in the speech of the bilinguals.

The phoneme /I/ regularly occurred in place of /ɛ/ before /m/ and /n/ in *ten, hem, pen,* and *men,* and other such words in Anglo speech. For at least some of the Anglo speakers (N, A1, A4, and A6) the distinction between /I/ and /ɛ/ was completely lost before /m/ and /n/. The other informants alternated between [I] and [ɛ] in such words.

Only L6 and L7 used /I/ in any of the words of the type listed above, indicating that this regional feature occurred only in the speech of the most truly bilingual Latin informants.

/e/ (T.S. /ey/)

This mid-front tense vowel occurred as in StAE in *bracelet, pane, plain, eight,* etc. in the speech of all the Anglos and Latins. The phoneme /e/, while it did occur as a monophthong [e] in the speech of A2 and A3, usually appeared before the semivowel /y/ as [e⁺] in the foregoing words.

Before /ŋ/ the phonemes /ey/ often substituted for StAE /I/ in *thing, swing, ink, spring, shrink,* (A6, A1, N).

Can't occurred with /ey/ in San Antonio in the records of N, A1, A4, A5, and A6, both in conversation and in the recorded readings. The same pronunciation occurred in the speech of L1, L5, L6 and L7, suggesting that this realization of *can't* was the conversational norm in San Antonio speech, since the highly educated Anglos, A4, A5 and A6, used it regularly.[21] However when asked directly for the form, A4 gave [kænt] as a citation form. This suggests a difference in style levels, at least in her speech.

/ɛ/ (T.S. /e/)

This mid-front lax vowel occurred as in StAE *bread, yellow, record,* and *seven* in the speech of both Anglos and Latins. The unilingual Latins sometimes used

/ɪ/ in place of /ɛ/ in *chest, getting,* etc. (L2 and L3).

/æ/ (T.S. /ae/)

This low-front open vowel occurred as in StAE in *bath, calf, dance, cattle, pallet,* in the speech of all the Anglos, ususally in the variants [aeꞁ], although [æ] occasionally occurred also, in *catch* for example (A1, 2, 3, and 6).

/ae/ occurred in the speech of the Latin bilinguals without the high off-glide, as [æˆ], but the unilinguals usually used [ɛ], indicating interference with the Spanish phoneme /e/. [ɛ] occurred in *daddy, man, candy, at, handle, pants,* and *bag* in unilingual Latin English. At other times the low-central Spanish /ɑ/ occurred in *Saturday, apple, Latin, bath, pantry,* and *aunt.*

A special feature of San Antonio speech, characteristic of Southern dialects, is the use of /æ/ followed by /w/ in various words where /ɑw/ occurs in other dialects, as in *plow, cow, down, out, loud, ground.* This feature was regular in the speech of A2, A4, and A6. N alternated the low-front /a/ and /æ/ before /w/ in such words, as did A1 and A5. Yet not one of the Latin speakers had /æw/ in his English phonological system. L6 and L7 had the fronted /aw/, the alternate sequence which is similar in quality to the Spanish low central /ɑ/. The unilinguals substituted the Spanish diphthong /ɑʊ/ in such words.

/a/[22]

This low-front lax vowel occurred regularly in the phone [a.] in the speech of most of the Anglo informants in words where /ɑy/ occurs in most American dialects. In San Antonio Anglo speech [a.] occurred in *right, night, nine, five, siding, mild, grind, my, I, nice, lima,* and before /r/ as [a] in *iron, tires, tired, hired, sire,* and *wire.* A6 had [a.] in all words of this type, both in citation forms and in conversational forms. N, A2, A4, and A5 had this feature more than half the time in citation, conversation, and reading forms. In the comic strip reading, [a] occurred with the highest frequency for all informants. A4 used it consistently in the readings although not in citation forms, indicating again that she had very definite differences in her formal and informal speech styles. A5 and A6 had the phone [a.] for such words as those listed above except under conditions of strong sentence stress at a point of terminal juncture. There they used the phones [aɪ].

This regional feature had not been acquired by any of the Latin speakers except the bilingual L6. All the others used either [ɑɪ], similar to the Spanish diphthong /ɑɪ/ in *baile,* or more often the phone [ɑ]. This seems to be a further substantiation of the evidence collected for San Antonio Anglo speech which indicates that the [a.] instead of [ɑꞁ] is the linguistic norm, since the former is the pronunciation which the Latin informants tried to acquire. Apparently this so-called "diphthong" in *knife,* for example, impressed the Latin unilinguals as being closer to the Spanish /ɑ/ than to the Spanish /ɑy/ (as in *baile*). /ɑ/ occurred also before /r/ in the speech of the Latins.

/ɑ/

This low-central or low-back open vowel occurred as in StAE in *Mama, father, hospital,* and *vomit* in the speech of both Anglos and Latins. In words with historic short "o" such as *rock, pot, slop, crop,* and *shop,* [ɑ] occurred generally. But all of the Anglo speakers also had the more rounded phone [ɒ] in some of these words[23] as well as in *palm, wasp, squash, wash, dauber, water,* and *swamp.*

We have already mentioned above that the Latin informants frequently substituted the [ɑ] of the low-central Spanish phoneme where /a/ occurred in Anglo English. The same phone was also found for /æ/ and /ə/, illustrating the Latin informants' difficulty in mastering a highly differentiated vowel system. In Latin English the interference in the lower part of the vowel spectrum produced a rather chaotic situation. [ɔ], an allophone of Spanish /o/, occurred in *on, hospital,* L2, 4, and 7; [ə] occurred in *on,* L1; and in *calm,* L6. [ə] occurred in *water* and *wash* for all Latin informants although the backed, rounded phone [ɒ] was customary here in Anglo speech.

The back rounded [ɒ] or [ɔ] without any characteristic off-glide was common in Anglo speech before /r/ both in words such as *tar, barb, war, quarter, parlor, card, warm,* and *farm,* and words such as *cord, chord, form,* and *born.* At least two of the younger informants, A4 and A5, had lost the phonemic contrast found in StAE between *card* and *cord,* etc. A6 mentioned that she had this feature in her speech until she entered college in Virginia and had it called to her attention by her classmates there. So A6 had corrected this loss, making the distinction very clear by using [ɑ] in *card* and employing the distinctive up-glide usually not found before /r/ in *cord:* [kɔᵁrd], more often breaking the word into two syllables [kɔᵁərd]. The husband of A6, also a native San Antonian, said that he had the identical experience when he attended school in the coastal South.

This regional feature was totally missing in Latin English; *tar, barb, war, card,* etc. occurred with [ɑ] and *cord, form, bore,* etc. occurred with [ɔ], following the Spanish pattern.

/o/ (T.S. /ow/)

This mid-back rounded vowel generally occurred as in StAE with the high-back rounded up-glide [oᵁ] in *rose, ago, froze, sofa, drove, close,* and *stone.*

The Latin unilingual informants used the phones [o] and [o.], corresponding to the close allophone of Spanish /o/. The bilinguals usually used the phones [oᵁ].

/ʊ/ (T.S. /u/)

This mid-high back vowel with some lip-rounding occurred as in StAE in *took, good, bushel, butcher,* and *pull* in the speech of all the Anglo informants.

The bilingual Latins, L1, L4, L6, and L7, generally used the [ʊ] correctly. The unilinguals alternated between [ʊ] and [u]. [u] occurred in *good,* L2, L4; *bull,* L2, 3, 5; and *wool,* L1, 2, 5. [ə] occurred in *bull,* L7. The Northern regional pronunciations of roof [rʊf] L6 and *root* [rʊt] L3 are rare in Anglo speech.

/u/ (T.S. /uw/)

This high-back rounded vowel occurred as a simple vowel in the fronted phones [ʉ] or [ʉ̞] in *room, broom, food, loose, goober.* The fronting of the vowel was a very noticeable feature in the speech of A4, A5, and A6. The fronted quality did not occur in Latin speech except in the records of L6.

/ə/

This mid-central lax vowel occurred as in StAE in *sun-up, plunder, hundred, bucket, hung,* and *come* in the speech of all the Anglo informants.

However, as is the case with English /ɑ/, /ə/ presents difficulty for a native speaker of Spanish since there is no similar vowel in Spanish. For this reason the unilinguals and the two least skilled bilinguals, L1 and L4, generally used the phones [ɑ] or [ɑ^] in such words as *onion, pumpkin, judge, one, mother, up,* and *flood.* The bilinguals, L6 and L7, usually used [ə] in such words, yet the distribution of the phoneme was not entirely in conformity with San Antonio speech even for these most able bilinguals since [ə] occurred in their speech in *broom* and *soot.* The pronunciation [sət] for *soot* was regarded as archaic by the Anglos, used by N and remembered by A2 as his earlier pronunciation of the word.

D. Latin Spanish Consonants

The analysis of the Spanish consonant system presented here is a somewhat simplified version of that made by Harold V. King:[24]

/b/ with allophones: [b] occurring initially and medially before [r] and [l], initially before a vowel, and medially after [m].

[β̞] occurring medially before vowels and voiced consonants.

[β̞] occurring before voiceless consonants or pause, partially voiceless.

/d/ with allophones: [d] occurring initially and medially before [r], initially before a vowel, and medially after [n].

[ð] occurring medially before vowels and voiced consonants.

[ð̥] partially voiceless, occurring before voiceless consonants or pause.

/g/ with allophones: [g] occurring initially and medially before [r] and [l], initially before a vowel, medially before a stressed vowel in free variation with [ɣ], and medially after [ŋ].

[ɣ] occurring medially before vowels.

/p/ with one allophone [p] rarely occurs finally.

/t/ with one allophone [t] rarely occurs finally.

/k/ with one allophone [k] rarely occurs finally.

/č/ with one allophone [č] rarely occurs finally.

/f/ with one allophone [f] rarely occurs finally.

/x/ with one allophone [x] rarely occurs finally.

/š/ with one allophone [š] occurs finally after vowels in a small number of sequences.

/s/ with allophones: [s] occurs in all positions and may be lax or [h]

[z] occurs in free variation with [s] before [l], [m], and [ŋ], and before voiced consonants.

/m/ with one allophone [m] occurs initially and medially before vowels, medially before [p] and [b], and rarely finally.

/n/ with allophones: [n] occurs before [č] and [s].

[n̞] occurs before vowels and consonants other than labials or velars and finally.

[ŋ] occurs before [g], [k], and [x].

/ñ/ with one allophone [ñ] occurs medially between vowels and rarely initially.

/l/ with one allophone [l] occurs initially, medially, and finally.

/w/ with one allophone [w] with varying amounts of voiced velar friction, occurs initially and medially before vowels.

/y/ with allophones: [y] with varying amounts of voiced palatal friction, occurs initially and medially before vowels.

[y̞] with varying amounts of voiceless palatal friction, occurs before pause.

/r/ with one allophone [r] occurs only between vowels, a voiced alveolar flap.

/r̄/ with allophones: [r̄] apical trill, occurs initially, medially before vowels, medially before consonants, and in free variation with voiceless trill finally.

[r̞̃] voiceless apical trill occurring before pause.

A comparison of the consonant systems of Spanish and English shows many divergences which will cause the learner of English difficulty. One type of conflict is obvious. Spanish /d/ occurs as [d] only when it is initial. Before vowels in the medial position it becomes a dental fricative [ð̶]. But English /d/ has no fricative allophones. In English /ð̶/ is a separate phoneme. Two other Spanish stops, /b/ and /g/, have allophones with a similar distributional pattern.

Two other features which are distributional are also of significance. Firstly, the Spanish stops, fricatives, and affricates are of rare occurrence at the end of words. Secondly, the voiced consonants which do occur in final position, in the allophones [β], [ð̶], [y], and [r̄], usually are devoiced before pause. Such patterns will also cause interference, in the speech of the unilinguals especially. In the analysis which follows, certain occurrences of phones in the English of the Latin informants will be readily explainable as instances of such interference. For example, the weak execution of final stops in English (or even the complete omission of final stops for some unilingual speakers) and the tendency to devoice English voiced consonants in final position before pause are clear cases of interference between the two very different consonant systems.

E. A Comparison of Anglo and Latin English Consonants

For /b/, a voiced bilabial stop (as in StAE *bag*, *February*, and *tube*), the bilinguals L4, L6, and L7 used the phone [b] regularly. The unilinguals and L1 often used a bilabial fricative phone [β] in the following words where /v/ occurs in English: *vest* [βest] L1, 3, 5; *river* [ríβer] L5; also in *very* L2; *veal* L2; *vase* L1, 3, 5. [p'] occurred in final position in *web* [wεp'] L2 and 5.

For /p/, a voiceless bilabial stop (as in StAE in *paper, pasture,* and *crop*), the Latins use the phones [p] and [p'].

For /d/, a voiced alveolar stop (as in StAE in *died, garden, band,* and *hundred*), the bilingual speakers regularly used the phone [d], indicating mastery of the phoneme, but the unilinguals showed interference from Spanish /d/. For example, a typical unilingual occurrence was the use of [t] for [d] in final position in words such as *sled* and *head* L2. [ð] often occurred between vowels, *widow* [wIðo] L2. [d] was omitted before pause in *good* L6; *feed, wild,* and *band* L2.

For /t/, a voiceless alveolar stop (as in StAE *tin, forty, posts, haunted, mountain,* and *pallet*), the Latin bilinguals used the phones [t] and [t'] but not always with the normal distribution. The aspirated phone [t'] which occurred only in initial position before a stressed vowel in Anglo English occurred also in final position before pause occasionally for all Latin informants, particularly in the speech of the bilinguals L1, 4, and 6 in words such as *bright, wait, that,* and *cost.* The aspirated phone also occurred medially for L1 and L2 in *fountain, twenty,* and *thirty* although the normal Anglo phone here was usually the alveolar flap [ř]. The phone [d] occurred intervocalically in the speech of the unilinguals L2 and L5 in *butter* and *thirty* (a phone common in such words in the speech of A6 also). The flapped phone, characteristic of Anglo speech, was regular in the speech of the other Latin informants in such words as *butter* and *water.*

For /k/, a voiceless velar stop (as in StAE in *car, casket, sack,* and *silk*), the phones [k] and [k'] occurred in the English of most Latin speakers. However, the aspirated stop [k'] was more general in the speech of the bilingual informants and occurred occasionally in final position in their speech.

For /g/, a voiced velar stop (as in StAE in *garbage, gave, ago, bag,* and *keg*), all of the Latin informants except L2 generally used the phone [g]. However the unilingual L2 often used the phone [k'] in final position, *pig* [pik'], *eggs* [εk's].

For /f/, a voiceless labiodental fricative (as in StAE in *father, fifth, afternoon, armful,* and *cough*), the Latin informants all used the phone [f] indicating a satisfactory employment of this English phoneme. But the /f/~/v/ distinction had not been mastered by L2, 3, 4, 5, and 6 (see below under /v/).

For /v/, a voiced labiodental fricative (as in StAE in *vase, vest, seven, five,* and *twelve*), the bilinguals L1 and L7 used the phone [v], indicating that they had mastered the /f/~/v/ contrast. But the unilinguals, L2, 3, 5 and the bilinguals, 4 and 6, used the phone [f] in final position occasionally: *five* [fɑif] L2, 5; *twelve* [twεlf] L3, 4, 5, and 6.

For /θ/, a voiceless interdental fricative (as in StAE in *three, Martha, nothing, bath,* and *fifth*), the phone /θ/ occurred generally for most Latin speakers. However, the unilinguals, L2, L3, and L5, occasionally used [t], a dental stop phone, in *three* and *throw* L2, *threw* L5, and *thin* L3.

For /ð/, a voiced interdental fricative (as in StAE in *the, father,* and *mother*), the Latin informants generally used the phone [ð]. However in initial position the unilinguals occasionally used the phone [d] in *those* L2 and L3. Unfortunately there were no occurrences of /ð/ in final position on the worksheets. This would undoubtedly have been a position of interference for the Latin speakers.

For /s/, a voiceless alveolar fricative (as in StAE in *sack, casket, yeast, cents, horse,* and *vase*), the phone [s] occurred generally for all Latin speakers. But such a statement belies the true problem since not even the best bilingual speakers had quite mastered the English /s/~/z/ distinction (see below, under /z/). In the phrase "twice better" the phone [z] occurred L5, but *twice* before pause ended in [s] L5. This is a total transfer of the Spanish distributional pattern for /s/ into English. In initial clusters such as /sk/ and /str/ an initial vowel was often introduced in unilingual speech, *strap* [ɛstrɑ̈p] L5.

For /z/, a voiced alveolar fricative (as in StAE in *zoo, houses, Tuesday, ashes, cleans,* and *dues*), not even the most expert bilinguals in the survey always used the phone [Z]. The pattern of occurrence of the phoneme /z/ after voiced sounds and the phoneme /s/ after voiceless sounds in various parts of the English grammatical system (noun inflections, verb inflections, etc.) is quite different from that of Mexican Spanish where /s/ has two principal allophones [s] and [z]. The later phone occurs only in close transition with a following voiced sound. The additional fact that /s/ is a phoneme of high frequency of occurrence in Spanish since it also marks noun inflections and verb inflections multiplies the degree of interference which occurs for Spanish speakers learning English. In general, L6 and L7 attained the English pattern, but a slight devoicing of /z/ as [Z̥] was characteristic in final position in their speech.

The phone [s] occurred medially in *raspberries* L2, 7; *Thursday* and *Wednesday* L4; *freezing* and *raising* L1. [s] occurred finally in *records* L1−7; *rose* L1, 4; *bedrooms* L1; *froze* L1, 4; *houses* L3, 4; *dishes* and *feathers* L2; as well as in numerous other words not listed here. The bilinguals, L6 and L7, either had a slight devoicing of /z/, using the phone [Z̥] before pause: *nails* [neᵁZ̥] L7, *rinse* [rɪnZ̥] L6, or the phone [s].

[Z̥] occurred in *grease* L4, L6; *greasy* L4, L6. This was the pattern of Anglo speech in San Antonio for these words. All the other Latins used [s] here, the pattern which happens to coincide with that of some Northern regional dialects.

For /š/, /č/ /ǰ/, there was great interference from Spanish patterns in the English of the unilinguals. One difficulty arises from the fact that /ǰ/ does not occur at all in Spanish and /š/ only rarely. In addition, neither /č/ nor /š/ appears regularly in final position. In unilingual speech [č] occurred in *shopping, sharp, sheep, shell,* and *insurance.* On the other hand [š] occurred in *chair, china, chocolates,* and *chew.* Medially, [š] occurred in *furniture* and *kitchen.* Finally, it occurred in *cinch* and *watch.* [j] occurred regularly as in StAE for the Latin informants with the exception of L2 who used [š] in *judge* and [č] in *jump.* A fricative phone of /y/, the Spanish voiced palatal semivowel (similar to [ǰ] in English), occurred in *yesterday* L5, *young* L2, *you* L2, and *yellow* L3 and L5.

Detailed discussion of the phonemes /m/, /n/, /ŋ/, and /w/ has been omitted since there was little that was significant in the dialect records for these phonemes.

For /l/, a voiced alveolar lateral (as in StAE in *law, class, careless,* and *wall*), all the Latin informants generally used [l]. However, in final position the bilinguals L6 and L7 often used the phones [ʊ] or [ə] in *wool, wall, towel, bull* L6, and *wool* L7. This feature was common in the speech of A4, A5, and A6. It occurred also in *milk* [mɪʊk] A2, A4, A5; *shoulder* [šoʊdər] N; *help* N, A1, A6; *knelt* A5; *melt* A1, A3, A6.

For /h/, a voiceless glottal fricative (as in StAE in *haunted, hen, hem, whip*), all the Anglos and Latins used the phone [h]. In the cluster /hw/ most Anglo informants retained the /h/ but A5 confessed that "/h/ is a very conscious thing with me," and he regularly lost it in *wheel, whinny,* and *whip.* A6 lost /h/ in *white* and *whip*; A3 lost it in *wheel.* Only L6 showed this Anglo loss, in *white* and *anywhere.*

For /y/, a voiced palatal frictionless semivowel (as in StAE in *year, yeast, your, onion,* and *stallion*), the Latin bilinguals L1, 4, 6, and 7 used the phone [y]. But the unilinguals L2, 3, and 5 often used a fricative phone [ǰ] instead. This phone occurred as stated above under /j/.

For /r/, a voiced alveolar retroflex (as in StAE in *rancid, roof, rinse, bread,* and *tree*), the bilinguals often used the phone [r]. However both the bilinguals and the unilinguals frequently used either a trilled [r̄] or a single flap [ř] similar to the British English [ř] between vowels (in *very*) or the American [ř] between vowels (in *butter*) since this is the type of articulation common to /r̄/ and /r/ respectively in Mexican Spanish. Strongly trilled /r̄/ occurred especially after consonant clusters, as in *three* [ɵr̄i.] L1, 2, and 3.

F. Latin English Stress

Interference in the suprasegmental system of stress was very striking in the English of the Latin informants. Stress is phonemic in both Spanish and English but Spanish has only two degrees of stress and English has at least three. The stress pattern for compound nouns in English is either a primary on the first noun and a secondary on the second noun or a primary on the first noun and a tertiary on the second noun: *pecán trêe* or *pecán trèe.* Syllables in Spanish are either strong or weak and equally timed. As a result, when the Spanish speaker uses his system in English, it sounds to an English speaker as if he had given each noun equal stress or stressed the second noun more heavily than the first: *pecán trèe* or *pecân trée.* Such a contrast as that between *whîte hóuse* and *Whíte Hòuse* is not possible in Spanish where both sequences are translated as *cása blánca.* The bilingual Latins generally achieved the English pattern although a strong stress often occurred on each of the two parts of the compound in their English. But L4 and the unilinguals L2, 3, and 5 commonly used the Spanish stress pattern on English compounds.

A strong stress occurred on the second part of each compound in the following: *pecan trée* L4; *cherry trée* L4; *strawbérries, raspbérries* L3, L4; *apple trée* L5; *hang óver* L5; *White Hóuse* L4, L5; *storage róom* L2, L4; *wash dáy* L2; *nigger shóoter* L2, 3, 4; *hot cákes* L2; *glow wórm, yellow jácket, grandfáther, midwífe, hill bílly* L3. The list of such stress occurrences is so long that only a sampling of the material has been presented here.

G. Summary of Phonological Patterns of Latin Informants

It seems fairly clear that the phonological norm which the Latin informants were striving to attain was not general American English but standard Southern American English in the regional variety spoken in San Antonio by the Anglo informants. Thus in making an analysis of their ability we could not consider them to be masters of English if they used [ɑʊ] in *cow* even if these phones happen to be found in many varieties of American English, since the Anglo informants of San Antonio used only [æʊ] or [aʊ] in such a word. None of the Latin informants included in this survey had achieved the English of San Antonio completely. However L6, although he had not mastered the /s/∼/z/ contrast for example, used most of the pronunciation variants common to the region including [aʊ], the monophthongal [a.], the fronted [ʉ], palatalization of /t/ ([ţ]) and /n/ ([ŋ]) in *Tuesday* and *new*.

IV. Lexical Peculiarities of the Latin Informants

The general cultural situation in San Antonio has been presented in Sections I and II. Here we will discuss the situation only as it was reported by the informants themselves and as it is illustrated by the workbook materials.

As has been mentioned in Section III, all the informants either were born in San Antonio or went there as small children, so they are truly representative of the Latin community. The older informants have had little formal education since, as L1 explained, in those days it cost too much to send children to school, especially when a man had a large family. Three of these five informants, L2, 3, and 5, have been classified as Latin unilinguals but two others, L1 and L4, have succeeded in educating themselves to a remarkable degree and are classified as Latin bilinguals along with the college students, L6 and L7, because of their proficiency in English.

The Latin informants represent a variety of occupations. All of them have worked outside the home—L1 as a seamstress, L2 as a ticket seller in a theater and as a *partera* (midwife), L3 as a printer's helper and as an expert gardener at the Alamo, L4 as a saleslady, and L5 as a professional actress. The two university students, San Antonians by birth, have had army training—L6 fought in the Korean War—and it was in the Army that they became truly bilingual.

All of the Latin informants were keenly aware of the cultural struggle that is going on in their community and of the prejudice against them as a minority group. For example L1's granddaughter, who was present during her interview, was a third generation San Antonian, very well educated, who had been doing highly skilled office work for several years in Los Angeles. The hard facts about the social situation in her home town and their economic repercussions had shocked her upon her return to San Antonio several weeks before. "Every ad for a good job says, only *Anglos* need apply!"

The Anglo informants also expressed their attitude toward the Latin minority in the community. The youngest Anglo, A6, product of a highly educated and wealthy San Antonio family, remarked, "Many of my friends and relatives don't think Negroes and Mexicans are human beings—just animals. I didn't even know we had many Mexicans in San Antonio until I came home from college in Virginia."

After a derogatory speech about the present efforts in San Antonio to improve the schools and education of the Mexican people, A1 spoke of the

Mexican family renting his house. "These Mexicans in my house speak as good English as we do. They're fine people. You couldn't say anything detrimental about them except that they're Mexican and they can't help that!"

One way in which a study of the dialect of an area mirrors the social and cultural situation is through a collection of the "nicknames" for the different racial groups. For example, each informant was asked, "What are the Mexicans called?" They were asked to classify the terms as neutral, polite, and derogatory. A4 said she would use the term *Spanish people* for those on a higher economic level (L7 uses *Spanish-speaking people* in this way). A5 used *Spanish people* for the "whiter skinned and more dignified" ones. N and A4 used *Latin Americans.* A4 said, "They resent *Mexican,* so I try not to call them that" (L6 suggested *Mexican* as a neutral term but added that some resented it, L2 reserved the term for those who live in Mexico). *Meskans* is a term A5 applied to the less-educated (L6 said that the Latins call themselves *Meskans* in fun but do not like to have others do it).

The only derogatory term that the Latins volunteered was *wet backs;* however many derogatory terms were given by the Anglos, especially the son of the German informant A3. He uses *pepper belly, bean bandits,* and *Brownies,* commenting that "The Mexicans have called me a *square-head."* (Several of the Latins spoke about discrimination against them by the German immigrant population of San Antonio, especially in earlier days when the Germans would not even admit them into their restaurants.)

Anglo informants also gave the terms *pilau* and *greaser* and in turn the Latins gave *gringo* and *agringados,* the later a term for Spanish-speaking people who adopt American cultural ways. *Tex-Mex* did not seem to be very common in San Antonio. It was given as *heard,* but not used, by N, A4, L2, and L3. L2 expressed dislike for the term. L7 used it in conversation to designate Texas Spanish which he felt to be very different from Mexican Spanish.

This, then, was the social situation for the Latin informants. It had been expected without question that a linguistic survey such as was conducted here would indicate the different degrees of language ability among these informants but it was at first not clear how the social situation would be reflected in their English. The preliminary vocabulary study revealed the fact that the Latin informants were to a great extent cut off from the Anglo culture. Their social isolation forced them to learn their English primarily from school and books and from "on-the-job" training rather than free association with the English-speaking members of the community. Thus the old words, which are the intimate reflection of tradition and regional culture, were for the most part absent from their vocabulary. Many of these words, familiar to the Anglos, are transmitted orally from parent to child and often never appear in standard dictionaries. Such words were seldom known even by the Latin bilinguals, illustrating how little they participate in the regional heritage of the community.

A number of words found to be key South and South Midland vocabulary items[25] had a high incidence of 53-percent occurrence in the speech of the Anglo informants. These words were: *light bread* 'white bread', *corn shuck* 'outer covering of an ear of corn', *clabber* 'curdled milk', *pallet* 'temporary bed spread on the floor', *jackleg preacher* 'itinerant preacher', *snack* 'quick bite of food', *pully bone* 'wish bone', *snake doctor* 'dragon fly', *haints* 'ghosts', *disremember* 'don't remember'. The percent of occurrence for the Latin informants was 9%. And if we omit the term *snack,* which is used in advertising (for example, *snack bar*), the percentage is only 7%. Actually L1, the oldest Latin informant, a bilingual, was the only Latin who knew *light bread, clabber and pallet.* L4 and L6 knew *corn shuck* and that was the sum total of their knowledge of these regional words. Other terms unfamiliar to the Latins, yet typical of the Anglo speech, were *Christmas Gift!* 'a term for a greeting on Christmas morning', *snap beans* (in other regions *green beans* or *string beans*), and *French harp* 'harmonica'. The Latins used the commercial terms for these last two items.

The English of the Latins reflects their cultural situation not only in the regional vocabulary but also in their rejection of words borrowed from Spanish. Instead of being proud of the Spanish terms which are proof of the colonial history of the Spanish culture in the area, they observe strict separation of the vocabularies of the two languages. The prestige language, English, must not be "corrupted" by Spanish vocabulary. Thus an important group of words considered a part of the region's cultural heritage from Spanish[26]—words used freely, especially by older members of the Anglo community—are completely rejected for use in English by the Latins.

Norther and *northern* (Spanish *norte,* 'north wind'): One or the other of these variants was used by A1–6, and N. But only L4 and 7 used either word. L2, who would use *norte* only in Spanish and who knew no English equivalent, made up "dark clouds" and "north" to fill in the gap in English.

Patio (Spanish 'the inner court of a house'): L4 gave it as English. The other bilinguals did not use it.

Bronco (Spanish 'rough' or 'morose', as in the expression *caballo bronco,* 'a wild horse'): This was used only in Spanish by L1, 3, and 7. L6 gave *mustang* as the English equivalent (no longer recognizable as Spanish *mesteño* 'a small wild horse of the Southwest'). L2 and L5 suggested *wild horse* as an acceptable English substitute.

Arroyo (Spanish 'a water course'), a generally known Spanish word in Anglo speech in the Southwest, was nevertheless rejected by L2, 3, 4, 5, and 7 as *Spanish* with the added objection that the Spanish word does not mean "dry gully," its most common meaning in English.

Mesa (Spanish 'table'), given in Webster's *New International Dictionary,* was nevertheless regarded only as Spanish by the Latin informants. However L7 said he would use it in English if he were in New Mexico or even in West Texas. He and L4 used *plateau* in English.

Alamo (Spanish 'poplar') has been applied to the sycamore and the cottonwood in America. None of the Latin informants had any English names for these trees.

Pilón (Spanish 'a bonus given with a purchase'): This term was used in English by A1, 2, 4, and 5. A1 said "Mexican, but I use it." L2, 3, 4, and 5 gave it as used only in Spanish.

Burro (Spanish 'small ass'): This is in general use in Texas English. Yet L1, 3, and 5 avoided it in English, although they had no alternate English word.

Plaza (Spanish 'town square') is a well-known Spanish borrowing in the Southwest used mainly to describe the public square of a town. L2 would not use *la plaza* in English nor would any of the other unilinguals.

Frijoles (Spanish 'beans') is in general use by the Anglos in west and central Texas but it was not used by any Latins in English.

Certain of the words given above, especially those which afforded no alternate English words, received special treatment from the bilingual Latins. These words (also the personal names of the Latin bilinguals and Spanish place names), which could not be avoided in English, were given a *Spanish* pronunciation when used in Spanish to other Spanish speakers and an *English* pronunciation when used in English to English speakers. For example, L6 and L7 separated *corral* into English and Spanish by giving it the Anglo pronunciation, [kəfǽl] in English and the Spanish pronunciation [koɾɑl] in Spanish. *Pinto* (Spanish 'spotted', applied to a horse) was given by L6 with two pronunciations [pɪ́ntoᵁ] and [pi̇́.nto], the first for use in English and the second for Spanish. (The unilinguals rejected the use of both these words in English.) *Arroyo* occurred as [ɑɾóyo] in Spanish and [ərɔɪyo] in English. *Canyon* appeared as [kɑñón] and [kǽnyən]. *Mesa* was [mesa] and [méɪsə]. *Burro* occurred as [búro] and [bɔ́ro]. Names had similar treatment: *San Antonio* [sɑ́n ɑntónio] and [sǽn æntóᵁniyoᵁ], *Dolores* [dolɔ́řes] and [dəlɔ́řəs], *Gonzalez* [gonsɑles] and [gənzáles].

V. Grammar of Anglo and Latin English

Only a few items of morphology such as variant verb forms and pronoun usage are treated in the workbook. But even this limited corpus revealed the wide gap between Anglo and Latin English. While standard forms of written English were known by all but the oldest uneducated Anglo informants, A1 and A2, standard regional variants were still preferred. For instance all the Anglo informants said *dived* (past tense of *dive*), the form used in the Midland and South. On the other hand, bilingual L6 used *dove*, apparently unaware that it was a Northern (Yankee) form.[27]

The Latin usage ranged from that of L2, who used present tense verbs almost entirely ("I sit yesterday"), to a considerable proficiency with standard formal written forms by L6 and L7. These educated bilinguals were very careful to conform to standard usage and frequently commented on the fact that they changed a given regional form either because a certain teacher preferred another or because another form was prescribed in standard text books. Thus the Latin bilinguals tended to deviate from Anglo regional usage. For example, *ought to/ought not to* is a Southern pattern while in the North the negative is either *hadn't ought to* or the substitute form *should not*.[28] Most of the Anglos used *ought not to*; all Latin informants except L6 and L2 used *should not*. L6 used *hadn't ought to* and L2 used the aberrant form *don't supposed to do it*.

VI. Evaluation of the Linguistic Findings

The linguistic evidence reveals that the Latins' isolation from the Anglo community is very profound. This results in a series of social isoglosses separating their speech from that of the Anglo community. Although these lines cannot be drawn on the map in the same manner as the geographical isoglosses which separate one regional dialect from another, they are quite as real and enduring.

In the long run, the acquiring of the regional standard speech cannot be completely accomplished even by the most enlightened efforts of the educational institutions, although greater linguistic sophistication and better understanding both of language styles and variations and of the difference between oral and written forms of English could certainly improve the situation. It is clear that the adoption of the regional standard speech depends mainly on *acculturation,* which is the elimination of social barriers. Only when this is achieved, an ideal situation from the point of view of democracy, can such social isoglosses be eliminated.

Notes

[1] The author's unpublished dissertation, "A Dialect Study of San Antonio, Texas: A Bilingual Community," (University of Texas, 1957), Microfilm Publication no. 25,178.

[2] Janet B. Sawyer, "Aloofness From Spanish Influence in Texas English," *Word,* XV, No. 2 (1959), 270-281.

[3] ——, "Social Aspects of Bilingualism in San Antonio, Texas," *Publications of the American Dialect Society,* 41 (1964), 7-15.

[4] William A. Stewart, "Foreign Language Teaching Methods in Quasi-Foreign Language Situations", *Non-Standard Speech and the Teaching of English,* Language Information Series 2, Center for Applied Linguistics, 1964. Stewart mentions this *dialect* in the body of his article and again in a note: p. 6 ". . . An example which comes immediately to mind concerns Mexican-American English. *Note 7.*" Here I do not refer to the kind of English which a monolingual Spanish speaker in Mexico may end up with after having taken English in school. Rather, I refer to a special dialect of American English spoken in the Southwest by a considerable number of Americans of Mexican descent, who are usually bilingual in it and some variety of Mexican or Southwestern Spanish.

[5] See E. Bagby Atwood, *The Regional Vocabulary of Texas* (Austin, 1962) for a more recent analysis of the larger dialect area.

[6] Hans Kurath, M. L. Hanley, B. Bloch, G. S. Lowman, Jr., and M. L. Hansen, *Linguistic Atlas of New England,* 3 vols. in 6 parts (Providence, 1939-43); Hans Kurath, *A Word Geography of the Eastern United States* (Ann Arbor, 1949); and Hans Kurath and Raven I. McDavid, Jr., *The Pronunciation of English in the Atlantic States* (Ann Arbor, 1961).

[7] Homer Lee Kerr, "Migration Into Texas 1865-1880" (University of Texas diss., 1953).

[8] Kerr, pp. 93-94.

[9] *La Prensa* (San Antonio, Texas), April 17, 1956, p. 2.

[10] ——, February 12, 1956, Editorial, p. 2.

[11] ——, March 15, 1956, Editorial, Montiel Olvera, p. 2.

[12] The term *bilingual* will be used throughout this study to designate Latin informants whose records demonstrate the fact that they have good command of the vocabulary, pronunciation, and grammar of English. The term *unilingual* will be used for Latin informants who have limited command of English vocabulary, pronunciation, and grammar.

[13] During years of contact with Spanish-speaking students from Central and South America at the University of Texas, the author observed a sharp difference between the pride and confidence that the foreign students felt for their language and culture and the insecure embarrassment which the Texas speakers of Spanish exhibited. The Texans avoided contact with the foreign students.

[14] Kurath and others, *Atlas.*

[15] George L. Trager and Henry Lee Smith, *An Outline of English Structure,* in *Studies in Linguistics,* Occasional Papers, No. 3 (Norman, Oklahoma, 1951).

[16] Hans Kurath, *A Word Geography of the Eastern United States* (Ann Arbor, 1949).

[17] Many of the socially prominent families of San Antonio send their children to Virginia to finishing school. Also, politically, Texas conforms to the rest of the "solid Democratic South" at least on the state and local levels.

[18] Harold V. King, "Outline of Mexican Spanish Phonology," *Studies in Linguistics,* X, No. 3 (1952), 51-62.

[19] The [I] and [ε] of Spanish are higher than the [I] and [ε] of English.

[20] Standard American English.

[21] Summer Ives, "Pronunciation of 'Can't' in Eastern States," *American Speech, XXVIII* (1953), 149-155. Professor Ives found [ke+nt] to be substandard in the East.

[22] This vowel, not provided for by Trager-Smith, was the subject of much discussion at the Linguistics Conference in 1956 at the University of Texas. Professor J. M. Sledd of the University of Illinois stated that the nine simple vowels of the Trager-Smith analysis would not adequately account for all the contrasts in his particular Southern dialect. At that time a tenth vowel /a/ was felt to be necessary for his dialect.

[23] If [ɒ] occurred as a monophthong or with a centralizing upglide, as [ɒ] or [ɒᶧ], it was assigned to the phoneme /ɑ/. If it occurred with a high back upglide[ɒᵁꟾ] or [ɒᵒ],it was assigned to /ɔ/ since /ɔ/ commonly occurred with such allophones in San Antonio speech.

[24] "Outline of Mexican Spanish Phonology."

[25] Kurath, *Word Geography.*

[26] Atwood, *The Regional Vocabulary of Texas.*

[27] For analysis of verb forms in the East consult E. Bagby Atwood, *A Survey of Verb Forms in the Eastern U.S.* (Ann Arbor, 1953).

[28] See Atwood, *Verb Forms,* p. 33.

Speech Mixture in New Mexico: The Influence of the English Language on New Mexican Spanish

Aurelio M. Espinosa

New Mexico was first colonized by the Spaniards in 1598, when Juan de Oñate conquered the country and occupied it in the name of Spain. The Indian rebellion of the year 1680 put an end to this first attempt at colonization. All the Spanish inhabitants who were not killed by the Indians fled to the province of northern Mexico. In 1693, however, the country was reconquered and permanently colonized under the leadership of Diego de Vargas. From 1693 to 1846, when the territory was invaded and occupied by the American army, New Mexico was the home of a Spanish speaking colony, which was often quite isolated from the culture centers of New Spain.

The admission of Texas as a state by the United States of North America in the year 1845, in open defiance to the Mexican government to which this territory had by right belonged since the Mexican independence, was the immediate cause of the Mexico-American war, which ended in the cession by Mexico to the United States of the vast Spanish territory now comprised in the states of California, Nevada, Utah, Arizona, Texas, New Mexico and part of Colorado, in the year 1848. The territory of New Mexico, which had been the permanent home of a Spanish speaking population since 1693, and which at the time of the American occupation included also what is now Arizona and part of Colorado and had a Spanish population of over 75,000 people, was invaded in 1846 by General Kearny, who entered New Mexico by the Santa Fé trail and took Sanda Fé without resistance. New Mexico was formally occupied, a provisional government was established and the territory declared a part of the United States of North America.

The New Mexican people offered no resistance whatsoever. General Armijo who had been charged with the defense of the country, finding his soldiers unprepared and too few to meet the American invaders, fled to Mexico, and the people, accustomed to revolutions and frequent political changes since the Mexican independence of 1810, accepted the new régime not only without resistance but even with pleasure, at least in some quarters. That the invaders were not everywhere welcome, however, is evident from the fact that only two years after the American occupation, in 1848, an anti-American revolt in Taos resulted in the murder of the American governor and the killing of many of the American settlers. American settlers, who had begun to enter the territory since the early part of the nineteenth century, came in large numbers after the American invasion of 1846, from the South and middle West, and in a few years the country was, politically, partly Americanized, since when the New Mexican people have been obliged to live in a reluctant but necessary submission.

For some seventy years, therefore, the Spanish people of New Mexico have

Reprinted by permission from H. Morse Stephens and H. E. Bolton (eds.), *The Pacific Ocean in History* (New York: The Macmillan Co., 1917), pp. 408-428.

been in continuous, direct, and necessary contact with English speaking people. Race antagonism has always been very pronounced, especially among the lower classes of both races, although they have freely intermarried and race fusion has been gradually taking place. These intermarriages were, relatively speaking, much more frequent in the first years of the American occupation, when young soldiers, merchants and adventurers from the southern and middle-western states settled in New Mexico and almost invariably and of necessity (there being very few American women) married Spanish women. From the Louisiana territory there came also after the early thirties many French settlers and many of these also remained in New Mexico and married Spanish women.

With the introduction of the railroads and the very rapid commercial progress of the last thirty years, together with the rapid growth of large cities and towns in New Mexico, there has come a check in the race fusion and the mutual contact and good feeling between the two peoples. This check has been caused, in part, also, by the great influx into New Mexico of peoples of other nationalities, especially Jews and Italians. In the new cities, such as Albuquerque, East Las Vegas, Silver City and Roswell, where the English speaking people are numerically superior, the Spanish people are looked upon as an inferior race and intermarriages are not very frequent at the present time. In some instances the high-browed Americans who in these cities look down on the New Mexican-Spanish inhabitants, are low class Jews and poor Americans who have become wealthy in New Mexico by very questionable methods. Outside of a few of these very recent American cities, however, the Spanish element is still the all important and predominant one. Santa Fé, Taos, Socorro, Las Cruces, Tomé, West Las Vegas and a score of other smaller towns and many more villages are predominantly Spanish and in these places the English influence in language, customs and habits of life is very insignificant. Some of the very isolated places like Taos and Santa Fé are yet thoroughly Spanish and will continue so, perhaps, for more than a century.[1]

At the time of the American occupation of New Mexico in 1846, the entire Spanish population of what is now New Mexico and southern Colorado was about 50,000. By 1885, or some forty years after the American occupation, the Spanish population of these regions had risen to 100,000, while the English speaking people numbered less than 40,000. The rapid influx and rise of the American population did not become important until after 1880, or after the introduction of the railroads and other means of rapid transportation and communication. At present, the Spanish people of New Mexico number about 175,000 or about one half of the entire population of the state. In southern Colorado the Spanish people number about 50,000. The Spanish inhabitants of New Mexico and southern Colorado, or the New Mexican territory, which is the special object of our present study, number, therefore, about 225,000.[2]

In the region in question, therefore, the Spanish and English speaking inhabitants are very evenly divided, numerically. The inhabitants of both races, however, are not everywhere evenly divided. Some of the very recent cities like Albuquerque and Roswell have twenty Americans to one Spaniard, while in cities like Taos and Tierra Amarilla the figures are easily reversed. The remote mountain districts of New Mexico are settled entirely by Spanish people and there is not found one American to fifty Spanish inhabitants. A very large portion of the New Mexican territory, therefore, has not yet come under the influence of American institutions, in spite of the fact that the public school system makes an attempt to introduce everywhere the use of English.

The New Mexico public school system dates from the year 1896. Since that time there has been a systematic attempt to have the English language taught in all the schools. Sometimes the American authorities have been very bitter in denouncing the use of Spanish in some of the country schools and in their enthusiasm for the English language have gone so far as to forbid the use of Spanish by the Spanish children during their play. All such measures have been fruitless. The fact of the matter is that previous to 1896, and in many instances even at the present time, Spanish has been taught in the private and public schools, and has been considered far more important than English; and where there were no schools, parents who could read and write taught their children to read and write in Spanish. At present, although the school laws demand the use of English in the public schools, in many places, where all the pupils and even the teacher are Spanish, more Spanish is taught than English, and the whole atmosphere of the school is decidedly Spanish.[3] The Spanish inhabitants of New Mexico have been, therefore, very zealous about the use of their native speech, and in spite of the present intellectual and commercial superiority of their American neighbors, have not abandoned their language, religion, customs, and habits of life. As to language, not one in a hundred is found who has entirely abandoned the use of Spanish and taken up English in his home. This fact speaks eloquently for the tenacity and vigor of Spanish tradition and culture.

With the new generation, however, and especially with the new Spanish population of the cities and towns where the Spanish and American inhabitants are evenly divided, the problem is becoming fundamentally different. The Spanish school children of the predominantly American cities and towns like Roswell, Albuquerque, East Las Vegas, etc., speak English as well as the English speaking people and speak very poor Spanish. The growth of the English influence in the schools has been, therefore, the greatest recent factor in the gradual encroachment of the English language on the Spanish language in New Mexico and southern Colorado. This is not, however, the only factor. The Americanization of the country has brought with it the introduction of all American institutions with their modes of expression. In many fields of activity and intercourse, for example, in commerce, political institutions, and machinery, the Spanish people readily adopted the English terminology, in many cases having no Spanish equivalents.

Of the entire New Mexican-Spanish population of New Mexico and southern Colorado, about 75,000, or one third of the population is entirely ignorant of the English language. Most of these are people about fifty years of age. Of the people under forty years of age nine out of ten have been in the public schools and speak English fairly well. There are, of course, great differences, if one distinguishes between town and country districts, social classes, etc. In some isolated districts and towns not ten per cent of the Spanish inhabitants speak English. In cities where the American influence is great the figures are easily reversed. But even where English is not wide-spread among the Spanish inhabitants the English influence, especially in language, is strong, for reasons already stated. Even in cases where race pride and the love of the mother tongue have been decidedly contrary to the acceptance of the English language, the necessary commercial and political intercourse with English speaking peoples, the introduction of American machinery, farming implements, household articles, etc., many of these of recent invention and previously unknown to the New Mexicans, and lastly, as we have said, the compulsory introduction of the English language in the schools, have of necessity caused the introduction of a large English vocabulary into New Mexican Spanish.

It is no easy matter to determine through what channels the English words have found their way into New Mexican Spanish. The way the words have been introduced has been in many cases, no doubt, associated with the time of introduction, although this is, generally speaking, as yet an unimportant matter. Such words as *cute* < COAT, *rinque* < DRINK, *jolón* < HOLD ON, *bogue* < BUGGY, *queque* < CAKE, *escrepa* < SCRAPER, *jaira* < HARROW, *reque* < RAKE, *jarirú* < HOW DO YOU DO, *esteble* < STABLE, *greve* < GRAVY, *broquis* < BROKE, *craque* < CRACKER, *parna* < PARTNER, are words of extremely wide usage, belong to general terminology, and must have been introduced in the early years of the American occupation. Such words as *boila* < BOILER, *breca* < BRAKE, *cabús* < CABOOSE, *chequiar* < CHECK, *espaique* < SPIKE, *guiangue* < GANG, *pulman* < PULLMAN, *reque* < WRECK, *suichi* < SWITCH, *taya* < TIE, *troca* < TRUCK, *yarda* < YARD, belong exclusively to the railroad vocabulary and have been introduced into New Mexican Spanish since this institution came to New Mexico or after 1880. In the same way, it seems fairly reasonable to suppose that such words as *esmart* < SMART, *felo* < FELLOW, *besbol* < BASEBALL, *crismes* < CHRISTMAS, *espichi* < SPEECH, *fain* < FINE, *fone* < FUNNY, *ful* < FOOL, *espeliar* < SPELL, *juipen* < WHIPPING, *rede* < READY, have been introduced through the public school channels and are of very recent introduction. Many social terms and words that have to do with recent factory and city employment terminology, such as *pare* < PARTY, *jaque* < HACK, *piquenique* < PICNIC, *quiande* < CANDY, *aiscrím* < ICE-CREAM, *sangüichi* < SANDWICH, *sete* < SET, *sute* < SUIT, *londre* < LAUNDRY, *somil* < SAW-MILL, *polís* < POLICE, *lonchi* < LUNCH, *žobe* < JOB, *cambasiar* < CANVASS, *bil* < BILL, *chachar* < CHARGE, *esprés* < EXPRESS, are also, clearly, of very recent origin.

The English influence on New Mexican Spanish has been slow and gradual. As a rule, the English words adopted have no Spanish equivalent. In most cases the adoption of the English word has not been a case of fashion, luxury in speech, neglect of Spanish, or mere desire of imitating the language of the invaders, but an actual convenience and necessity. Of the entire New Mexican-Spanish vocabulary of English source by far more than 50 per cent of the words have been introduced since the year 1880, or rather within the last thirty-five years.

The New Mexican-Spanish vocabulary of English source is very unequally distributed throughout New Mexico and Colorado. Of the entire vocabulary, perhaps 50 per cent is of general use among the Spanish inhabitants, while the other 50 per cent is used only by those who are continually in daily and necessary contact with English speaking people in the cities or places and institutions where certain special vocabularies are in constant use. The mechanic who works in the railroad shops uses continually and unconsciously such words as *žopes* < SHOPS, *estraique* < STRIKE, *estiple* < STAPLE, *boila* < BOILER, *forman* < FOREMAN, *guaša* < WASHER, *reile* < RAIL, and a score or more of other words peculiar to his trade, words absolutely unknown to the New Mexican wood-seller or inhabitant of the mountain districts. The same applies to other trades and professions.

It is a surprising thing, however, to observe the general diffusion of a large part of the English borrowed words. Words that are once adopted and which become phonetically Spanish, become a part of the New Mexican-Spanish vocabulary and no one is cognizant of their English source. The New Mexicans who come from the mountain districts, or from the remote country villages and who speak only Spanish, and on arriving at a town enter a drug store to ask, *'Quier' una boteit'e penquila* (< PAIN-KILLER, a patent medicine), or a saloon to ask, *'Quier' un frasquitu e juisque* (< WHISKEY), are speaking as far as they are concerned, pure Spanish.

Besides the use of the regularly developed words of English source, there presents itself in the cities where English is predominant the problem of actual speech mixture. In the streets, in the factories, shops, stores, and other places of employment and amusement, and even in the homes, especially when all those in the family can speak good English, one continually hears the New Mexican-Spanish people speaking Spanish and English mixed. In such cases regular English words and phrases are used mingled with Spanish words and phrases. The part of speech least used in such mixtures is the verb, which when used at all is regularly developed and takes the Spanish verb endings. The line between the regularly developed New Mexican-Spanish words of English source and the English words and phrases used at random and with the usual English inflection, is, as a rule, easy to draw. On the other hand this very kind of speech mixture is at present the great factor in introducing English words into New Mexican Spanish. A word frequently used, even if known to be English by those who use it, can be easily adopted as a regular Spanish word.

The kind of speech mixture which brings into the Spanish of New Mexico the use of regular English words and phrases has no fixed limits and cannot follow regular laws. There is no limit to the use of such curious phenomena, and they are most common among those who work in the cities, the school children and the educated who know English well. Even the uneducated, however, partake in this phenomenon, so that the English influence on the Spanish language of New Mexico and Colorado is very strong in various ways. It has introduced some 300 regular hispanized words of English source,[4] has caused the curious speech mixture of which we have just spoken, and has influenced the syntax of the Spanish language itself.[5]

Since the examples of the speech mixture just mentioned could be multiplied almost *ad libitum,* I made no systematic attempt to record all those heard. As in most such cases the English words or phrases used remain unchanged, there seemed no great value for the philologist in collecting examples. A few of those which are found among my notes are the following:

¡qué *ice-cream* tan *fine*!
¡qué *fine ice-cream*!
¡qué hombre tan *sporty*!

Well, boys, vámonos.
¿how are you, señoritas?
señorita, *come in.*
well, come along, chicos.
you bet que sí.
va (a) haber una feria muy *fine.*
este *team* tieni un *fine pitcher.*
tuvimos un grand *time.*
ayer juimos á los *movies.*
quería andar de *smart and he got it in the neck.*
yo no voy a bailar este *two-step.*
¿comieron *turkey* pa *Christmas?*
¿ónde stá mi *silk hat?*
¡qué *waist* tan bonito traía la novia!
¡qué muchacha tan *fool!*
es el niño más *cute* que he visto.
no andes ai de *smart Alek.*
vamos ir al *foot-ball game* y después al baile a tener *the time of our lives.*
he is doing the best he can pa no quedarsi atrás pero lo van a fregar.
no seas tan *cheater.*
Well, compadre, *¿how is your* vieja?
quítate di aquí, *cry-baby.*
sean hombres y no anden *fooling around* tanto.
esa sí que fué una *first class* cochinada.
No le hagas caso a ese *fool.*

The English influence appears also in other important spheres of linguistic development, construction, word order and in the development of new meanings in the Spanish language itself. The commercial and political superiority of the English language in these regions has caused the Spanish to be considered by necessity the less important and under the continuous influence of English in every respect. Even the local Spanish newspapers (and there are about a score of these in New Mexico and some six or seven in Colorado) are full of phrases and constructions which have been literally translated from the English. Since the Spanish newspapers publish American news taken from the English newspapers the influence is direct. The New Mexicans are educated in English schools, and necessarily all possible influences are changing gradually the Spanish constructions into English constructions with Spanish words. From a Spanish population that is in continual and necessary contact with English speaking people who make no effort to learn Spanish,[6] and whose language they must study and speak, the influence just mentioned is exactly what is to be expected. The people are beginning to think in English and for expression seek the Spanish words which convey the English idea.

The English influence in question is one of the most interesting problems in linguistic investigation. We have before us, not the gradual and natural development of syntax, word-meaning, etc., as one can observe in the gradual development of popular Latin into the Romance Languages, but the somewhat unnatural and necessary development which comes from urgent economic causes. The complete materials for this part of our work have not been yet worked out in detail, and we shall content ourselves with a few examples of the phenomena in question.

The most difficult part of the study above mentioned is that involving mere idea expressions which involve no necessary association with American institutions. The problem is made all the more complicated when one has to decide whether the new construction could have been evolved without the English influence. Expressions and constructions evolved in New Mexican Spanish directly under the influence of the English construction are very numerous. Of the following, some are taken from my notes, others are taken from the local Spanish newspapers. To show clearly how parallel the constructions run, I give the English equivalent, in good English. As for the Spanish, in some cases it would have to be translated again into Spanish to make it clear.

los prisioneros fueron puestos libres, the prisoners were set free.

haga fuerza venir, make an effort [to try] to come.

si gusta, if you please.

la mejor cosa en el proyecto, the best thing in the bill.

consiste de tres partes, it consists of three parts.

nadie debe interferir en este asunto, no one must interfere in this affair.

el comité se convino á las dos, the committee convened at two o'clock.

todas otras apropiaciones se harán en decretos separados, all other appropriations shall be made in separate bills.

fué ordenado de ir á la cárcel, he was ordered to go to jail.

¡venta nunca vista! ¡precios quebrados! ¡vengan a ver para ustedes mismos! los que vengan primero serán servidos primero, wonderful sale! prices smashed! come and see for yourselves! first come, first served.[7]

la familia de la viuda será soportada por el estado, the widow's family will be supported by the state.

fueron recipientes de muchos presentes, they were the recipients of many presents.

niños de decendencia española jamás serán negados el privilegio de admisión y atendencia a las escuelas públicas, children of Spanish origin shall never be denied the privilege of admission, etc.

todo poder político esta investado y emana del pueblo, all political power is invested in and emanates from the people.

la constitución tomará efecto y entrará en plena fuerza, the constitution will take effect and come into full force.

nada en este artículo será construído de prohibir el giro de bonos, nothing in this article must be construed to prohibit the floating of bonds.

dos de sus hijos atienden á las escuelas públicas, two of his sons are attending the public schools.

The Spanish translations used for governmental, political, educational, industrial, farming, and household terminologies, alone furnish material for a long and interesting study. The English words in question must of necessity be translated and the New Mexicans draw from their own resources and easily find some word or words to express the idea. The phrases and word groups joined with the preposition *de,* in origin a Spanish construction, are very abundant.

Since I have not made a special study of these terminologies in any of my publications, the complete list from my notes is given below. The list, no doubt, is a small part of those in actual usage.

aceite di olivo, olive oil.
administrador de terrenos, land administrator.
aliansa de los rancheros, farmers' alliance.
asistente estafetero, assistant postmaster.
auditor ambulante, travelling auditor.
boleta republicana, republican ballot.
cama que se dobla, folding-bed.
carta enregistrada, registered letter.
carne de bote, canned meat.
casa di alto, two story house.
casa de corte, court house.
colegio di agricoltura, College of Agriculture.
comisionado de condado, county commissioner.
compañía de l'aseguransa, insurance company.
común de cadena, water-closet.
corte suprema, supreme court.
corte de distrito, district court.
cuerda de la lus eléctrica, electric light wire.
día de Crismes, Christmas day.
día, di acción de gracias, Thanksgiving day.
dipo de l' unión, union depot.
diputau alguasil, deputy sheriff.
diputau asesor, deputy assessor.
diputau escribano, deputy clerk.
el de las órdenes, the order man (grocer).
enumerador del censo, census enumerator.
escuela alta, high school.
escuela de minas, school of mines.
escuela normal, normal school.
escuela de reforma, reform school.
espíritos di alcamfor, spirits of camphor.
esteque de pierna, round steak.
fondo de escuelas, school fund.
frijoles de jarro, canned beans.
frutas evaporadas, evaporated fruits.
gran jurau, grand jury.
gran marcha, grand march (at balls).
hospital de mineros, miners' hospital.
implementos de rancho, ranch implements.
ispetor de caminos, road overseer.
jamón di almuerso, breakfast bacon.
jamón de pierna, ham.
jues de distrito, district judge.

jues de la corte suprema, supreme court judge.
jues de pas, justice of the peace.
leche de bote, condensed milk.
leva de cola, swallow tail coat.·
leva larga, Prince Albert coat.
leva de tasación, tax levy.
máquina de cortar sacate, hay-mower.
máquina de cortar trigo, harvester.
máquina de coser, sewing machine.
máquina de trïar, threshing machine.
máquina de rajar, saw-mill, lumber mill.
maquinita de moler carne, meat-chopper.
mariscal de la su̯idá, city marshall.
mariscal de los Estaus Unidos, United States marshal.
mayor de la su̯idá, city mayor.
medesina de la patente, patent medicine.
mesa de librería, library table.
mesa de cosina, kitchen table.
mesita del cuarto de recibo, parlor table.
notario público, notary public.
orden de estafeta, post-office money-order.
oya del eslope, slop bucket.
olivas, olivos, olives.
palita de los panqueques, pancake paddle.
palito de los dientes, toothpick.
palo de telégrafo, telegraph pole.
patio de maderas, lumber yard.
pinturas, moving pictures.
pipas del agua, water pipes.
pipas del gas, gas pipes.
procurador de distrito, district attorney.
procurador general, attorney general.
planta de la eletresidá, electric light plant.
regentes de l'Universidá, University regents.
sarsaparila del dotor ayer, Dr. Ayer's Sarsaparilla.
sete de platos, set of dishes.
superintendente de instrusión pública, superintendent of public instruction.
supervisor de florestas, forest supervisor.
supervisor del censo, census supervisor.
tienda de grocerías, grocery store.
tienda de l'unión, union store.
tíquete de paso redondo, round-trip ticket.
túnico de tienda, ready-made dress.
vestido de tienda, ready-made suit.
viaje redondo (also *paso redondo*), round trip.
yarda, yard of a house, lot, courtyard.
yardas del ferrocarril, railroad yards.

yave del agua, water-faucet.
zapatos bajitos, low shoes, slippers.

Phonetic Developments

The phonetic changes involved in the hispanized words of English origin are of the greatest interest to the philologist. The study of these changes does not concern us here, and it is sufficient to point out a few of the most general. The phonetic processes in question forcibly remind the philologist of the similar processes in the old Vulgar Latin and early Romance words derived from the old Germanic dialects. In both the old and modern developments we have the case of a Germanic language furnishing hundreds of vocables for adoption by a Latin language. It would not be strange to find a few parallel developments, but it is indeed surprising to find that many of the important phonetic processes involved are essentially the same. These facts speak eloquently for the ethnical unity, vigor, and force of these important branches of the Indo-European languages, and at the same time give testimony to the existence and solidarity of phonetic laws. Some of these changes are now given:

1. *Vowels*

English accented *ŭ* becomes New Mexican-Spanish *o*, BŬGGY > *bogue,* LŬNCH > *lonchi,* BŬNCH > *bonchi,* FŬN > *fon.* In the same manner Germanic *ŭ* becomes *o* in Romance, Franconian HŬRDI > Old French *horde,* Old High German KŬPPHIA > Old Spanish *cofia.*

English accented *ŏ* becomes New Mexican-Spanish *o*, BŎSS > *bos,* LŎT > *lote.* In the same manner Germanic *ŏ* often becomes *o* in Romance, Old English NŎRTH > Spanish *norte,* Fr. *nord.* The law of *ŏ* > *ue* does not operate any longer.

English accented *ō* may become New Mexican-Spanish *u* (generally *o*), CŌAT > *cute,* HIGH-TŌNED > *jaitún.* Likewise Germanic *ō* often became *u* in Romance, *URGŌLI > Sp. *orgullo,* Germanic HLŌDWĪG > O. French *Louis.*

English accented *ē* becomes New Mexican-Spanish *i*, SPEECH > *espichi,* LEASE > *lis.* Likewise Germanic *i* (*ee*) became Romance *i*, Gothic RĪKS > French *riche,* Sp. *rico,* Old H. German ESLĪZAN > O. French *eslicier.*

2. *Epenthetic Vowels*

Between certain English consonant groups epenthetic vowels develop in New Mexican Spanish, in the same manner as in Germanic groups which passed over into Romance.

English NICKEL > *niquel,* English MACNALLY > *Mequenale,* SHOTGUN > *sotegón.* Likewise Germanic BOLLWERK > Old French *boulevard,* English PARTNER > Fr. *partenaire.*

3. *Consonants*

English initial *w* becomes New Mexican-Spanish *gu̯*, WAIST > *gu̯eiste,* WINCHESTER > *gu̯incheste,* WILLY > *Gu̯ile.* In the same way all the early

Romance languages converted Germanic *w* into *gu̯*, Old High German WERRA >
Old Spanish *guerra,* Germanic WARJIAN > *guarir,* etc.[8]

English *f* becomes New Mexican-Spanish *f* (> bilabial *f* or *j*), FŨN > *fon,*
FOOL > *ful, jul.* Likewise Germanic initial *f* became Romance *f* (often >
bilabial *f* in Spanish).

Résumé

The influence of the English language on the Spanish of New Mexico and
Colorado must be studied, therefore, according to the following divisions, the
phenomena of each division given in the order of relative importance from the
viewpoint of the comparative philologist:

1. The study of the phonetic development of all popularly and regularly
developed New Mexican-Spanish basic words of direct English source (about
three hundred in number), a list of which is given at the end of this article.

2. The study of the morphological development of these words with the
additional forms of non-phonetic development, from the viewpoint of inflection
and conjugation, together with all derivatives therefrom.

3. A complete etymological vocabulary of all the New Mexican-Spanish
words of English origin, with all derivatives, proper names, surnames, names of
places, etc., with meaning if different from the English.

4. The study of the New Mexican-Spanish words and phrases used to
translate the English governmental, political, educational, industrial, farming and
household terminologies.

5. The study of the problem of speech mixture in New Mexican Spanish.

6. The study of the English influence on New Mexican-Spanish syntax and
general phraseology and grammatical construction.

7. The historical, racial, and political problems.[9]

Vocabulary

A complete list of all the basic[10] New Mexican-Spanish words of English
origin follows. The English words from which the New Mexican-Spanish words
are derived are given in all cases. The New Mexican-Spanish words are
transcribed as accurately as possible in the Spanish alphabet. The symbol *š* is
equivalent to English *sh.*

1. *Nouns*

áiscrím < ICE-CREAM.
alcojol < ALCOHOL.
ale < ALLEY.
otomobil < AUTOMOBILE.

bágachi < BAGGAGE.
baisíquel < BICYCLE.
balún < BALLOON.

balís < VALISE.
bel < BĀLE (of hay).
bil < BILL.
béquenpaura < BAKING POWDER.
besbol < BASEBALL.
bisnes < BUSINESS.
bísquete < BISCUIT.
blofe < BLUFF.

bogue < BUGGY.
boil < BOIL (furuncle).
boila < BOILER (of engine).
bonchi < BUNCH.
boquebor < BUCKBOARD.
bos < BOSS.
brande < BRANDY.
breca < BRAKE.
brel < BREAD.
bugabú < BUGABOO.
buquipa < BOOK-KEEPER.

cabús < CABOOSE.
cláun < CLOWN.
clica < CLIQUE.
clósete < CLOSET.
cofe < COFFEE.
cumplén < COMPLAINT.
craque < CRACKER.
crismes < CHRISTMAS.
crobar < CROWBAR.
cuara < QUARTER (coin).
cun < COON.
cuque < COOKY.
cute < COAT.
Chales < CHARLES.
chansa < CHANCE.
cheque < CHECK.
chipas < CHIPS.
Chochis < GEORGE.
choque < CHALK.

daime < DIME.
daique < DIKE.
daun < DOWN (football).
dipo < DEPOT.
dola < DOLLAR.

escrachi < SCRATCH.
escrapes < SCRAPS.
escrepa < SCRAPER.
escrín < SCREEN.
eslipa < SLEEPER (car).
esmaši < SMASH.
espaique < SPIKE.
espelen < SPELLING.
espichi < SPEECH.

espor < SPORT.
esprés < EXPRESS.
esprín < SPRING (bed).
estaile < STYLE.
esteble < STABLE.
estepes < STEPS.
esteque < STEAK.
estiple < STAPLE.
estraique < STRIKE.
evrebore < EVERYBODY.

faila < FILE.
faya < FIRE.
fayamán < FIREMAN.
felo < FELLOW.
faul < FOUL (baseball).
flaya < FLIER (train).
fon < FUN.
forman < FOREMAN.

ǧele < JELLY.
Ǧimes < JIMMY.
ǧobe < JOB.
gondeme < GOD DAMN (= insult).
greve < GRAVY.
grimbaque < GREENBACK.
griso < GREASER (Mexican).
guaša < WASHER (mech.).
güeiste < WAIST.
guiangue < GANG.
Güile < WILLY.
güincheste < WINCHESTER.
güisque < WHISKEY.
guoque < WALK.

jaira < HARROW.
jaque < HACK.
jolón < HOLD ON (=insult).
juipen < WHIPPING.
juisque < WHISKEY.
jupencofe < WHOOPING COUGH.

laya < LIAR.
lere < LADY.
léreschois < LADIES' CHOICE.
lis < LEASE.
lon < LAWN (grass).

lonchi < LUNCH.
londre < LAUNDRY.
lote < LOT.

Mague < MAGGIE.
Maques < MAX.
Marí, Marrí < MARIE.
méchica < MEXICAN.
místar < MISTER.
mompes < MUMPS.
monquerrenchi < MONKEY WRENCH.

nicle, niquel < NICKEL.

otemil < OAT MEAL.
ovarjoles < OVERALLS.

panqueque < PANCAKE.
pantre < PANTRY.
pare < PARTY (social).
parna < PARTNER.
pene < PENNY.
penquila < PAINKILLER.
picha < PITCHER (baseball).
picle < PICKLE.
piquenique < PICNIC.
ploga < PLŬG.
poca < POKER.
polís < POLICE.
ponchi < PUNCH.
pone < PONY.
ponšope < PAWN SHOP.
porchi < PORCH.
pul < PULL.
pulman < PULLMAN.
puši < PUSH.

queque < CAKE.
quecha < CATCHER (baseball).
quiande < CANDY.
quiaši < CASH.
quido < KĬDDO.
quimona < KIMŌNO.
quique < KICK.

raide < RIDE.
rapa < WRAPPER.

redes < RADISHES.
reile < RAIL.
remarca < REMARK.
renchi < RANGE.
renganchi < TRAINGANG.
reque < RAKE.
reque < WRECK.
resensaque < DRESSING SACK.
rigue < RIG.
ril < DRILL.
rinque < DRINK.
risés < RECESS.
roles < ROLLS.
roši < RUSH.
rula < RULER.

saibor < SIDEBOARD.
saiguoque < SIDEWALK.
salún < SALOON.
sanamabichi < SON OF A B -.
sanamagón < SON OF A GUN.
sángüichi < SANDWICH.
sarsaparila < SARSAPARILLA.
selesute < SAILOR SUIT.
sete < SET.
sinque < SINK (kitchen).
somil < SAW-MILL.
suera < SWEATER.
suichi < SWITCH.
suitejarte < SWEETHEART.
sur < SEWER.
sute < SUIT.
šaine < SHINE (shoe shine).
šampú < SHAMPŌO.
šante < SHANTY.
šerife < SHERIFF.
šo, cho < SHOW (circus).
šopes < SHOPS.
šorgüeiste < SHIRTWAIST.
šotis, šotís < SCHOTTISCHE.
šotegón < SHOTGUN.

taya < TIE (railroad).
telefón, telejón < TELEPHONE.
tíquete < TICKET.
trampe < TRAMP.
transe < TRANSOM.
triques < TRĬCKS.

trite < TREAT.
troca < TRUCK.
tustepe < TWO-STEP (dance).

yarda < YARD.
yel < YELL.

2. *Adjectives*
broquis < BROKE (poor).

cranque < CRANKY.
crese < CRAZY.

dochi < DUTCH (American, German).

esmarte < SMART.
espore < SPORTY.

fain < FINE.
fone < FUNNY.
ful, jul < FOOL.

griso < GREASER.
güilo < WILLY (= foolish).

jaitún < HIGHTONED.

méchica < MEXICAN.

ponque < PUNK.

quiute < CUTE.

rede < READY.

sanamabichi < SON OF A B-.
sanamagón < SON OF A GUN.
sor < SORE (offended).

trampe < TRAMPY (tramp-like).

3. *Verbs*
   New Mexican-Spanish verbs of English origin take the English verb as the stem and add the regular endings. Nearly all add -*iar* to form the infinitive.

baquiar < BACK + IAR.
bonchar < BUNCH + (I)AR.
bosiar < BOSS + IAR.

cambasiar < CANVASS.
craquiar < CRACK.
cuitar < QUIT.
chachar < CHARGE.
chequiar < CHECK.
chitiar < CHEAT.

deschachar < DISCHARGE.

escrachar < SCRATCH.
esmašar < SMASH.
espeliar < SPELL.
estraiquiar < STRIKE.

fuliar < FOOL.

jairiar < HARROW.

lonchar < LUNCH.

monquiar < MONKEY.

puliar < PULL.
pušar < PUSH.

quiašar < CASH.
quiquiar < KICK.

requiar < RAKE.
riliar < DRILL.
risquiar < RISK.
roseliar < RUSTLE (=WORK).

suichar < SWITCH.
šainiar < SHINE.
šutiar < SHOOT.

telefoniar < TELEPHONE.
trampiar < TRAMP (steal).
tritiar < TREAT.

4. *Adverbs* (some are
              also adjectives)

crese < CRAZY.

enejau < ANYHOW.

fain(e) < FINE.
fone < FUNNY.

olraite < ALL RIGHT.

rede < READY.

tumoro < TOMORROW.

5. *Exclamations, greetings, etc.*

albechu < I'LL BET YOU.
auchi < OUCH.

bai bai < BYE BYE.

càmíar < COME HERE.
càmón < COME ON.
chi clai < JEE CLY.

ǧijuís < GEE WHIZ.
gódèmete < GOD DAMN IT.
gorejèl, gorijèl < GO TO HELL.
guirepe, guirape < GET UP.
gurbái < GOOD BYE.

jaló < HELLO.
jamachi < HOW MUCH.
jariru < HOW DO YOU DO.
jàrirúsa < HOW DO YOU DO, SIR.
je < HEY.
jolón < HOLD ON.
jurá, juré < HURRAH.

op, opa, ope < UP.

plis < PLEASE.

šarap(e) < SHUT UP.
šo < PSHAW.
šoquis < SHUCKS.

yubete < YOU BET.

yubechu < YOU BET YOU.
yubechu laif < YOU BET YOUR LIFE.

Notes

[1]The Spanish inhabitants of New Mexico and Colorado are descendants of the old Spanish families which entered the country with the *conquistadores* in 1598 and 1693. They very rarely intermarried with the native Indian population and are, therefore, in every sense of the word, Spanish. See also, *Studies in New Mexican Spanish,* Part I, pp. 334, 335.

[2]My previous estimate was a little exaggerated. See *The Spanish Language in New Mexico and Southern Colorado* (Santa Fé, New Mexico, 1911), p. 17, and *Studies,* vol. 1, p. 1.

[3]In the summer of 1910 I had charge of the four weeks' Teachers' Institute of Socorro County in central New Mexico. There were in attendance some twenty-five school teachers, all but four Spanish, and of the twenty-one who were Spanish, not one half could carry on correctly an ordinary conversation in the English language. They taught in districts where only Spanish is spoken and gave some of the instruction in Spanish.

[4]This number does not include derivations. One single noun of English origin may give two or even three or more derivatives, so that counting in all derivatives, including diminutives, augmentatives and post-verbal nouns, the number of words of English origin may easily reach 600 or more. In the number above given, 300 words of English origin, are included only basic words developed in *tota forma* from the English original, such as *quique* < kick, a regular phonetic development, whereas *quiquiada, quiquiadita, quiquiadera* are derivatives which have Spanish endings.

[5]An English influence similar to the one found in New Mexican Spanish exists no doubt in the Spanish of Arizona, Texas and California. In the region of Santa Barbara in Southern California, a strong Spanish Community since the early part of the eighteenth century, I have found some 150 basic words of direct English source, regularly developed and in common use among the Spanish inhabitants. Their phonetic development differs very little from the New Mexican.

[6]The New Mexico-English Americans are prejudiced, as a rule against the Spanish inhabitants and do not care for their language or culture. In California, where the English speaking population is more enlightened, we find no racial prejudice, and the cult for Spanish things is general.

[7]The English imitation reaches the height of ignorance and stupidity in the following announcement (Albuquerque, 1909): *¡Gran venta de salvaje para hombres y mujeres y niños!* Great salvage sale for men, women and children! Even the uneducated New Mexicans remarked that only the final *s* of *salvajes* was missing.

[8]*Studies in New Mexican Spanish,* vol. 3, § 48.

[9]Practically all these problems have been studied in detail by the author in various publications; especially in *The Spanish Language in New Mexico and Southern Colorado* (Santa Fé, New Mexico, 1911), and *Studies in New Mexican Spanish*, Part III, *The English Elements of (Revue de Dialectologie Romane*, Hamburg, 1914).

[10]Derivatives from the words phonetically developed are not included. These can be formed almost *ad libitum.* In our *Studies, op. cit.,* all these have been carefully studied.

Adaptation of English Borrowing

J. Donald Bowen

Borrowing in the Spanish of San Antoñito. Besides the numerous borrowed forms inherited from Castilian and possibly other dialects of Spain, the Spanish of San Antoñito parallels the growth of American Spanish in general in its acceptance of new vocabulary forms in its lexicon from surrounding linguistic environments. This tendency to borrow vocabulary is probably stronger in the Spanish speaking areas of the United States, where English has replaced Spanish as the official language.

Bilingualism is a common characteristic of most native Spanish speakers in the United States, and in urban centers it is not uncommon to find children speaking only English, although their grandparents spoke only Spanish. Given the tremendous prestige English enjoys over Spanish in the United States and the traditional willingness of Spanish to accept borrowings, it is not difficult to understand the reason for the tremendous influence English has had on Spanish. This influence has largely been felt in vocabulary, though earlier the initial glottal stop was discussed as a possible influence on the phonology. No noticeable effect on the morphology is apparent, and no major syntax patterns have been changed. A few loan translations of English idioms show a mild patterning in a few phrases for the only possible syntactical influence: /tubímos um bwén tyémpo, isímos bwén tyémpo en el kamíno/, etc.

If English is the major source of borrowings in San Antoñito Spanish, it is certainly not the only one. Native Indian languages which have had contact with Spanish have left their mark on the Spanish vocabulary. We are quite sure that the following words are contributions that have come ultimately from Aztec:

/čilakayóte	nistamál
ixóte	pičikwáte
kamóte	tekolóte
koyóte	xakál/

Other words which are apparently not of Spanish or English origin are very likely borrowings from Indian languages, such as /íčite, čakéwe, čimaxá, očá, pitisáya, púnči/, etc. The sources for checking the probable provenience of these forms either do not exist or they are so inaccessible and unreliable that it seems hardly worth the effort to try to trace them down.

English borrowings in San Antoñito Spanish. A significant factor in describing the adaptation of borrowings, if the criteria are based upon phonemic and syllabic structure, arises from the fact that English is considerably more complex than Spanish: there are more phonemes in English and fewer limitations of distribution. Adapting English to Spanish patterns, then, involves the changing

From "The Spanish of San Antoñito, New Mexico." University of New Mexico Ph.D. dissertation, 1952. Reprinted by permission of the author.

115

or dropping of sounds or sound sequences to conform to permitted sounds and combinations of sounds in Spanish. English words with sounds and structures similar to those permitted in Spanish have little difficulty being adapted; others are usually, though not always, adapted.

To explore all of the equivalences and shifts of sounds in the process of borrowing would take more information than is at present available. For instance, nearly all bilinguals have a characteristic English phonemic system which does not correspond to that of native English speakers. Certain features of borrowings might well be traced to bilingual phonemics, such as: the complete elimination of open high vowels, the frequent lack of vowel length, accent shifts, the lack of retroflexion, etc. The present study will therefore not attempt to chart sound equivalences, but will merely list borrowings from English as they are adapted formally and semantically.

Formal adaptation. Under this heading borrowings from English will be discussed and presented in the order they comply with Spanish formal patterns. It is noteworthy that the large majority of borrowings are well adapted. Many of those not adapted may not be current through the entire village, and some that are unadapted by some informants are completely adapted by others.

Borrowings adapted to common patterns. To show the operation of derivational morphemes, the borrowings that follow are subdivided into two groups. The first group, comprised of nonderived nouns, adjectives, and exclamatives, are forms that are adapted to the phonemic and syllabic patterns of Spanish. The second group, comprised of derived nouns and verbs, shows the phonological adaptation of the English form plus the addition of a native Spanish derivational morpheme.

1. *Borrowings phonologically adapted:*

/el ansestór	la čáke
el árme	la čalúpa
los babipínes	un čánte
un balún	un čáte
el baskeból	el čategón
el baté	el cíngle
el baysíko	el čó
el beysból	el čópe
el bléte	(el) čóre
la blóka - el blóke	los čórtes
el bóge	čú
el bómpe - la bómpa	un dáyme
um bónče	un díče
las brékas	un dípo
um búčale	un díso
un dóče	el gríso
los eskrápes	el kalsamán
la eskrépa	el káyte
un eskrín	un kéke
el eslíke	un kíke

un espáyke	el klóče
un espíče	el kóke
un esprínge	el kórpo
un estéble	la kórsa
un estéke	el kráke
un estráyke	el kránke
un eswíče	la krayóla
el fáyte	krísmes
el férlo	la króča
um fláte	el króče
el fón	el kúke
fóne	el kúte
forblís	el líste
el fuból	el lónče
un galón	el lóndre
un garáče	el lóte
el gaselín	el magasín
gidónya	el mápe
el gránte	la mentoláte
el grébe	la míra
la gréda - el gréyder	modeláče
los mómpes	la rróla
un monyórden	el rrisés
el morosáyko	el rrúče
un níkle	el sakaról - sararól
el ólyo	la salepátika
el párče	el santaklós
el párna	el sanwíce
el páte	un sasefón
las payámas	el satín
um péne	el sáyne
el pikeníke	el sáyren
las pínčes	el saywóke - saywáke
la plóga	un séte
el plóge	el sínke
la póka	el sitixól
el polbéro	la sóda
um pónče	el súte
el pópe	la swéra
la púča	la tasasyón
um púče	la táya
um púle	táyte
el rráfete	el telefón
el rrayadóre	la tórca
un rréke	el tórke
un rríl	el tráke
el rrín	el trámpe
un tréle	la xáyra

él tríke	el xáywe
la tróča	xé
la tróka	la xóka
la wáca	la xolestín
el wayín	el xwíle - la xwíla
el wáyno	el xwípe
un wéče	la xwípen
el wíske - xwíske	el yáke
xálo	la yárda
el xakéke	la yérse/

2. *Borrowings phonologically adapted plus Spanish derivational morphemes:*

/arroyárse	desčarčár
el asesamyénto	enwečár
asesár	eskračár
bakyár	eskrinyár
batyár	fulyár
blofyár	kečár
bompyár	kikyár
bončár	el kotón
čarčár	krankyár
čaynyár	kročár
čekyár	kwityár
čusár	likyár
čutyár	el listyadór
listyár	saynyár
lofyár	sikyár
lončár	swičár
la lončéra	taypyár
la lončería	testyár
mapyár	tičár
mistyár	trampyár
monkyár	tročár
parkyár	la trokáda
pičár	el trokéro
plogyár	el trokón
la pompíta	el wačadór
pompyár	wačár
pončár	weldyár
praymyár	el weldyadór
pučár	xayrár
rrekyár	xwipyár/
rrolár	

Borrowings adapted to less common patterns. The following borrowings are adapted to patterns that exist in Spanish but have limited occurrence. Criteria for placing forms in this category include: a final /-i/, occurrence of the sequences /oy, ay, aw/ especially when followed by a consonant in the same syllable, a final unaccented syllable /-l, -r/, and a sequence of three consonants in one syllable. Nonderived nouns and exclamatives occur in this group:

/el ármi	el kéčer
áwči	kíti
el bekenpáwra	el nébi - néybi
el bómper	el páynte
la bóyla	el píčer
el brándi	el púdi
el čáyn	la rryúla
el eskigráwn	el séleri
un estéymen	los táwnses
el filistéče	xáni
el foretrí	la yéli/
el grábel	

Borrowings forming new patterns. The following borrowings show phonological patterns which do not conform to those of native Spanish words. Features of syllable structure and accentuation usually enter into these new formations. Nonderived nouns, adjectives, and exclamatives occur in this group:

/el basketból	gidáp - gidyáp
los blúmers	el kalsamáyn
un dáym	el kláwn
un déyt	un kók
el eskárf	el kómbáyn
el futból	lébordé
un garáč	el rrím
un sét	el xaloín
las sísers	el xám
swít	el séspúl
el tíčirt	la skúl/

Borrowings containing English phonemes. Some words with one or more English sounds are fairly common. The English sounds, of course, are those which have no closely equivalent sound in Spanish. Some of the following words appear with changes which adapt them to Spanish patterns in the lists that precede. Several of the following forms are proper names which may have Spanish equivalents, but whose English-sounding variants are preferred:

/á[ɹ]mi	k[ǽ]mb[l̩]
[ǽ]lis	lo[ɹ]éyn
b[ɔ́ɹ]ni	pá[ɹ]adays
d[ǽ]di	p[ǽ]tsi
[dž]ó[ɹdž]	pí[ɹ]yod
[dž]ín	rí[ɸ]matik
est[é]di	[vaé]li/
f[éɹ]lo	

Borrowings of English words without adaptation. With many bilinguals there is an almost constant use of English words in Spanish contexts. An expression such as /béngan por mi/ "early in the morning" /porke tenémos ke salír tempráno/ is not at all uncommon. Some English expressions like "uh huh" have been accepted in the speech of informants who do not normally use an excess of English forms. It would seem that children reared in a bilingual atmosphere tend to use both languages and intermix them, using an English word whenever the Spanish word does not readily come to mind, and vice versa.

Possible English influence on form. The following words are phonologically closer to English forms than to similar forms in standard Castilian, according to the criteria set forth in Tomás Navarro Tomás' *Manual de pronunciación española.*[1] Some of these forms are probably pure borrowings from English; others may be Spanish forms that have been changed by phonologically and semantically similar forms in English. No attempt to distinguish causal relationships is made here because of insufficient evidence to verify any conclusions reached. Underscoring calls attention to changes:

/aluminár	makániko
aropláno	kimóna
atomátiko	rrubárbo
atomobíl	sasefón_
báysikleta	telefón_
kangratulár	gaselín_/

Semantic adaptation. Under this heading borrowings or possible borrowings from English will be discussed as they affect meanings. Sometimes the loan is a form, but under this classification it is usually an idea adapted to a native form. Authority for the meanings of standard Castilian is the *Diccionario de la lengua española,* 17th ed., of the Real Academia Española.[2]

Loan translations. An idea or usage typical to English is expressed by corresponding Spanish words or phrases:

/alambrár/	to wire (a house for electricity)
/el aséyte/	oil (oiled road)
/la barréna/	drill (well-digging outfit)
/el béynt-i-dós/	twenty-two (caliber rifle)
/el gáto/	cat (caterpillar tractor)
/la kása de kórtes/	court house
/la kórta/	(hair) cut
/el kórte/	cut (off), short cut
/el kwarénta-y-kwátro/	forty-four (caliber rifle)
/un kwatr-óxos/	four-eyes (boy wearing glasses)
/mákina de labár/	washing machine
/mákina de para kosér/	sewing machine
/mama-gránde/	grandmother
/mantekía de kakawáte/	peanut butter
/papa-gránde/	grandfather
/el papél/	newspaper

/rryáles/	
/dós rryáles/	two bits (twenty-five cents)
/kwátro rryáles/	four bits (fifty cents)
/séys rryáles/	six bits (seventy-five cents)
/el sesénta-y-séys/	(highway) sixty-six
/los sobre-sapátos/	overshoes
/el tréynta/	thirty (caliber rifle)

Words semantically similar to those of English rather than, or in addition to, similar forms in standard Castilian. These are forms which combine the semantic characteristics of both English and Spanish. Whether they are coincidentally borrowings or there was actually an influence felt through the association of the English and Spanish forms is not easy to say:

/agradárse	el kondutór
atendér	la méča
el bíl ·	o
el bós	los oxáles
la depresyón	la párte
deskargár	la rrénta
é	el túbo
la estámpa	la unyón
las groserías	xalár
el kárro	yá/

Words of limited extension, meaning, or use in standard Castilian, but which are common in English, that are of frequent occurrence in the Spanish of San Antoñito. Again the following forms may be borrowings that happen to partially coincide with words that exist in Castilian. I suspect that most of them are borrowings from English:

/el ákre	el tánke
la kámara	el tratór
la pómpa	

Notes

[1]6th ed. (New York, 1950), 326 pp.
[2](Madrid, 1947), 1345 pp.

Some Lexical Characteristics of San Jose Spanish

Anthony Beltramo and
Antonio de Porcel

1. Introduction

The Spanish of Mexican American bilinguals reveals considerable word borrowing from the dominant language, English. In one respect, this effect must be viewed as a sign of acculturation by the minority group, and the gradual displacement of Spanish by English. At the same time, however, it is a device for achieving diversity within Spanish, through further refinement of the vocabulary. It is one of the implements for creating a bilinguals' dialect, appropriate to its unique social and physical environment.

It is easy, and entertaining, to talk about loanwords with bilingual Californians. Practically everyone is aware of them. However, when it comes to identifying the source language of these words in Spanish contexts, bilinguals are not equally sure of themselves in every case. The purpose of this paper is to explore whether this variation in the ability to judge words as borrowings is associated more closely with linguistic or non-linguistic factors. On the linguistic side, we find that there is not just one, but several processes available for the adaptation of English lexical items to Spanish. Depending on their adaptation, some borrowings remain perhaps "more English" than others. On the non-linguistic side, we might find that the awareness of borrowing varies according to characteristics of the speakers who use them, for example, their occupational status or length of residence among English speakers.

Field work for this study was conducted in San Jose, California, where Mexican Americans represent approximately 25 percent of the total population. Owing primarily to geographic and sentimental closeness to Mexican borderlands, the Spanish language remains in wide use.

The ease with which individuals could talk about words "half Spanish," "mostly English," etc. suggested arranging a controlled situation in which bilingual subjects were asked to describe lexical items representing the various loan types. The kind of description sought refers, like our linguistic classifications (see following section), to formal characteristics of lexical items and not to subjects' evaluation of them (pro-con) or inclination to use them. It is not concerned with the question of whether bilinguals actually accept or resist words on the basis of their "Englishness." In other words, with respect to the attitudes that speakers hold toward these borrowed words, we are seeing only their cognitive side, and not conative (actual speech behavior) or emotive aspects.[2]

It seemed reasonable to assume that (1) more highly acculturated individuals, by doing better at a task of placing loan types in their "correct" descriptive categories, would show a higher awareness of the varieties of English influence and, (2) certain loan types would be generally easier to identify as English than other types.

122

2. Variables

In order to study the relation between acculturation and the bilinguals' own classification of borrowings we sought (1) a translation of linguistic classifications of borrowings into everyday language, and (2) some non-linguistic indicators of acculturation for individuals.

2.1 Linguistic Factors

Bilinguals often give plain-language descriptions, which correspond roughly to linguistic labels for loan types, as illustrated below.

(1) "An English word:" Phonological adaptation or lexical switch.
Examples: Este *jaiwei* es muy peligroso. ('highway')
　　　　　Quiero limpiar mis *clósets* este fin de semana.

(2) "A word part English, part Spanish:" Morphological adaptation.
Examples: Mi abuela nos hizo una *cuilta* bonita. ('quilt')
　　　　　Las más baratas son llantas *recapeadas.* ('recapped')

(3) "A Spanish phrase that translates an English phrase:" Loan translation.
Examples: Su hijo va a la *escuela alta.* ('high school')
　　　　　Luego llegaron Roberto y su *mejor mitad.* ('better half')

(4) "A Spanish word being used a new way:" Loanshift extension.
Examples: *Atendemos* a la misma escuela. ('to attend,' std. 'to heed')
　　　　　Me dió una *lectura* porque llegué muy tarde. ('lecture,' std. 'reading')

(5) "Completely Spanish." This type includes Spanish words which have cognates in English with a different usage but no attested influence on Spanish. Although given in perfectly acceptable standard usage, these might be doubted as to their "purity" because of an awareness of the English.
Example: Tuvieron una *discusión* sobre la propina. 'They had an *argument* over the tip.'

In this case, for example, hesitations as to whether *discusión* is "pure Spanish" could arise due to familiarity with English *discussion.* In itself, this is a type of lexical influence which would characterize linguistic acculturation.

Thus, within type 5, there are words which would have this possibility of confusion with an English cognate, and words which do not.

2.2. Non-Linguistic Factors

Only adult bilinguals were chosen for this study (age 15 and older).

The literature on typologies of Mexican Americans and on acculturation has suggested the variables to consider.[3] Among the most important are sex, age, generation, extent of the use of Spanish, occupation, and education.

A. Sex.

In general, the role differences between men and women in this group are probably not so exaggerated as those described, for example, by William Madsen for south Texas. The woman is "the perfect counterpart to the Latin male," inclined to be submissive and respectful while he is aggressive and condescending. Her goals are completely subordinate to his.[4] It seemed possible that different role expectations between women and men might be reflected in the language variation sought here. To be consistent with the leader-follower roles as described, we could assume that the male, for his greater exposure to the world, is more acculturated.

B. *Generation and Age.*

The history of migration from Texas to Santa Clara County makes available several generations of adults. We can distinguish (a) those born in California of Texan parents, from those born in Texas. The latter can be meaningfully separated into (b) those who immigrated to Santa Clara County before age 10, and (c) those who immigrated to Santa Clara as young adults. We would expect (a) to be the most acculturated, (b) less, and (c) least. On the other hand, a simple grouping by age might be more revealing: the younger, the greater evidence of assimilation to the majority culture.

C. *Extent of the Use of Spanish*

Sociological and sociolinguistic studies on the Mexican American often employ some kind of index of usage by individuals. It would be helpful to obtain a single score for each subject, expressing the extent of his use of Spanish as compared with English. A 25-point scale was devised by Patella et al,[5] recording information for five types of situations. We have adapted this scale and simplified the scoring to ten points. Since we interviewed subjects individually, it was possible to complete the questioning without use of a questionnaire, and tabulating could be done afterward.

The set of questions used, with scoring indicated for each response, is as follows:

1. (Family) What language do you usually use at home?
   0 English   1 About the same   2 Spanish
                         amount of both
2. (Peers) What language do you usually use in social contacts (neighbors, organizations, etc.)?
   0 English   1 About the same   2 Spanish
                         amount of both
3. (Job) What language do you usually use at work?
   0 English   1 About the same   2 Spanish
                         amount of both
4. (Mass media: listening) How many of the radio and TV programs you listen to are in Spanish?
   0 None   1 Some   2 More than half or all
5. (Mass media: reading) How many of the magazines and newspapers you read are in Spanish?
   0 None   1 Some   2 More than half or all

This allows a maximum potential of ten points, for the subject who uses Spanish most of the time, and a minimum of zero for very restricted usage.

For this study, scoring was still further abbreviated, as explained later. It was assumed that acculturation is negatively associated with the degree of Spanish use.

D. *Occupation and Education.*

Three occupational categories were broadly defined, with the help of scoring used by the U.S. Census Bureau.[6] For this study, examples of the occupations represented in each category are:

Lowest scores, 0-34 (laborers, service workers): sheet metal laborer, beer truck driver, housewife, field laborer, butcher, kitchen worker.

Middle scores, 35-80 (operatives, craftsmen, foremen, clerical, sales): bookkeeper, printer, house painter, auto mechanic apprentice.

Highest scores, above 80 (managers, officials, proprietors, professional, technical): teacher, industrial engineer, draftsman, editor, social worker, electrician.

The assumption was that the acquisition of higher job skills and higher occupational status indicate further acculturation. Higher schooling was assumed to be associated with generalized acculturation in the same direction.

In short, linguistic acculturation, as an aspect of generalized acculturation, might be associated positively with later generation, male sex, higher occupational status, and higher schooling, and negatively with age and the degree of Spanish use.

3. Subjects

The subjects themselves or their parents were all of Texas origin, from south of the Nueces River. A further requirement was that none had studied Spanish formally. More than eighty adult bilinguals were located by word of mouth, through friends and contacts in school districts, organizations, and businesses. Individuals were asked questions regarding place of birth, schooling, etc., in a single session during which the loanword test was also given (see below). Information on subjects was continually reviewed, and when 50 qualified persons had been interviewed, data gathering stopped.

The fifty respondents are described in Figure 1. For the meaning of the code numbers, refer to the Key.

4. Procedure

A. *Loanword Test*

The test consisted of sixty Spanish sentences, forty of which contained loanwords (one per sentence) from the various categories described in section 2.1 (above), and twenty without English loanwords. Four distinct types of loans occurred in ten sentences each: phonological adaptations, morphological adaptations, loan translations and loanshift extensions. Of the remaining twenty sentences, which were standard Spanish, ten contained the deceptive (non-loanword) cognates described under "linguistic variables" above, and ten were without these. The sixty sentences are reproduced in the Appendix.

Test items were randomized and recorded on tape by a native-speaking

Figure 1
Loanword Test Subjects and Subject Variables

Subject	sex	age	gen	use	occ	ed	Subject	sex	age	gen	use	occ	ed
1.	1	1	1	1	2	1	26.	2	1	1	1	2	2
2.	1	1	1	1	3	3	27.	2	1	1	1	3	2
3.	1	1	1	2	3	3	28.	2	1	1	1	3	3
4.	1	1	2	1	2	1	29.	2	1	1	2	2	1
5.	1	1	2	1	3	2	30.	2	1	1	2	3	2
6.	1	1	2	2	2	1	31.	2	1	1	2	3	2
7.	1	1	2	2	3	2	32.	2	1	1	2	3	2
8.	1	1	2	2	3	2	33.	2	1	2	1	2	1
9.	1	1	3	2	2	1	34.	2	1	2	1	3	2
10.	1	2	1	2	3	2	35.	2	1	2	2	2	1
11.	1	2	1	2	3	2	36.	2	1	2	2	2	1
12.	1	2	3	3	2	3	37.	2	1	3	2	2	1
13.	1	2	3	3	2	3	38.	2	2	1	2	3	2
14.	1	2	3	3	3	2	39.	2	2	1	2	3	3
15.	1	2	3	3	3	3	40.	2	2	2	2	1	2
16.	1	2	3	3	3	3	41.	2	2	2	2	1	3
17.	1	3	3	1	1	1	42.	2	2	2	2	3	3
18.	1	3	3	1	2	1	43.	2	2	3	2	3	2
19.	1	3	3	2	1	2	44.	2	2	3	3	3	2
20.	1	3	3	2	1	2	45.	2	2	3	3	3	3
21.	1	3	3	2	1	1	46.	2	2	3	3	3	3
22.	1	3	3	2	1	1	47.	2	3	3	1	3	2
23.	1	3	3	2	1	3	48.	2	3	3	2	1	2
24.	1	3	3	2	2	2	49.	2	3	3	3	3	2
25.	2	1	1	1	2	1	50.	2	3	3	3	3	3

Key: Code numbers indicate the direction expected for the association with linguistic acculturation: 1, highest; 2 and 3, lower. The total number of subjects in each subgroup is given in parentheses.

Variables			*No. of Subjects*
Sex:	1	Male	(24)
	2	Female	(26)
Age:	1	Ages 15 - 25	(22)
	2	Ages 25 - 45	(16)
	3	Ages over 45	(12)

Generation:
	1	Born and raised in San Jose	(15)
	2	Born in south Texas, emigrated between ages 4 - 10	(12)
	3	Born in south Texas, emigrated as adult	(23)

Use of Spanish (see the scoring procedure described above):
	1	Uses Spanish less than half the time (scores 1-3)	(13)
	2	Uses Spanish about half the time (scores 4-6)	(27)
	3	Uses Spanish more than half the time (scores above 6)	(10)

Occupation (see the explanation above):
	1	Highest occupational status scores	(9)
	2	Middle occupational status scores	(15)
	3	Lowest occupational status scores	(26)

Education:
	1	Nine or more years of formal schooling	(14)
	2	Between four and eight years of formal schooling	(21)
	3	Three or fewer years of formal schooling	(15)

graduate student from Monterrey, Nuevo León (northern Mexico). Intelligibility was excellent; there were no comments from subjects concerning voice, dialect, or the playback (cassette, portable Sony TC-100A). On an answer sheet, subjects responded to each item by placing a mark in one of five columns, thus evaluating the stimulus word along the following scale: "Pure Spanish–Mostly Spanish–Half and Half–Mostly English–Certainly English." A copy of the answer form is included in the Appendix.

The following instructions were found adequate for the loanword test:

When I listen to Spanish around here, I hear a lot of words that come, I think, from English. Some of the words sound just like they do in English, but some have been changed a little, to sound more like Spanish. Others were always Spanish words, but now people use them with a new meaning, like 'asistir,' meaning 'assist' instead of 'go to.' On this tape, there are sixty sentences I made up. Some of the sentences are pure Spanish. Some of them have words from English. There will only be one word from English in a sentence like that. Listen for the number, then the sentence. If you think the sentence is all Spanish words, mark 'pure Spanish.' If not, then tell whether it is 'certainly English,' or anything in between.

B. Scoring

The norm used in scoring was intended to reflect speakers' common judgments about borrowings. Thus, in each of the six categories, a response received a score of one when it occurred in either of the columns marked below:

	Spanish	Almost Spanish	Half	Almost English	English
All Spanish	x				
All Spanish, with known cognate	x				
Loanshift Extension		x	x		
Loan Translation		x	x	x	
Morphological Adaptation			x	x	
Phonological Adaptation				x	x

That is, words which are standard Spanish, cognates or not, should be judged as "Spanish." Loanshift extensions are familiar Spanish words in new environments; the same is true of loan translations, except that these consist of more than one word whose order of placement suggests a still closer resemblance to English. Morphological adaptations have English stems, and so they should be felt as closer to English than to Spanish. Most "English" of all are phonological adaptations. Ten points was the possible score in each category, for a grand total of 60.

5. Data Analysis and Results

A. *Subject Variables.*

To test the effects of the non-linguistic variables on subjects' ability to identify borrowings, a one-way analysis of variance with unequal group sample sizes (see Figure 1) was carried out for each category of loan types, using a BMDOIV computer program package.[7]

Table 1 presents the means for male and female groups, as well as the results of the one-way analysis of variance comparing the male and female means for each loan-type category.

TABLE I

Variable: *Sex*

| | Group Means | | Analysis of Variance Results | | |
| | 1 | 2 | Mean Squares | Mean Squares | |
Loan Types	Male	Female	Between Groups	Error	F
Spanish Word	8.6	9.1	2.55	1.66	1.54
Span. w/cognate	7.8	7.4	1.70	4.39	.39
Loanshift	2.8	3.2	2.04	4.25	.48
Loan Trans.	3.1	4.0	9.63	5.10	1.89
Morph. Adapt.	4.4	4.2	.42	8.33	.05
Phon. Adapt.	7.6	5.7	46.46	11.12	4.18*

*Significant at .05, $F(1,48) \geq 4.04$. That is, for a difference to be significant it is necessary for the F ratio to be at least 4.04 at the .05 level of significance, with 1 and 48 degrees of freedom.

It appears that only for a single loan type was the difference in perception of English influence a significant one with regard to sex. In identifying phonologically adapted words as "definitely English," men did significantly better than women.

Table 2 presents means for each of the three age groups, and the results of the one-way analysis of variance for each loan-type category.

It is apparent that at no point do differences in the way these bilinguals group loanwords correspond to differences in age.

In Table 3, we can compare mean scores for each loan type in the three generation groups, and the analysis of variance results.

The mean scores for the various categories here suggest that comparing recent immigrants with native-born residents, it is the recent arrivals who actually do better at each task. In fact, in the identification of "pure Spanish" words, the lead is significant.

Means for the three groups differing in their use of Spanish are presented in Table 4, along with the analysis of variance.

The general tendency across the groups differing in their use of Spanish is also opposite to that expected. Those who use Spanish more seem to do better at sorting words by type of English influence, but only significantly so when it comes to telling which words appear "half and half," or morphologically adapted.

TABLE 2

Variable: *Age*

| | Group Means | | | Analysis of Variance Results | | |
| | **1** | **2** | **3** | **Mean Squares Between** | **Mean Squares** | |
Loan Types	Youngest	Middle	Oldest	Groups	Error	F
Spanish Word	8.5	9.1	9.2	4.10	1.66	1.19
Span. w/cognate	7.1	7.8	8.3	10.16	4.30	1.18
Loanshift	2.5	3.3	3.3	8.32	4.20	.99
Loan Trans.	3.4	4.2	3.0	10.89	5.18	1.05
Morph. Adapt.	3.9	5.3	3.7	22.60	8.03	1.41
Phon. Adapt.	6.3	6.0	7.9	28.90	11.73	1.23

TABLE 3

Variable: *Generation*

	Group Means			Analysis of Variance Results		
	1	**2**	**3**	**Mean Squares**		
	Born	Im. as	Im. as	Between	**Mean Squares**	
Loan Types	San Jose	Child	Adult	Groups	Error	F
Spanish Word	8.1	9.5	9.0	13.29	1.46	4.54*
Span. w/cognate	7.1	7.2	8.1	11.99	4.26	1.41
Loanshift	2.2	3.1	3.4	13.13	4.10	1.60
Loan Trans.	3.5	2.9	3.9	7.16	5.26	.68
Morph. Adapt.	3.3	3.8	5.2	38.98	7.68	2.54
Phon. Adapt.	5.3	7.1	7.1	33.32	11.64	1.43

*Significant at .05, $F(2,47) \geq 3.20$.

TABLE 4

Variable: *Use of Spanish*

	Group Means			Analysis of Variance Results		
	1	**2**	**3**	**Mean Squares**		
	Least		Most	Between	**Mean Squares**	
Loan Types	Use	Half	Use	Groups	Error	F
Spanish Word	8.7	8.9	9.1	.94	1.73	.27
Span. w/cognate	7.2	7.4	8.6	12.77	4.24	1.51
Loanshift	2.5	2.7	4.2	19.46	3.97	2.45
Loan Trans.	3.0	3.7	3.8	5.19	5.30	.49
Morph. Adapt.	2.5	4.6	5.6	60.15	7.23	4.16*
Phon. Adapt.	7.0	6.7	5.6	12.59	12.08	.52

*Significant at .05, $F(2,47) \geq 3.20$.

Table 5 gives the means for the three occupational status groups as well as results of the analysis of variance.

TABLE 5

Variable: *Occupation*

| Loan Types | Group Means | | | Analysis of Variance Results | | |
	1 High Status	2 Med Status	3 Low Status	Mean Squares Between Groups	Mean Squares Error	F
Spanish Word	9.2	8.6	8.9	2.21	1.70	.65
Span. w/cognate	7.4	7.3	7.8	3.46	4.44	.39
Loanshift	3.3	2.3	3.2	10.37	4.16	1.25
Loan Trans.	3.6	4.2	3.2	10.41	5.19	1.00
Morph. Adapt.	3.4	5.5	3.9	31.47	7.84	2.00
Phon. Adapt.	8.3	7.7	5.3	84.96	10.54	4.03*

*Significant at .05, $F(2,47) \geq 3.20$.

Only when these bilinguals are confronted with the most minor deviations from English, i.e. phonological adaptations, do achievement groups form corresponding to occupational status. This variable has no effect on the other scores.

Means and analysis of variance results for the three educational groups are shown in Table 6.

Amount of time spent in school has no effect on the awareness of English influence except, again, in identifying phonological adaptations.

Summarizing to this point, we have seen that higher acculturation, as defined here, is associated with higher scores on the loanword test in only a single category: phonological adaptations. Moreover, this is significant in only three of the subject variables: sex, occupation and education.

TABLE 6

Variable: *Education*

| Loan Types | Group Means | | | Analysis of Variance Results | | |
	9 yrs. or more	4-8 yrs.	3 yrs. or less	Mean Squares Between Groups	Mean Squares Error	F
Spanish Word	8.6	9.0	8.9	.92	1.73	.27
Span. w/cognate	6.9	7.9	7.9	10.78	4.28	1.26
Loanshift	2.5	3.0	3.4	5.87	4.26	.69
Loan Trans.	4.4	3.4	2.9	15.13	5.09	1.49
Morph. Adapt.	4.7	3.9	4.4	5.81	8.39	.35
Phon. Adapt.	8.6	5.7	5.9	77.53	10.69	3.62*

*Significant at .05, $F(2,47) \geq 3.20$.

B. Linguistic Variables.

We will now turn from subject variables and consider linguistic differences in loan types as the source of variance in performance on the test.

As illustrated in Tables 1-6, practically no variance is accounted for by differences between subgroups defined within each of the six social variables. For the group as a whole, however, a glance at any one of these will reveal a striking consistency in the relative sensitivity to English in each of the loan types. Disregarding social factors now, we can compute mean scores for all subjects together, for each subtest ("pure Spanish words," "loanshifts," etc.). These are plotted in Figure 2.

FIGURE 2.

Mean Scores for All 50 Subjects in Each Loan Type Subtest

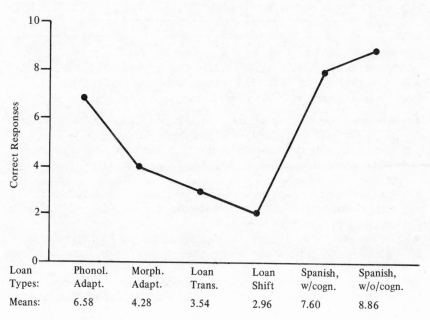

Loan Types:	Phonol. Adapt.	Morph. Adapt.	Loan Trans.	Loan Shift	Spanish, w/cogn.	Spanish, w/o/cogn.
Means:	6.58	4.28	3.54	2.96	7.60	8.86

By means of a statistical procedure known as orthogonal comparisons,[8] we may now ask which of the loan types are significant sources of variability. This technique allows us to ask specific questions regarding the linguistic effects of each of the loan types on the awareness of English influence. It is possible, from a linguistic point of view, to group together those types deviating least from Spanish and English (native words, phonological adaptations) under the label "pure" types, apart from those perceived as "mixed" (morphological adaptations, loan translations and loanshifts). The reader will note that the mean scores in Figure 2 were reordered in Table 7, according to these linguistic groupings. Table 7 also presents the contrast coefficients being used for each of the five orthogonal questions.

TABLE 7

Means and Contrast Coefficients For Orthogonal Questions
Concerning Linguistic Effects of Loan Types

		"Pure" Types			"Mixed" Types	
		Spanish Words		English Words (phonol. adapted)	English Form and Meaning (morphol. adapted)	English Meaning Only	
		without cognates	with cognates			Loan Trans.	Loan Shift
Mean:		8.86	7.60	6.58	4.28	3.54	2.96
Contrast Coefficients	L1	1	1	1	-1	-1	-1
	L2	-1	-1	2	0	0	0
	L3	-1	1	0	0	0	0
	L4	0	0	0	2	-1	-1
	L5	0	0	0	0	-1	1

The overall significant variability attributable to loan types has been broken down into single degree of freedom orthogonal comparisons (L1, L2, etc.). The five orthogonal questions we are asking are:

L1: Are those loan types which are grouped here as "pure" significantly easier to identify as to English influence, than the "mixed" types?

L2: Concerning only the "pure" items for both languages, is there a significant difference in the confidence with which bilinguals assign them to their respective languages?

L3: Concerning only the "Spanish words," is there a difference between the recognition as "Spanish" a word without a "deceptive cognate" in English, and that of a word with a cognate?

L4: Within the "mixed" types, is the recognition of English influence in morphological adaptations easier than that in loan translations and loanshifts?

L5: Concerning loanshifts and loan translation, which adopt only English meaning and not form, is either of them more "anglicized" than the other from the users' point of view?

The answers to each of these questions are summarized in Table 8.

6. Conclusions

Four of the five orthogonal questions are shown in Table 8 to be significant sources of variability. More specifically, the data show clearly that:

Native words, and English words transferred to Spanish by mere phonological adaptation, are indeed more easily recognized with respect to English influence than the "mixed" loan types. (L1)

Within the perceptually more "pure" types, pure native words (with and without English cognates) are significantly more easily recognized as Spanish than are phonologically adapted borrowings recognized as English. (L2)

TABLE 8

*Analysis of Variance Including the Partitioning of Linguistic
Variable Source (L) into Five Single Degrees
of Freedom Orthogonal Questions*

	Source	Degrees of Freedom	Sum of Squares	Mean Square	F Ratio
	Lingusitic Variables (L)	(5)	(1,426.78)	285.36	47.94**
L1:	"Pure" vs. "Mixed" Types	1	1,252.60	1,252.60	210.52**
L2:	"Pure Spanish" vs.				
	"Pure English"	1	90.73	90.73	15.25**
L3:	Spanish: with vs.				
	without cognate	1	39.75	39.75	6.68*
L4:	Morph. Adapt. vs. L.				
	Trans. & Shifts	1	35.30	35.30	5.93*
L5:	Translations vs. Shifts	1	8.50	8.50	1.43
Individual Differences		49	276.23	5.64	.95
Error		245	1,458.33	5.95	

*Significant at .05 level.
**Significant at .01 level; .01, F (5,200) $\geq$ 3.11; .05, F (1,200) $\geq$ 3.89; .01, F (1,200) $\geq$ 6.75; .05, F (50,200) $\geq$ 1.41.

The existence of cognates in English appears to interfere significantly with the recognition of native words as "pure Spanish." (L3)

Within "mixed" types, an English influence involving form and meaning is more easily recognized as English than an influence affecting meaning only. (L4)

No significant difference appears between the recognition of English influence in loanshifts and loan translations. (L5)

It is also interesting to note that none of the variation in bilingual judgment was due to differences between subjects. In fact, individual differences are not a significant source of variability (see Table 8). Thus, it seems clear that linguistic differences between the various loan types we have examined account quite heavily for the differences in speakers' awareness of English influence. The second of the two assumptions stated in the introduction, concerning the importance of linguistic differences, was confirmed, but not the first, concerning social differences. These findings are in agreement with those of Haugen for bilingual *usage,* in Norwegian. He reports finding "a high degree of uniformity of practice with respect to the adoption of English materials."[9] Similarly, we can report a high degree of uniformity in the bilinguals' awareness of borrowing.

It should be stressed again that it is neither the speakers' evaluative responses nor actual usage that we have been concerned with here, but with the cognitive awareness of borrowing. What is suggested by the results is that regardless of how much bilinguals differ in their use of Spanish (as long as they use it), or in age, education or other social variables which may reflect acculturation to the larger society, their bilingual competence is about the same where the awareness of English influence in the lexicon is concerned. The curve shown in Figure 2, which expresses how well just about everyone does at sorting loan types, is one profile of this competence.

Notes

[1] This research was carried out while the first author held a Ford Foundation Dissertation Fellowship in Ethnic Studies. The computational work was done by the second author.

[2] An investigation of bilingual norms in the *use* of borrowed words is included in Einar Haugen's *The Norwegian Language in America,* Vol. I, pp. 60-61.

[3] For example, see Fernando Peñalosa et al, "A Socio-economic Class Typology of Mexican-Americans," *Sociological Inquiry* XXXVI, 1 (Winter, 1966), 19-30.

[4] William Madsen, *Mexican-Americans of South Texas* (New York: Holt, Rinehart and Winston, 1965), p. 20.

[5] V. M. Patella et al, "Language Patterns of Mexican Americans: Are the Ambitious Un-Mexican?" Unpublished paper, Texas A&M University, 1970, p. 6.

[6] *Methodology and Scores of Socioeconomic Status,* U.S. Bureau of the Census, Working Paper No. 15 (Washington: G.P.O., 1963).

[7] Wilfred J. Dixon, ed., *Biomedical Computer Programs* (Berkeley: University of Calif. Press, 1968), pp. 486-94.

[8] Roger E. Kirk, *Experimental Design Procedures for the Behavior Sciences* (Belmont: Wadsworth, 1968), pp. 69-82.

[9] Haugen, *loc. cit.*

References

Agheyisi, Rebecca and Joshua A. Fishman. "Language Attitude Studies: A Brief Survey of Methodological Approaches," *Anthropological Linguistics* (May, 1970), 137-57.

Beltramo, Anthony F. *Lexical and Morphological Aspects of Linguistic Acculturation by Mexican Americans in San Jose, California.* Unpublished Ph.D. dissertation, Stanford University, 1972.

Dixon, Wilfrid J., ed. *Biomedical Computer Programs.* Berkeley: University of California Press, 1968.

Haugen, Einar. *The Norwegian Language in America: A Study in Bilingual Behavior.* Reprinted, Bloomington: Indiana University Press, 1969. 2 vols.

Kirk, Roger E. *Experimental Design Procedures for the Behavioral Sciences.* Belmont: Wadsworth, 1968.

Madsen, William. *Mexican-Americans of South Texas.* New York: Holt, Rinehart and Winston, 1965.

Patella, Victoria M. and William P. Kuvlesky. "Language Patterns of Mexican Americans: Are the Ambitious Un-Mexican?" Paper presented at the annual Rural Sociological Society meetings. Texas A&M University, 1970.

Peñalosa, Fernando and Edward C. McDonagh. "A Socio-economic Class Typology of Mexican-Americans," *Sociological Inquiry* XXXVI, 1 (Winter, 1966), 19-30.

U.S. Bureau of the Census. *Methodology and Scores of Socioeconomic Status.* Working Paper No. 15. Washington: Government Printing Office, 1963.

Appendix

Loanword Test

Test items.

1. El pasaje de ida y vuelta es muy caro. (F)*
2. Carlos buscó una silla y se sentó. (F)
3. Van a cantar en el *hall* de la escuela. (A)
4. Mi hermana quiere trabajar como *taipista*. (B)
5. Es el único salón de belleza, pero tiene seis *operadoras*. (D)
6. Mi abuela nos hizo una *cuilta* bonita. (B)
7. La tienda está cerrada para *remodelar*. (C)
8. Nos echó uno de sus *espiches*. (A)
9. Hay tres cuartos con *tapetes de pared a pared*. (C)
10. Quiere que su *yarda* sea la mas bonita de la calle. (C)
11. ¿Tienen Uds. unas *questiones*? (D)
12. Estuvimos solos por tres horas. (F)
13. Le ofrecieron un *shower* en casa de sus padres. (A)
14. Llamé, y me abrieron la puerta. (F)
15. Este clima es muy *conveniente* para él. (E)
16. ¿Cuándo te *blicheaste* el pelo? (B)
17. José es el *manejador* de nuestro conjunto. (C)
18. Es un cuento casi sin *argumento*. (E)
19. Andrés es muy alto para su edad. (F)
20. De vez en cuando compro cosas en esa *marqueta*. (B)
21. Su hijo va a la *escuela alta*. (C)
22. ¿Cuáles de los candidatos estan *corriendo* todavia? (D)
23. Devolvió el dinero sin decir nada. (F)
24. Este *highway* es muy peligroso. (A)
25. No es rica, pero gasta mucho dinero. (F)
26. Mi tía nos *congratuló* de la comida. (E)
27. ¿Ha venido el cartero? (F)
28. Luego llegaron Roberto y su *mejor mitad*. (C)
29. El lunes me van a *interviuar* para un empleo. (B)
30. Elena es muy *sensible* a los cambios de clima. (E)
31. En este pueblo a las once de la noche no hay nadie en las calles. (F)
32. Rafael y yo *atendemos* a la misma escuela. (D)
33. A mí me gusta el chorizo *home made*. (A)
34. El trabaja muy poco por su *disabilidad*. (C)
35. María se va a *registrar* en esa escuela. (D)
36. Este libro puede *influenciar* a Juan. (B)
37. Su padre fue un magnífico cantante *amateur*. (A)
38. El niño necesita enseñanza *remedial*. (C)
39. He oído contar esa *historia* mil veces. (E)
40. Hay tres o cuatro *individuales* que no han pagado todavía. (D)
41. Quiero limpiar mis *clósets* este fin de semana. (A)

*See Key at End of Loanword Test.

42. Los *aplicantes* calificados pueden pedir dinero prestado. (C)
43. Me gustan estos encuentros *ocasionales*. (E)
44. Manuel no quiso comer, porque no tenía *apetito*. (E)
45. Dejemos esto para después, porque ya tengo sueño. (F)
46. El postre fue un sabroso *keik*. (A)
47. En esta ciudad los muchachos se juntan en *gangas*. (D)
48. El Sr. Torres trabaja en una *canería*. (B)
49. Lo quiso vender en un *mercado de la pulga*. (C)
50. Mi hermana tiene muy buena *letra*. (E)
51. La casa es vieja pero tiene *carpetas* nuevas. (D)
52. Tuvieron una *discusión* sobre la propina. (E)
53. Las más baratas son llantas *recapeadas*. (B)
54. Dice que lo compró *cash*. (A)
55. Roberto está *determinado* a ganar. (E)
56. ¿Cuál es la opinión de la *mayoridad*? (C)
57. Ellos quieren que yo vaya a la universidad, pero no me dan la *soporta*. (D)
58. Mañana podemos comprar los *tíketes* para el baile. (A)
59. Dicen que José va a *cuitear* su trabajo. (B)
60. Mi padre me dió una *lectura* porque llegué muy tarde. (D)

Key:
A. "An English Word"
B. "A word part English-part Spanish"
C. "A Spanish word that translates an English word"
D. "A Spanish word being used a new (wrong) way"
E. "A cognate, but used correctly in Spanish"
F. "Acceptable Spanish"

RESPONSE SHEET FOR LOANWORD TEST

	puro ESPAÑOL	casi español	mitad y mitad	casi inglés	cierta- mente INGLÉS		puro ESPAÑOL	casi español	mitad y mitad	casi inglés	cierta- mente INGLÉS
1						31					
2						32					
3						33					
4						34					
5						35					
6						36					
7						37					
8						38					
9						39					
10						40					
11						41					
12						42					
13						43					
14						44					
15						45					
16						46					
17						47					
18						48					
19						49					
20						50					
21						51					
22						52					
23						53					
24						54					
25						55					
26						56					
27						57					
28						58					
29						59					
30						60					

Spanish-English Code Switching

Donald M. Lance

One of the fascinating phenomena in the linguistic behavior of true bilinguals in all parts of the world is the tendency to switch from one language to the other in the middle of a sentence. It occurs primarily in relaxed social settings where the speakers are aware that the other members of the conversation group have a good speaking knowledge of both languages. As will be shown by examples below, the language switching does not occur simply because the speaker does not know a particular word in one language or the other; rather the word or phrase that is most readily available at the moment for some usually unexplainable reason is the one that comes out. Nor is there a distinct tendency for the shifting to go in one direction rather than the other, though when only one word from the other language is used it is most often an English word in a Spanish sentence.

In the first part of this discussion, only the language of the two women will be considered; the children's language will be treated later in the paper. The discussion will be largely anecdotal, treating three general types of switching, in the following order:

1. Single words or terms inserted into a sentence
   a. Quasi-technical terms
   b. Brand names
   c. Place names
   d. Personal names
   e. Tag questions
   f. Interjections, adverbs, etc.
   g. Numbers
2. Longer phrases or clauses
   a. Spanish to English
   b. English to Spanish
   c. Spanish to English to Spanish
   d. English to Spanish to English
3. Quotations
   a. Spanish introductions to English quotations
   b. Quotations with switching within them

One of the most common uses of English words in otherwise Spanish sentences is the adoption of what might be termed quasi-technical terminology,

---

Reprinted, with minor revisions, by permission of Texas A&M University from Donald M. Lance, *A Brief Study of Spanish-English Bilingualism: Final Report, Research Project ORR-Liberal Arts-15504*, Texas A&M University, August 25, 1969. See the Introductory Note in "Dialectal and Nonstandard Forms in Texas Spanish" in this volume for a brief description of the informants in this study.

words that have specialized uses in American culture or technology. Often the word is adapted morphologically and becomes at least temporarily a loan word, such as *troca* (truck), *diche* (ditch), *pompa* (pump), *paipa* (pipe), *queque* (cake), etc., but there are others that phonologically and morphologically appear to be simply English words used in Spanish sentences, as in the following examples:

(1) MOTH: ¿ Sabes componer *flats*? [flaets]
(2) NEIGH: Pero cuando tienen que hacer muchos, y tienen ese— ¿ cómo se nombra?—piece work, . . .
(3) MOTH: Más antes yo antes de trabajar sí les hacía *pies*.
(4) FATH: A mediodía, pos, uno podía comer *hamburgers*.
(5) NEIGH: Ya lo compra mixteado.
       MOTH: No, nomás la *filling*. La *pie crust* la hago con harina, manteca, y poquita espauda y sal. Y luego la meringue la hago con . . . los *egg whites* . . . la clara.

Some of these terms can be translated into Spanish rather easily, as in the use of *trabajo por pedazo* (which was also used earlier in the same conversation) and the recently adopted *hamburguesas* for *hamburgers*, but the word *pasteles* may not fully suffice for *pies* since it also applies to cakes, and there does not appear to be a word for *flat* except for recent coinages such as *puntura, ponche,* etc.—at least no single word has been included in recent editions of bilingual dictionaries available to the author. The terms in (5) also could be translated, but with some loss in specificity. In each of these words the phonology used was that of English, though produced with the speaker's own particular accent.

Spanish words used in English sentences were limited largely to such terms as *tortilla, enchilada,* and *taco,* for which there are no equivalent terms in English. The speakers, however, occasionally pronounced Spanish words with some English phonology (e.g., with a retroflex [r] and a final [ə] in *tortilla* and with a slightly aspirated [t'] in *taco*). When one considers the implication of the cultural dominance in the area, this contrast is not surprising. Other terms have near equivalents in English which could be used but usually are not. *Chile* can be translated as *pepper,* but references to *chile* in Mexican cookery would include only certain kinds of pepper. Likewise, the English word *hamburger* does not have a culturally equivalent term in Spanish. On a different, but still cultural topic, we always used the term *curandero* because *witch doctor* has connotations that do not apply to the South Texas *curandero.* (The second generation in this discussion disclaimed having faith in *curanderos,* though they commented that the older generations still depend on them. There are no *curanderos* in Bryan, they reported.)

Many individual words and terms receive ambivalent treatment because they are not always translatable. For instance, Lupe said,

(6) MOTH: Vivo 'horita en siete . . . seven hundred por la *Lucky Street,*
with a burst of nervous laughter as she switched to English for the numbers, but her husband, with a little less hesitation, but some nervous laughter said,

(7) FATH: Vivo en . . . este . . . sieto cero cero *Lucky.*

Both pronounced the street name with the English vowel [ə ˌ], and by no means would either have translated the street to "La Calle de la Suerte." Though neither of the women used *calle*, the mother consistently used the feminine article with street names, as when she was explaining the location of a bakery:

(8) MOTH: . . . en la *Bryan* (Street) . . . al otro lado del del *A&P* . . .

with both *Bryan* and *A&P* receiving standard English pronunciation. Occasionally the switching back and forth between the phonology of Spanish and English caused problems, as shown in this short exchange in which both trade names and quasi-technical terms are used.

(9) NEIGH: ¿ La . . . la marca?
     MOTH: La *Betty Crocker*.
     NEIGH: Ay, tú! (Laughter) Veces la *Hines*.
     MOTH: *Pillsburr* . . . (laughs) Ya no podía hablar.
     CARM: Ya se trabó la lengua.
     MOTH: No, este . . . a mí me gustó los queques así . . . de cajita.
     CARM: A mí me gustan porque son rápidos.
     NEIGH: Están más sabrosos . . . están más sabrosos los *homemades*.

The names of cities, unlike street names, often are translatable since so many of them are Spanish in origin. In referring to *San Antonio* and *San Benito* the speakers sometimes said them in English and sometimes in Spanish (including *San Antone*), regardless of which language the sentence was in. For other names, such as *Bryan* and *Houston*, the usual Spanish pronunciation would not be appreciably different from the pronunciation in English with a Spanish accent, but others such as *Caldwell* are not easily adapted to Spanish phonology. None of these names are ordinarily changed much from the English pronunciation. The most interesting exchange regarding place names occurred with the grandparents, who understandably would have more difficulty in adapting place names to English pronunciation. The grandmother said that she was born in *'l Hondo*, with the reduced proclitic article. I perceived it as *Londo* or perhaps *London* but knew of no such town in South Texas. Her husband, who knows more English, clarified the matter by saying it in English, "Hondo City," using the English pronunciation [hando] without the Spanish article. The article is not included in the official name of the town, though Spanish-speaking citizens apparently use *El Hondo* for both the town and the river by that name. The grandfather said that they also had lived in Jourdanton, pronounced [jeᵈn̩tən], which I could not understand until I realized that he had used a predictable phonological translation of the rather interesting pronunciation used by the English-speaking citizens of the town: [jə̆dn̩tən].

The pronunciation of personal names also receives ambivalent treatment, as does the naming of children in families that are becoming anglicized. The names of the third-generation informants in this project are Rachel, Tom, Richard, Mollie, and Janie, the latter from a family across the street. As the mother talked about her older daughter, she sometimes said *Rachel* [réčəl] and sometimes *Raquel* [řàkél], and the final vowel in Mollie's name was sometimes the tense Spanish [i] and sometimes the lax English vowel [I], the latter with the appropriate vowel and [i] in the root syllable. Likewise, the younger boy was sometimes called *Richard* and sometimes *Ricardo*, whether he was present or simply the topic of conversation—regardless of the language being used. The mother also used several different forms for the name of her husband:[soteɾo], [sətɛro], [teɾo], [teᵊro], and [tɛrɪ]. (The [r] here indicates a retroflex English *r* and the [ɾ] the flapped Spanish *r*.) The neighbor when speaking English pronounced her name [gǽᵊlvéᵊz], but [gálβes] in Spanish conversations. No attempt was made in this study to explore the psychological implications of the use of both language systems in the use of personal names, though perhaps it should be mentioned that one cannot assume that any particular individual responds the same to, for instance, *Richard* and *Ricardo*. For example, if an individual's name is *Ricardo* and he identifies very strongly with Mexican-American culture and has certain anxieties regarding anglicization (or de-hispanicization), he may resent having a teacher or even his parents call him *Richard*—even more Anglo, *Rick* or *Rickey*.

Often the additional word from the other language is a simple phrase like a tag question, interjection, adverb, or false start, as in these:

(10) MOTH: I mean, I can't drive standard, *¿tú?* (meaning a car with standard transmission)
(11) NEIGH: Oh, they make like invitations and all that, *¿ no?*
(12) NEIGH: It's about the same, *¿ no?*
(13) MOTH: *Pero, . . . este . . .* I'm so tired on Fridays, *que ¡ij!*
(14) MOTH: *Pues,* yeah, I want to go.
(15) MOTH: *Pos* they didn't know who it was.
(16) NEIGH: *Pos* if you want something good, that's the way to make 'em.
(17) NEIGH: *Since . . .* como a gusta, este, sí.
(18) NEIGH: *Pero . . .* what I think about that is they're way out there.
(19) NEIGH: *Y . . . y . . .* and you've seen 'em in things, you know.

The switching process is not always instantaneous and complete, however; in (18), for example, the speaker pronounced *pero* with a strong Texan English accent, including a diphthongized [ɛᵊ], a retroflex [r], and an off-glide at the end of the word.

Rather often brief little English phrases carrying little semantic information are inserted into Spanish sentences:

(20) MOTH: Porque perdió un libro que resultó rompido, *or something like that.*
(21) NEIGH: Hay unos que son muy—cómo se dice—muy rancheros *or something.*
(22) MOTH: *I mean* cuando voy a comprar algo, al pueblo, . . . I don't like to take them with me.
(23) NEIGH: *I think,* yo gasto más gas en ir pa' 'llá a camprar esa cosa barata.
(24) NEIGH: *I mean,* si hay una persona que no puede hablar inglés, tengo que hablarlo.
(25) NEIGH: [El padre] quiere hablar español, pero—*I mean,* mejicano—pero habla más como hablan en España que aquí.

No such Spanish expressions were used in English sentences, though it would not have been surprising if an occasional *y todo eso, tú sabes,* or *este* were to be interjected into English sentences, since they occurred so often in Spanish sentences.

Many of the lapses into English in otherwise Spanish sentences are related to the fact that certain terms, in addition to the quasi-technical expressions mentioned earlier, are used most often in situations that call for English. The street address in (6) is one such example. There is ample evidence in the tapes that the informants knew the numbers in Spanish, because when talking about such topics as the number of children in the family, there was no hesitation in producing them, and the children did some counting. The following examples reveal the tendency to think of prices in English, though they also can be expressed in Spanish very easily:

(26) NEIGH: I think yo gasto más gas en ir pa' 'llá a comprar esa cosa barata cuando podía comprarla aquí.

     MOTH: And then you can buy it here for two or three pennies más.

    NEIGH: Maybe two-three pennies more, but you usates más pa' ir pa' 'llá. I think you use more than two pennies or three pennies worth of gas.

(27) MOTH: En la tienda trae un paquetita por . . . I think it's seventeen.

(28) MOTH: Las tortillas [de la tortillería] se los venden en. . .let's see, I think it's a dozen for fifteen, las las dos docenas por thirty. En el paquete. . . .En las tiendas están más caro. Me parece diecisiete o dieciocho.

(29) MOTH: La otra vez me hizo que comprara un roast asina grandote. Costó como four something.

Other examples of dependence on English numbers were found but not in large enough quantity to indicate a distinct tendency.

(30) NEIGH: Fíjate, yo me levanto a las cuatro de la ma . . . cuatro . . . four thirty.

(31) MOTH: Bajé yo creo, como ten pounds.

In many sentences much longer phrases or clauses from the two languages occur. The scope of this paper is not broad enough to allow for a detailed analysis of the interplay between the two grammatical systems in these sentences, though it would be both possible and desirable to do so; instead only a few representative samples will be given here, in four groups—Spanish-to-English (32-35), English-to-Spanish (36-42), Spanish-to-English-to-Spanish (43-45), and English-to-Spanish-to-English (46-47):

(32) NEIGH: Como digo, they don't try.

(33) MOTH: Te digo que este dedo has been bothering me so much.

(34) MOTH: A Sotero le gusta mucho cocinar barbecue every Sunday . . . every Saturday.

(35) MOTH: Entonces me dijeron que la pusiera una en el cuarto, pa' que it'd get rid of the dust or todo eso.
(36) MOTH: I think I was mopping y me pegué asina.
(37) MOTH: It doesn't matter if you tore it or . . . o lo que haigas hecho.
(38) MOTH: When, you know, I buy one que tiene hueso.
(39) MOTH: Oh, I mean, you can buy the [taco] shells ya ya hechas asina.
(40) NEIGH: But this arthritis deal, boy, you get to hurtin' so bad you can't hardly even . . . 'cer masa pa' tortillas.
(41) NEIGH: ¿Are you sure que hay asina, porque pos no en todos hay?
(42) MOTH: Just when they get shoes or les voy a comprar vestido o algo asina, 'tonces sí los llevo.
(43) MOTH: Se me hace que I have to respect her porque 'tá . . . (older).
(44) NEIGH: Le saco la semilla esa y se le echa el hamburger meat y el queso y todo eso y you let 'em fry real slow en . . . en el sartén.
(45) MOTH: Y en ratos me dan ganas de pop up and dicir, "Ay . . . ."
(46) NEIGH: Yeah, but I buy 'em mostly pa' 'l hamburger meat.
(47) MOTH: Yeah, and one thing about them . . . les gusta tochar todo, and I'm afraid they're gonna break it and I don't have enough money to pay for it.

The variety found in these sixteen citations suggests that there are perhaps no syntactic restrictions on where the switching can occur, for it takes place in the following environments:
1. In compound structures
    a. compound sentences: before (36,47) or after (42,44) the conjunction, or with the conjunction repeated (37)
    b. compound sentence elements: before (44) or after (45) the conjunction
2. Between major syntactic elements
    a. between the subject and the verb (33)
    b. between the verb and the complement (34,41)
    c. between a noun and post-posed modifier (38,39)
    d. between adverbial clauses or phrases and the main clause (32, 35, 43, 44)
    e. between the verb and an adverb of place (46)
3. Within major syntactic groups
    a. between the article and the noun (44, 46)
    b. between the auxiliary and the main verb (40)
    c. after a preposition (45)
    d. after a subordinating conjunction (35, 43)
The reader will recall from the preceding discussion that the primary criterion for considering these to be examples of switching rather than borrowing is that, for example in *hamburger meat* in (44), the phonology, morphology, and syntax are basically English.

Another interesting instance of switching within longer segments occurs in quotations. When the conversation was in English, both the introduction and the quotation itself were in English, but in conversations with switching the introduction was often in Spanish and the quotation usually in the language used by the persons being quoted:

(48) MOTH: Dice, "Ay," dice, "you're gonna hit it . . . ." He says I'm a
            reckless driver. Le digo, "I don't think so." I mean, I just drive
            the normal way I'd drive to College Station.

(49) NEIGH: Les dije yo, l'ije, "Well, if she has to pay for it, you let me know
            and I'll pay for it."

When we were using either English or code switching, the neighbor said both the
introductions and the quotations in English and said both in Spanish during the
Spanish conversation, but in the Spanish interview with Carmen she produced
the following rather interesting passage:

(50) NEIGH: Y una vez me dijo mi chamaca, dijo, "Mami, you go there, order
            me a hamburger basket deluxe." "Are you sure que hay asina,
            porque pos no en todos hay?" Dijo, "Si, nomás diles que quieres
            un hamburger basket deluxe."

The mother tended to translate the quotation into Spanish when we were
speaking either Spanish or both languages, but she also produced these
interesting passages:

(51) MOTH: Y luego dice, "Has he been eating' good?" y le dije, "no," y luego
            dice " ¿Por qué no lo llevas a this lady que cura eso?"

(52) MOTH: Y luego le dije, "No, Patty," pues este, "get your mother . . . .,"
            le dije and, I mean, "Si vas a ir a la escuela," I mean . . . . "Pues,
            yeah, I wanna go." 'Tonces salió eso que she wanted to take
            mechanic.

(53) MOTH: Y luego las huercas ahi besándose enfrente. Y le dije, "Mira,
            Rachel, that's what I don't want to bring you," . . . este . . .
            "porque mira si vienes tú sola," le dije, " ¿ cómo andarás tú
            también?"

There were no instances of an English introduction to a Spanish quotation in the
data collected.

As one can see by observing the preceding examples, the reason for switching
from one language to the other is apparently not motivated by gaps in the
vocabulary of the speaker. Sufficient evidence was found to indicate that the
speaker knew the appropriate words in both languages and simply produced the
one that was closest to the tip of the tongue. On a number of occasions they
produced both expressions within the same or subsequent utterances—perhaps
suggestive of stylistic implications. There are twelve such instances in the
mother's speech and four in the neighbor's. Also there were many other
instances in which there is overt evidence that the two women knew both the
Spanish and English expressions, but only a few examples will be treated in
detail here.

In a conversation about different ways to prepare beans, we had been talking
in both languages and had used both *frijoles* and *beans*. When I asked, in English,
about the expression "refried beans," the following exchange took place:

(54) DL: Do you ever say "refried beans"?
     MOTH: Refritos.
     DL: Refritos.
     NEIGH: Um huh. Um huh. Les gustan más.
     MOTH: Yo . . . yo cuando hago *refritos beans,* . . .

Not only the word itself but also the placement and concordance restrictions in
the use of the adjective became involved, though *beans* for some reason was
pronounced with Spanish phonology.

Several times the mother produced the word in one language and immediately
thereafter repeated it in the other.

(55) MOTH: It's his . . . ¿ cómo se dice?
     NEIGH: Nephew.
     MOTH: Sobrino. Nephew.
(56) MOTH: Hay a pasearse por los . . . pa' 'l colegio, de *just driving.*
                  Paseándose.
(57) MOTH: It's *real* easy. 'Tá *bien* easy.
(58) MOTH: No, eso lo compro de *cajita.* Es una *little box* asina y ya
                  viene . . . .

In three instances she inserted an expression like *tú sabes*:

(59) MOTH: Parece que los tapaba pa' que se . . . el vapor . . . que se les cayera
                  el *skin*, el, tú sabes, *cuerito.*
(60) MOTH: Pos la mitad de él lo hice come en *slice*, tú sabes, en *rebanadas.*
(61) MOTH: Y luego los metía ahi y luego en la fat . . . en la *grease* . . . tú
                  sabes, en la *manteca* y quedan bien tostadas.

One might be tempted to assume that in these sentences the *tú sabes* is a hint
that the speaker was asking for confirmation of her choice of words, but since
the intonation was very much like that of the current *you know* in English, this
interpretation is rather doubtful. In a couple of other sentences she inserted
questions that appear more clearly to be asking for confirmation, but the
intonation used was also like that used for *tú sabes*. A more plausible
explanation is that she was searching through her personal lexicon for the one
word that would carry the narrowest or most precise range of semantic
information in order to satisfy her (subconscious) assessment of the range of her
auditors' lexicons.

(62) MOTH: Lo hago con los *egg whites* . . . la *clara* . . . ¿Cómo le dicen a los
                  blanquillos?
(63) MOTH: Qué comidas! Puro *atole* me dieron, atole de . . . de . . . ¿ cómo
                  se llama?. . . ese *soup* de avena, "cream and wheat" que le dice
                  ella, y el . . . este . . . me dieron este . . . *soup* . . . y . . . puros
                  caldos.

In (63) the ellipses indicate pauses. Since *atole* is a Nahuatl borrowing for porridge, or cornmeal mush, it is an appropriate word for *cream of wheat*, but since there is no common term in English for cream of wheat, oatmeal, etc. in popular use in this area, the mother was "at a loss for words" in describing the liquid diet that she had received during a recent stay in the hospital. At the time, she was talking only with Carmen and the neighbor, both of whom knew *atole*. There was one very interesting instance in which the interviewer pretended not to understand the English expression and got an immediate translation, though the English words were still closest to the tip of her tongue:

(64) MOTH: Yo le echo muchos short cuts.
     CARM: ¿ Mucha qué?
     MOTH: Muchos *short cuts . . . travesías.*

The neighbor's bilingual repetitions are very much like the mother's, though she used fewer, with this contrast paralleling the number of Spanish words used in the mixed conversations (1492:12::484:4, or approximately 120:1). Three of the repetitions occurred in the same utterance:

(65) NEIGH: Más *chicken* y turkey asina. *Pollo.*
(66) NEIGH: But what I usually buy are those thick ones, las más *gruesas.*
(67) NEIGH: You know, *fry* that, y luego . . . guisar los frijoles en ese.

In the fourth instance about a minute of conversation intervened between her use of the last expressions:

(68) Ella iba por su 'pelativo antes que se casara.
   . . .   .
   Asina de . . . en lugar de . . . nomás el *last name.*

In two instances the two women produced the two expressions in response to the same question:

(69) CARM: Pastel sí, ¿pero de qué?
     NEIGH: *Lemon* . . . the most.
     MOTH: Andale, a Sotero le gusta tanto el *limón.*
(70) NEIGH: I mean, she sounds different than us.
     CARM: ¿Diferente?
     MOTH: Sí, porque ella está *educada* y . . . .
     NEIGH: Muy *educated* y nosotros pobremente . . . .

It may have occurred to the reader that well over half of the preceding examples are from the same speaker. This fact reflects the relative amount of English and Spanish that the two speakers used, and the contrast also might be interpreted as rough measure of language dominance in the two women. Altogether four tapes were made on which the use of the English and Spanish of the two was elicited. Table A shows the total number of words in each language on the tapes.

TABLE A: Words Used by the Adults

Interview		English	%	Spanish	%
IX	Mother	487	75	164	25
	Neighbor	750	89	92	11
	DL	154	86	25	14
XIV-A	Mother	317	48	346	52
	Neighbor	1294	89	161	11
	DL	410	73	149	27
XIV-B	Mother	810	65	415	35
	Neighbor	1016	95	51	5
	DL	418	88	72	12
XV-A	Mother	233	29	567	71
	Neighbor	248	58	180	42
XV-B	Mother	174	8.5	1854	91.5
	Neighbor	180	15.5	983	84.5
	Carmen			829	100
VIII-B	Mother	20	6.6	283	93.4
	Neighbor	46	3	1505	97
	DL	5	.7	665	99.3

Interviews IX and XIV consist of conversational interviews conducted by the author in English and Spanish mixed together so as to encourage, though not specifically elicit, sentences like those given in the earlier part of this paper. Interview XIV is divided into two parts because about half-way through the tape I commented that "in mixing English and Spanish the mixture is that you [mother] are speaking Spanish and you [neighbor] are speaking English." They reacted with surprise and said that they had not noticed. My intention was to encourage the neighbor to use more Spanish, but as the table shows, the comment apparently just made all three of us more self-conscious and resulted in our using a higher percentage of English. The first portion of Interview XV consists of both English and Spanish with only the two women present in the room; for the last portion of the tape, Carmen Reyna, the project secretary, entered the room and conducted an interview in Spanish. Interview VIII consists of one portion in English and a longer interview in Spanish; only the second part is used here since no Spanish was used in the first portion.

The statistics in Table A are consistent with other facts that merit some discussion at this point. The mother's family speaks primarily Spanish at home because her parents and in-laws do so. The neighbor's family, on the other hand, speaks English almost exclusively because when she married she had not spoken Spanish for ten years. When the neighbor was seven her mother died and her father married a "bolilla" (as she said it, meaning "Anglo") who forced the family to speak only English. When she married, she had to relearn Spanish because her mother-in-law could not speak English; she continued to speak English at home, however. Thus, the mother is closer to being Spanish-dominant and the neighbor is decidedly English-dominant, and it is not surprising that the mother consistently used proportionately more Spanish than the neighbor did, with the sole exception of Interview VIII-B.

The principal reason for the mother's increased use of Spanish in XIV-A, the second of the interviews, is that when I told her that I wanted to have another session in mixed language I probably hinted that there was an inordinately low amount of Spanish used in the first interview. Interestingly enough, the neighbor, who was simply asked to come over after I arrived, used almost exactly the same percentage of each language in IX and XIV-A. Also, the mother, being the hostess, would naturally be accommodating in regard to my implicit desires in the interview. Neither informant, however, displayed the least awareness of when she was switching from one language to the other; in fact, on a couple of occasions—but not in a recorded interview—I asked them if they knew whether they had used a Spanish word or an English word in a particular instance, and they truly did not know which they had used. The only such incident caught on tape was in the English interview with the sister. In a conversation about her trip to the Houston Zoo I asked her if she knew a word for *monkey*, to which she replied "changos." Then when I asked if she knew another one, she asked her father in Spanish and in the ensuing conversation she and I spoke both languages, with her father using only Spanish. Suddenly, she looked surprised, said "We talked both languages," and laughed. As the results of the comment at the end of XIV-A show, calling attention to the switching process can cause a marked change in linguistic behavior. Another indication of the success, or naturalness, of the interviewing done for this project—subjective though it is—is that I could not estimate the proportionate amount of Spanish that I had used and was surprised by the differences in my own speech shown in the statistics for Interviews IX, XIV-A, and XIV-B; I thought I had used much more Spanish in each of the interviews.

Also of interest is that the neighbor tended to dominate the conversation in my interviews, whereas the mother dominated it in the others. Because her step-mother was an Anglo she perhaps is able to identify with Anglos more readily. As well, she is eleven years older. The age factor also partially explains why the mother spoke approximately twice as much as the neighbor did in the interview with Carmen. (Their ages: neighbor 39, mother 28, Carmen 22; the author's 37.)

The reason why the informants used more English with Carmen than with me is that she did not use instructions explicitly designed to give them the right psychological set to be relaxed but to stick to only one language. Had she done so, there is little doubt that they would have used even less English with her than with me. Appendix I contains a tabulation of all the interviews in which an appreciable amount of code switching occurs.

Another possible index to language dominance is the frequency with which a particular speaker uses the opposite language in his response to either a question or a statement made by another person.

Table B contains a tabulation of the total number of such responses in the interviews listed in Table A.

It is interesting to note that the mother responded in Spanish to something either the neighbor or I said in English over eight times as often as the neighbor

TABLE B: Responses to Questions or Statements

	Spanish Response to English	English Response to Spanish
Mother	34	9
Neighbor	4	37
DL	6	0
Carmen	2	0

did, and the latter gave an English response to Spanish three times as often as the mother did. The fact that neither Carmen nor I ever responded in English to a Spanish utterance can be attributed largely to our desire to get the informants to speak Spanish as much as possible. The statistics for these responses are also included in the data in Appendix I.

The switching from English to Spanish by the children was not included in the preceding discussion because the interviews were not entirely satisfactory. As Tom explained to me, it is "too hard" to speak Spanish in a situation in which English would appear to be appropriate. Nevertheless, with more time to become better acquainted with the children, either Carmen or I could surely have gotten them to feel completely relaxed and speak with ease in a Spanish interview, because they were friendly and helpful and apparently were not unduly inhibited at any time in our presence. A large enough sample of their Spanish was collected, however, to justify some speculative analysis. Statistics on the incidence of English and Spanish in their speech are included in Appendix I.

Two tapes were made with the children speaking Spanish. The first one, about five minutes long, consists of three of the children telling stories to Gail Smith, a graduate student working on the project, who had conducted two very successful interviews with them in English, but who cannot speak Spanish though she can read it and understand it when spoken fairly slowly. Mollie, the eight-year-old girl, demurred when her turn came. The second tape is a topical interview about fifty minutes long conducted by Carmen Reyna. Richard, the nine-year-old boy, was not feeling well and did not participate in the second interview.

The number of English words used by each child is a good indication of how ill-at-ease he was in the interview for various reasons, but it should not be interpreted as an indication of his knowledge of Spanish. See Table C.

TABLE C: Words Used by the Children

		English	%	Spanish	%
	Rachel	74	43	97	57
VII	Tom	48	34	93	66
	Richard	20	7	282	93
	Rachel	20	4	481	96
XIII	Tom	145	42	202	58
	Richard	118	30	269	70
	Carmen	10	.7	1499	99.3

One might assume from studying the data that the age of each child has a lot to do with his linguistic behavior in these interviews, though with this study being as limited as it is, I have had to rely rather strongly on my impressions about them as I observed them during each of the four visits in their home. Many interviews with these and other children would be necessary for more than rather speculative comments. Rachel, who is twelve, is becoming very much "the young lady" and appeared to be drawn very strongly to both Mrs. Smith and Miss Reyna. Thus, she had a great deal of difficulty forcing herself to speak a language that Mrs. Smith could not speak, but she quite readily spoke the native language of Miss Reyna and did so with no apparent difficulty. Richard appeared to be very much "Daddy's boy" and entered into the task of telling a story in his family language with much enthusiasm but still had difficulty talking a language foreign to Mrs. Smith, whom he also liked very much. (On the first visit he gave her a piece of his art work as a gift.) Tom revealed no overt signs that could be used to interpret his linguistic behavior, but his playing Little League baseball suggests that he has become rather strongly oriented toward the dominant element of the local culture and thus might be subconsciously suppressing Spanish as a means of communicating with people outside the immediate family or peer group.

The statistics on the number of sentences in each language show the nature of the language switching that the children were undergoing as they told their stories:

TABLE D: Sentences in Interview VII

	E	%	S	%	M	%	Total Sentences	Total Words
Rachel	1	6	2	13	12	81	15	171
Tom	2	18	3	27	6	55	11	141
Richard			14	56	11	44	25	302

The reason for the high number of words per sentence is that they made many false starts and repeated many words; the repeated words were counted so as to indicate the frequency of hesitations and repetitions. Rachel had 35 words in her repetitions and false starts, 28 of which were English, thus reducing the percentage of English words in the *intended* story to 33 per cent; Tom had 19 in his, 17 of which were English, adjusting his intended story to 25 per cent English; Richard had 26, four in English, adjusting his to 6 per cent English. Of the remaining 16 English words in Richard's story, 8 were *bear* or *bears* (he never did use the word *oso*); thus, adjusting for this one word, one might argue that only 3 per cent of the words in his story were English.

Representative examples are given here, with all their repetitions and hesitations, to demonstrate exactly what Tom meant when he said that it is hard to speak Spanish in such circumstances:

(71) RACH: Uh. . .They [the lions] were. . .they were nice to him [Daniel] and all, and then. . .he. . .él vino. . .a nice man and todo eso,. . .and. . .

> (sighs)...y 'pues [después que] los quitaron, él...él...he...él became on good con Jesús y todo eso.

(72) TOM: They wouldn't ... they didn't believe in ... uh ... no creían en Jesús and then He sent this man, este hombre pa' ... dijo que ... que if he didn't ... that ... si no quería (creía) en Jesús que juía (fuera).

(73) RICH: Su 'amá 'tole (atole) ... eh .,.. uh ... tres bowls ... soperas, y un ... un bear ... dijo que 'taba bien caliente y la 'amá dijo que 'taba bien caliente también, y el ... el chiquito bear dijo que 'taba bien cold ... frío.

In relating the story Richard's memory of the details apparently got ahead of his telling of it and he collapsed the bears' and Goldilock's comments about the soup into one long but highly inaccurate indirect quotation. This segment of uncomfortably contorted phrasing is not by any means representative of Richard's true linguistic competence or his knowledge, for in other interviews he would often correct or add details when the other children were telling stories or just talking. After the ordeal was over, the research team felt somewhat guilt-stricken for having posed such an unnecessarily difficult task for the children. For the sake of perspective, it should be pointed out that repetitions and false starts are not uncommon even in adult speech and are quite prevalent in all children's speech, though there clearly are more than the usual number in these examples. If one edits the sentences and deletes the false starts and repetitions in these three examples, the sentences are much easier to read, but they still contain some nonstandard and stylistically immature constructions:

(71) RACH: They were nice to him and all, and then él vino a nice man and todo eso, y después que los quitaron él became on good con Jesús y todo eso.

(72) TOM: No creían en Jesús and then He sent este hombre, y [Jesús] dijo que si no creía en Jesús que juía.

(73) RICH: Su mamá hizo atole—tres soperas—y un bear dijo que estaba bien caliente y la mamá dijo que estaba bien caliente también, y el chiquito bear dijo que estaba bien frío.

As the statistics in Table D reveal, the task of speaking Spanish was made much easier for the children in Interview XIII, when Carmen was interviewing them. As in interviews with the parents, there was some rather automatic switching between English and Spanish, particularly when the topics had non-domestic overtones. It is interesting that the relative amount of English and Spanish that Rachel used in Interview XIII is rather close to that of her parents when I interviewed them in Spanish in Interviews III and VIII-B. One would guess, on the basis of his performance on Tape VII, that Richard would also have used Spanish more than 95 percent of the time. The relative frequency with which each responded in the opposite language also is parallel to the figures shown for the adults in Table B:

TABLE E: Responses to Questions or Statements

	Spanish Response to English	English Response to Spanish
Rachel		1
Tom	2	11
Mollie		10
Carmen	7	

A representative passage is given here to show the nature of the mixing in the children's speech:

(74) CARM: Cuéntame del juego.
     TOM: Primero they were leading diez pa' nada.
     CARM: Mmm. ¿Diez a nada? ¡Isssh! ¿Y luego?
     TOM: Then there was our team to bat and we made . . .'cimos dos carreras. And then ellos fueron a batear. Hicieron una and then nojotros 'cimos cinco. Después 'ciron six, 'ciron cinco.
     MOLL: Siete.
     TOM: And then they made dos and then it was our time to bat and we made . . .
     CARM: ¿Cuántas?
     TOM: Ah . . . five or six. And then they beat us by five runs.
     CARM: ¡Ay! ¡Ay! ¿Cómo te sentiste?
     TOM: No muy bien.
     CARM: ¿Mal? ¿Por qué?
     TOM: Porque ellos nos ganaron.
     CARM: Les ganaron. ¿Y les van a ganar ustedes?
     TOM: Yo no sé.
     CARM: ¿Quieres ganar?
     TOM: Sí.

After he had told about the English-environment baseball game, Tom had no marked tendency to mix the two languages; it should be noted also that in his description of the baseball game he used *carreras* as well as *runs, batear* as well as *bat, ganaron* as well as *beat*, and numbers in both languages. Thus, as with the adults, linguistic competence is not the principal parameter in the processes underlying the switching between the two languages.

Appendix I

TAPE	WORD				SENTENCE						RESPONSES	
	E	%	S	%	E	%	S	%	M	%	S/E*	E/S**
IX												
Mother	484	75	164	25	61	67	13	15	16	18	3	1
Neighbor	750	89	92	11	70	83	8	10	6	7		2
DL	154	86	25	14	24	84	4	13	1	3	1	
XIV-A												
Mother	317	48	346	52	61	41	70	47	17	12	22	5
Neighbor	1294	89	161	11	152	75	34	17	16	8	1	15
DL	410	73	149	27	74	62	36	30	9	8	4	
XIV-B												
Mother	810	65	415	35	93	59	38	24	27	17	6	2
Neighbor	1016	95	51	5	110	91	9	7	2	2	2	4
DL	·418	88	72	12	51	77	13	20	2	3	2	
XV-A												
Mother	233	29	567	71	9	11	46	56	27	33	2	1
Neighbor	248	58	180	42	16	29	27	49	12	22	1	5
XV-B												
Mother	174	9	1854	91	9	3	213	76	59	21	1	
Neighbor	180	16	983	84	19	9	161	78	28	13		11
Carmen			829	100			198	100			2	
VIII-B												
Mother	20	<7	283	93+								
Neighbor	46	3	1505	97								
DL	5	<1	665	99+								
III												
Father	2	1+	157	99								
Mother	18	3	581	97								
Corrales	5	<3	179	97+								
DL	12	2+	527	<98								
X												
Grdfather	19	1+	1297	<99								
Grdmother	1	<1	413	99+								
Sister	14	<4	375	96+								
DL	16	1+	1251	<98								
VII												
Rachel	74	43	97	57	1	6	2	13	12	81		
Tom	48	34	93	66	2	18	3	27	6	55		
Richard	20	7	282	93			14	56	11	44		
XIII												
Rachel	20	4	481	96	3	2	113	92	8	6		1
Tom	145	42	202	58	23	23	64	66	11	11	2	11
Mollie	118	30	269	70	19	17	84	83	12	10		10
Carmen	10	<1	1499	99+	5	3	434	94	4	3	7	

*Spanish responses to English questions or statements.

**English responses to Spanish questions or statements.

E = English   M = Mixed
S = Spanish

Cognitive Aspects of Bilingual Communication

John J. Gumperz and
Eduardo Hernández-Chavez

Socio-linguistic studies of bilingualism for the most part focus on the linguistic aspects of the problem. Having discovered that speakers alternate between what, from a linguistic point of view, constitute grammatically distinct systems, investigators then proceed to study where and under what conditions alternates are employed, either through surveys in which speakers are asked to report their own language usage (Fishman, 1965), or by counting the occurrence of relevant forms in samples of elicited speech. The assumption is that the presence or absence of particular linguistic alternates directly reflects significant information about such matters as group membership, values, relative prestige, power relationship, etc.

There is no doubt that such one-to-one relationships between language and social phenomena do exist in most societies. Where speakers control and regularly employ two or more speech varieties and continue to do so over long periods of time, it is most likely that each of the two varieties will be associated with certain activities or social characteristics or speakers. This is especially the case in formal or ceremonial situations, such as religious, or magical rites, court proceedings, stereotyped introductions, greetings, or leave-takings. Here language, as well as gestures and other aspects of demeanour, may be so rigidly specified as to form part of the defining characteristics of the setting—so much so that a change in language may change the setting. Similarly, ethnic minorities in complex societies often maintain a clear separation between the native language which is spoken at home and with in-group members and the outside language used in commercial transactions or at work with outsiders.

There are, however, many other cases where such correlations break down. Consider the following sentences from a recently recorded discussion between two educated Mexican Americans.

1. a. W. Well I'm glad that I met you. O.K.?
   b. M. *Andale, pues* (O.K., swell) And do come again. Mm.
2. M. *Con ellos dos* (with the two of them). With each other.
   La señora trabaja en la canería orita, you know? (The mother works in the cannery right now). She was... *con Francine jugaba* ... (She used to play with Francine ...) with my little girl.
3. M. There's no children in the neighbourhood. Well... *sí hay criaturas* (There are children).
4. M. ....those friends are friends from Mexico *que tienen chamaquitos* (who have little children).

Reprinted by permission from *Language Use and Social Change* edited by W. H. Whitely, London, Oxford University Press, 1970. pp. 111-125.

5.   M. . . .that has nothing to do *con que le hagan esta* . . .(with their doing this).
6.   M. But the person . . . *de* . . . *de grande* (as an adult) is gotta have something in his mouth.
7.   M. And my uncle Sam *es el mas agabachado* (is the most Americanized).

It would be futile to predict the occurrence of either English or Spanish in the above utterances by attempting to isolate social variables which correlate with linguistic form. Topic, speaker, setting are common in each case. Yet the code changes sometimes in the middle of a sentence.

Language mixing of this type is by no means a rarity. Linguists specializing in bilingualism cite it to provide examples of extreme instances of interference (Mackey, 1965), and middle-class native speakers in ethnically diverse communities are frequently reluctant to recognize its existence. Yet it forms the subject of many humorous treatises. In spite of the fact that such extreme code switching is held in disrepute, it is very persistent, occurring whenever minority language groups come in close contact with majority language groups under conditions of rapid social change. One might, by way of an explanation, simply state that both codes are equally admissible in some contexts and that code switching is merely a matter of the individual's momentary inclination. Yet the alternation does carry meaning. Let us compare the following passage from a recent analysis of Russian pronominal usage (Friedrich, 1966) with an excerpt from our conversation.

An arrogant aristocratic lieutenant and a grizzled, older captain find themselves thrust together as the only officers on an isolated outpost in the Caucasus. Reciprocal formality at first seems appropriate to both. But while the latter is sitting on the young lieutenant's bed and discussing a confidential matter he switches to *ty* (tu). When the lieutenant appears to suggest insubordination, however, the captain reverts to *vy* (vous) as he issues a peremptory demand . . . (p. 240).

8.   M. I don't think I ever had any conversations in my dreams. I just dream. Ha. I don't hear people talking; I jus' see pictures.
9.   E. Oh. They're old-fashioned, then. They're not talkies, yet, huh?
10. M. They're old-fashioned. No. They're not talkies, yet. No. I'm trying to think. Yeah, there too have been talkies. Different. In Spanish and English both. An' I wouldn't be too surprised if I even had some in Chinese. (Laughter.) Yeah, Ed. *Deveras* (Really). (M. offers E. a cigarette which is refused.) *Tú no fumas, ¿verdad? Yo tampoco. Dejé de fumar.*

The two societies, the social context, and the topics discussed differ, yet the shift from English to Spanish has connotations similar to the alternation between the formal (second person pronoun) *vy* (vous) and the informal *ty* (tu). Both signal a change in interpersonal relationship in the direction of greater informality or personal warmth. Although the linguistic signs differ, they reflect similar social strategies. What the linguist identifies as code switching may convey important social information. The present paper is an attempt to elucidate the relationship between linguistic form, interactional strategies, and social meaning on the basis of a detailed study of a natural conversation. The conversation was recorded in an institution specializing in English instruction for Mexican immigrants. The staff, ranging in age from recent high-school graduates to persons in their middle fifties, includes a large number of people of Mexican or Mexican-American descent, as well as some English-speaking Americans. Of the latter group several speak Spanish well. The recording was made by a linguist (E), a native American of Mexican ancestry who is employed as an adviser for the programme. His interlocutor (M) is a community counsellor employed in the programme. She is a woman without higher education who has been trained to assist the staff in dealing with the local community. She has had some experience in public affairs. In spite of the difference in education and salary, both participants regard each other as colleagues within the context of the programme. When speaking Spanish they address each other by the reciprocal *tú*. The programme director or a Spanish-speaking outside visitor would receive the respectful *usted*. Conversations within the office are normally carried on in English, although, as will be seen later, there are marked stylistic differences which distinguish interaction among Mexican Americans from interaction across ethnic boundaries.

For analysis the taped transcript was roughly divided into episodes, each centering around a single main topic. Episodes were then subdivided into "turns of speaking" (i.e. one or more sentences reflecting a speaker's response to another's comment). The author and the interviewer co-operated in the analysis of social meaning. Two types of information were utilized. Turns containing a code switch were first examined as to their place within the structure of the total conversation in terms of such questions as: what were the relevant antecedents of the turn and what followed? What was the turn in response to, either in the same or preceding episodes? The purpose here was to get as detailed as possible an estimation of the speaker's intent. In the second stage the switched phrase would be substituted with a phrase from the other language in somewhat the same way that a linguistic interviewer uses the method of variation within a frame in order to estimate the structural significance of a particular item. By this method it was possible to get an idea of what the code switch contributed to the meaning of the whole passage.

Linguistic Aspects of Code Switching

Before discussing the social aspects of code switching some discussion of what it is that is being switched is necessary. Not all instances of Spanish words in the text are necessarily instances of code switching. Expressions like *ándale pues* (I) *dice* (he says) are normally part of the bilingual's style of English. Speakers use such expressions when speaking to others of the same ethnic background in somewhat the same way that Yiddish expressions like *nebbish, oi gewalt,* or interjections like *du hoerst* characterize the in-group English style of some American Jews. They serve as stylistic ethnic identity markers and are frequently used by speakers who no longer have effective control of both languages. The function of such forms as an ethnic identity marker becomes particularly clear in the following sequence between M and a woman visitor in her office.

Woman: Well, I'm glad that I met you. O.K.?
M: *Andale, pues.* (O.K. swell) And do come again. Mm?

The speakers, both Mexican Americans, are strangers who have met for the first time. The *ándale pues* is given in response to the woman's O.K. as if to say: 'Although we are strangers we have the same background and should get to know each other better.'

Apart from loan-word nouns such as *chicano, gabacho,* or *pocho,* the ethnic identity markers consist largely of exclamations and sentence connectors. For example,

11. M. I says Lupe *no hombre* (why no) don't believe that.
12. M. *Sí* (yes) but it doesn't.
13. M. That baby is . . . *pues* (then).

Mexican Spanish is similarly marked by English interjections. Note, for example, the 'you know' in the sentence:

14. M. *Pero como,* you know . . . *la Estela* . . .

The English form here seems a regular part of the Spanish text, and this is signalled phonetically by the fact that the pronunciation of the vowel *o* is relatively undiphthongized, and thus differs from other instances of *o* in English passages. Similarly, words like 'ice-cream' have Spanish-like pronunciations when they occur within Spanish texts and English-like pronunciations in the English text.

The greater part of the instances of true code switching consist of entire sentences inserted into the other language text. There are, however, also some examples of change within single sentences, which require special comment. In the item below the syntactic connection is such that both parts can be interpreted as independent sentences.

15. M. We've got all these kids here right now, *los que están ya criados aquí* (those that have been raised here).

This is not the case with the noun qualified phrase in item (4) and the verb complement in (5). Other examples of this latter type are:

16. M. But the person . . . *de* . . . *de grande* (as an adult) is gotta have something in its mouth.
17. M. *¿Será que quiero la tetera? para* pacify myself.   (It must be that I want the baby bottle to . . .)
18. M. The type of work he did *cuando trabajaba* (when he worked) he . . . what . . . that I remember, *era regador* (he was an irrigator) at one time.
19. M. An' my uncle Sam *es el más agabachado* (is the most Americanized).

Noun qualifiers (4), verb complements (5), parts of a noun phrase (16), the predicate portion of an equational sentence (19), all can be switched. This does not mean, however, that there are no linguistic constraints on the co-occurrence of Spanish and English forms. The exact specification of these constraints will, however, require further detailed investigation. Clearly, aside from single loan words, entire sentences are most easily borrowed. Sentence modifiers or phrases are borrowed less frequently. And this borrowing does seem to be subject to some selection constraints (Blom and Gumperz, 1970). But some tentative statements can be made. Constructions like: *que* have *chamaquitos* (who have boys) or, *he *era regador* (he was an irrigator) seem impossible.

The Social Meaning of Code Switching

When asked why they use Spanish in an English sentence, or vice-versa, speakers frequently come up with explanations like the following taken from our conversation:

> If there's a word that I can't find, it keeps comin' out in Spanish. I know what word I want and finally when I...well I bring it out in Spanish, and I know the person understands me.

Difficulty in finding the right word clearly seems to account for examples like: *para* pacify myself (17). In other instances some items of experience, some referents or topics are more readily recalled in one language than in another, as in:

20. M. I got to thinking *vacilando el punto este* (mulling over this point).
21. M. They only use English when they have to . . . like for *cuando van de compras* (when they go shopping).

Linguistically motivated switches into English occur when the discussion calls for psychological terminology or expressions, e.g. 'pacify', 'relax', 'I am a biter'. Such expressions or modes of talking seem rarely used in typically Mexican American settings. On the other hand, ideas and experiences associated with the speaker's Spanish-speaking past, such as items (20) and (21), trigger off a switch into Spanish.

In many other instances, however, there seems to be no linguistic reason for the switch. *Si hay criatures* (item 3) is directly translated without hesitation pause in the following sentence. Many other Spanish expressions have English equivalents elsewhere in the text. Furthermore, there are several pages of more general, abstract discussion which contain no Spanish at all.

One might hypothesize that codes are shifted in response to E's suggestion and that M answers him in whatever language he speaks. This is clearly not the case. Several questions asked in English elicit Spanish responses, and vice-versa.

In discussing the social aspects of switching it is important to note that while the overt topic discussed is the use of English and Spanish, much of the conversation is dominated by a concern with Mexican versus non-Mexican, i.e. common middleclass values or group membership. Spanish occurs most in episodes dealing with typically Mexican American experiences. In several places fears are expressed that Mexican American children are losing their language, and thus, by implication, denying their proper cultural heritage. To some extent the juxtaposition of English and Spanish symbolizes the duality of value systems evidenced in the discussion.

At the start of the conversation several exchanges dealing with the mechanics of tape-recorder operation are entirely in English. Code shifts begin with a sequence where M asks E why he is recording their talk and E responds:

22. E. I want to use it as a . . . as an example of how *chicanos* can shift back and forth from one language to another.
23. M. *Ooo. Como andábamos platicando* (Ohh. Like we were saying).

M's switch to Spanish here is a direct response to his (E's) use of the word *chicanos*. Her statement refers to previous conversations they have had on related subjects and suggests that she is willing to treat the present talk as a friendly chat among fellow *chicanos* rather than as a formal interview.

Codes alternate only as long as all participants are *chicanos* and while their conversation revolves around personal experiences. Towards the end of the recording session, when a new participant enters, talk goes on. The newcomer is an American of English-speaking background who, having lived in Latin America, speaks Spanish fluently. Yet in this context she was addressed only in English and did not use her Spanish. Furthermore, in the earlier part of the session, when E and M were alone, there was one long episode where M spoke only English even when responding to E's Spanish questions. This passage deals with M's visit to San Quentin prison, to see an inmate, and with prison conditions. The inmate was referred to only in English, and the conversation contained no overt reference to his ethnic background. Further inquiries made while analysis was in progress revealed that he was a non-*chicano*. It is evident from the first example that it is social identity and not language *per se* which is determinant in code selection. The second example indicates when conversations have no reference to speakers or their subjects' status as *chicanos* and when, as in the present case, a subject is treated in a generally detached manner without signs of personal involvement, code switching seems to be inappropriate.

On the whole, one has the impression that except for a few episodes dealing with recollections of family affairs, the entire conversation is basically in English. English serves to introduce most new information, while Spanish provides stylistic embroidering to amplify the speaker's intent. Spanish sentences frequently take the form of pre-coded, stereotyped, or idiomatic phrases.

While ethnic identity is important as the underlying theme, the actual contextual meanings of code alternation are more complex.

Turning to a more detailed analysis, many of the Spanish passages reflect direct quotes or reports of what M has said in Spanish or of what other Mexicans have told her, eg.

24.   Because I was speakin' to my baby . . . my ex-baby sitter. And we were talkin' about the kids you know, an' I was tellin' her . . . uh . . . *'Pero, como,* you know . . . uh . . . *la Estela y la Sandi . . . relistas en el telefón. Ya hablan mucho inglés. Dice, 'Pos . . . sí. Mira tú, dice, 'Pos yo no sé de*

> *dode' dice, 'Pos. . . el. . . las palabras del televisión. Y ya que me dice. . .
> ya me pide dinero pa'l "ayscrin" y. . .'* You know?. . .'*Y hue. . . y eso
> no es nada, espérate los chicharrones,* you know, when they start school'
> ('But, how, you know . . . uh . . . Estela and Sandi are very precocious
> on the telephone. They already speak a lot of English'. She says, 'Well,
> yes, just imagine' she says, 'well I don't know where they get it from',
> she says, 'well, the words on television. And she already tells me . . . she
> already asks me for money for ice cream and' . . . you know? 'And
> then . . . and that isn't anything, wait for the *chicharrones,* you know,
> when they start school')

Throughout the conversation Spanish is used in quoting statements by
individuals whose *chicano* identity is emphasized. The following passage, in
which Lola, who is of Mexican origin, is quoted in English, seemed to at first
contradict this generalization.

25.   An' Lola says, 'Dixie has some, Dixie'. So Dixie gave me a cigarette.

Lola, however, is in her late teens, and members of her age group, although
they know Spanish, tend to prefer English, even in informal interaction. Later
on, however, if they marry within the *chicano* community they are quite likely
to revert to the predominate usage pattern. The use of English in her case
reflects the fact that for the present, at least, Lola identifies with the majority
group of English monolinguals with respect to language-usage nouns.

The pattern of quoting *chicanos* in Spanish and talking about them in English
in reversed in the following passage, in which M. reports on the way she talks to
her children.

26.   Yea. Uh-huh. She'll get . . . 'Linda, you don' do that, *mija* . . . (daughter)
        La vas . . . (You are going to . . .) you're going to get her . . . give her . . .
        a bad habit.' *Le pone el dedo pa' que se lo muerda,* (she gives her her
        finger to bite), you know, '*Iiya,* she'll bite the heck out of you'. 'Ow!'
        La otra grita, (the other one yells). *So, una es sadist y la otra es
        masochist* (So, one is a sadist and the other is a masochist). (Laughter.)

Further inquiry again reveals that in M's family children are ordinarily
addressed in English.

Aside from direct quotes, Spanish occurs in several modifying phrases or
sentences such as: 'those from Mexico', *que tienen chamaquitos* (Item 4). The
effect here is to emphasize the ethnic identify of the referent. The use of *si hay
criaturas* is particularly interesting in this respect. It is preceded by the following
exchange:

27. M. There's no children. The Black Panthers next door. You know what I
        mean.
    E. Do they have kids?
    M. Just the two little girls.

E. No, no. I mean do some of the other people in the neighbourhood have kids?

M. They don't associate with no children . . . There's no children in the neighbourhood. Well . . . *sí hay criaturas* (yes there are children).

M. goes on to talk about the one other Mexican family in the building. The *sí hay criaturas* here serves to single out Mexican children from others and in a sense modifies the 'there's no children' several sentences above. The implication is that only the other *chicano* children are suitable playmates.

In a last group of examples the switch to Spanish signals the relative confidentiality or privateness of the message. The first example cited as item 2 above is a case in point:

28. With each other. *La señora trabaja en la canería orita,* you know. (The mother works in the cannery, you know.)

Here M's voice is lowered and the loudness decreases in somewhat the same way that confidentiality is signalled in English monolingual speech. Next consider the following:

29. E. An' how . . . an' how about now?

M. *Estos . . . me los hallé . . . estos Pall Mall's me los hallaron.* (These . . . I found . . . These Pall Mall's . . . they were found for me.) No, I mean . . .

M has been talking about the fact that she smokes very little, and E discovers some cigarettes on her desk. Her Spanish, punctuated by an unusually large number of hesitation pauses, lends to the statement an air of private confession. She is obviously slightly embarrassed. Note the almost regular alternation between Spanish and English in the next passage:

30. Mm-huh. Yeah. An' . . . an . . . an' they tell me 'How did you quit, Mary?' I di'n' quit. I . . . I just stopped. I mean it wasn' an effort I made *que voy a dejar de fumar porque me hace daño o* (that I'm going to stop smoking because it's harmful to me, or) this or tha', uh-uh. It's just . . . that . . . eh . . . I used to pull butts out of the . . . the . . . the wastepaper basket. Yeah. (Laughter) I used to go look in the (. . . unclear . . .) *se me acababan los cigarros en la noche.* (my cigarettes would run out on me at night). I'd get desperate, *y ahi voy al basurero a buscar, a sacar,* you know? (Laughter) (and there I go to the wastebasket to look for some, to get some, you know?).

The juxtaposition of the two codes here is used to great stylistic effect in depicting the speaker's attitudes. The Spanish phrases, partly by being associated with content like 'it is harmful to me' or with references to events like 'cigarettes running out at night' and through intonational and other suprasegmental clues, convey a sense of personal feeling. The English phrases are more neutral by contrast. The resulting effect of alternate personal involvement and clinical detachment vividly reflects M's ambiguity about her smoking.

Our examples of bilingual communication indicate that language usage is closely tied to the position of *chicanos* as a minority group within the English-speaking majority. Selection of alternate forms is related to a variety of social factors such as ethnic identity, age, and sex (as in the case of Lola in item 25), degree of solidarity or confidentiality, etc.

In our conversational contexts at least the relationship of such factors to verbal messages is quite different from what the sociologist means by correlation among variables. We could not take a rating of, for example, ethnicity or degree of solidarity as measured by the usual survey techniques, or other scaling devices and expect this rating to predict the occurrence of Spanish and English in our texts. Such ratings determine the likelihood of a switch, but they do not tell us when a switch occurs in a particular case, nor do they predict the meaning of a switch. What seems to be involved rather is a symbolic process very much like that by which linguistic signs convey semantic information. Code selection, in other words, is meaningful in much the same way that lexical choice is meaningful. The regular use of particular speech varieties in speech events specific to certain classes of speakers and speaker-related activities sets up associations between these varieties and features of the social environment which are like the associations between words and objects. As long as the forms in question are used in their normal or regular setting, these associations convey no new information. But in contexts where—as in the examples cited here—there is an option, where one variety is merely normal and speakers can juxtapose another variety, selection becomes meaningful. The second, juxtaposed set of forms becomes socially marked in the sense that it introduces into the new context some of the semantic features of the speech events with which it is normally associated in the minds of the participants.

In the present conversation English is normal, except in a few passages with special content, and here the objective information is introduced in English, while the Spanish is marked and typically occurs in modifier phrases and sentences. Items such as 'there are no children' followed a few sentences later by *sí hay criaturas* or 'I got to thinking', or *vacilando el punto este,* where the Spanish elaborates on previous subject matter, exemplifies what we mean by marking through juxtaposition.

The decoding process by which speakers judge the significance of marked forms bears close similarity to normal semantic decoding. In other words, speakers select from alternate dictionary meanings or semantic features in accordance with the contextual constraints imposed by semantic and syntactic rules. In the present case Spanish derives its basic meaning from its association with communication among *chicanos.* But for *chicano* speakers in-group communication also carries secondary meanings of solidarity or confidentiality when compared to verbal interaction in a mixed group. The speakers judge what is meant in each case by evaluating the reasonableness of a particular interpretation in the light of the topic discussed and his own knowledge of social norms. Social structure, like syntax, aids in the interpretation of sentences. It is part of what a speaker has to know in order to judge the full import of what is said. Two speakers will make similar interpretations of a sentence only if they interpret it in terms of the same social assumptions.

Conclusion

The foregoing analysis has some important implications for the cross-cultural study of bilingualism. Since there is more to communication than grammar alone (I am using the term 'grammar' in the sense in which that term is usually defined by linguists), mere knowledge of the alternating varieties is not enough. The investigator must control the speaker's own system and must pay particular attention to the often quite arbitrary signs by which these values are signalled in speech.

To be sure, any analysis which, like ours, relies on a single case raises some question about the generality of the results. Are the processes discovered here peculiar to the present conversation and speakers, or do they account for the behaviour of larger groups? Goffman has shown that to assign others to social roles or categories is a common behavioural strategy. What seems to be peculiar about the present case is not what is done but how and by what linguistic means it is done.

As a behavioural strategy, code switching bears considerable similarity to the use of polite and familiar address pronouns in other societies. Our findings regarding the relation of ethnic identity and confidentiality parallel Brown's findings (1965) about the connection between high status and social distance. English forms ordinarily associated with non-members, i.e. non-*chicanos*, are like high-status pronouns, in that they convey formality or distance when used to refer to members, while customarily forms used among members, i.e. *chicanos*, are like familiar pronouns, in that they convey secondary meanings of solidarity and confidentiality.

How does the cognitive approach to bilingual usage relate to the more usual survey methods? Obviously, it does not eliminate the need for surveys. In the many little-known areas of the world language-usage surveys are essential tools for assembling basic data on usage norms and attitudes. But in the present rudimentary stage of our knowledge of language usage survey questions tend to reflect the analyst's, not the native's, theory of speaking. Analyses such as the present one which are not too difficult or time consuming may provide important background information to improve survey content.

Note: Work on the present paper was supported in part through grants from the Institute of International Studies, University of California, Berkeley; and Office of Education, Bureau of Research, Department of Health, Education and Welfare, Washington, D.C.

References

Blom, Jan-Petter and John J. Gumperz (1970). 'Social Meaning in Linguistic Structures: Code-switching in Northern Norway', in John J. Gumperz and Dell Hymes (eds.), *Directions in Sociolinguistics.* New York: Holt, Rinehart and Winston.

Brown, Roger (1965). *Social Psychology.* New York: Free Press.

Fishman, Joshua A. (1965). 'Who Speaks what Language to Whom and When', *La Linguistique* 2: 67: 88.

Friedrich, Paul (1966). 'Structural Implications of Russian Pronominal Usage', in William Bright (ed.), *Sociolinguistics.* The Hague: Mouton. 214-53.

Mackey, William F. (1965). 'Bilingual Interference: its Analysis and Measurement', *Journal of Communication,* 15, 239-49.

Chicano Multilingualism and Multiglossia

Fernando Peñalosa

Among social scientists and educators it is virtually axiomatic that the Mexican American population is both "bilingual" and "bicultural," yet such an axiom has not yet been subject to any intensive scrutiny or questioning. It has generally been taken for granted and then one goes on from there, to conduct one's study of social stratification, the school dropout problem, police-community relations, or whatever else happens to interest the scholar. Yet such an axiom should be scrutinized, for upon further examination, Chicano "bilingualism" turns out not to be so much an established fact, as an extremely problematic field for research; virtually unexplored in any depth at all. True, there is bilingualism among Chicanos, but what is its extent? What is its nature? In what social contexts and for what purposes are the various linguistic codes[1] used? What are the educational and other social consequences? We do not yet have sufficient data to answer these questions; still it would seem useful to map out our area of concern through a rather cursory examination of Chicano multilingualism and multiglossia[2] as they might appear from the perspective of current sociolinguistic theory.

Diglossia and Bilingualism

One of the peculiarities of traditional concern with bilingualism has been the viewing of it as an abnormal phenomenon, or at least a temporary one, in the "normal" type of society ordinarily envisioned by sociologists of the structural-functional persuasion. Gumperz has pointed out the fact that total bi- or multi-lingualism is the rule rather than the exception in a wide variety of societies.[3] Chicano society (or culture, or subculture) is certainly then in this respect neither abnormal nor unusual. And inasmuch as the situation has persisted for more than a century and is still in full vigor, it is certainly not a mere temporary phenomenon which will be disappearing in the near future.

Before we proceed any further, the important distinction between bilingualism and diglossia must be made. (Below, reasons will be given for preferring the terms multilingualism and multiglossia in their stead.) For the concept diglossia we are indebted to Ferguson, who coined the term to refer to situations where either two varieties of the same language or two different languages are coextensively used in the same society, i.e. one colloquial variety (or varieties) for everyday affairs, and one more respected variety used for writing and formal affairs, as for example, colloquial and classical Arabic, *katharevousa* and *dhimotiki* in Greek, or Yiddish and Hebrew in traditional Eastern European Jewish culture.[4] In such societies, some individuals may be bilingual in the two

---

Reprinted by permission of the author. [ERIC ED 056 590.]

languages, but others are monolingual colloquial speakers. Since Ferguson's pioneer formulation, however, sociolinguists have come to accept the idea that diglossia exists not only in multilingual societies which officially recognize several languages, but also in societies which are multilingual in the sense that they employ separate dialects or other functionally differentiated codes or language varieties in different social settings.[5]

Thus the concept "diglossia" refers to the recognition and acceptance of different forms of speech within a given society, and "bilingualism" refers to the linguistic behavior of individuals within that society. As Fishman puts it, "Bilingualism is essentially a characterization of individual linguistic behavior whereas diglossia is a characterization of linguistic organization at the socio-cultural level."[6] A further distinction has been made by Kloss who suggests that we use the term "in-diglossia" to refer to a relationship between closely related languages, and "out-diglossia" to refer to a relationship between languages not closely related.[7]

Applying the concepts just discussed it would seem that in the Chicano community, we can recognize both in-diglossia and out-diglossia. Thus, with reference to Spanish we can identify the use both of standard Mexican Spanish as well as of that variety of Spanish characteristic of the peasantry and lower class of Mexico. As far as English is concerned, there is the use both of colloquial English and of standard English. Thus we have in-diglossia with reference to each of the two languages, but we also have out-diglossia because English and Spanish is each used by the Chicano in its own spheres. The term "complex diglossia" is suggested to describe those societies such as the Chicano, which are charac-terized by both in-diglossia and out-diglossia.

With reference to bilingualism on the other hand there is the question of its definition, and the nature of the types or forms in which it occurs. At the present time there appears to be a general consensus among sociolinguists that anyone is bilingual who can produce meaningful utterances in more than one language. Hence bilingualism manifests itself in a range of degrees, from complete, symmetrical native control of two languages, to the asymmetrical case, where there is extreme weakness in one of the two languages. In this sense, then, virtually all Chicanos are bilingual; it still remains an empirical question to what degree they are so. Whatever tentative answers to this question can be mustered in the near future should be of enormous practical significance particularly to those professionally concerned with the education of the Mexican American student. Perhaps the most significant variables with which they are dealing are the ones least clearly understood, i.e. the range and dimensions of multilingualism.

The compound-coordinate distinction is a useful one. Compound bilinguals are those who learned both languages in a bilingual home or neighborhood or one language through the medium of another, hence have fused two meaning systems; coordinate bilinguals, having learned their two languages in different contexts, have somewhat different meanings for corresponding words in the two languages. In the Chicano case, we would be interested in the potentially different effects in this connection of a child being reared in a home where Spanish only was spoken as opposed to a home where both languages were used on a more or less equal basis. Ony might speculate that the compound bilingual

Chicano child might miss some of the subtleties of the English used in his school, while the coordinate bilingual might avoid this type of difficulty. There appears to be a general tendency for coordinate bilingualism to shift to compound bilingualism, although formal education can help to keep the two semantic systems distinct if only one language is used at a time. The planning of bilingual education programs which ignores these distinctions may be imperilling the very success of these programs. For example, the question as to whether both languages shall be used in the same time period to discuss the same subject, or whether only one language is to be used in a given time period should be settled, taking into consideration sociolinguistic as well as administrative factors.

Perhaps the relationship of linguistic to sociocultural variables might profitably be explored by utilizing the concepts of "compound biculturals" and "coordinate biculturals." Thus, for example, perhaps Mexican immigrants become bicultural in coordinate fashion, while most barrio residents become enculturated in such a fashion that they are bicultural in compound fashion. (It may very well be that those who are compound bilinguals are also compound biculturals; the same being true for the coordinate.) In any case, the relationship between the two sets of variables seems worth some exploration. This is not a new idea. Soffietti has suggested the term "cultural accents," to refer to conflicting habit patterns persistently interfering with each other and resulting in any number of distortions or outright substitutions.[8] Again the practical implications are obvious. Are we interested in bicultural education or are we trying to blend two cultures into one?

Types of Codes

Whether different varieties of speech are languages, dialects, or whatever, depends not on linguistic grounds, but on sociopolitical considerations. Thus as indicated above we would prefer to avoid the spurious language-dialect distinction and use the more neutral term "code." Determination of the varieties of speech or codes in the Chicano community must be based in part on an examination of its social structure and in part on perceptions and attitudes of community members. This topic still remains virtually unexplored more than two decades after Barker's pioneering Tucson study.[9] Barker identified three varieties of Spanish spoken in Tucson and these would seem to be fairly common elsewhere in the Southwest. They are (1) Standard Mexican Spanish, the language spoken by educated persons in Mexico; (2) Rural-lower-class Mexican Spanish spoken in Mexico by the uneducated, and which Barker identifies, too narrowly in my opinion, as "Southern Arizona Dialect of Spanish"; (3) Youth argot, often called "Pachuco" dialect. It seems, tentatively at least, that a fourth language variety could be added, one which in certain loci or for certain purposes may be the predominant one, and which has no widely recognized name, but which conveniently might be called "pochismos," i.e. speaking with pochismos. Estelle Chacón suggests (somewhat facetiously) that pochismos might be defined in the United States as "an unpredictable scattering of Spanish words and phrases used throughout an English conversation," and that Mexicans might define it as precisely the opposite.[10] (My own thinking is that the scattering is systematic, not random, and that much systematic scattering could indeed be predicted from social and psychological variables, had we the necessary data.) Chacón claims, "It is my mother tongue."[11] A very important theoretical point is raised here. Is "pochismos" Spanish with English interference, English with Spanish interference, simple code switching, all of these, or a separate code that can properly be said to act as "mother tongue?"[12]

Certainly "pochismos" merits careful study in view of its very importance to the entire Mexican American population. The practical implications are no less significant than the theoretical ones. Educators might ponder the feasibility of trilingual education. For example, the poetry of Alurista, who writes in this code, has found an exceptionally favorable emotional and intellectual response among Chicano intellectuals, students, and activists (these three categories are not mutually exclusive, of course). There seems to be continuum from interference to code switching. When does interference become code switching: When a word from the other language is introduced? a phrase? a sentence? a paragraph? any utterance? Whatever the conceptualization, observers from both north and south of the border have noted the large amount of code switching among Chicanos. A possible explanation derives from an observation of Weinreich: Abnormal proneness to switching has been attributed to persons who, in their early childhood, were addressed by the same familiar interlocutors indiscriminately in both languages.[13] Apparently at a later age, however, the person has no difficulty communicating with other persons reared similarly, and even extreme interference will not lessen intelligibility.

Now what about the Chicano child? Does he speak with pochismos? If he does so, was it because he was addressed by his parents and/or barrio chums indiscriminately in both English and Spanish, or addressed by such interlocutors in pochismos, in all three, or perhaps in pochismos and only one of the other two codes? Certainly the range of variation to be found in Mexican American communities in this regard is deserving of serious research. Equally significant are the possible social psychological correlates of such linguistic behavior. Hymes suggests that unless the roles and setting of the languages are kept distinct, the child may develop personality difficulties.[14] Lambert notes that students "who face an unresolved conflict of cultural allegiances are held back in their progress in both languages."[15] Attitudes towards one's own ethnic group or a different one are believed to be strong predictors in success or failure in learning the language of each group. Thus the success of bilingual education of the Chicano, at least as far as the mastery of Spanish and English is concerned, is likely to be heavily dependent on the students' attitudes toward the majority culture and their own.

In this connection it should be noted that the Chicano is not really a marginal man so much as he is part of a marginal culture, neither Mexican nor American. As directly implied above, the linguistic marginality is also salient. "Pocho" may well be the "mother tongue" in this marginal culture. When bilinguals interact primarily with bilinguals, they reinforce bilingual behavior as well as strengthen their marginal culture. As Homans notes, "the more frequently persons interact with each other, the more alike in some respects both their activities and their sentiments tend to become."[16] Thus also Ervin-Tripp concludes that where bilinguals have been interacting mainly with other bilinguals for a long time the model for each of their languages is not monolingual usage of these languages but rather the languages as spoken by the bilinguals themselves.[17] This last statement raises some interesting questions. While the barrio Chicano's model for English may be the English of his barrio peers, is the model for his Spanish the speech of his peers or the speech of his parents? On the other hand the models for "pochismos" and "pachuco" are most likely to be the speech of his peers for when bilinguals communicate primarily with bilinguals, linguistic interference is likely to be very high in both languages.

At this point it should be obvious that indeed what we have in the Chicano community is not a simple case of diglossia and bilingualism, but rather a case of multiglossia and multilingualism, with very complex relationships among the half-dozen codes in use among Chicanos. Which of these codes do educators for example wish to take into account in their planning? At the very least, if we insist on a simplistic definition of bilingual education, we should be fully aware of what we are doing.

Choice of Code

An emergent sociolinguistics of the Chicano would need to identify the different contexts or "registers" in which codes available to Chicanos are used, and attempt to ascertain the conventions and social psychological factors which determine the use of which codes in which registers. There is in principle no difference whether we are talking about in-diglossia or out-diglossia. As Gumperz remarks, "The same social pressures which would lead a monolingual to shift from one language to another."[18]

To a certain extent diglossia exists in both the U.S. among the English-speaking, and in Mexico among the Spanish-speaking, in the sense of that one code is used in the schools and usually a different one in the home and neighborhood, i.e. standard vs. folk (or colloquial). In each case the situation is therefore one of in-diglossia. For the Chicano child, however, the situation is usually one of out-diglossia. As Barker explains it, "Young children do not learn formal Spanish at home. Instead, at the age when they ordinarily would be learning formal Spanish, they go to school and learn formal English. For many children English thus becomes identified with most types of formal relationships."[19] If the student decides to study Spanish in high school he is faced with a different type of problem. In high school his Spanish teacher (frequently an Anglo) tells him the Spanish he learned at home is not "good" Spanish, with the implication that his parents are uneducated and illiterate peasants. Chicano students consequently become demoralized. The result? With a small percentage of brilliant exceptions, Anglos get better grades in Spanish classes than Chicanos. Defeating the student thus on his home ground is a particularly insidious method of demonstrating the cultural "inferiority" of the Mexican American student. The teacher who is party to such a fraud is ignorant not only of linguistics and social structure, but also of his educational responsibilities to his students. Further clarification of Chicano multilingualism and multiglossia is indeed urgent if educators are realistically to plan *with* the Chicano community for the education of the Chicano student. These phenomena must be made clear to the teacher himself, and he must make them clear to his students, so there will be mutual respect for the different varieties of speech and their speakers. At the same time students should be learning or improving those varieties of speech (codes) which will be needed or useful in the different life situations in which they will be finding themselves and for which their education is supposedly preparing them.

Notes

[1] By "codes" are meant languages, dialects, or other varieties of speech.

[2] Because I believe more than two codes are in use among Chicanos, I prefer the prefix "multi-" to the prefix "bi-" in discussing our linguistic situation.

[3] John Gumperz, "Types of Linguistic Communities." *Anthropological Linguistics* IV (1962), pp. 22-40.

[4] Charles A. Ferguson, "Diglossia." *Word* XV (1959), pp. 325-340.

[5] A more acceptable term than "multilingual" would be "multicodal." Despite its greater conceptual clarity, however, I refuse to add to the already overburdened repertoire of sociological jargon.

[6] Joshua A. Fishman, "Bilingualism with and without Diglossia; Diglossia with and without Bilingualism." *Journal of Social Issues* XXIII, No. 2 (April 1967), pp. 29-38.

[7] Heinz Kloss, "Types of Multilingual Communities: A Discussion of Ten Variables." *Sociological Inquiry* XXXVI, No. 2 (Spring 1966), pp. 132-145.

[8] James P. Soffietti, "Bilingualism and Biculturalism." *Journal of Educational Psychology* XLVI (1955), pp. 222-227.

[9] George Barker, "Social Functions of Language in a Mexican American Community." *Acta Americana* V (July - September 1947), pp. 185-202.

[10] Estelle Chacón, "Pochismos." *El Grito* III, No. 1 (Fall 1969), pp. 34-35.

[11] *Ibid.*

[12] Linguistic interference is the "tendency for the phonological, lexical, and semantic systems of one language to intrude on those of another." (John McNamara, "The Bilingual's Linguistic Performances," *Journal of Social Issues* XXIII, No. 2 (April 1967), pp. 58-77.) Code switching is "The constant alternating in discourse between two languages." (Daniel N. Cárdenas, "Dominant Spanish Dialects Spoken in the United States," Washington, D.C., ERIC, 1970, p. 43).

[13] Uriel Weinreich, *Languages in Contact* (New York: Linguistic Circle of New York, 1953, p. 74).

[14] Dell H. Hymes, "The Ethnography of Speaking." in *Anthropology and Human Behavior* (Washington, D.C.: Anthropological Society of Washington, 1962), pp. 15-53.

[15] W. E. Lambert et al, "A Study of the Roles of Attitudes and Motivations in Second-Language Learning," pp. 473-549 in Joshua A. Fishman, ed., *Readings in the Sociology of Language* (The Hague' Mouton, 1968).

[16] George L. Homan, *The Human Groups* (New York: Harcourt, Brace, 1950).

[17] Susan Ervin-Tripp, "An Issei Learns English." *Journal of Social Issues* XXIII, No. 2 (April 1967), pp. 78-90.

[18] John Gumperz, "On the Linguistic Markers of Bilingual Communication." *Journal of Social Issues* XXIII, No. 2 (April 1967), pp. 48-57.

[19] Barker, *loc. cit.*

Social Functions of Language in a Mexican-American Community

George C. Barker

The language of any human society may be studied not only from the standpoint of its content and structure but also from that of its functions in the society. This paper describes an inquiry into how language functions in the life of a bilingual minority group in process of cultural change. Since the subjects of this study are individuals of Mexican descent living in the community of Tucson, Arizona, sixty miles north of the Mexican border, the type of cultural change involved would seem to be both acculturation, involving the continuous firsthand contact of representatives of two different cultures, and assimilation, involving the gradual engulfing of representatives of one culture, and their absorption into the dominant group.

The central problem of this inquiry may be stated as: "How, if at all, may the linguistic behavior of members of the bilingual minority group be related to other aspects of their social behavior?" This question was brought forth by the observation that bilinguals who are members of the same ethnic minority group often display wide variations in their linguistic behavior, both in respect to their usage of the ancestral language and in their usage of English. Are these variations the result of unrecognized uniformities in the way language functions in the lives of these people, or must such variations be attributed to chance? How does it happen, for example, that among bilinguals, the ancestral language will be used on one occasion and English on another, and that on certain occasions bilinguals will alternate, without apparent cause, from one language to another? Again, how is it that certain bilinguals will deliberately avoid speaking the ancestral language with outsiders, even though they know that the outsider understands and speaks their language, while other bilinguals will go out of their way to get outsiders to speak the language, and will take great pleasure in helping them learn its subtleties?

The problem of how languages change under conditions of culture contact already has received careful attention on the part of anthropologists and linguists. Also, some valuable work has been done on the problem of the relation between linguistic change and other aspects of the acculturation process. The work of Spicer[1] has indicated that the introduction of loan-words from Spanish and English into the Yaqui vocabulary may be correlated, to some degree, with different historic periods in Yaqui acculturation. A parallel study, made by Jean Bassett Johnson,[2] has indicated that while the Spanish language has influenced every aspect of the Yaqui language and social life, it has not destroyed or altered the fundamental integrity of Yaqui culture. Comparatively little study has been made, however, of the precise relation between the linguistic and non-linguistic behavior of a group in process of cultural change.

Reprinted by permission from *Acta Americana* 5.185 - 202 (1974). This paper is an abstract of the writer's doctoral dissertation.

Anthropologists and sociologists engaged in field studies of the life of a group in process of culture contact frequently have noted that, where two languages are involved, the functions formerly performed by one language come to be divided between two or more. This division seems to be based partly on convenience and partly on necessity. Individuals brought up in the language of their ancestral culture seem to find it easier to talk to each other in that language and to talk to outsiders in the language of the outsider's culture. Some investigators have suggested that a logical outcome of this division is that for individuals both inside and outside the ethnic group, the ethnic language comes to symbolize the group and its cultural background, or, in terms of its social function, to identify the group as a group. This point has been advanced by many students of acculturation and assimilation. Redfield,[3] in his study of Tepoztlan, showed how the native Indian language, rather than Spanish, became a symbol of local patriotism. Similarly, Reuter,[4] discussing culture contacts in Puerto Rico, has shown how the impact of Western culture has "outmoded" the folk language of Puerto Rico, and at the same time has changed it from a tool to a sacred value.

A second and equally important hypothesis regarding this division in linguistic function is that the individual's skill in using the language of a second or adopted culture comes to symbolize his status in the new society. For the uneducated immigrant this situation seems to impose a heavy penalty. Ruth Tuck,[5] in her study of a Mexican-American community in California, suggests that the failure of Mexican laborers to use English in public, together with their faulty use of English, constitutes the principal reason for the feeling on the part of many Anglo-Americans that the Mexican cannot be assimilated or, in short, that he should have no status at all in the community. Bossard[6] summarized this relation of language to status of bilingual groups by pointing out that in the United States and in all countries where there are linguistic minorities, the process of linguistic identification with status operates in two dimensions rather than in one. Here, he points out, in addition to the determination of status on the basis of conformity to one socially accepted form of expression, there is the added dimension of bilingualism, operating against an historical background of immigrant sequence and minority group status. In this added dimension, he suggests, a second language and its vestiges are bound up with the status of the particular minority group which speaks that language.

Whether or not one accepts the above hypotheses, the fact is apparent that in any given situation, members of a bilingual group have the opportunity of a choice between two or more alternate languages and dialects. It thus becomes possible to describe the linguistic behavior of any given bilingual individual in terms of patterns of usage and response to both languages, and to see precisely what relation may exist between these patterns and the non-linguistic behavior of the same individual with respect both to his own group and to outsiders. Comparisons may be further facilitated if the bilinguals studied have similar backgrounds and live in the same general community.

With these primary considerations in mind, the writer outlined a linguistic research program which was approved in 1943 by the Department of Anthropology, University of Chicago. The general method suggested, and later followed, was that of the case study. Out of some one ethnic community it was proposed to select a number of individuals as representing (1) a cross-section of the community's social system and (2) a proportionate sampling of the community in terms of length of residence. Through informal observation and contacts over a period of at least six months it was proposed to examine the language usage of these individuals from the standpoint of both in-group and out-group relations. The type of ethnic community chosen for this study, it was felt, preferably should be a fairly compact, definitely set-off group within an urban area. It was decided to study a Spanish-speaking group, inasmuch as the writer understands and speaks the language. It was felt that the group should include a stable element of older immigrants and their children as well as an element representative of more recent migratory movements, thus making possible the comparative study of these three segments (parental generation, younger native-born generation, and recent immigrants) with their correspondingly different social backgrounds.

In 1945, after a series of survey trips to various California and Arizona towns having Mexican minorities, the city of Tucson was chosen as a testing ground for the hypotheses of this inquiry mainly for two reasons: first, the range of social positions occupied by the town's Mexican-American population was unusually wide, thereby permitting a comparative analysis of linguistic and other social behavior of individuals in different social settings and, second, an investigation of ethnic relations in Tucson, already being conducted by Mr. Harry Getty of the anthropology staff, University of Arizona, had made available to the writer much basic data on Tucson's social structure. This material, collected by Getty over a period of three years, provided the foundation for the present inquiry.

Before attempting to summarize the field methods and conclusions of this study, a brief statement should be made in regard to the nature of the social and linguistic background on the Mexican population in Tucson. Of Tucson's total population, approximately one-fourth, or about twenty-thousand persons, are of Mexican descent. Some of these people take little or no part in the life of the Mexican community, but the vast majority, either because of family connections, residence, occupation or social background, or a combination of these factors, are involved in it in one way or another.

The most striking feature of Tucson's social structure is its division into main parts—Anglo[7] and Mexican. Without attempting to trace in detail the development of this division, we may say that it goes back at least to the beginning of the United States occupation of this originally Mexican pueblo some seventy-five years ago. While U.S. authorities have never pursued a policy of deliberate segregation, there was, from the very earliest U.S. settlement, a tendency for the Anglos to settle in the northern part of town and to leave the south very largely Mexican in composition. This tendency was reinforced after the coming of the railroad from California in 1880, as new Anglo settlers preferred to live on higher ground on the north and east sides of town. By 1915, at the beginning of a new and heavy Anglo influx, almost all the newcomers were settling on the east side of the tracks.

The Anglos immigrating to Tucson during the first half century of American occupation were almost without exception drawn from the upper and middle classes of people in other American cities. Many of these people were retired businessmen and their families; others were health-seekers who could afford to spend at least a part of their time in the beneficial climate of Tucson. Anglo laborers were not attracted to Tucson for a number of reasons: one of the most important was that Tucson had no large industries, and another was that the town already had an abundant supply of Mexican Indian labor. From this situation it is apparent that from the very start of Tucson's U.S. occupation, the town's lower class has been drawn almost exclusively from its large Mexican population.

The railroad tracks are significant not only in the division between the Anglo and Mexican communities, but also in the structure of the Mexican community itself. The bulk of the Mexican population lives on the westerly side of the main Southern Pacific tracks, which bisect the city diagonally from northwest to southeast. A comparative handful of Mexican people, however, live among the Anglo-Americans on the east side of the tracks. Practically all of the people on the west side have some share in the life of the Mexican community. A few of those living on the east side also take part in the life of the Mexican community, but their participation is relatively slight, and they are important to this community more as eminent figureheads than as leaders.

Besides this basic division of east and west, there are other geographic divisions which further differentiate those parts of the Mexican population living on the west side. There is, first of all, the "centro" or nucleus of the old Mexican pueblo, in the downtown section of the city where many Mexican families still live. Then radiating outward both to the northwest and south are the various "barrios" or neighborhoods. Those to the south include Barrio Libre and Barrio Millville, and to the northwest, Barrio Anita, and the newer Hollywood and El Río, and Barrio Pascua and Belén, this latter adjoining the Yaqui village of Pascua.

According to Mr. Getty's and the writer's observations, as well as the testimony of our informants, the barrios are primarily geographic units and do not differ sharply from one another in social composition. However, there is some evidence that the barrios are socially distinct neighborhoods, each with its peculiar characteristics. It seems significant, for example, that the younger generation, as well as the older, is familiar with the barrio names and areas occupied by each.

From the standpoint of the present study, by far the most important of the geographic divisions mentioned above is that between the east and west. This sharp difference is immediately apparent in a comparison of house types and streets in the two parts of town. The houses of the barrios are generally small box-like adobe structures, often with no inside plumbing or even cement floors. The yard surrounding the house usually is bare, with perhaps a few straggling patches of grass fronting the street. In the back, there is generally a wood pile, outhouse and chicken shed. In contrast, the houses of people of Mexican descent on the east side of town are much larger, patterned after upper class Anglo standards, with inside bathrooms, gas or electric appliances for heating and cooking, and with pleasingly landscaped yards. Also, unlike the rough and dusty streets commonly found on the west, the streets on the east side are far more frequently paved and tree-lined.

The above physical differences mirror differences in the socio-economic statuses of Mexican people living in the two areas. In occupation, the people of the barrios are generally unskilled or skilled laborers, tradesmen, small shop owners or clerical assistants. On the other hand, those people of Mexican descent who live on the east side are generally either professional people, owners of medium or large-sized business enterprises, or white-collar employees having responsible positions in such enterprises.

Important as the railroad tracks are, however, they are by no means a hard and fast dividing line of social class in the Mexican community. Many people of considerable social distinction still live on the west side of town. Included in this group are many younger members of the exclusive Club Latino, whose roster supposedly is limited to Tucson's sixty Mexican families of highest social prestige. Some of these people have moved from the crowded central sections of the city to the new residential locations in the south part of town. Despite its position west of the railroad tracks, South Tucson has an attractive residential area in which homes of Mexicans and Anglos are interspersed, and which compares favorably with lower middle-class Anglo neighborhoods on the east side of the city.

As between the barrios themselves, the contrasts are much less sharp than those between the east and west. The most marked differences are those between the unplastered shack-like adobe huts in the southwest part of the Barrio Libre, along the Santa Cruz river, and the neatly plastered and painted adobe or concrete-block houses of El Río. These differences, again, reflect differences in socio-economic statuses. The people in the southwest part of Barrio Libre are mainly families of migrant workers or day laborers, and represent the lowest economic level in the city. In the other barrios, and especially El Río, most of the families have one or more members with steady year-round jobs either as unskilled or semi-skilled laborers. As we have already noted, these other neighborhoods also have a fair scattering of skilled laborers, clerical assistants, and small shopowners.

In terms of socio-economic class, then, there seem to be at least five groups represented in the Mexican community in Tucson. The highest or "upper" of these may be said to be composed of those wealthy "Old Families" of Mexican descent who live on the east side of the railroad tracks. The lowest is the group of unskilled migrant worker families in the southwest while in between are, first, the steadily employed unskilled or semi-skilled laboring groups, who might be regarded as a sort of "upper-lower" class and, second, the group of skilled laborers, tradesmen, clerical workers, and small merchants who comprise what might be called the Mexican community's middle class and, third, that less prominent and less well established younger element of the upper group whose members live on both sides of the tracks, and which might be said to compose the Mexican community's "lower-upper" class.

Cross-cutting the divisions of geography and social class in the Mexican community are two other important divisions—those of age-group and national origin. From the estimates of informants, government reports and the writer's own survey, it seems evident that about half of the Mexican residents of forty years of age or older are immigrants from Mexico. Most of these people came to the United States in the two decades following the collapse of the Diaz regime in 1910, and permanent immigration since then has been relatively slight. The result has been to increase the separateness of this group not only as immigrants but as an age group. In the Hollywood Barrio, for example, a majority of the adults who are forty years of age are immigrants from the Mexican state of Sonora.

In regard to linguistic background, limitations of space necessitate elimination of all but the barest essentials. We may simply note here that four main variants of Spanish may be distinguished in Tucson. These are, first, the Southern Arizona dialect of Spanish; second, standard Mexican Spanish; third, the Pachuco dialect; and fourth, the Yaqui dialect of Spanish. Of these four, the Southern Arizona dialect is by far the most widely used in Tucson. It is characterized by the use of some archaic forms of Spanish, by the use of many pochismos,[8] and by the tendency of its speakers to rely almost entirely upon the familiar verb endings, and by its intonation patterns or *sonsonete*, which may easily be distinguished from that of the standard Mexican Spanish of Mexico City. Pachuco is an argot of youth which borrows heavily from Mexican and American slang. Its use in Tucson is perhaps wider than that of the Yaqui dialect of Spanish, which is confined to a few hundred persons of Yaqui Indian descent.[9]

Field Methods

In the course of this inquiry, the field work for which extended over a six-months period in Tucson, the writer collected as much material as possible on the language usage and social life of representative individuals and families of Mexican descent. In all, the work included data on more than one hundred individuals, who were members of twenty families. This group of families represent an attempt by the investigator to obtain a cross-section of the families of Mexican descent living in Tucson. Viewed from the standpoint of geographic location, six of these families live on the east side of the railroad tracks, while fourteen live on the west and south sides of town. Of these fourteen, eleven live in the strongly Mexican barrios, while three live in neighborhoods which might be described as neutral or intermediate in ethnic composition.

In socio-economic status, five of the families were evaluated as belonging to the upper-lower class, nine to the lower-middle class, and six to the upper-middle class in the general Tucson community.[10] From the standpoint of length of residence, four of the families are those of P_1 immigrants (persons who came to the United States at the age of eighteen or over), three are of P_2 immigrants (persons who came to the United States under eighteen) and thirteen are of the F_1 or succeeding American-born generations. Of these thirteen, three may be classified as among the "Old Families," the topmost group in Tucson's Mexican-American population.

The main field method of this study was that of observation. During the writer's residence in Tucson he had opportunity to see how people of Mexican descent talked and acted, both in the Mexican sections, in Anglo neighborhoods, and in the privacy of their own homes. The effort was made to observe individuals and families in a variety of situations and to see how their usage of Spanish and English compared with their actions in each case. To put people at their ease regarding his presence, the writer did not conduct formal interviews or take down conversations as they occurred. Rather, he attempted to become acquainted with people simply through casual and informal social and business contacts. In the Mexican neighborhood in which he lived he was known as a student who was interested in Mexican customs. As such he was not too obstrusive a figure, and was able to witness many conversations in which the participants took little or no notice of his presence.

At the beginning of his stay, and also at the end[11] the writer had a series of informal interviews with individuals prominent in Mexican and Anglo society in Tucson. The object of these interviews was not so much to obtain data on the subjects' language usage as it was to obtain background material on the languages and dialects used in Tucson and on the social structure and Mexican participation in the life of the town. These interviews were supplemented by others obtained by Mr. Getty over a three-year period.

A third type of field method used in this study was that of questionnaires. These were of two types. The first was a series of eighteen questions which was submitted to sixth grade school children by their teachers or principals while the writer was still in the field. The information sought in this questionnaire included data on the child's family, period of residence in Tucson, language usage, and cultural interests. This questionnaire was filled out by about two hundred Mexican pupils and about sixty Anglo pupils. The second questionnaire was far more limited in scope and number. It was designed simply to fill out blank spots in the writer's information on the family language usage of some of his subjects, and was sent out by mail after the writer had left the field.

Conclusions

The study resulted in the following conclusions, each of which may be stated in the form of a tentative hypothesis, subject to the check of similar investigations among other bilingual minority groups.

1. *Division of the social functions of language.* In a bilingual minority group in process of cultural change, the functions originally performed by the ancestral language are divided between two or more languages, with the result that each language comes to be identified with certain fields of interpersonal relations. In the Tucson Mexican-American group, four such linguistically identifiable fields of interpersonal relations readily may be distinguished. These are, first, the field of intimate or familial relations; second, the field of informal relations; third, the field of formal relations; and, fourth, the field of Anglo-Mexican relations.

In the field of intimate or familial relations, Spanish is almost universally dominant in Tucson's Mexican-American community. Almost without exception, the Southern Arizona dialect of Spanish is the language of early childhood and the language used by parents to children in the home. By extension, the informal Spanish of the home is used in close friendships and in Parish social life and ceremonial relationships in the community. The Southern Arizona dialect thus comes to be identified with family background and minority group membership.

In the field of formal relations among bilinguals—a field which includes many types of economic relations and some formal social relationships—English is widely used. The substitution of English for formal Spanish may be traced to the fact that, as has been noted among other bilingual groups, young children do not learn formal Spanish at home. Instead, at the age when they ordinarily would be learning formal Spanish, they go to school and learn English.[12] For many children, English thus becomes identified with most types of formal relationships. Exceptions are events in the Mexican community having a religious or patriotic social context, in which formal Spanish customarily is used.

In relations between Anglos and Mexicans in Tucson, English is the standard language. Even though the bilingual individual knows that the Anglo he is addressing speaks Spanish, he will almost always use English. Exceptions to this are some immigrants from Mexico who, if they feel that the Anglo to whom they are speaking is favorably inclined toward Mexico, will encourage him to speak Spanish. So strongly is the speaking of Spanish identified with participation in the Mexican community in Tucson that some bilinguals who wish to improve their relations with Anglos will even deny that they speak Spanish.

2. *Congruity of the individual's linguistic behavior patterns with his social relations.* For each bilingual individual, the languages he speaks take on different symbolic values which vary according to the individual's social experience. The character of this experience, in turn, depends on, first, the position of the minority group in the general community; second, the relation of the individual to the minority group; and, third, the relation of the individual to the general community, or, in short, to the above-described fields of interpersonal relations. The different values resulting are expressed in correspondingly different linguistic behavior patterns. Thus, among the individuals in this study, four main types of linguistic behavior patterns may be defined. These patterns, and the types of social experience with which they were found to be correlated, may be outlined briefly as follows:

Bilinguals, type 1: (usually American-born) speak Southern Arizona dialect of Spanish and sub-standard English; favor English and avoid Spanish in conversations with Anglos. Seek mobility through Anglo contacts.

Bilinguals, type 2: (including many immigrants) speak standard Mexican Spanish and sub-standard English; favor Spanish in conversation with Anglos and tend to be shy about their English. Seek mobility through Mexican community or are apathetic.

Bilinguals, type 3: (mostly children of types 1 and 2) speak Southern Arizona dialect of Spanish, Pachuco, and sub-standard English. Favor special language. Reject both Mexican and Anglo groups and seek to form a society of their own.

Bilinguals, type 4: (including many "Old Families") speak standard Spanish, Southern Arizona dialect, and standard English. Favor both standard English and standard Spanish. Marginal to both Mexican and Anglo groups.

In interpreting this classification, it should be emphasized that the Mexican people of Tucson are more or less bicultural. Mexican cultural interests, aided by religious influence, are dominant in the field of familial and intimate relations, while in the field of Anglo-Mexican relations the influence of Anglo urban culture competes with Mexican cultural interests for their attention. For individuals in the Mexican community, these fields may be represented as a kind of continuum, at one end of which are the intimate relations with others of Mexican descent, while at the other end are the purely formal relations with Anglos. In between are formal and informal relations with people of Mexican descent outside the family circle, and in some cases with Mexicans from Mexico.

Paralleling the above-described continuum in fields of interpersonal relations is a continuum in language usage, and we find that the categories of interpersonal relations are reflected by corresponding variations in linguistic behavior. At one end of this linguistic continuum Spanish is dominant in the individual's contacts and at the other end English is dominant. In between are the pochismos, the Pachuco dialect, and the various mixtures of the two languages. Carrying this comparison a step further, we find that the position of each individual on the cultural continuum is roughly paralleled by his position on the linguistic continuum. The four groups of individuals described above thus may be broadly ranged according to (1) type of linguistic behavior pattern, or language usage, and (2) position with respect to Mexican and Anglo fields of interpersonal relations.

In their relation to these fields, the "Pochies," individuals of the first type described above, may be described as oriented toward Anglo culture in all fields except that of intimate and familial relations. The members of the second type, the immigrant group, are oriented toward Mexican culture not only in familial relations but also in the field of informal and formal relations with other bilinguals. Their leaders, all of whom use standard Spanish on formal occasions, represent a small minority of the total Mexican population but are the backbone of what might be called the "Colonia Mexicana" in Tucson. The third main type, the Pachuco group, rejects the cultural norms of both the Anglo and Mexican groups for its fields and substitutes those of its own, drawn from anti-social aspects of both cultures. The fourth type, that of the "Old Families," tries to maintain an even balance between Anglo and Mexican fields.

3. *Congruity of the group's linguistic behavior patterns with its social relations.* The data accumulated by Getty clearly indicates that the Tucson Mexican community occupies a subordinate social position in the town's social structure. This position is reflected in the characteristic ways in which the group uses and reacts to English and Spanish, or, in brief, in its linguistic behavior patterns. As we have seen, the group tends to preserve Spanish as the language of intimate and familial relations, while reserving English for relations of a more impersonal type. This tendency holds not only for members of the immigrant generation but equally for many Arizona-born and educated bilinguals. Of equal significance is the tendency, already mentioned, of many bilinguals to avoid the speaking of Spanish in social relations with Anglos, even though they are aware that the Anglos speak Spanish.

The social segregation of the Mexican population in Tucson is nowhere more clearly indicated than in the linguistic behavior patterns of children in the barrios. It is a curious fact that one of the institutions fostering the speaking of Spanish among Mexican-American children in Tucson is the playground of the neighborhood public school. Inside the school buildings children are required to speak English, but outside there are no restrictions, and schools which once tried to require English on the playground have given it up as unenforceable. Once outside the formal atmosphere of the classroom, Mexican-American pupils seem to have an almost irresistible impulse to revert to the informal Southern Arizona dialect at play. The one factor which might prevent this reversion—the presence of a large number of pupils of other ethnic groups—is missing, since there are few non-Mexicans living in the Mexican neighborhood. The use of Spanish in informal games is carried over to informal relations generally on the playground. At lunch time the use of Spanish is encouraged in the lunch stands just across the street from the school yard, where children may go to get tortillas and cokes, and to play Mexican records on the jukebox.

In addition to their tendency to avoid Spanish in relations with Anglos, many Tucson bilinguals manifest a feeling of inferiority with respect to their "Mexican accent" in speaking English. The association of inferior social standing with this accent would seem to support Bossard's hypothesis regarding linguistic identification with status. The social function of the Mexican accent in Tucson's economic structure is clearly summed up by one of the writer's bilingual informants who remarked, concerning his own group, "People on the east side of town speak English to their children because they don't want them to grow up with an accent, and endanger their chances of getting a job."

Inferior social status in Tucson is associated not only with the "Mexican accent" but with the Southern Arizona dialect of Spanish. The dialect is the language *par excellence* of the barrios on the west side of town. While its use is not confined to these lower-class areas, Mexican-Americans living on the east side avoid speaking it in conversation with cultured persons from Mexico. Conscious of its "errors," they seek to substitute standard Spanish forms wherever possible. Similarly, Mexican-Americans who move from the barrios to the east side of town tend to drop the dialect in favor of English and standard Spanish. In making this change, they are perhaps influenced by their awareness that the Tucson Anglo community accepts them not as "Mexicans" but as "Spanish-Americans" or "Latin-Americans." Here again, there is evidence of linguistic identification with the socio-economic status of the minority group. As one Anglo informant frankly admitted when asked what term she used for the Spanish-speaking people of Tucson: "Why, I use Mexican, unless I'm talking to or about those in the upper brackets; then it's customary to use Spanish-American."

4. *Correlation of linguistic behavior patterns with acculturation conditions.* Analysis of linguistic behavior patterns in the Mexican-American minority group in Tucson leads to the following inferences regarding the basic conditions of acculturation in the Tucson area:

i. Psychological, as well as social, subordination of the Mexican population in the general Tucson community, as indicated by:

   a) reticence of many Mexicans to speak Spanish with, and in the presence of, Anglos.

   b) identification of the term "Mexican" with lower-class status in Tucson, and corresponding substitution of the term "Spanish-American" for Mexicans having higher status.

   c) lack of informal interpersonal relations between Anglos and Mexicans as indicated by lack of informal linguistic categories common to both. Very few Mexicans can "kid" and use small-talk entirely in English in a manner common among Anglos. Also, very few Anglos can speak the mixed Spanish-English common in informal usage among Tucson Mexicans.

   ii. Cultural, as well as physical, segregation of the Mexican population in the general Tucson community as indicated by:

      a) inability of many young bilinguals to free themselves of "Spanish accent" in speaking English.

      b) inability of many young bilinguals to translate freely from one language to the other.

      c) dependence of American-born bilinguals on Spanish in certain fields of interpersonal relations: i.e. family life and close friendships.

      d) use of pochismos and other hybrid linguistic forms.

   iii. Divergent types of cultural orientation, and correspondingly divergent social goals, in the Tucson Mexican population, as indicated by the four main types of linguistic behavior patterns found among members of the minority group.

In evaluating the usefulness of linguistic behavior patterns in the analysis of acculturation and assimilation problems, one may well ask, "What advantages does this method offer as contrasted to existing sociological methods of solving the same type of problem? To answer this question it will be necessary to review briefly the concept of the linguistic behavior pattern, or language usage. This concept rests on the postulate that the linguistic behavior of any given individual exhibits a systematic patterning which can be defined objectively in terms, first, of the limits of the system; second, of the parts of which it is composed; and, third, of the relative frequency of use of the various parts in standard situations. Thus the student of linguistic behavior is concerned not so much with what an individual says are his attitudes and values (i.e. how he rationalizes) as with how he uses and reacts to the linguistic symbol systems at his command in the course of his daily contacts. An Anglo resident of Tucson may say he is "very fond of the Mexican people," but such a statement cannot be given much weight in comparison to data on his linguistic behavior which show that in his social and economic relations he clearly places them in a subordinate role, while he refers to those who are his social equals not as Mexicans but as "Spanish-Americans" or members of "Old Families." The analysis of linguistic behavior, then, would seem to have an advantage over direct questions obtained through formal interviews and questionnaires, which too often are rationalizations of what the subject considers his attitudes should be.

A second principal advantage of the method would seem to lie in the fact that it offers a means of obtaining an independent check on other sociological data. Since the linguistic system of an individual or group functions as an autonomous, self-contained system, this system may be analyzed and reported on independently of other cultural data. Here again, the fact that language enters intimately and almost unconsciously into the defining and constant redefining of all interpersonal relations, makes possible a relatively high degree of objectivity in the analysis of interpersonal relations from the data of linguistic behavior.

In summary, it is hoped that this exploratory study of linguistic behavior patterns may contribute to the development of a new and useful method of sociological analysis. Further research in this field of the social functions of language may be expected to follow along two main lines: first, the development of language usage as a more precise tool of sociological analysis, and second, the application of this tool in the study of that aspect of social behavior in which it may be most effectively used, namely, in the investigation of interpersonal relations, with special reference to attitudes. Progress along the first line will be dependent upon the more precise description and analysis of variations of linguistic behavior in social situations, and upon the statement of these relations in quantitative terms. Research along the second line may be conducted on several different levels: these range from the psychological level, on which the concern is with individual personalities, to the cultural level, on which the concern is with the language, goals and values of larger groups of people.

Finally, a note may be added on the need for extending this type of research to other frontier areas. The sociological problems arising from the drawing of boundary lines through a zone in which people of two cultures mingle are not confined to southern Arizona. We may predict that similar problems will exist wherever political boundaries are established between contiguous cultures having different languages. We also may predict that in any such area there will be a large number of bilinguals, and that these will tend to develop a hybrid culture and language of their own. "Assimilation" in such an environment thus takes on a significance quite different from the traditional ethnocentric use of the term. In the long run, the assimilation process in such areas would seem to consist not so much in the engulfing of a minority group by a majority group as the fusion of the two to produce something new. If such is found to be the case, a modification of traditional political and educational policies with respect to such border peoples would seem to be in order.

Notes

[1] Spicer, E. H. "Linguistic Aspects of Yaqui Acculturation", *American Anthropologist*, Vol. 45, no. 3.

[2] Johnson, J. B. "A Clear Case of Linguistic Acculturation", *American Anthropologist*, Vol. 45, no. 3.

[3] Redfield, Robert. *Tepoztlan: A Mexican Village.* University of Chicago Press, 1930.

[4] Reuter, Edward B. "Culture Contacts in Puerto Rico." *The American Journal of Sociology,* September, 1946.

[5] Tuck, Ruth D. *Not With The Fist: A Study of Mexican-Americans in a Southwest City.* Harcourt Brace & Co., 1946.

[6] Bossard, James H. "The Bilingual As A Person – Linguistic Identification With Status". *American Sociological Review,* December, 1946.

[7] This term will be used in this paper to denote persons whose cultural background is that of the Anglo-American majority in the United States.

[8] This term refers to hispanized English words which are commonly used by the "Pochies", persons of Mexican descent who were born in the United States.

[9] Speakers of Yaqui, and of the Yaqui dialect of Spanish, were not included in this study, as they were felt to constitute a separate ethnic group.

[10] The above terminology is used only as a scheme of classification. The categories suggested

are not to be regarded as fixed or absolute and are intended simply to indicate the relative position of the subjects studied in the general socio-economic structure of Tucson.

[11]The major part of the writer's field work was accomplished between the months of July, 1945, and February, 1946. In this study no attempt has been made, therefore, to deal with the effects of the introduction into Tucson elementary schools of the teaching of Spanish, an innovation which came later in the spring of 1946.

[12]cf. Trager, George L. "Number, Gender, and Personal Reference in Pennsylvania Windish (Slovene)." Unpublished paper read before the Linguistic Society of America, 1941.

Pachuco: An American-Spanish Argot and Its Social Function in Tucson, Arizona

George C. Barker

Introduction

In many cities of the American Southwest there are today Mexican-American boys who are known to local authorities and to members of their own community as pachucos. These boys may be said to constitute a small minority of the total Mexican-American youth in any given town, and may be distinguished from the latter by certain peculiar characteristics of dress, behavior, and language. This paper is a study of the speech of these boys and their followers as found in one southwestern city—Tucson, Arizona. The aim of this paper is first, to obtain some insight into the origin and nature of the Pachuco argot and, second, to examine its social functions—that is, to see what relation may exist between the usage of the Pachuco jargon and the social positions, goals and values of its speakers in the Tucson community.

Webster defines an argot as a secret language or conventional slang peculiar to a group of thieves, tramps or vagabonds; or, more broadly, a cant or class jargon.[1] The same authority defines a jargon as a hybrid speech or dialect arising from a mixture of languages.[2] Pachuco[3] justly may claim both titles, for while it is basically a variant of Spanish, Spanish-speaking people living in Tucson find it almost as unintelligible as do English-speaking people. This situation may be explained in part by the fact that Pachuco borrows heavily not only from Mexican slang, but from American slang as well. In part, also, it may be due to the fact that many of the commonest Pachuco words have been imported from the colloquial Spanish dialect of New Mexico and western Texas, and are not commonly known in Arizona. These points will be discussed further in a later section of this paper.

Dialects of Spanish in Tucson

As a means of defining the usage of the Pachuco argot in Tucson, it will be well first to review briefly the other common variants of the Spanish language which are heard in the town. These are, in the order of their numerical strength, first, the southern Arizona dialect of Spanish, second, standard Mexican Spanish, and third, the Yaqui dialect of Spanish. Since the Yaqui dialect of Spanish has only about 900 speakers in the Tucson area and since we are not concerned with this group in the present study, our discussion will be limited to the other two dialects and Pachuco.

Southern Arizona Spanish has many points in common with the type of Spanish spoken by the Hispano-American of New Mexico. Older speakers of both dialects use many forms which were brought into the new world during the sixteenth and seventeenth centuries, and which, due to the isolation of these speakers, have changed in locally limited ways, and have not been subject to the leveling effect of the standard language.

The southern Arizona dialect seems to have retained fewer of these local forms than has the dialect of New Mexico. Perhaps one reason for this is that Tucson children are studying standard Spanish in high school, junior high school, and, since 1946, in grammar school. In their school Spanish, the children are being taught to substitute the standard forms for the colloquial ones. Another point is that Tucson, located on a direct rail route to Mexico City, is less isolated from Mexico than many of the New Mexican communities.

Besides its archaic forms, another outstanding characteristic of southern Arizona Spanish is its heavy use of Hispanized English words, commonly known as "pochismos." A list of some of the more common of these will be found at the end of this paper. These forms are used most frequently by younger speakers, but older persons are by no means free of them. Not only words, but expressions, are borrowed and transposed by young and old alike. A priest told the writer that children making confession to him often told him that they had "hablado para atrás" (talked back to) their elders. A teacher of Mexican descent said she sometimes used the expression "me agarró el chivo" (he got my goat). A craftsman, fixing a window-lever on his car, told the writer, "Está fuera de orden" (it's out of order). An elderly gentleman wrote concerning his children "Tubieron muy buen tiempo" (They had a very good time).

A third prominent characteristic of southern Arizona Spanish is the tendency of its speakers to rely largely on the familiar verb forms (second person), even though they may never previously have met the person to whom they are speaking. This is especially true among younger speakers. A boy goes up to a soft drink stand, for example, and asks, "¿Qué tienes?" (what hast thou?) even though he may never have met previously the girl who waits on him.

A fourth major characteristic of southern Arizona Spanish is its similarity to the Spanish of the northern part of the state of Sonora, Mexico. Speakers of southern Arizona Spanish have a pronounced sentence melody or "sonsonete," which is very similar to that of northern Sonora. Storz describes the Sonoran intonations as follows: "the sentences and phrases have a rising inflection with a sharp fall toward the close, the words themselves being spoken with a drawl when emphasis is desired."[4] This intonation is so firmly established as a linguistic pattern that Tucson children of Mexican descent frequently carry it over into their English. The main difference in the Spanish of the two areas seems to consist in: first, the much greater use in southern Arizona Spanish of Hispanized English words of "pochismos," second, the greater use in Sonora of polite forms, and third, the wider substitution in Sonora of standard forms in place of archaic words and expressions. The writer's informants seemed to agree that these differences could be explained largely in terms of language training in school and especially in the family. In Sonora, for example, the use of many archaic forms seems to be limited to poor and uneducated people while in southern Arizona their use extends through a much wider segment of the Spanish-speaking population.

To describe the type of standard Spanish spoken in Tucson as Mexican

Spanish is perhaps an over-simplification, as the republic of Mexico seems to be divided into at least five main dialect areas. The northern Sonora area we have described may perhaps be regarded as a subregion of one of these major areas, the norteño. Four other areas, each of which is characterized by similarly distinct differences in accent and vocabulary, are outlined by the Mexican linguist Henríquez Ureña, as the central area, or "el centro" comprising the highlands of central Mexico; the south including Morelos, Guerrero, and Oaxaca; the Mexican gulf coast or costeño, comprising Tamaulipas, Vera Cruz, Tabasco, and Campeche; and the region of Yucatán.[5]

Of these five areas, the central one is the one that might best be described as the standard of Mexico, since it is the area in which is situated Mexico City, the capital, and accordingly, the one which enjoys the greatest prestige. Of course, the Spanish of Mexico City has many features in common with the Spanish of the Mexican provinces which together distinguish Mexican Spanish from the Castilian Spanish of Spain. Perhaps the chief ones of these are "yeísmo," the lack of distinction between the *ll* and *y*; "seseo," failure to distinguish the *c* before *e* and *i* from the sibilant sound of *s*; and the many Mexicanismos and words of Nahuatl origin.[6] From the standpoint of our study, however, the most interesting features of the Spanish of Mexico City are those which serve to distinguish it from the northern Sonora dialect and the southern Arizona dialect. Perhaps the most obvious of these is the fact that the standard intonation patterns or "sonsonete" of the Mexico City Spanish, differ from the "rustic" patterns of Sonora which some of the writer's informants have described as "clipped." From the standpoint of vocabulary, the Spanish of the central area contains relatively few archaisms, and has been influenced more by the classical forms introduced into Spain in the seventeenth and eighteenth centuries.[7] In contrast to southern Arizona Spanish, also, there is a much more strict use of formal Spanish between individuals who are not on intimate terms with each other. For a clerk in Mexico City to use familiar Spanish to a customer, for example, would be grossly insulting.

In contrast to the southern Arizona dialect and standard Mexican Spanish, the usage of Pachuco in Tucson may be defined in terms of a particular sex and age group. For this reason Pachuco is referred to in this paper as an argot or jargon rather than as a dialect. The speakers of Pachuco are very largely adolescents and young men of Mexican descent who move in lower-class[8] social circles. Since, in Tucson, most Mexicans having lower-class status live on the west side of town the Pachuco speech community may be defined in terms of geography as well as of age, sex, social-economic class. Many adults of Mexican descent living on the east side of town have little or no knowledge of Pachuco.

As has been mentioned, Pachuco borrows heavily not only from Mexican but from American slang. It is perhaps this latter element of its vocabulary which makes it so difficult for Mexican speakers to understand. Words like "chante" (shanty), "flicas" (flickers, movies) reflect American slang origin, while "Guaino" (a wine drinking souse), and "rolante" (automobile) indicate the Hispanization and adaptation of English words.

Other prominent characteristics of Pachuco are its use of a sonorous drawl, or as the pachucos say, a "cola" (tail); its exclusive reliance on the formal verb forms of Spanish; and finally its use of gesture and signs to supplement its vocabulary. Several of the most obscene terms in Pachuco are indicated by signs made with the hands of the speaker. In general, it may be said that habitual speakers of Pachuco try to keep it an exclusive language, restricted to the initiated through the frequent introduction of new slang terms.

The Structure of Pachuco

In its syntax, or sentence structure, the Pachuco jargon is more closely related to the southern Arizona dialect than to standard Mexican Spanish. Speakers of Pachuco, like Spanish-speaking persons in many other new world areas, use colloquialisms that would be frowned upon by teachers of "good Spanish." An example is the construction "vamos a ir" (we are going to go) instead of "vamos" or "iremos" (we will go). Pachuco differs from the southern Arizona dialect, however, in its exclusive reliance on formal verb forms, already noted, and in its frequent use of attention-getting forms of address, prefatory to statements and questions. Following are examples:

"Nel pues sabe, carnal, me fué a una cantina, ve."
(Well you know, pal, I went to a bar, see.)
" ¿Ese, Crow, 'onde 'stá su ramfla?"
(Say, Crow, where's your car?)
"Pues nel ve, Crow, que yo tengo un datile con una chavala que le dicen Dora."
(Well look here, Crow; I've got a date with a gal named Dora.)
"Sabe qué el bato que me la hizo chillar no anda aquí."
(You know, the guy who gave me trouble didn't come here.)

The similarity of these expressions to colloquial substandard English expressions, as shown above, indicates to what extent Pachuco has been influenced by these American forms.

To make any over-all statements concerning the nature of Pachuco word structure, or morphology, would be a difficult if not impossible task, since its vocabulary is a "duke's mixture" of words from several linguistic sources, each of which has its own rules of morphological construction. As a means of simplifying this presentation, therefore, examples of the words drawn from these different sources will be given, and after each of these groups of words, some remarks will be added concerning their structure and origin.

The vocabulary used by the pachucos of Tucson consists largely of words drawn from at least four and possibly five immediate linguistic sources. These sources are: first, southwestern Spanish, including southern Arizona Spanish; second, the New Mexico dialect of Spanish; third, Mexican slang; fourth, standard Spanish; and fifth, a tentative category—words invented by the pachucos or their antecedents. These sources will be considered in the above-mentioned order.

One of the main characteristics of southwestern Spanish is its heavy use of Hispanized English words and expressions. These "pochismos" or "Anglicismos" are of two main types: first, English words that have been made into Spanish nouns or verbs through Hispanization, or changes in spelling and pronunciation and, second, English or American slang expressions which have been translated into Spanish. Speakers of Pachuco have taken over many words and expressions in both of these categories. The following are examples:

Hispanized English words

English	Spanish
beer	birria
bunk	bonque
control	controlar
spot	espatiar
look (watch)	guachar
gang	ganga
song	songa

Translated American slang words and expressions

English	Spanish
to get a kick out of	agarrar patada
to cut it out	cortarse
to beat it	pegarle
to give one the air	dar aire
to paint the town red	pintar el pizo en colorado
to blow one's top	volar la tapa

As will be seen from the above, the Hispanized English words have been altered to conform to the Spanish pattern of word structure. Verbs have been given "ar" or "iar" endings, thus permitting their conjugation along orthodox Spanish lines. Nouns also have been altered to fit Spanish orthography; thus, as noted, American "shanty" becomes Pachuco "chante" (house), and by parallel construction with the standard Spanish "casa" (house) and "casarse" (to get married), becomes "chantarse" (to get married). This conformity to Spanish linguistic structure is apparent even in the literally translated words and expressions, which, while they have meaning only in the light of American usage, are typically Spanish in their construction.

From the Spanish dialect of New Mexico and western Texas[9] the Pachuco jargon has picked up some of its most distinctive words and phrases. Among these are the following:

Dialect	New Mexico meaning	Pachuco meaning
bato, bata	sweetheart	guy, girl
chale	shut up	no
cantón	house	home
chuchuluco	toy	candy
entabicar	to put in jail	to put in jail
guisa	girl friend	girl
garras	rags	clothes
jando	money	money
jefe, jefa	father, mother	father, mother
el mono	humorous cartoon	movie
pisto	(pistón) drunkard	liquor
rolar	to lie down to sleep	sleep
simón	yes	yes

tando	hat	hat
tecla	cigarette stub	doped cigarette
trapos	dry goods	clothes
trola	match	match
rucqo	(ruquito) old man	old man
rucqa	out of style	old woman

From colloquial Mexican usage Pachuco has adapted many words and expressions not found in standard Spanish dictionaries. The following are examples.

Mexican	Pachuco	Meaning
andar aguetando	andar huitado	to feel low
colero (chronic borrower)	colerar	to borrow
el congal (brothel)	el congal	hangout
chanate (blackbird)	chanate	Negro
ficha (an IOU note)	ficha	money
filero (a type of knife)	fileriar	to knife someone
mayate (June bug)	mallate	Negro
panocha (sweets, brown sugar)	panocha	wine
ramfla (old vehicle)	ramfla	auto
tecolate (cigarette stub)	tecolata	cigarette stub
trompa (mouth)	trompear	to neck

Perhaps the largest single source of words in the Pachuco vocabulary is standard Spanish. By this term, "standard Spanish" is meant not only words current in the standard Spanish of the present day, but also some words and expressions now generally archaic or obsolete, yet which still are listed in modern dictionaries of Spanish. These standard Spanish words conveniently may be divided into three groups; first, words used by the pachucos with a change in meaning; second, words used with a change in form; and third, words which have been changed both in form and meaning.

In the first group, Spanish words which have been changed in meaning, the following examples may be cited:

Spanish	Standard meaning	Pachuco meaning
atizar	to stir up (the fire)	to beat up
al alba	at dawn	sharp, smart
abusado	to take advantage of	smart, alert
aquellas	those	swell, super
clavar	to nail, to cheat	to steal
chaveta	bolt, pin, key	head
carnal	related by blood	brother, pal
gabacho	derogatory term applied by Spanish to French	American
grifo[10]	kinky, entangled	marijuana addict
refinar	to refine	to eat

In the second group, Spanish words changed in form, the following are common examples:

Spanish	Pachuco	Meaning
Arizona	araisa	Arizona
mexicano	chicano	Mexican
California	califa	California
el corazón	la cora	heart
El Paso	El pachuco	El Paso
Juárez	Juarilez	Juarez
Los Angeles	los	Los Angeles
México	Mejicle	Mexico
restaurante	resta	restaurant
el retrato	el retra	picture

In the third group, Spanish words changed in both form and meaning, the following examples may be cited:

Spanish	Meaning	Pachuco	Meaning
al alba	at dawn	alalvar	wise up
borrar	to blot out	borrarse	to scram (get away quickly)
cacarear	to cackle	la cácara	girl
caldear	to heat	calear	to bawl out
Calvario	Calvary	Calvito	God
cantón	corner	cantonear	to live
refinar	to refine	refín	food
yesca	tinder	yesco	marijuana addict

A fifth group of words in the Pachuco vocabulary consists of terms which cannot at present be traced to any outside source, and thus presumably have originated among the pachucos or their antecedents in the Mexican underworld. This grouping is of course tentative as new evidence may indicate that many of the words so classified may be reassigned to one of the sources already mentioned. In this fifth group, the following examples may be cited:

Pachuco	Meaning
bola	shoe shine
bute	very much
cachuquear	to double-cross
catear	to beat up
carlongo	coat
entacucharse	to dress up
estramos	pants
frajo	cigarette
gacho	bad, lousy
jambo	thief
jaspia	hunger
lisa	shirt
liquellar	to see
órale	O.K.

princer	on foot
pucha	cigarette butt
relizar	to give, trade
rufo	freight train
tacuchi	zoot suit

Any discussion of the Pachuco vocabulary would be incomplete without reference to its rapid change in content. As is the case with all such jargons, words which have become hackneyed and colorless through overuse constantly are being replaced by new expressions. The word for girl is a good example. In Tucson, at different times, the writer noted the following terms in current use: chavala, guisa, haina, cuerpo, jedionda, cácara.

A similar variety exists with reference to the expression "I'll be seeing you," which in Tucson has been modified successively from "Ay lo guacho" to "Ay lo guareo" and "Ay lo liquello."

In part, such variations may be attributed to the desire of Pachuco speakers to keep "hep" with their gang and to appear sophisticated to their friends. In part, also, the introduction of new synonyms serves to maintain the secretive character of the jargon. This secrecy is convenient when discussing "dangerous" topics such as marijuana, for which the writer has heard at least eight different names.

Paralleling the above-mentioned differences in vocabulary are minor variations in intonation patterns among different speakers of Pachuco in Tucson. Those most familiar with the jargon affect a whining nasal drawl common among the pachucos in Los Angeles. Those less familiar with the jargon speak it much as they do the southern Arizona dialect of Spanish. In general, we may say that the differences in the Pachuco jargon in Tucson do not vary according to neighborhood, as has been reported in Los Angeles,[11] but are rather due to differences in the speaker's knowledge and practice of what one informant has called pachuco "style" in language, dress and behavior.

Origin and Spread of Pachuco

The presence in the Pachuco vocabulary of a large number of words peculiar to the New Mexico dialect of Spanish would seem to point to that general area as a possible point of origin of the argot. This evidence is supported by the testimony of six of the writer's best informants, all of whom are agreed that the argot originated in the border area of El Paso and Juárez. As further evidence, many of the writer's informants have pointed out that the word "pachuco" is a colloquial way of saying El Paso. Similarly, a person from El Paso commonly is referred to as "Del pachuco." Of course, this does not necessarily mean that the pachucos were the first group to speak the jargon. On the contrary, three of the writer's older informants have pointed out that the jargon goes back at least to the early 1930's, thus antedating by several years the pachucos themselves. Two of these same informants have suggested that the jargon originated among "grifos," or marijuana smokers and dope peddlers, in the El Paso underworld.

The most conclusive single piece of evidence on this point is contained in a letter to the writer from Gabriel Córdova, graduate student at the El Paso School of Mines, who was for several years court interpreter for the El Paso police court. Córdova says the jargon originated with original members of the 7-X gang, a group of marijuana smokers and peddlers who first met in the neighborhood of Florence and Eighth streets, El Paso.[12] It seems probable that these individuals, in turn, obtained a substantial part of their vocabulary from the *Caló* or argot of the Mexican underworld. Caló, in its turn, may be traced back to the gypsies in Spain, for Caló was the term used by the gypsies to refer to their own language.

With the origin of the Pachuco jargon thus briefly indicated, we may now go on to inquire into the route and manner of its spread in the Southwest. There seems little doubt that this was accomplished largely by single men and boys who for various reasons migrated from El Paso to other southwestern towns along the Southern Pacific railroad. For example, Lalo Guerrero, one of the writer's older informants, reports that he first heard the jargon about 1933 when he obtained work in a Tucson bakery run by a group of El Paso youths. He reports that he and other boys in the neighborhood picked up the jargon from these El Paso boys.

The greatest single impetus to the spread of the jargon seems to have come in 1942, when a large group of El Paso boys migrated to Los Angeles. As in previous instances, this migration took place by means of "hopping freights." This time, however, the wholesale migration was instigated by a "floater" or "flora" from the El Paso police department, which placed suspended sentences on a number of the boys. Under the terms of the floater, these pachucos were to receive prison sentences if they ever returned to El Paso.

In Los Angeles during World War II the pachucos became identified—along with many Filipino and Negro youths in the metropolitan area—as "zoot-suiters." This arose through their custom, apparently borrowed from the Filipinos, of wearing "zoot suits"—radically styled men's clothing marked by their long coats, pancake hats, pants with narrow cuffs and thick-soled shoes. Added touches were heavy gold watch chains and long hair slicked back to a duck's tail effect in the back of the head.

Just how great was the influence of the original El Paso pachucos in the spread of "pachucoism" remains problematical, but the fact is apparent that by the end of 1942, there were self-styled pachucos in many Mexican districts of Los Angeles. These boys aped the manners, dress, and speech of the original pachucos, and fraternized in informally organized neighborhood gangs. These neighborhood groups of course brought pressure to bear on all boys of Mexican descent living in their "territory" to conform to the group's style. Those who did not were called by such names as "squares," "venados," "pacoimas," and "Pepsi-Cola kids."

As these neighborhood gangs continued to grow, they became increasingly dangerous in the eyes of the police. Tension was heightened by occasional fights between gangs from different neighborhoods. After one such fight, which occurred at a place called Sleepy Lagoon, between Los Angeles and Long Beach, a man was found murdered. In the resulting dragnet arrests, twenty-three Mexican-American boys, most of them minors, were taken into custody and tried for first-degree murder. In an atmosphere of public hysteria, a jury convicted seventeen of the boys of responsibility for the murder. Thanks to the efforts of a Citizen's Committee, all of these boys later were re-tried and exonerated, but the incident illustrates the ill repute now linked to the pachuco type of Mexican youth.

Gang fights and the wearing of the zoot suits were, of course, not the only reasons for the notoriety of the pachucos in Los Angeles during the war. Of greater importance in this connection was sensational newspaper publicity accompanying their participation in the zoot suit riots of 1943. These fights and riots involved various pachuco gangs and members of the U.S. armed services in the Los Angeles metropolitan area. Most of them seem to have originated with the dating of pachuco girls by servicemen. The riots were ended after protests from the government of Mexico and after the downtown area of Los Angeles had been declared out-of-bounds for men in the armed services.

While the Los Angeles area thus became the center or "capital" of the pachuco world, it should not be forgotten that the pachucos were making themselves felt in other communities as well. Impelled partly by economic insecurity, partly by police pressure, and partly by the desire to become "big shots" in their home communities, many boys who had taken on pachuco ways "apañeron el rufo" (hopped a freight) and went home, there to spread the pachuco influence among less sophisticated boys of their own acquaintance. The railroads in this way became carriers of the pachuco style and speech, and main railroad towns in the Southwest became subcenters for pachuco activity. To this infiltration, Tucson was no exception and in 1944 and 1945 the town experienced several disturbances in the form of street fights between pachucos and non-pachucos. The most serious of these occurred in 1945 when a group of high-school boys paraded through the downtown Mexican area in search of pachucos.

The end of the war brought a lessening of the pachuco disturbances in Tucson and elsewhere, but it did not provide a permanent solution to the problem of "pachuquismo." Mexican-American youths who had been in the armed forces returned to their home towns to find social conditions little different than when they left. Some of these boys were able to take advantage of their army training to get good jobs, but others drifted back to their old street corners and poolroom haunts, and soon were pachucos again. The only important difference in their style was that in place of "drapes" they now wore parts of their old army uniform.

As a social phenomenon, postwar pachucoism has differed from the wartime brand in two important ways. First, there is a strong trend among the younger Mexican-Americans to glamorize the pachucos—or to see them as a type of beloved vagabond or Robin Hood; and second, the jargon borrowed by the pachucos from the El Paso-Juárez underworld has become an important part of colloquial slang or jive talk, and thus has come to symbolize the ways and attitudes of the pachucos and of Mexican-American youth in general.

The first trend may be illustrated by the experience of Lalo Guerrero, a Tucson-born singer who became interested in the pachucos while leading a band in a Los Angeles night club just after the war. Guerrero had scored some success by composing and conducting his own songs, and conceived the idea of writing one about the pachucos. His original objective, he told the writer, was simply to make fun of the pachucos in music, but to do this he made a serious study of the Pachuco jargon and manner of speaking. The effect of this song, called "El

Pachuco," was quite different from what he expected. Instead of discouraging the pachucos, the song had the effect of dramatizing and popularizing their life in the eyes of other Spanish-speaking people. A record company in Los Angeles obtained the reproduction rights to the song and made it an extremely popular hit. Then Guerrero wrote a second song called "La Pachuquilla" (the pachuco girl). Within a few months sixty thousand copies of this record were sold in southwestern cities. From then on Guerrero found himself being prodded by the record company to write more Pachuco songs. To date he has produced eight, all of which are popular recordings and now other companies are beginning to come out with their own Pachuco records.

The second trend, a development of the Pachuco argot as a symbol of Mexican-American youth and its ways and attitudes, may be illustrated by the varying reactions of different individuals in Tucson to the jargon. Many well-educated persons, especially those in the upper classes of the Mexican population, are inclined to look upon the jargon with disgust or alarm. A parish priest spoke sadly to the writer about the "disintegration" of the Spanish language and a professional stenographer accused the youth of Tucson of murdering their mother tongue. Persons less well educated including many of those in the middle class of the Mexican population are inclined to be amused by the jargon. The tendency in this group is to look upon some of the jargon's terms as droll and spicy, and even to use them on occasions when they can do so without risk to their own reputation. Finally, among younger men of lower-class status, including many among the laboring group, the words of the argot form an important part of almost every conversation. As one young clerk in a furniture store put it, "We couldn't understand each other without it." In short, the individual's knowledge and use of terms and expressions in the argot indicates that he is in step with the younger generation.

As a means of enabling teen-age children to keep "hep," the Pachuco recordings have an important function. While these records are expensive, many of them selling for one dollar apiece, their main customers are young persons. The same may be said for Pachuco numbers in Tucson jukeboxes. When the song "Pachuco Boogie" first appeared in the machine at the Jukeland concession on West Congress street, a crowd of boys stood around it for hours at a time, trying to catch each word of the spoken Pachuco monologue contained in the song. Children also like to memorize the lyrics of these songs. One of Guerrero's compositions was included in the 1948 graduation program of a public school in Miami, Arizona, and proved extremely popular.[13]

Usage of Pachuco in Tucson

While, as the foregoing discussion indicates, many young persons understand and use some Pachuco terms, this should not be taken to mean that they speak the argot fluently. This brings us to the question of why some youths seem to depend on the argot as their chief means of communication, while others, living in the same general neighborhood, resort to it only for colorful words and phrases and still others refrain from using the jargon at all. To answer this question it may be helpful to examine a number of individual cases and to see what relation, if any, may exist between social behavior on the one hand, and variations in the usage of Pachuco on the other.

As a basis for this inquiry the writer interviewed fifteen boys and young men all of whom lived in the Mexican sections of Tucson, on the westerly side of the Southern Pacific tracks. While several of these youths could be interviewed only once, the majority of them were interviewed several times over a six-month period. From the standpoint of social behavior, ten of the boys were participants in gangs or cliques which included one or more known pachucos. The other five had no social relations with Tucson pachucos, although one of them reported that he himself had been a pachuco when he lived in Los Angeles. To facilitate comparisons, brief notes on the background, social relations, and language usage of the ten participants will be described first, and that of the five non-participants, second.

The boys in this study who associate with pachucos, or who are pachucos themselves, are members of one or the other of two distinct gangs or cliques. Five of them are in a clique in which the leading figure was a boy nick-named Toro, and the other five are in a group centering around a boy nick-named Sapo. For convenience, these two groups will be referred to as Toro's gang and Sapo's gang, respectively.[14] Most of the boys in Toro's gang live in the Mexican section known as Barrio Libre. This section of town is one of the poorest, economically, in the city, and is reported to be the home of most of the "bad" pachucos.[15] The boys in Toro's gang do not hang out in this neighborhood, however, as much as they do around the Capitol Theater and Jukeland Arcade on West Congress street. They vary in age from seventeen to twenty-two years, and only one of them is still in school.

The boys in Sapo's gang live fairly close to the center of town on Cushing, Meyer, and Simpson streets. They occasionally go down to West Congress, but generally hang out in the neighborhood of Sapo's house on South Meyer street, and around the Burlesque Theater on Convent street. They vary in age from fifteen to twenty-one years, and as is the case in Toro's gang, only one is still in school.

Notes on Toro will be presented first, as he is the individual who, of all those interviewed, most nearly fits what might be called the pachuco stereotype. He is of medium height, about twenty-two years of age and of athletic build. His dark-complexioned face might be considered handsome were it not for numerous scars and pockmarks on his cheeks. He has a wide mouth, fringed by a thin moustache, and when he smiles, his nostrils dilate broadly, a feature which may be the source of his nickname of Toro (bull). His coarse black hair is combed straight back, and he wears an old army shirt open at the neck, army pants with narrow cuffs, and thick-soled shoes. When he talks Pachuco he constantly uses his hands, and his voice drawls out the endings of words in a sonorous manner.

At the time of the writer's first interview, Toro lived with his father in an adobe house in Barrio Libre. Toro has two brothers, one older than he, and three sisters. Toro's mother died when he was twelve years old and the father has not remarried. Toro has lived in Tucson all his life except during World War II, when he was in the U.S. Army. He has visited Los Angeles, and during his army service was stationed for several months in New York. Since his return from service,

Toro has been working as helper to his father, who operates a dump truck. This work is sporadic, however, and gives Toro much time to spend with his "carnales" on West Congress street where he is a well-known figure, not only to Mexican-American boys but to the police. He customarily hangs out around the Jukeland Arcade, one of Tucson's most notorious pachuco meeting places. When he is not to be found there, he is likely to be in trouble. On one occasion when he was missing, the writer discovered that Toro's father's dump truck had been involved in a collision with another car, and that both Toro and his father had been injured. On another occasion the writer learned that Toro was in the city jail for two weeks, presumably on a charge of disturbing the peace. Toro later told the writer that the police let him go after they could find nothing against him. On still another occasion, Toro's disappearance was explained by a newspaper story based on police records indicating that Toro had been involved in a knife battle with another pachuco by the name of Leonardo. The knifing occurred as the climax of an argument which arose during a party at Toro's house. He was cut several times on the chest and abdomen and had to be taken to the hospital to have one of his wounds stitched up.

A few weeks after this knifing incident, the writer happened to meet Toro at noon in front of a furniture store on West Congress street. He looked worried and appeared not to have shaved for three or four days. He said he had been waiting all morning for his girl friend, and that they were supposed to get married the same day. He said he and Luey G. had been out in Luey's car several nights ago and he, Toro, had gotten into a "jam" with this girl and now he either had to marry her or go to the "pen." Two days later, on the occasion of the writer's last interview with him, Toro said the wedding had been postponed until the following Saturday. To date the writer has received no further information as to whether he went through with the wedding, or whether he went to prison. Toro did say, however, that if he got married he was not going to change his style.

Luey G. is a sharp-eyed, wiry youth, nineteen years old, who lives with his mother near Toro's house in Barrio Libre. When he was in the ninth grade, at the age of sixteen, Luey enlisted in the U.S. Army and spent one and a half years in Germany with the American Army of Occupation. He now speaks English, Spanish, and German as well as Pachuco, which he says he picked up from other Spanish-speaking boys in the army. Following his return from service Luey decided not to go back to school, and instead got a job in a brickyard on West Congress street where he is working with eight other fellows. He has bought a car, and thus has become a pivotal member of Toro's gang. He frequently takes Toro and his other friends around to dances and parties, and it was on one of these occasions that Toro got into the "jam" mentioned above.

Bill S. is a quiet good-looking youth of seventeen, who lives with his father and mother, one brother and two sisters on the west side of town. He quit school after reaching the sixth grade and has been working for the past few weeks in the same brickyard where Luey is employed.

Pete R., twenty years of age, a tall thin boy, is known as Goofy among the pachucos. He is a native of Tucson and lives with his parents and two brothers and sisters in an adobe house on Meyer street. He was never in the army but has made brief trips to Los Angeles and El Paso. Since he quit school several years ago he has worked as a miner. He is at present unemployed.

Frank T. or Goat,[16] as he is known among the Tucson pachucos, is seventeen years old and lives on Eighteenth street in Barrio Libre. Goat is of medium height, with very dark complexion, heavy black hair and protruding lips, a combination which may account for his sometimes being called Crow by his friend, Toro. Goat lives with his mother and is the oldest of five children in the family. He is now in the tenth grade in Tucson high school. At the time he was first interviewed by the writer, Goat was a habitué of the pachuco hangouts on Congress street, but more recently Toro and his other friends have not seen him. One reason for this is that Goat has obtained a Saturday job. Another may be that he is beginning to regard Toro's company as too risky for his (Goat's) security. Still another reason may be his mother's strong anti-pachuco attitude. For a long time Goat has refrained from speaking Pachuco to anyone who knows his mother, and especially to her friends and relatives, for the reason that this would create a "bad impression." On his last interview with the writer, Goat emphasized that "respectable married people" don't approve of the pachucos, and that boys forget Pachuco after they get married. From Goat's changing attitude and natty appearance at this interview, it might be inferred that he is thinking of getting married himself.

Sapo, the central figure in the second gang, is twenty-one years old and lives with his parents on South Meyer street. In appearance Sapo is large and of massive build, with a round face, small moustache, and bulging eyes, which may account for his nickname (Spanish for toad). He is a veteran of World War II, and since his return from service has been working with his father, a plasterer. Sapo has his own car, an old Pontiac sedan with his name stenciled prominently on one side. He also has the use of his father's car, an expensive and swank-appearing machine, for special occasions. Sapo's house is a meeting place for his crowd, and the boys frequently go out with him in his car. When the writer first met Sapo, he and three of his carnales were out driving in the neighborhood of a Papago Indian village nine miles south of Tucson, where the writer's father was making a sketch of the old San Xavier Mission. On two subsequent occasions the boys traveled in the car of Sapo's father to visit the writer's cabin.

Sapo told the writer he learned most of the Pachuco he knows from boys in Tucson. He learned some of it from friends and cousins, and some from records. Besides talking Pachuco with his companions, Sapo says, he sometimes speaks it to his father and mother, but reports they do not understand him.

Rudy J., the model pachuco of the Sapo gang, is eighteen years of age and lives with his parents on Simpson street. He is undersized for his age, and his head, with its heavy black mane of hair combed back ducktail style, appears out of proportion to his slight body, an incongruity which his companions have recognized by calling him Tack. The prestige of Tack as a pachuco is due largely to a three months' trip he made last year to California. During this trip he worked as a celery picker in Southern California and also in an airplane "cocooning" project at an air depot near San José. In both localities he picked up much of the Pachuco argot and also learned several Pachuco songs. Since his return home, Tack has learned more Pachuco on Congress street, but says he never speaks Pachuco to his parents or to his seven brothers and sisters all of whom speak Spanish at home.

Freddy P., sixteen years of age, lives on Cushing street at the home of his father and stepmother. He is of medium build, but thin, with a fair complexion and unruly black hair. The corners of his mouth habitually are turned down and unlike his companions, he does not laugh easily. His mother, who was Mexican, had been married before she met Freddy's father, an American, and had a son named Joe by her first marriage. Then, by her second marriage, she had two boys, a girl, and the youngest, Freddy. She died of tuberculosis the year after Freddy was born. When Freddy was four years old his father remarried and now has another family. Freddy reports that he learned to speak Pachuco in Tucson and in Los Angeles. Besides speaking Pachuco to his companions, Freddy says, he sometimes speaks it to his uncle at home, but says his uncle doesn't understand it.

Like his pal, Freddy, Joe F. was born of a Mexican mother and an American father. He also is of medium build but is heavier than Freddy, and smiles more frequently. He is eighteen years old and lives on Meyer street. He finished junior high school but dropped out of school after a year of high school. For a short time, he worked in a large furniture store on West Congress street. In May, 1948, he lost his job.

Ernest S., youngest and smallest of the Sapo gang, is only fifteen years old. Perhaps because of his small stature, comparative youth, and inexperience, he does not talk much with his friends, which seems to account for his nickname of "Noisy." Noisy lives in the house of his parents on Convent street and is attending Safford Junior High School. There are two other children, both girls. Noisy was born in Tucson but went with his parents to live in Phoenix at the age of three. He reports that he learned a few Pachuco words in Phoenix but has acquired most of his vocabulary since the family returned to Tucson four years ago. He says he speaks Pachuco with other boys at school, at home with his father (who he says likes to hear it) and with the fellows at Sapo's house.

We now come to the final group in this study—boys who at present have no pachuco associations. In discussing this group it should be made clear at the outset that the boys included do not form a social unit but are grouped together simply to facilitate comparison with the two groups which do have pachuco associations.

Of the five boys in this third group, one, Alex B., may be described as a former pachuco. Alex is about twenty-two years of age, a veteran of World War II and is now married and has two children. Born in Los Angeles, Alex has lived in Tucson only about a year. Of medium build, he is the youngest of eight brothers. He says he was a pachuco while attending junior high school, between the ages of fourteen and seventeen, in the Negro-Mexican district of Watts near Los Angeles. "You're a square if you don't," he said in explaining how he got into a gang through pressure from pachucos at school. To conform with the others he wore drapes, much to the disapproval of his parents and brothers, all of whom were in the bakery business. Then, at eighteen, Alex entered the U.S. Army and was overseas two years. When he returned to Los Angeles, he says, pachuco drapes and ways were "out" for him. He married and settled down to be respectable, and came to Tucson with several of his brothers to start a branch of the family baking business.

Like Alex, Enrique C., the second youth in this group, learned the Pachuco jargon in Los Angeles. In appearance, Enrique is tall and good looking. He was born in Tucson, but at the age of sixteen, in 1942, he went to Los Angeles and lived for nine months with relatives in the Boyle Heights district, a cosmopolitan neighborhood on the east side of town. While there he attended Roosevelt High School and also worked during the summer in the Continental Baking Company. In this work, and in conversations with his cousins, he picked up most of his Pachuco vocabulary. The fellows in the bakery, he reports, were not pachucos but they knew the words. During his residence in Los Angeles Enrique came in contact with many pachucos but did not mix with them. He states that he and his cousins were known by the pachucos as the Pepsi-Cola kids.

Following his return to Tucson, Enrique finished high school and then entered the U.S. Army. When he came back from the service he registered as a freshman at the University of Arizona, but dropped out within a year to go into business. Still only twenty-one, he is living at home and speaks Spanish with his parents and sister. He speaks both English and Spanish with his friends and reserves his Pachuco for occasions when he wants to amuse them.

Ralph Z., another non-pachuco, has lived most of his life in Tucson, and knows only a few words of Pachuco. Ralph's father is a member of a distinguished and wealthy Tucson family. At the time of the writer's interview he was seventeen and had just dropped out of his senior year in high school to go into professional baseball. Until his marriage recently, he lived with his parents, two brothers, and a sister at the family home on the west side of town. While in junior high school Ralph came into contact with a number of pachucos but never mixed with them. In high school his interest in baseball led him into close association with American boys, so that he has tended to develop his English rather than Pachuco.

Carlos L., another non-pachuco, is seventeen and is making good marks in high school. He is of dark complexion and undersized but is a bright boy with an aggressive disposition. He is the younger of two sons in a family of seven children and lives in the El Rio district. Carlos' father is a grocer and the boy helps him in the store after school hours. He is also much interested in sports and is on a high-school team. As is the case with Ralph Z., Carlos' ambition and associations with American boys in junior high school and high school sports have led him to develop his English vocabulary rather than Pachuco.

Pablo T., the fifth boy in this non-pachuco list, seems to know hardly any Pachuco words. Pablo, who now is twenty-three, was raised in Nogales on the Mexican border, sixty miles south of Tucson, and lived in that city until he was seventeen years of age. His mother was a member of a distinguished old Mexican family which had large property holdings in the Nogales area. His father was an apprentice carpenter who deserted his wife shortly after their marriage. Pablo lived with his mother in a "poor but nice" neighborhood on the American side of town. He reports that while there were pachucos in town when he lived there, he never had any friends that were pachucos. He thinks that one reason for this was that the pachucos lived on the Mexican side of town. When the war began, Pablo enlisted in the navy and his mother moved to the El Rio neighborhood in Tucson. After his return from service, Pablo settled in Tucson and married the older sister of Carlos L. Pablo and his wife are now managing a drugstore recently opened in El Rio by his wife's father, a former resident of El Paso who knows many Pachuco words.

While the number of boys interviewed in this study is too small, and the information collected too fragmentary, to make definite conclusions, a few simple generalizations may now be suggested as to the ways in which the usage of the Pachuco argot may be related to the social behavior of boys of Mexican descent in the Tucson community.

Social Functions of Pachuco

Relation of Usage to Gang Participation

The usage of Pachuco in Tucson is by no means restricted to members of pachuco gangs. To know some Pachuco expressions is a mark of sophistication among many boys of Mexican descent in Tucson. The knowledge and use of some Pachuco words indicates that the individual is modern and in step with his own generation. However, there are two main differences in the usage of boys who are gang members from that of those who are not. These differences are, first, that gang participants speak Pachuco habitually, as a means of communication, and second, that gang members have a larger and more up-to-date vocabulary than nonparticipants.

Relation of Usage to Socio-economic Status

In this study eight of the ten boys having pachuco associations were doing some form of manual labor and the two remaining ones were still in school. While this should not be taken to imply that all pachucos are laborers, or vice versa, it does seem to indicate a connection between laboring groups and the spread of the Pachuco argot. Not only the boys interviewed but also other informants of the writer have indicated that the jargon may be picked up in such places as railroad yards, brickyards, bakeries, construction projects, and even furniture stores employing Mexican labor. All of this may be taken as evidence that Pachuco is definitely an argot of the lower class of the Mexican population. For this reason it is not difficult to see why socially ambitious boys tend to refrain from using the jargon as an habitual means of communication.

Relation of Usage to Goals and Values

The habitual use of the argot, then, may be taken to indicate that the speaker is not interested in raising his social status above that of the laboring group. Such usage may also indicate his rejection of some of the conventional values of Mexican and American culture. This brings us to the question of what light the study of Pachuco usage may throw on the nature of pachuco values. The following brief appraisal of pachuco values is based partly on the above case notes and partly on six Pachuco texts recorded by the writer and his bilingual assistant, Raúl R. Three of these texts were recorded manually in cafes on West Congress street, while the other three were recorded by machine in the writer's cabin. All of the informants in Toro's and Sapo's gangs participated in making the texts, but members of the two groups were not brought together. In each instance the writer told the boys that he was interested in their language and the instructions given them were simply to talk in Pachuco as they would when with each other in various situations around town. The content of their remarks was left strictly up to the boys themselves, and in this way they received no indication that their remarks would be examined from the standpoint of the values involved.

Pachuco values may be said to have two basic premises, which may be stated briefly as follows: (1) We'll probably die young so we may as well get our thrills out of life now; and (2) the laws are against us but we can outsmart them. The values stemming out of these premises conveniently may be divided into two groups. The first of these relates to the way in which the pachuco regards himself; the second concerns his relations with others.

The pachuco has a strong feeling of insecurity about himself. His parents have come from a society which is different from that in which he is now growing up. They are near the bottom of the social ladder and cannot or do not care to give their children much help in achieving the goals and values of the new society. The school system is similarly of little help. The pachuco does not see how school can do him much good as he doesn't think he has much chance of getting a white collar job. So he loses interest and drops out of school as soon as he can. He now finds himself one of a group of fellows who are in much the same position as he is. He has had enough contact with American urban life not to want to work the way his father has. So he hangs around the street corner with the other boys and works only to accumulate enough money to maintain his personal prestige and "style" and to have a high time. The high time, with plenty of drinks and girls, is his supreme goal and value. Beyond that, he sees little or nothing.

The pachuco feels that he belongs neither to the society of his parents nor to that of the Americans. He therefore tries to create one of his own. The pachuco looks to his carnales as allies in a conspiracy to get what they want from society without having to suffer its penalties. In his quest for a high time, the pachuco is not hampered by conventional morals. Petty theft is considered smart if the thief is not caught. The pachuco accepts little or no responsibility about the girls he takes out with him. His main concern is that the girls don't squeal (que no sean gritonas). The pachuco may use a guitar to attract a girl, but his attitude is far from chivalrous. The smart pachuco gets the girl to pay for his dinner (que paguen las chavalas).

It is of course open to question as to what extent the writer's ten gang participants subscribe to the system of values implied in their records and in their recorded conversations. The point cannot be denied, however, that they set up these converstions as fair samples of Pachuco talk. It seems fair to assume that the habitual use of Pachuco implies the substitution of such pachuco values for the more conventional ones of Mexican and American society.

Summary

In summary, the Pachuco argot may be said to have two main social functions in the Tucson community. The first and basic of these is its function as the private language of groups of boys who find themselves not fully accepted in either American or Mexican society. As such, Pachuco transmits a set of values which runs counter to the accepted social order and tends to isolate the users from the type of social contacts which would assist their assimilation into American life.

The second function of Pachuco is as a symbol of sophistication among members of the younger generation. In this use it may be compared to the jive-talk of some teen-age Americans. In both cases the argot is sufficiently diluted in conventional speech so that its exclusive character is lost. Instead of indicating the separation of the speaker from the general society, this limited use indicates that he is modern and en rapport, or, in short, that he "gets around."

To the extent that Pachuco persists as a private language in Tucson, it might be taken as symptomatic of the continuing disorientation of one element of the younger Mexican generation. We may venture to predict that only when the goals of American society can be demonstrated as obtainable to him—perhaps then through such means as vocational education—will the pachuco as a linguistic and social type disappear from the Tucson scene.

Notes

[1] Webster's New International Dictionary, p. 146.

[2] *Ibid.* p. 1329.

[3] To aid in distinguishing between references to the pachucos and their jargon, the term "pachuco" will be capitalized in this paper only when it designates the jargon.

[4] George C. Storz, *Mexican-Spanish.* p. 14.

[5] Henríquez Ureña, Pedro, *El español en Mejico, los Estado Unidos y la América Central,* xvii-xx.

[6] Cf Entwistle, William J., *The Spanish Language,* also, Semeleder, R., "El español de los Mexicanos," in Ureña, *op. cit.*

[7] Cuervo, in *El Castellano en America* notes (p. 69) that in early times there was not the great distance between the "cultured" and popular languages that later developed under the influence of classical studies; and that in books written at the time of the Conquest are many forms still heard among the common folk of Latin America.

[8] "Lower class" as here used has reference simply to the relative socio-economic position of one segment of the Mexican population in Tucson.

[9] Cf. Kercheville, F. M. *A Preliminary Glossary of New Mexico Spanish,* 1934. 10. Cf. English "reefer."

[11] Griffith, Beatrice, "The Pachuco Patois," Common Ground, Summer, 1947.

[12] Letter to the writer, June 7, 1948.

[13] Information from Miss Gloria Howatt, teacher in the public schools, Miami, Arizona.

[14] The term "gang" is used in this paper to indicate a loosely organized neighborhood group, and the social units so designated should not be thought of as limited only to the members here described.

[15] One informant described the pachucos of Barrio Libre as being the only ones in Tucson who used chains to threaten and intimidate "squares."

[16] The reason for using the nickname goat is uncertain, but it may be a shortened form of the term "monigote," meaning bumpkin, dolt, or lout.

Assessing Language Maintenance in Spanish Speaking Communities in the Southwest

Andrew D. Cohen

The Treaty of Guadalupe Hidalgo in 1848, which ended the Mexican American War, provided protection under the law for Spanish language and Mexican culture. Yet educational practices for the past 120 years have worked against such provisions. Many Mexican Americans feel that the United States government assumed the attitude of conqueror to vanquished, and that Spanish language and Mexican culture were viewed by many education officials as shackles that had to be stripped off before full partnership in American society could be attained.

Over the years Mexican Americans have been asking what happened to the "Great American Dream" of freedom, democracy, and plurality. However disadvantaged they are economically and socially, many Mexican Americans feel advantaged linguistically and culturally in that they have two languages and share at least two cultures.

Christian and Christian (1966), in Fishman's *Language Loyalty in the United States,* state that the Spanish-speaking population is perhaps the fastest growing population in the Southwest. They note that the Spanish-speaking population in California increased by 88% between 1950 and 1960. Factors such as the proximity of Mexico to the United States and the availability of low-status jobs have encouraged immigration. The recent immigrants have come seeking greater prosperity, as most of them were among the very poor in Mexico.

Some thirty years ago the Mexican immigrants in California were subject to exploitation and abuse (Bustamante and Bustamante 1969). Now they find somewhat more favorable circumstances under which to live and work. For example, a UCLA report suggests decreasing discrimination against Mexican Americans in the labor market (Fogel 1965). At the same time, Mexican Americans are more vocally asserting pride in *la raza*—in their Mexican heritage and in the Spanish language, and the majority culture is coming to accept cultural differences as enriching and worthwhile for the society.

European colonies in the United States are fast losing native speakers of their respective languages and familiarity with their "old world" cultures for lack of renewed contact with the home country or with recent immigrants (Fishman 1966b). Mexican Americans, on the other hand, return frequently to Mexico, renewing cultural and linguistic ties, and the recent immigrants fraternize with the established immigrants and native-born. Factors such as these lead to speculation that the Spanish language may be used in California for many years to come (Christian and Christian 1966).

Within the last few years, the United States Office of Education finally moved to recognize and foster within the school system this linguistic and cultural "advantage" of the Mexican American. Under Title VII of the Elementary and Secondary Education Act (ESEA), a Bilingual Education Program was set up. In its first academic year (1969-70), some seventy-six bilingual programs were funded nationally. Of these, twenty-three were projects in California for Mexican Americans. During the 1971-72 school year, 163 bilingual education programs were funded.

Now that a potential means for preserving native Spanish language ability and Mexican American culture has been instated in the form of bilingual schooling, the question is whether this bilingual schooling will foster the use of Spanish and identification with Mexican American culture among Mexican American students. It would seem that answers to this question would be of paramount importance both to educators who are considering starting bilingual programs and to educators who have current programs and are interested in the long-range effects of such programs.

Until recently, the schools could claim little or no role in Spanish language maintenance. Spanish classes were not geared for native Spanish speakers, and Mexican Americans were often criticized for seeking an easy "A" if they enrolled in Spanish.[1] The result was that while the United States was spending millions of dollars a year teaching Spanish to native English speakers, hundreds of thousands of native Spanish speakers were losing their native language competence (Gaarder 1967). Now, however, the bilingual school can claim a role in Spanish language maintenance, while at the same time teaching English language skills. The research task for the sociolinguist is to determine how extensive a role this is.

This article discusses the measurement of bilingual proficiency and language use and then gives guidelines as to how to assess Spanish language maintenance in a bilingual community in the Southwest. The sociolinguistic assessment of a bilingual education project in Redwood City, California, is described briefly as illustrative of studies that can be done on language maintenance.

Definition of Bilingualism

Although the terms "bilingualism" and "bilingual" are frequently used, the users rarely define what they mean when they use the terms (see John and Horner 1971). Individuals are referred to as "bilinguals" as if there were some fixed notion of what that meant. Bartlett observes the following about bilingualism:

> Despite the widespread appearance of the phenomenon, we do not yet have a satisfactory general theory of bilingualism. Indeed, it was not until this century that attempts were made to analyze the phenomenon scientifically, and to assess its effects on human behavior and its influence on social structures. From what evidence we have of earlier periods, bilingualism appears as a rare and unusual quality, suspect except in those societies which valued another language as a key to culture. Indeed, in former times the word had overtones of deceitfulness, and a little of this aura still hangs about it. (Bartlett 1969, v-vi.)

Jakobovits (1970) points out that both nonprofessional and professional judges have their own versions of "folk bilingualism." To the nonprofessional judge, accent, pronunciation, and fluency may be given a disproportionate degree of importance. Thus, a speaker with a poor accent and less fluency but with greater knowledge of the language might not impress them as being bilingual. Some professionals require equal facility in two languages before they are willing to talk of bilingualism, while others are willing to speak of "incipient bilinguals" (Diebold 1961). Jakobovits (1970) asserts that there is no particular advantage in setting arbitrary limits for a definition of bilingualism. Instead, emphasis should be placed on specifying the extent of an individual's knowledge of his two languages.

Figure 1 provides a three-dimensional model, based on Macnamara (1967), Cooper (1968; 1970), and Bordie (1970), showing five elements of each of the four major skills in each language. This particular model is set up, for illustration purposes, to measure a speaker's ability in one variety of Spanish and one variety of English. A language "variety" refers either to a dialect, a register, a style, or a level of formality. Notice that four of the five elements of each of the four skills are the same. Speaking, writing, listening, and reading all involve semantics (the meaning of words and phrases), syntax (the arrangement of words in sentences), morphology (the grouping of parts of words into words), and lexicon (a listing of all the words and word particles in a language). Phonemes (the meaningful sound units in a language) are the fifth element in the *oral* skills—speaking and listening—and graphemes (the units that represent the phonemes in the orthography) comprise the fifth element in the *written* skills—writing and reading.

Macnamara terms bilinguals as "persons who possess at least one of the language skills even to a minimal degree in their second language" (Macnamara (1967, 59-60). I prefer the definition of a bilingual as a person who possesses at least one language skill in one variety of each of two languages. This then takes into account both very young children with some listening comprehension in each of two languages but no speaking ability, as well as English-speakers who read a little French or understand a little German. The one remaining problem with the above definition is that of determining what constitutes a language. As Gumperz (1967; 1969) has documented, peoples' perceptions of language may cross-cut long-existing notions of what languages are, especially in places where languages are in contact (see Weinreich 1953). It is possible, for instance, that one variety of a Chicano's speech may be viewed by an outsider as mixing English and Spanish, but the speaker views it as a language in its own right. For our purposes, if a variety cross-cuts two languages, it will be designated as such.

Measurement of Bilingualism

Social scientists have devised a series of measures of bilingualism, including both reports of language use and language proficiency, and actual measures of performance such as word recognition or word naming (see Macnamara 1967; Kelly 1969; and Fishman 1971a, for detailed descriptions of different approaches to measurement of bilingualism).

Hoffman (1934) devised an instrument for measuring the extent of bilingual background or environment to which an individual is exposed by asking the subject to estimate the extent to which each of his languages is used in his home. More recent research is still using the Hoffman Bilingual Scale (see Jones 1960; Lewis and Lewis 1965; Riley 1968) to assess degree of bilingualism. However, as

Figure 1

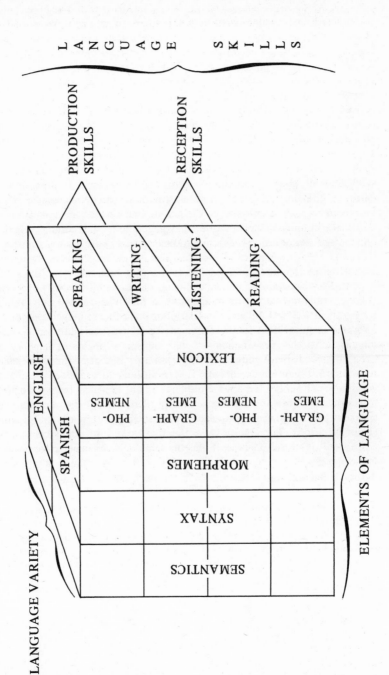

Haugen points out (Haugen 1956, 94-95), this is a rather imperfect instrument when trying to assess where and when one language would be chosen instead of the other. Bilingualism is viewed as present or not present, with no attempt to differentiate the conditions under which a person speaks one language, the other language, or both. Macnamara (1969) used a Hoffman-type scale in his own research with sixth-grade pupils in Montreal and also found it to be a weak measure of bilingualism when related to performance measures of bilingual proficiency.

Fishman (1964; 1965; 1966a), drawing on Weinrich (1953) and Gumperz (1964), provides a theoretical framework for a more complete study of bilingualism than that suggested by Hoffman. Fishman advanced the notion of the bilingual dominance configuration, which describes an individual's bilinguality in terms of language use and proficiency for each of the four language skills across language varieties and across societal domains. Fishman (1971b) also defines a domain as a cluster of social situations which are typically constrained by a common set of behavior rules. The domains which are relevant for a given bilingual community may vary, but they generally include family, neighborhood, religion, education, and the occupational sphere. Note that a domain is more than a context or a place. A domain also comprises the roles of interlocutors within the particular setting and the topics that these interlocutors are likely to discuss. For instance, within the occupational domain the boss and an employee (two interlocutors in a socially prescribed role relationship) may be talking in the boss's office (setting) about a salary boost for the employee (topic).

A major innovation in the Fishman model was the addition of the domain dimension to the measurement of bilingualism. Domains of language use had been discussed by Weinreich (1953) but not operationalized in sociological research. Fishman observed that the traditional measures of degree of bilingualism which subtracted a score obtained in one language from a score obtained in another may be insufficiently revealing of relative proficiency since bilingual speakers may use each language under socially-differentiated circumstances (Fishman 1965). The traditional difference-score approach labeled a person a "balanced" bilingual if his score was the same in each language for the particular linguistic task required (Macnamara 1969). Yet Fishman points out that the notion of balance is unrealistic for the following reason:

> . . .Socially patterned bilingualism can exist as a stabilized phenomenon *only* if there is functional *differentiation* between two languages rather than merely global dominance or balance. From the point of view of sociolinguistics any society that produces functionally balanced bilinguals (i.e., bilinguals who use both their languages equally and equally well in all contexts) must soon cease to be bilingual because no society needs two languages for one and the same set of functions. (Fishman 1971a, 560)

While degree of bilingualism is an attribute of a person, the term "diglossia" has emerged (Ferguson 1959; Gumperz 1964; Fishman 1967; 1971b) for describing this "functional differentiation between two languages" at the societal level (mentioned in the above quote by Fishman). For a bilingual Mexican-American community to remain diglossic, for example, one language must be used more in certain domains, while the other is used more in other domains. For example, English may be the predominant language in the occupational sphere (particularly at the higher levels of employment), while Spanish is the language of the home. As soon as the uses of the two languages begin to overlap, Spanish will give way to English—the socially-dominant, more prestigious language—unless conscious efforts are made to create functional specialization of Spanish and English. Efforts such as bilingual education in the schools and special practices in the homes (see Christian 1971) may not be enough.

Fishman (1971a) criticizes the measures of bilingualism that do not take into account the bilingual respondent's use and proficiency as related to domains of social interaction. Unfortunately, the bulk of research on bilinguals makes no allowances for differences by domain. Riley (1968), for instance, made an effort to relate word recognition abilities in bilinguals to their degree of bilingualism. However, he used the Hoffman scale (Hoffman 1934) which falls short of a domain analysis.

The insights of Fishman into the field of bilingualism are of importance because they suggest a research direction to help shed new light on a controversy that has been raging for decades, primarily among educators and psychologists, over the supposed detrimental effects of being bilingual. John and Horner (1971) point out that between the ages of five and seven, children use language at an accelerating rate for the purposes of problem solving. In early learning, the child is ordering the world around him and language is critical in this ordering process. Does the introduction of a second, weaker language at this point simply confuse the ordering process? The authors point out that if bilinguals have the opportunity to develop two languages fully, they may demonstrate cognitive skills superior to those of their monolingual peers. Jones (1969) cites psychological, neurological, pedagogical and socio-political research supporting the favorable effect of early introduction to learning a second language.

Only with the work of Fishman, Cooper, Ma, et al (1971), employing Fishman's bilingual dominance configuration theory, did there begin to appear research on the bilingual that truly considers factors such as domains of bilingual proficiency and use. These authors studied 431 Puerto Ricans ranging in age from under six to sixty-four, from a four-block neighborhood of Jersey City, New Jersey. The major intent of the research was to pioneer a series of techniques for better describing bilinguals, and to determine the interrelationships and relative effectiveness of these techniques.

Two pieces of research from the massive study, Cooper (1971) and Edelman, Cooper, and Fishman (1971), are perhaps illustrative of some of the approaches used. Cooper (1971) took 38 subjects, thirteen-years-old and above, and administered tasks of word naming by domain and word association to them. The word naming task asked subjects to name, in one minute, as many different words referring to a specified domain as they could. This task was administered first in one language and later in the other. For "family," they were asked to name things seen or found in a kitchen; for "neighborhood," things seen or found in the street; for "religion," things seen or found in a church; for "education," subjects studied in school; and for "work," the names of jobs, occupations, or professions. On the word association task, respondents were asked to give, within one-minute periods, as many continuous associations as possible to each of the following stimulus words in English and Spanish: *factory, school, church, street,* and *home.*

Cooper related word naming and word association to six criterion measures— years in the U.S.A., occupation, accentedness of speech in English, English repertoire range (number of English speech styles), and listening comprehension in Spanish and English. Relative proficiency in word naming varied significantly as a function of context, age, and recency of arrival in the United States. The bilinguals were more proficient in Spanish than in English word naming in the tradition-oriented domains of home and religion. In the domains of neighbor-hood, education, and work, some age groups performed better in English. In interpreting the results, the authors pointed out that if word naming had not been broken down by domain, the performance of the six demographic subgroups (ages 13-18, 19-34, or 35 and above, with more than 11 years or less than 11 years on the mainland) would have been described as "balanced" in terms of the difference between their English and Spanish average *total* scores. Yet all but one of these groups exhibited significant differences between English and Spanish average scores in one or more domains.

Edelman, Cooper, and Fishman (1971) tested 34 6-12-year-old Puerto Rican boys and girls attending a parochial school in Jersey City. All were born in the United States. The students were asked how much they used Spanish and English with various bilingual interlocutors in school, at church, in the neighborhood, and at home (representing the domains of education, religion, neighborhood, and family, respectively). Students also received a word naming instrument similar to the one used in the Cooper research mentioned above. However, the occupational domain was eliminated because it did not apply.

Results showed that the children reported using more Spanish in the domains of family and neighborhood and more English in the domains of education and religion. There were no differences for the domain of family. In comparing the results from self-report of language use with those on word naming, we see that children reported using more Spanish than English in the neighborhood and yet performed better on word naming for the domain of neighborhood in English than in Spanish.[2] Ervin-Tripp (1971) points out that perhaps the problem here is one of using self-report rather than recordings of natural conversation. She suggests that perhaps the children's conversations *were* in Spanish, but that vocabulary for nameable shapes and objects was primarily in English and that the children could actually be using considerable English when believing their conversations were normally in Spanish.

Ervin-Tripp is perhaps pointing out one major weakness in the Jersey City research. Fishman plays down the importance of the languages-in-contact aspect of bilingual use and proficiency (see Fishman 1971a), and except for passing mention in an article by Ma and Herasimchuk (1971), *Bilingualism in the Barrio,* all but ignores the phenomena of loan words and language mixing.[3] Considerable language mixing has been observed in U.S. bilingual communities (see Espinoza 1917; Lance, 1969; Gumperz and Hernandez, 1970[4]), but it is increasingly evident that some bilinguals do not model their speech on any variety used by unilingual speakers of their language, but on local bilingual usage, which shows considerable linguistic fusion of two languages (Gumperz 1967; 1969).

Relating Measures of Bilingualism to Bilingual Education Programs

With 163 bilingual education programs funded under Title VII[5] during the 1971-72 school year and numerous other projects receiving funding from another source, an attempt is being made to meet the linguistic and cultural needs of minority school children. However, the proliferation of bilingual education programs has prompted sociolinguists to call attention to the lack of investigations of existing language situations as part of program planning. Whereas there does exist a small legacy of sociolinguistic studies of bilingual communities (see Barker 1947; Weinreich 1951; Haugen 1953; Diebold 1961; Rubin 1968; Fishman, Cooper, Ma, et al 1971), there has not been a truly sociolinguistic study of a bilingual schooling program.

Fishman and Lovas (1970) state that most existing bilingual programs have not utilized recent insights into societal bilingualism in their program designs. Staff personnel offer educational, psychological, or linguistic reasons for project characteristics, but ignore the language situation existing in the community involved. The only quoted statistics refer to the number of people with Spanish surnames, and it is assumed that this is enough to give reliable and meaningful data about the language situation. Valdez (1969) warns against the mistake of trying to assess bilingual proficiency from surnames. Fishman and Lovas (1970) point out that more than census data and school records are necessary. They emphasize that a survey should be undertaken to identify the languages and varieties used by parents and children by social domain, an estimate of relative proficiency in each language by domain, an indication of the community attitudes toward the language varieties in the community, and an indication of community attitudes toward changing the community language situation.

Sociolinguists have shown how language can be studied in relation to its social environment. As Fishman defines it, *sociolinguistics* is "the study of the characteristics of language varieties, the characteristics of their functions, and the characteristics of their speakers as these three constantly interact, change, and change one another within a speech community" (Fishman 1971b, 4). As both Hymes (1967) and Ervin-Tripp (1964) have pointed out, language exists and functions within some social context. Therefore, the description of language should reflect its function in the local society.

Studies which trace the progress of children schooled bilingually have appeared abroad and are beginning to appear in the U.S. Mention is made of tests that the students took and of their charted progress. Occasionally mention is also made of the language used in the home, but rarely is there any systematic study of how the child's language behavior in school relates to his language behavior out of school and to the language patterns of parents and siblings. Nor is there mention of the effect of bilingual schooling on his language behavior over time.

The language use and proficiency of Mexican American children schooled bilingually in California is a virtually untapped field, but one of great importance in determining the effectiveness of bilingual education in the state. The only language use studies that I have been able to find were conducted in Texas and New Mexico, and not on children in bilingual programs. Patella and Kuvesky (1970) related language use of Texas high school children to aspirations and occupations. Mahoney (1967) did a secondary analysis of data collected by the Texas Agricultural Experiment Station in 1962. Language use items were one part of a 14-page questionnaire designed to find out more about the Spanish-American labor force in Texas. Mahoney studied the language choices of rural and urban household heads and their children in a variety of language use situations. She then related language use information to demographic variables such as age, birthplace, education, income, and occupation. Timmins (1971) studied the relative bilingualism of 60 Spanish-surnamed school children grades 1-4 in the Armijo Elementary School in Albuquerque, New Mexico. An attempt was made to determine if language usage and proficiency varied in relation to the number of years in public school and in relation to social domain. A Spanish usage rating schedule was used to assess language usage with various "bilingual" interlocutors in the domains of education, religion, neighborhood, and family. A word naming task and a picture response task were used to assess aspects of language proficiency in the same domains.

Ornstein (1971) introduces a "sociolinguistic research kit" aimed at specifying categories of information that should be given priority in sociolinguistic research projects in the Southwest. His "kit" includes the following:

1) *Linguistic Data*
   a) regional and non-standard variants of Spanish in the fields of phonology, grammar, and lexicon, according to use by different social strata;
   b) non-standard features of the English employed by various socio-economic groups;
   c) interference phenomena.
2) *Socio-Attitudinal Data*
   a) attitudes toward the different varieties of Southwestern Spanish and English and the degree of "language loyalty";
   b) attitudes toward comparative life-styles and value systems of the *anglo* and *hispano.*
3) *Bilingual Communication Data*
   a) patterns of linguistic dominance;
   b) distributive roles of Spanish vs. English in Southwest communication networks;
   c) ranges of codes employed;
   d) code switching. (Ornstein 1971, 56)

Gaarder (1971) also provides a framework for research in sociolinguistics, as he lists twenty-two sociocultural factors affecting the maintenance or shift of Spanish in the U.S. Some of these factors were originally identified by Weinrich (1953). Among the factors are the following:

1. Size and homogeneity of the bilingual group.
2. Access to renewal from hinterland.
3. Reinforcement by in-migration and immigration.
4. Relative proficiency in both languages.
5. Modes of use (reading, writing, listening, speaking).
6. Specialized use by domain and interlocutor.
7. Status of the bilingual groups.
8. Attitudes toward each language.
9. Function of each language in social-advance.

Kjolseth (1972) points out that there is a lack of hard evidence on the effects of bilingual education programs upon community language use patterns. He registers a plea for research on shifts in the bilingual dominance configurations of specific groups. He calls for the consideration of changes in subgroup language use patterns in domains outside of the school. He views the real innovation to be the investigation of language use patterns, as opposed to measuring only changes in individual language skills and language attitudes.

Since one of the aims of the Redwood City Bilingual Education Project was to maintain the minority group's language and culture, a longitudinal study was implemented to assess whether the program was achieving that aim. The Redwood City School District began its bilingual schooling in the fall of 1969, under the auspices of the ESEA Bilingual Education Program, Title VII. The Redwood City project was initiated with one Pilot first-grade class of twenty lower-class Mexican Americans and ten middle-class Anglos at the Garfield Elementary School. The following school year 1970-71 a new first grade and kindergarten were added, referred to as the Follow Up I and Follow Up II groups, respectively. In the fall of 1970 a longitudinal study of the Pilot, Follow Up I, and Follow Up II groups was begun. At that time comparison groups of Mexican Americans were selected. At the end of the 1971-72 school year, tests were administered and interviews conducted to measure change over the two-year period.

In the fall of 1970, parents of bilingual and comparison group children were administered a home interview schedule which asked about the language use and proficiency patterns of all family members. Parents and older siblings of children in the bilingual and comparison groups were also given a language orientation questionnaire to determine their "language loyalty." See the Appendix for copies of the Language Use and Proficiency, and Language Orientation Instruments. A series of questions relating to demographic and socioeconomic factors were included in the home interview. At the same time, pretest or baseline data on language use and proficiency were collected directly from the children in the Bilingual and Comparison groups, using a pupil language use inventory, story telling, word naming, oral comprehension, and reading.

At the end of two years of schooling, the bilingual and comparison groups were given the same instruments as a post-test, plus a language use observation instrument and a writing sample (for the Pilot group only). At that time, the students' parents were asked to describe the current language use and proficiency patterns of their children in the bilingual or comparison group, and the language loyalty of the parents was again assessed. The cultural attitudes of the bilingual and comparison students were also assessed. In keeping with Tucker and d'Anglejan (1971), the students' content mastery and intellectual development were measured at the end of the two-year period, using the Cooperative Primary Test of Math and the Inter-American Subtest of Nonverbal Ability.[6]

This study incorporates many of the suggestions for research contained within the sociolinguistic frameworks of Ornstein and Gaarder (see above). The research concerns itself with patterns of language proficiency in four skills in both languages and with the distributive roles of Spanish and English by social domain, and with attitudes toward language maintenance and attitudes toward culture (Ornstein, see above points 3a, 3b, 2a, 2b; Gaarder, see above points

4-9). Baseline data also includes information on the size and homogeneity of the bilingual group, access to renewal from the hinterland, and reenforcement by in-migration and immigration (Gaarder, see above, points 1-3).

The intent of this article has been to stimulate others to replicate my research in these same areas, as well as to promote research in other areas of concern to sociolinguistics (see the Ornstein and Gaarder variables above). It is the task of the sociolinguist to determine how rapidly and completely Spanish is being displaced by the socially and culturally dominant language, English, and the effect that bilingual schooling has upon this process.

Notes

[1] See *Chicanismo* 1.5:2 (Stanford University, May 4, 1970) for an attack by Chicano students on Stanford University's Spanish Department.

[2] An earlier version of this article (Edelman 1968) reports this discrepancy.

[3] See Weinreich (1953) for a detailed description of the phenomenon of languages in contact.

[4] All three articles appear in this volume.

[5] The Bilingual Education Act, within the Elementary and Secondary Education Amendments (ESEA) of 1967.

[6] A full report on this research by the author, entitled "Innovative Education for La Raza: A Sociolinguistic Assessment of Bilingual Schooling in California," will appear as a Ph.D. Dissertation at Stanford University in the fall of 1972 and as a book for Newbury House in 1973.

References

Barker, George C. 1947. "Social Functions of Language in a Mexican-American Community," *Acta Americana,* V, pp. 185-202.

Bartlett, D. W. 1969. "Preface" to *Description and Measurement of Bilingualism.* L. G. Kelly (ed.), U. of Toronto, Canada, pp. v-vi.

Bordie, John G. 1970. "Language Tests and Linguistically Different Learners: The Sad State of the Art." *Elementary English,* 47:814-28.

Bustamante, Charles J. and Patricia L. Bustamante. 1969. *The Mexican-American and The United States.* Mountain View, Calif.: Patty-Lar Publications.

Christian, Chester. 1971. "Differential Response to Language Stimuli Before Age 3: A Case Study, " Conference on Child Language, Chicago, Nov. 22-24, Les Presses de l'Université Laval, Quebec.

Christian, Jane M. and C. C. Christian, Jr. 1966. "Spanish Language and Culture in the Southwest," in J. Fishman (ed.), *Language Loyalty in the United States.* The Hague: Mouton & Co., pp. 280-317.

Cooper, Robert L. 1968. "An elaborated language testing model." *Problems in Foreign Language Testing. Language Learning.* Special Issue No. 3, pp. 57-72.

_____. 1970. "4. Testing." In R. C. Lugton, ed., *Preparing the EFL Teacher.* #7. Philadelphia: The Center for Curriculum Development.

_____. 1971. "Word Naming and Word Association." In Fishman, Cooper, Ma, et al. *Bilingualism in the Barrio.* Indiana U. Publications, Language Science Monographs #7. The Hague: Mouton & Co., pp. 286-294.

Diebold, A. Richard. 1961. "Bilingualism and Biculturalism in a Huave Community." Unpublished Ph.D. dissertation, Department of Anthropology, Yale University.

Edelman, Martin. 1968. "The Contextualization of Schoolchildren's Bilingualism." In Fishman, J. A., R. L. Cooper and R. Ma, et al. *Bilingualism in the Barrio.* Two Volumes,

Final Report. Yeshiva University, Contract No. OEC-1-7-062817-0297, U.S. Department of Health, Education and Welfare. ED 026 546.

———, R. L. Cooper, and J. A. Fishman. 1971. "Young Puerto Rican Schoolchildren." In Fishman, Cooper, Ma, et al. *Bilingualism in the Barrio.* Indiana U. Publications, Science Monographs #7. The Hague: Mouton & Co., pp. 298-304.

Ervin-Tripp, S. M. 1964. "An analysis of interaction of language, topic, and listener." *The Ethnography of Communication, American Anthropologist,* 66:2:86-102.

———. 1971. "Social Dialects in Developmental Sociolinguistics." In R. Shuy, ed. *Sociolinguistics: A Crossdisciplinary Perspective.* Washington, D.C.: Center for Applied Linguistics, pp. 35-64.

Espinosa, Aurelio M. 1917. "Speech Mixture in New Mexico: the Influence of the English Language on New Mexican Spanish," in H. M. Stephens & H. E. Bolton, eds., *The Pacific Ocean in History.* New York: MacMillan Co., pp. 408-428.

Ferguson, Charles A. 1959. "Diglossia," *Word,* 15:325-340.

Fishman, Joshua A. 1964. "Language Maintenance and Language Shift as a Field of Inquiry." *Linguistics,* 9:32-70.

———. 1965. "Who speaks what language to whom and when?" *Linguistique,* (2) 67-88. (Reprinted in Fishman, Cooper, Ma, et al. *Bilingualism in the Barrio.* Indiana U. Publications, Language Science Monographs #7. The Hague: Mouton & Co., pp. 583-604.

———. 1966a. "The Implications of Bilingualism for Language Teaching and Language Learning." In *Trends in Language Teaching,* Valdman, A., ed. New York: McGraw-Hill, pp. 121-132.

———. 1966b. *Language Loyalty in the United States.* The Hague: Mouton and Co. ERIC ED 036 217.

———. 1967. "Bilingualism with and without Diglossia; Diglossia with and without Bilingualism." *Journal of Social Issues,* 23.2:29-38.

———. 1971a. "Sociolinguistic Perspective on the Study of Bilingualism." In Fishman, Cooper, Ma, et al. *Bilingualism in the Barrio.* Indiana U. Publications, Language Science Monographs #7. The Hague: Mouton & Co., pp. 557-582.

———. 1971b. *Sociolinguistics: A Brief Introduction.* Rowley, Mass.: Newbury House.

———. 1970. "Bilingual Education in Sociolinguistic Perspective." *TESOL Quarterly,* 4.3:215-222.

———, R. L. Cooper, and R. Ma, et al. 1971. *Bilingualism in the Barrio.* Indiana U. Publications, Language Science Monographs #7: The Hague: Mouton and Co.

Fogel, Walter. 1965. Education and Income of Mexican Americans in the Southwest. Mexican-American Study Project Advance Rep. 1. L.A., Division of Res., Grad. School of Bus., U. of Ca., 28 pp.

Gaarder, A. Bruce. 1967. "Organization of the Bilingual School." *Journal of Social Issues,* 23.2:110-120.

———. 1971. "Language Maintenance or Language Shift: The Prospect for Spanish in the United States." Paper presented at the Child Language Conference, Chicago, November 22-24, 1971. 49 pp. To appear in collected conference papers, University of Laval Press.

Gumperez, John J. 1964. "Linguistic and Social Interaction in Two Communities." In John J. Gumperz and Dell Hymes, eds. *The Ethnography of Communication.* Washington, D.C.: American Anthropological Association, 1964, pp. 137-153.

———. 1967. "On the Linguistic Markers of Bilingual Communication." *Journal of Social Issues,* 23.2:48-57.

———. 1969. "How Can We Describe and Measure the Behaviour of Bilingual Groups?" In L. G. Kelly (ed.), *Description and Measurement of Bilingualism.* U. of Toronto Press, Toronto, Canada, pp. 242-249.

———. and Eduardo Hernández 1970. "Cognitive Aspects of Bilingual Communication." In

W. H. Whiteley, ed. *Language Use and Social Change.* London: Oxford University Press, pp. 111-125.

Haugen, Einar I. 1953. *The Norwegian Language in America: a Study in Bilingual Behavior.* (2 Vols.) Philadelphia: U. of Penn. Press.

_____. 1956. *Bilingualism in the Americas: A Bibliography and Research Guide.* University of Alabama, The American Dialect Society.

Hoffman, Moses N. H. 1934. *The Measurement of Bilingual Background.* New York: Teachers College, Columbia U.

Hymes, Dell. 1967. "Models of the Interaction of Language and Social Setting." *Journal of Social Issues,* 23.2:8-28.

Jakobovits, Leon A. 1970. *Foreign Language Learning.* Rowley, Mass.: Newbury House.

John, Vera P. and Vivian M. Horner. 1971. *Early Childhood Bilingual Education.* New York: Modern Language Association of America Materials Center.

Jones, R. M. 1969. "How and When Do Persons Become Bilingual?" In L. G. Kelly, ed. *Description and Measurement of Bilingualism.* U. of Toronto Press: Toronto, Canada, pp. 12-25.

Jones, W. R. 1960. "A critical study of bilingualism and nonverbal intelligence," *British Journal of Educational Psychology,* 30:71-76.

Kelly, Louis G. (ed.) 1969. *Description and Measurement of Bilingualism/Description et Mesure du Bilinguisme.* Canadian Commission for UNESCO, University of Toronto Press.

Kjolseth, Rolf. 1972. "Bilingual Education Programs in the United States: for Assimilation or Pluralism?" In Paul Turner, ed., *Bilingualism in the Southwest.* Tucson: University of Arizona Press.

Lance, Donald M. et al. 1969. *A Brief Study of Spanish-English Bilingualism: Final Report, Research Project ORR-Liberal Arts-15504,* Texas A&M U., College Station, Texas. August. ED 032 529.

Lewis, Hilda P. and Edward R. Lewis. 1965. "Written language performance of 6th-grade children of low SES from bilingual and from monolingual backgrounds." *Journal of Experimental Education,* 333:237-42.

Ma, Roxana and Eleanor Herasimchuk. 1971. "The Puerto Rican Speech Community." In J. Fishman, Cooper, Ma, et al. *Bilingualism in the Barrio.* Indiana U. Publications. Language Science Monographs #7. The Hague: Mouton & Co., pp. 357-364.

Macnamara, John. 1967. "The Bilingual's Linguistic Performance—A Psychological Overview." *Journal of Social Issues,* 23.2:58-77.

_____. 1969. "How can one measure the extent of a person's bilingual proficiency?" In Kelly, L. (ed.), *The Description and Measurement of Bilingualism.* U. of Toronto Press, Toronto, Canada, pp. 80-97.

Mahoney, Mary K. 1967. "Spanish and English Language Usage by Rural and Urban Spanish-American Families in Two South Texas Counties." Unpub. MS Thesis, Texas A&M Univ.

Ornstein, Jacob. 1971. "Sociolinguistics and the Study of Spanish and English Language Varieties and Their Use in the U.S. Southwest, With a Proposed Plan of Research." Albuquerque: SWCEL.

Patella, Victoria M. & W. P. Kuvesky. 1970. "Language Patterns of Mexican Americans: Are the Ambitious Un-Mexican?" Paper presented at the Rural Sociological Society meetings, Washington, D.C., August 26-30, 1970.

Riley, John E. 1968. *The Influence of Bilingualism on Tested Verbal Ability in Spanish.* Texas Woman's Univ., June 7, 1968. ERIC ED 026 935.

Rubin, Joan. 1968. *National Bilingualism in Paraguay.* The Hague: Mouton & Co.

Timmins, Kathleen M. 1971. "An Investigation of the Relative Bilingualism of Spanish Surnamed Children in an Elementary School in Albuquerque." Ph.D., The University of New Mexico.

Tucker, G. Richard and Alison d'Anglejan. 1971. "Some Thoughts Concerning Bilingual Education Programs." *Modern Language Journal,* 491-493.

Valdez, R. F. 1969. "The Fallacy of the Spanish Surname Survey." *California Teachers Association Journal* (May), 65.3:29-32.

Weinreich, Uriel. 1952. "Research Problems in Bilingualism with Special Reference to Switzerland." Unpub. doct. dissertation. Department of Linguistics, Columbia U.

_____. 1953. *Languages in Contact: Findings and Problems.* New York: Linguistic Circle of New York. Reprinted 1968, The Hague: Mouton & Co.

Appendix: Home Interview with Parents

Language Proficiency	Household Members			
Spanish (2=yes; 1=a little; 0=no)	1	2	. . .	15
1. Can _____ understand a conversation in Spanish?				
2. Can _____ engage in an ordinary conversation in Spanish?				
3. Can _____ read a newspaper in Spanish?				
4. Can _____ write letters in Spanish?				
English (2=yes; 1=a little; 0=no)				
5. Can _____ understand a conversation in English?				
6. Can _____ engage in an ordinary conversation in English?				
7. Can _____ read a newspaper in English?				
8. Can _____ write letters in English?				

Language Use	Household Members			
(3=Sp; 2=both; 1-Eng; 0=no)	1	2	. . .	15
9. What language does _____ use most frequently at home for conversation with adults?				
10. What language does _____ use most frequently at home for conversation with children?				
11. What language does _____ use most frequently to read books or newspapers at home?				
12. What language does _____ commonly use at home for writing letters?				
13. What language does _____ use most at work for conversation with fellow workers?				
14. What language does _____ use most at work for conversations with the supervisor (boss)?				

	Household Members			
	1	2	. . .	15
15. What language does _____ common- ly use when talking to people of the same age in the neighborhood (on the street)?				
16. What language does (did) _____ use at school? (2=Sp; 1=Eng & Sp; 0=Eng)				
17. What language does _____ like most for conversation with adults?				
18. What language does _____ like most for conversation with children?				
19. In what language does _____'s priest (minister) give the _____ when _____ attends services?				

Pupil's Language Use Inventory (2=Sp; 1=both; 0=Eng)

1. In what language does your mother usually talk to you at home?
   What language do you use to talk to her?

2. What language does your father use to talk to you at home?
   What language do you use to talk to him?

3. What language do your parents speak when they talk to each other at home?

4. What language do your older brothers and sisters use when they talk to you at home?
   What language do you use when you talk to them?

5. What language do your younger brothers and sisters use when they talk to you at home?
   What language do you use to talk to them?

6. Who are the kids you hang out with in school?
   When you are with _____ in the school playground, what language do you usually speak?

7. What kids do you hang out with where you live?
   When you're with _____, what language do you use?

8. Who do you go to church with?
   When you're standing outside the church along with _____ , what language do you speak?

Language Orientation

A. Is this a good reason for your children to learn Spanish?	very good reason	good reason	neither good nor bad	bad reason	very bad reason
1. It will help them to preserve their own native language and culture.					
2. It will someday be useful to them in getting a job.					
3. It will enable them to maintain friendships among Mexican Americans.					
4. It will enable them to continue to think and behave as true Mexican Americans (Chicanos).					
5. No one is really educated unless he is fluent in the Spanish language.					
6. It will allow them to meet and converse with more and varied people.					
7.* They need it for some specific educational or business goal.					

8. How important is it for your children to be able to speak and understand Spanish?
   Very important_____ Somewhat important _____ Not important _____
9. How important is it for your children to read Spanish?
   Very important____ Somewhat important ____ Not important_____
10. How important is it for your children to write in Spanish?
   Very important ____ Somewhat important _____ Not important _____

B. Is this a good reason for your children to learn English?	very good reason	good reason	neither good nor bad	bad reason	very bad reason
1. It enables them to make friendships among Anglos (Gavachos).					
2. It will someday be useful to them in getting a job.					
3. They need a good knowledge of English to be respected by the Anglo community.					

*After the respondent has finished item #7 in A and B, he is to choose the two best reasons and the one least acceptable for learning Spanish and English.

	very good reason	good reason	neither good nor bad	bad reason	very bad reason
4. It will enable them to think and behave as Anglos do.					
5. No one is really educated unless he is fluent in English.					
6. It will allow them to meet and converse with more and varied people.					
7.* They need it for some specific educational or business goals.					

8. How important is it for your children to be able to speak and understand Spanish?

      Very important _____ Somewhat important _____ Not important _____

9. How important is it for your children to be able to read English?

      Very important _____ Somewhat important _____ Not important _____

10. How important is it for your children to be able to write in English?

      Very important _____ Somewhat important _____ Not important _____

The Acquisition of Grammatical Structures by Mexican-American Children

Gustavo Gonzalez

In the pages that follow, I will summarize what I consider to be the most important stages in the acquisition of Spanish grammar in young children. I will also present some hypotheses and raise some questions that cannot be resolved on the basis of the present data, but which will deserve close attention in subsequent studies.

The present study was concerned primarily with linguistic performance, i.e., the actual forms produced in speech, and not directly with linguistic competence (the abstract knowledge of the language underlying performance). This choice was made for the purpose of providing a basis from which the development of competence could better be studied. Although the size of the sample of each age level was limited to three children, we believe that the developmental sequence is relatively clear, and that the data (based on a total of fifty-four hours of recorded interviews) are sufficient to allow us to establish a tentative schedule for the appearance and establishment of various grammatical structures.

Age 2;0. (SUBJECT) - *SER* - NOUN PHRASE is used for the first time by all informants, as is (SUBJECT) - *ESTAR* - LOCATIVE ADVERB. Negation in the form of *no* is present at this level. Full-sentence negation is present, but not yet established. Full-sentence information questions are shared by all three informants. Direct object and direct object pronouns occur, but are used sparingly by the children. All utterances are short; the average length of intelligible utterances was three syllables. Locative adverbs are present at this age. Subjects appear in the surface structure; only nouns appear as subjects. Imperatives consisting of verb only and verb + direct object pronoun are noted.

Age 2;6. An increase is noted in the use of direct object pronominalization; it is possibly established at this level. The indirect object pronoun made its initial appearance here, and possibly became internalized also. The present progressive and periphrastic future tenses appear regularly at this level. The imperfect indicative, the past progressive, and the present subjunctive, tenses that will be established at a subsequent level, are introduced at this level. Full-sentence negation is established by this time. The *de* + NP formulation for the possessive makes its debut here, as does comparison through the use of *como*. The verb + infinitive structure has been internalized, and the process of substantivization was already much in evidence. Imperatives included verb + indirect object pronoun, verb + reflexive pronoun, and one instance of verb + indirect object pronoun + direct object pronoun.

Age 2;9. The reflexive pronoun appeared for the first time in a construction with the direct object pronoun. The *andar* progressive made its initial

Reprinted by permission of the author from "The Acquisition of Spanish Grammar by Native Spanish Speakers," Phd dissertation, University of Texas at Austin.

appearance. Full-sentence negation is fully established by now, while negatives other than *no* also begin to emerge. The negative concord transformation was also noted and appeared to be internalized. Post-noun possessives were used here for the first time (including *mío* and *Tuyo; suyo* does not appear until age 3;6, its place being taken by the more explicit *de* + NP sequence. Only nouns are used in the NP slot at this level). Imperatives involving indirect object, direct object, and reflexive pronouns appear to be established. Temporal adverbs appear at this stage but are limited. Locative adverb clauses make their debut here (one example), as do the impersonal reflexive construction and the noun clause used as direct object.

Age 3;0. Expansion of the indirect and direct object pronouns through the use of *a* + noun phrase cross-reference increases in variety (it appears first at 2;9). Present subjunctive and imperfect indicative verb tenses appear to be established. The past subjunctive appears for the first time. The use of the noun clause as a direct object increases. The reflexive for unplanned occurrences construction has been internalized by now. Appearing for the first time are the *si* conditional clause and the construction of comparisons with *más*.

Age 3;3. The tag question makes its first appearance here, as does the indirect command. Temporal adverb clauses emerged, with the use of both indicative and subjunctive moods (properly distinguished). Compound sentences appear to be established. The use of noun clauses and relative clauses is frequent at this level. Noted for the first time at this level are the *es que* + *sentence* pattern (=English *It's just that* + sentence) and the *se* form of the indirect object pronoun.

Age 3;6. Constructions utilizing pronominalized forms of both the indirect and direct objects increase in frequency. The use of *usted* verb forms was observed for the first time, though they were not consistently distinguished from *tú* forms (this distinction was not achieved by any of our informants through age 5;0).

Age 4;0. Locative adverbs appear as modifiers of *ser*. There is a noticeable increase in the number of temporal adverbial phrases. The conditional *si* clause appears to be established.

Age 4;6. A greater variety of *ser* and *estar* syntactic patterns was observed at this level. The temporal adverb as complement of *ser* made its initial appearance. The past subjunctive and *ir* + *-ndo* tenses appear established, as do compound-complex sentences.

Age 5;0. A peak of seven varieties of *a* + NP expansion of direct and indirect object pronouns is encountered, two of which are common to all three informants at this level.

On the basis of this sample of data from twenty-seven children, then, we are able to determine a number of consistent trends in the acquisition of features of Spanish grammar. Although the data are still too limited to permit the establishment of a definitive schedule for the development of particular structures, some fairly concrete observations can be made. The evidence for the sequence of appearance of different grammatical features is summarized in the sections below.

Verb Tenses

Since verbs play such a central role in any language, the development of verb tenses is of special interest. Table 1 provides a summary of verb tense activity from age 2;0 to 6;0.

According to the data, only the present indicative tense is established by age 2;0; the preterit indicative, the present progressive, and the periphrastic future are added at age 2;6. Four other tenses are noted at 2;6 but are not established: the imperfect indicative, the past progressive, the past perfect, and the present subjunctive. No new tenses are internalized at level 2;9, and only one tense makes its debut (the *andar* progressive). The present subjunctive is the only additional tense established at 3;0, although four new tenses make their initial appearance (conditional, *ir + -ndo*, present perfect, and past subjunctive). Level 3;3 introduces the future progressive (through use of the periphrastic future formulation) and establishes the imperfect indicative tense. No new tenses are established or introduced at 3;6. At four years of age, there is the incorporation of the past progressive and the *andar* progressive. The inflected future form makes a marginal appearance.

The four-and-a-half-year-old informants appeared to have mastered the *ir + -ndo* tense, and introduced the past perfect subjunctive to the verb tense inventory. Nothing new was introduced or established at the 5;0 level. As can be seen in the table, the introduction of a tense form at one level did not guarantee its appearance in subsequent levels.

In dealing with verb tenses and their establishment or non-establishment, several problems arise. Attempts at eliciting certain forms are not always successful. Some forms, such as the present progressive or the periphrastic

TABLE 1

Summary of Verb Tenses: 2;0 – 6;0

AGE LEVELS		Present Indicative	Preterit Indicative	Imperfect Indicative	Conditional	Present Progressive	Past Progressive	Future Progressive	Andar Progressive	Ir + -ndo	Present Perfect	Past Perfect	Present Subjunctive	Past Subjunctive	Periphrastic Future	Inflected Future	Past Perfect Subjunctive
	6.0	E	E	E	NE	E	E	?	?	?	E	NE	E	NE	E	NE	NE
	5.0	E	E	E	–	E	E	–	E	NE	NE	–	E	NE	E	–	–
	4.6	E	E	E	NE	E	E	–	E	E	–	NE	E	E	E	NE	NE
	4.0	E	E	E	–	E	E	–	E	NE	NE	NE	E	NE	E	NE	–
	3.6	E	E	E	–	E	NE	–	NE	NE	–	–	NE	NE	E	–	–
	3.3	E	E	E	–	E	NE	NE	–	NE	–	–	E	NE	E	–	–
	3.0	E	E	NE	NE	E	NE	–	NE	NE	NE	–	E	NE	E	–	–
	2.9	E	E	NE	–	E	NE	–	NE	–	–	NE	NE	–	E	–	–
	2.6	E	E	NE	–	E	NE	–	–	–	–	NE	NE	–	E	–	–
	2.0	E	NE	–	–	–	–	–	–	–	–	–	–	–	–	–	–

LEGEND: E = established at this age level
               NE = not established at this age level
               – = not occurring at this level
               ? = no data available

future, pose no problem at all. Other tenses, however, require the creation of complex situations for their elicitation, for it is only under these conditions that the forms occur. Among such are the perfect tenses and the past perfect subjunctive.

Even when the appropriate elicitation situations can be set up, there is no guarantee that the child will not produce an alternate form in the response. In several instances, for example, when a child was asked a question incorporating the use of the inflected future to test for his use of this form, the child responded using the present indicative or the infinitive form. Usually, however, the response would take the form of the periphrastic future, showing that the child probably had *receptive,* but not productive knowledge of the inflected future.

Another favorite response, this time possibly involving dialect difference, is that given to questions in the conditional tense: *viz,* the imperfect indicative. This may be explained in part by the fact that the imperfect indicative alternates with the past subjunctive tense, especially in *si* clause sentences in which the dependent verb is in the past subjunctive and the independent verb is in the conditional tense. There appears to be more alternation between imperfect indicative and past subjunctive forms of *-ar* verbs (i.e., *jugaba, jugara*) than between corresponding forms of *-er, -ir* verbs, probably due to the phonetic similarity of the former forms. The evidence on this point, however, is not conclusive.

The preceding considerations, coupled with the ever-present problem of sampling error, account for the apparent establishment of a verb tense at one level, only to be considered not established at a later level. The data can thus be taken as showing a possible trend of development and nothing more. If present comments concerning verb tenses seem a bit cautious, it is because they are so intended. The area under investigation is so complex that excessive caution is preferable to the assertion of prematurely definitive conclusions.

Sentence Patterns

Syntactic structures grow greatly in number and variety during this three-year span. Some structures occur only once anywhere in our corpus; others become firmly established as time goes along. In the following pages, a list of the principal syntactic structures encountered in our study will be presented, along with their frequency of occurrence at each age level (Table 2). Given this information, it is possible to devise graphs illustrating the growth and/or fluctuation of each of the syntactic patterns noted in our corpus, as well as the development of different component constituents.

For purposes of illustration, I have selected six syntactic patterns (all of which were shared by our three 5;0 informants) and plotted the information in graph form. The patterns chosen were the following (numbers correspond to the numbers given in the summary list):

11a. (SUBJECT) - VERB - DIRECT OBJECT - (ADVERB)
12a. (SUBJECT) - REFLEX. PRON. - VERB - DIRECT OBJECT - (ADVERB)
13a. (SUBJECT) - D. O. PRON. - VERB - (ADVERB)
14a. (SUBJECT) - REFLEX. PRON. - D. O. PRON. - VERB
15a. (SUBJECT) - I. O. PRON. - VERB - DIRECT OBJECT - (ADVERB)
16a. (SUBJECT) - I. O. PRON. - D. O. PRON. - VERB - (ADVERB)

Unified List of Principal Syntactic Structures: Age 2;0 - 6;0

1a.   (SUBJECT) - *SER* - NOUN PHRASE
1b.   *SER* - NOUN PHRASE - SUBJECT
1c.   *SER* - SUBJECT - NOUN PHRASE
2a.   (SUBJECT) - *SER* - ADJECTIVE
2b.   *SER* - ADJECTIVE - SUBJECT
3a.   (SUBJECT) - *SER* - ADVERB
3b.   ADVERB - *SER* - SUBJECT
4a.   (SUBJECT) - *ESTAR* - ADJECTIVE
4b.   *ESTAR* - ADJECTIVE - SUBJECT
5a.   (SUBJECT) - *ESTAR* - LOCATIVE ADVERB
5b.   LOCATIVE ADVERB - *ESTAR* - SUBJECT
5c.   *ESTAR* - LOCATIVE ADVERB - SUBJECT
5d.   (SUBJECT) - LOCATIVE ADVERB - *ESTAR*
6.   *ESTAR* - SUBJECT - (ADVERB)
7a.   (SUBJECT) - INTRANSITIVE VERB - (ADVERB)
7b.   (ADVERB) - INTRANSITIVE VERB - SUBJECT
8a.   (SUBJECT) - REFLEX. PRON. - INTRANS. VERB - (ADV.)
8b.   REFLEX. PRON. - INTRANSITIVE VERB - SUBJECT
9.   (SUBJECT) - TRANSITIVE VERB - (ADVERB)
10a. (SUBJECT) - REFLEX. PRON. - TRANS. VERB - (ADVERB)
10b. REFLEX. PRON. - TRANSITIVE VERB - SUBJECT
11a. (SUBJECT) - VERB - DIRECT OBJECT - (ADVERB)
11b. (SUBJECT) - DIRECT OBJECT - VERB
11c. VERB - DIRECT OBJECT - SUBJECT
11d. VERB - SUBJECT - DIRECT OBJECT
11e. DIRECT OBJECT - VERB - SUBJECT
12a. (SUBJECT) - REFLEX. PRON. - VERB - DIRECT OBJECT - (ADV.)
12b. REFLEX. PRON. - VERB - DIRECT OBJECT - SUBJECT
12c. REFLEX. PRON. - VERB - SUBJECT - DIRECT OBJECT
12d. (SUBJECT) - DIRECT OBJECT - REFLEX. PRON. - VERB
13a. (SUBJECT) - D. O. PRONOUN - VERB - (ADVERB)
13b. D. O. PRON. - VERB - SUBJECT
14a. (SUBJECT) - REFLEX. PRON. - D. O. PRON. - VERB
14b. REFLEX. PRON. - D. O. PRON. - VERB - SUBJECT
15a. (SUBJECT) - I. O. PRON. - VERB - DIRECT OBJECT - (ADV.)
15b. I. O. PRON. - VERB - SUBJECT - DIRECT OBJECT
15c. I. O. PRON. - VERB - DIRECT OBJECT - SUBJECT
15d. DIRECT OBJECT - I. O. PRON. - VERB - SUBJECT
16a. (SUBJECT) - I. O. PRON. - D. O. PRON. - VERB - (ADV.)
16b. I. O. PRON. - D. O. PRON. - VERB - SUBJECT
17a. (SUBJECT) - DIRECT OBJECT - D. O. PRON. - VERB
17b. DIRECT OBJECT - D. O. PRON. - VERB - SUBJECT
18a. (SUBJECT) - I. O. PRON. - VERB - INDIRECT OBJECT
18b. (SUBJECT) - INDIRECT OBJECT - I. O. PRON. - VERB
19a. (SUBJECT) - INDIRECT OBJECT - I. O. PRON. - VERB - DIRECT OBJECT
19b. (SUBJECT) - I. O. PRON. - VERB - INDIRECT OBJECT – DIRECT OBJECT
19c. (SUBJECT) - I. O. PRON. - VERB - DIRECT OBJECT - INDIRECT OBJECT
20.   (SUBJECT) - VERB - I. O. PRON. - INDIRECT OBJECT - DIRECT OBJECT
21a. (SUBJECT) - INDIRECT OBJECT - I. O. PRON. - D. O. PRON. - VERB
21b. (SUBJECT) - I. O. PRON. - D. O. PRON. - VERB - INDIRECT OBJECT

TABLE 2

Summary of Syntactic Structures and Their Frequency of Occurrence: Age 2;0 - 6;0

	2;0	2;6	2;9	3;0	3;3	3;6	4;0	4;6	5;0	6;0
1a.	7	6	9	9	9	8	9	9	9	9
1b.	–	–	–	1	–	–	–	–	1	ND
1c.	–	–	–	–	–	–	–	1	–	ND
2a.	–	–	5	4	5	2	5	6	7	3
2b.	–	–	3	–	–	–	–	1	–	ND
3a.	–	–	–	–	–	–	–	1	1	.5
3b.	–	–	–	–	–	–	2	2	–	ND
4a.	2	6	7	8	8	8	7	8	8	5
4b.	–	–	1	2	1	1	2	4	1	ND
5a.	4	3	3	5	3	6	5	6	6	ND
5b.	5	3	5	8	7	6	4	2	4	ND
5c.	–	–	–	–	1	–	–	1	1	ND
5d.	1	–	–	–	2	2	3	3	–	ND
6.	–	–	–	–	–	–	–	1	4	ND
7a.	6	7	–	6	4	7	3	9	7	9
7b.	–	2	3	–	5	4	6	4	5	ND
8a.	4	4	9	8	8	8	9	8	7	9
8b.	–	1	2	5	–	–	2	5	2	ND
9.	–	–	–	3	3	–	4	2	7	ND
10a.	–	–	6	3	4	5	4	9	9	9
10b.	–	–	2	–	4	5	6	4	–	ND
11a.	5	8	8	9	9	8	9	9	9	9
11b.	–	–	–	–	2	2	2	1	2	ND
11c.	–	2	2	3	2	3	2	3	2	ND
11d.	–	1	2	1	1	2	–	2	–	ND
11e.	–	–	–	1	3	1	–	–	–	ND
12a.	–	–	3	4	5	7	6	8	8	9
12b.	–	–	–	1	–	–	–	–	1	ND
12c.	–	–	–	–	–	–	–	–	1	ND
12d.	–	–	–	–	–	2	–	–	–	ND
13a.	2	3	8	9	8	9	9	9	9	9
13b.	–	2	1	5	2	2	1	2	5	ND
14a.	–	2	2	1	5	5	5	6	5	2
14b.	–	–	–	–	–	–	1	2	–	ND
15a.	–	3	3	8	8	9	9	9	9	9
15b.	–	–	–	–	–	3	2	–	2	ND
15c.	–	–	1	–	3	4	–	–	1	ND
15d.	–	–	–	2	–	–	–	–	–	ND
16a.	–	3	2	–	3	5	7	8	7	3
16b.	–	–	–	–	–	–	3	3	–	ND
17a.	–	–	–	–	–	–	4	2	–	ND
17b.	–	–	–	–	–	–	–	1	–	ND
18a.	–	–	–	–	–	–	–	–	2	ND
18b.	–	–	–	–	1	–	–	–	–	ND
19a.	–	–	–	2	–	2	–	4	1	ND
19b.	–	–	–	–	2	2	2	1	3	ND
19c.	–	–	–	1	–	2	1	1	6	ND
20.	–	–	–	–	–	–	–	–	1	ND
21a.	–	–	–	–	–	–	–	–	1	ND
21b.	–	–	–	–	–	–	1	–	3	ND
AGE LEVELS	2;0	2;6	2;9	3;0	3;3	3;6	4;0	4;6	5;0	6;0

(Row axis label: SYNTACTIC STRUCTURES)

ND = no data available

FIGURE 1. (SUBJECT) - VERB - DIRECT OBJECT - (ADVERB) [11a]

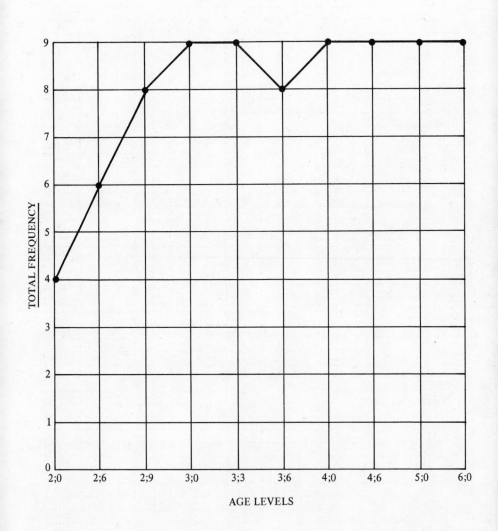

FIGURE 2. (SUBJECT) - REFLEXIVE PRONOUN - VERB - DIRECT OBJECT - ADVERB [12a]

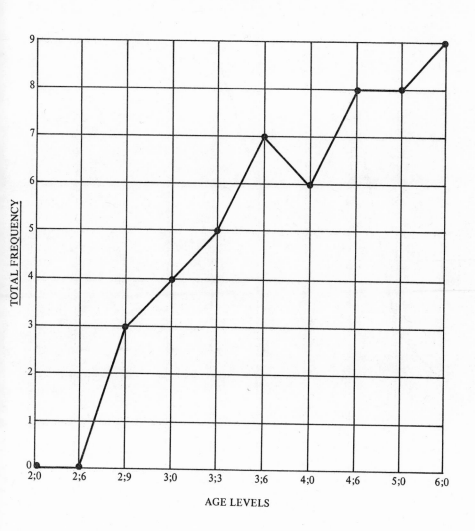

FIGURE 3. (SUBJECT) - DIRECT OBJECT PRONOUN - VERB - (ADVERB) [13a]

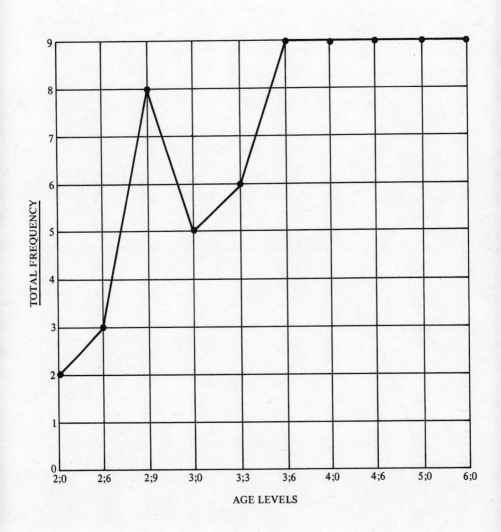

FIGURE 4. SUBJECT - REFLEXIVE PRONOUN - DIRECT OBJECT PRONOUN -
VERB [14a]

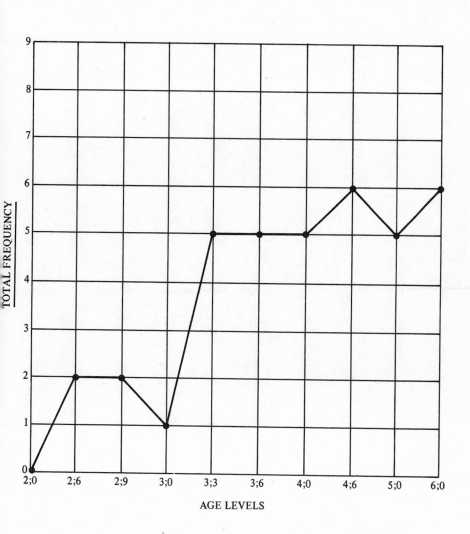

AGE LEVELS

FIGURE 5. (SUBJECT) - INDIRECT OBJECT PRONOUN - VERB - DIRECT
OBJECT - (ADVERB) [15a]

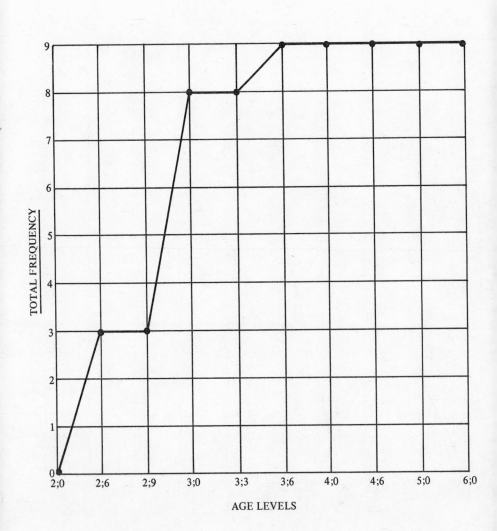

FIGURE 6. SUBJECT - INDIRECT OBJECT PRONOUN - DIRECT OBJECT
PRONOUN - VERB — (ADVERB) [16a]

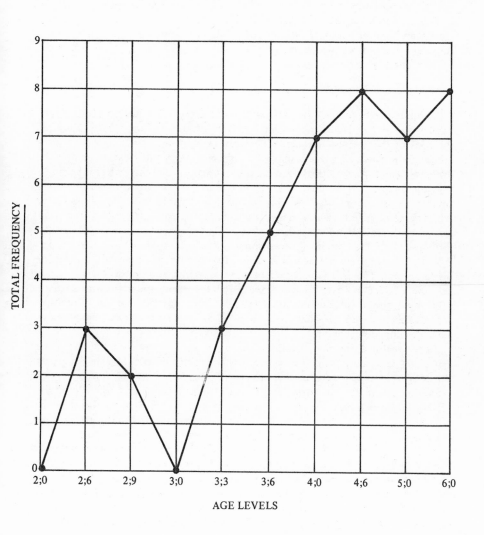

The figures given on the graphs represent the composite frequency at each age level for the structure under consideration. The figure given for Total Frequency (y axis) was derived by adding the figures of frequency of occurrence (0 = non-occurrence, 1 = one occurrence, 2 = two to three occurrences, 3 = more than three occurrences) for the three children in a given age group.

This quantification of the data helps to level out the effect of individual variation. Presenting the information in graph form should also make for easier cross-sample comparison. This kind of treatment might further permit cross-language comparison, which is necessary if any universal norms of syntactic development are to be defined.

Other Syntactic Features

The number of distinct syntactic structures grew from thirteen at age 2;0 to twenty-one at 2;6, increasing to thirty at 2;9. By age 3;0, thirty-three structures (or 85% of the greatest number of structures found at any one age level) were noted. Subsequent age levels showed minor increases; the greatest number of different structures was thirty-eight, noted at age 4;6. Relative clauses began to develop at age 2;6, as did the noun clause used as a direct object. Locative adverb clauses appeared at 2;9, and conditional *si* clauses were first observed at 3;0. Temporal adverb clauses made their debut at 3;3, as did the use of the noun clauses as a predicate noun.

Omission of the copular *ser* was noted in the speech of all informants at age 2;0. At 2;6, only one example was noted; two informants exhibited this at 3;6 (once apiece). The fact that it decreases in occurrence and is absent at our other age levels indicates that this is a developmental feature, found also in language acquisition studies of English-speaking children. It should be pointed out that the informants who omitted the copula at 3;6 were considered linguistically underdeveloped in general.

Other features are not established so easily. Lack of consistent subject-verb agreement is observed as late as level 5;0; the majority of cases involve the use of the subject after the verb in the sentence. Examples of lack of adjective-noun gender agreement occur infrequently at 2;6, 3;0, 3;6, 4;6 and 6;0 (González, 1968), indicating that the child has not completely eliminated this type of deviation by the time he enters school. Adjective-noun number agreement does not seem to cause as great a problem, the last example being noted at 3;3.

English influence on the syntactic arrangement of Spanish elements was evident only twice in our entire corpus, once in the possessive construction used by one informant at 3;3 (*"Mi papa casusa (cachucha)*," RG, I:36), and once at 3;6, when one informant translated the English expression *to be x years old* into Spanish literally (*"Joe es uno."*). At 6;0 (González, 1968) the English possessive still exerts influence (*monjitas escuela*), and literal translations continue to occur:

". . .hago *dishes*. ."   =English *I do the dishes* LG, I:11
". . .estaba tarde."   =English *You were late.* EE, II:29

Influence from English may increase as the child enters the public school system and his contact with English increases, but this needs to be studied.

There were surprisingly few ungrammatical sequences involving deviations in word order (other than those due to English influence), possibly because of the wider variability of syntactic arrangements allowed in Spanish. Only two examples, both at 3;3, were observed:

"¿Mucho, mucho tenes carros?"   RM, I:15
"Hay más otro pato."   RF, I:39

Negation

No was the only negative present at age 2;0; it was joined at 2;6 by *nada* (uttered in isolation). By 2;0, *nada* (=English *nothing*), *ni* (=English *not even, neither*), *nadie* (*nobody*), *tampoco* (*either*), and *nunca* (*never*) were observed; the negative concord transformation was in evidence for the first time. *Nada, nadie,* and *ni* were the only negatives (other than *no*) at the 3;0 level. Only *nada* appears to be established at this time. *Nunca, nada,* and *tampoco* comprised the list of negatives at 3;3; the latter two plus *ni* and *nadie* were noted at age 3;6. All forms observed at 3;6 were in evidence at age 4;0, with the addition of a new member: *ningún* (*not any*). The last two groups, age 4;6 and age 5;0, exhibited identical inventories of negatives: *nunca, ni nadie, nada,* and *tampoco*. It can safely be stated that by age 3;6, the child has a full set of negatives and the accompanying concord transformation.

Interrogatives

As early as 2;0, all forms of interrogatives (*yes-no*, information, and one-word information) are present; only the full-sentence information question was shared by all three informants. *Qué, dónde,* and *quién* were the question words utilized at this level. At 2;6 the following question words were used (in addition to the above): *para qué, cuándo, por qué,* and *cómo*. Full-sentence information questions continued to be the most popular type of interrogative. *Cuál* is the only addition at 2;9; two compounds with *quién* are noted: *de quién* and *con quién*. At 3;0, full-sentence information questions continue to be the favorite type. One-word information questions decline in use. No new question words were used. The tag question was introduced at our 3;3 level. Two new interrogatives are used in full-sentence information questions at 4;6: *de qué* and *cuántos*.

Imperatives

At age 2;0, imperatives consisting of verb only and verb plus direct object pronoun were noted. Verb plus indirect object pronoun and verb + reflexive pronoun were observed initially at 2;6; one instance of verb + indirect object pronoun + direct object pronoun was in evidence. This level also saw the use of the first negative command. The indirect command was introduced at 3;3.

Adverbial Modification

Single-word locatives are the first to appear (age 2;0); these are followed by single-word temporals (age 2;6). The next stage of development is the locative adverb clause (age 2;9), followed by the temporal adverb clause (age 3;3). There is a strong possibility that development is primarily by concept area, i.e., locative before temporal.

Sentence Complexity

Sentence types progressed from simple at age 2;0 to complex and compound at 2;6 (the complex seems established here; the compound is making its debut). Compound-complex sentences were not observed until age 4;0.

Grammatical Deviations

The acquisition of new patterns or processes does not seem to depend on mastery of previous patterns or processes. The child continues to acquire new constructions, but may still exhibit deviations in his use of earlier patterns. The most common type of deviation is regularization of irregular verb forms; this is followed closely by lack of subject-verb agreement when the subject follows the verb. This suggests that in the child's grammar, the agreement transformation is not yet firmly fixed before the subject-postposing transformations. All types of deviation encountered in the investigation were previously observed at the 6;0 level with varying degrees of frequency. Casual observation revealed that children with a smaller number of linguistic structures were generally unable to repeat sentences containing the structures missing from their inventory.

Problems for Future Research

A number of questions arose as a result of our exploratory study. Further investigation needs to be undertaken before any definitive statements can be made about these areas, though in many cases testable hypotheses can be framed on the bases of the present research. Among the questions needing investigation are the following:

1. In order of acquisition, does use of pronominalized forms necessarily follow the use of the corresponding noun?
2. Is there an order of acquisition of interrogative types, i.e., is the *yes-no* question type acquired before the full-sentence information question? Do single-word questions precede full-sentence questions?
3. Is there a sequence of development involved in the acquisition of question words, i.e., does *dónde* precede *por qué*, and so forth? Can the same type of sequence be determined for negatives other than *no*, i.e., *nada* before *nadie*, etcetera?
4. At what stage of development does the child's competence include perfect tenses? How much of this internalization can be expected to show in the child's performance?
5. For the child, is the *andar* progressive a more complicated form of the progressive than the regular *estar* progressive?

6. Is there any sequence involved in the acquisition of imperatives, i.e., do verb-only commands appear before verb + direct object pronoun commands? Do negative commands necessarily develop later?

7. At what stage does the child begin to use *tú* and *usted* forms other than indiscriminately?

8. Do the *si* clauses progress from using present indicative to using the past subjunctive tense?

9. In what ways and to what extent does the child's receptive competence differ from his productive competence?

10. How do children in our investigation compare language-wise with those in completely Spanish-speaking situations?

11. What influence does contact with English have on the child's attainment in Spanish?

12. What effect does socio-economic level have on the development of language in the child?

Exploratory investigations by their very nature often pose more questions than they answer, and the present study is no exception. Some general developmental tendencies have been presented and areas that require further scientific study have been pinpointed. Among the most important of these for any interpretation of results such as those obtained is an adequate study of regional and social dialects in the area, since without this it is impossible to know whether a structure used by the child is developmental in nature or represents a regional or social dialectal characteristic.

The present information should serve as a helpful guide for teachers, especially those at the kindergarten and primary grade level. It should indicate what type of structures the child is capable of producing at a given level; comparison with the children in her classroom could indicate to her whether her pupils are developing normally for their age. It would enable her to group them according to their language ability in Spanish. It might also suggest which tenses and structures perhaps should be avoided for a given age level.

Curriculum writers could also use the findings as a guide in determining the structures to be used at a given age level, from the language and conceptual point of view, and the sequencing of materials from a language structure point of view. The findings will enable them to construct materials for a specific age level and not for an adult population. It would also enable curriculum writers to avoid spending valuable time on structures that the child already knows. The Mexican American child in our investigation is not retarded in language development, as is often assumed. It is important that this be realized so that curriculum materials that "talk down" to him (through use of overly simple language structures) can be avoided.

The results of this investigation should also provide some guidelines in the area of test development. Knowing what structures the child can manipulate should enable evaluators to determine which tenses and how complex a sentence to use when testing a child at a given level. Above all, the information collected in this study is of crucial importance for anyone concerned with the design, conduct, or evaluation of bilingual programs for Mexican Americans and Spanish-speaking students generally. If such programs are to be effective, they must be based on a realistic understanding of the child's language, and of his linguistic capabilities and limitations. This information should serve to effectively dispel the educationally dangerous myth that Mexican American children have no grammar, and speak a supposedly corrupt mixture of Spanish and English called "Tex-Mex." Our study provides emphatic proof that the Mexican American child follows a quite consistent upward growth in his acquisition of Spanish grammar, and that the grammar he acquires, far from being corrupt, is probably as purely Spanish as that found anywhere in the Spanish-speaking world. This knowledge should inspire the teacher to a greater respect for the speech of the child, and for the truly impressive nature of his linguistic achievement.

It is my hope that this study will be followed by many others. There is, for example, an immediate need for a comparative study among economically deprived groups to test for the effect, if any, of economic deprivation on language development. Real-time case studies are needed to supplement the present apparent-time study, and the time limits need to be extended in both directions. Carefully-controlled competence tests are needed, and more detailed studies of particular grammatical features need to be carried out, using a variety of theoretical models. The present study can contribute to our understanding of universals in child language acquisition, but it is only a beginning. The field is relatively new, and much remains to be done.

APPENDIX A: SERIAL ORDER POSITION OF INFORMANTS

AGE	NAME	SEX	SERIAL ORDER POSITION
2;0	MJR	M	Only child
	LV	M	Sixth of six
	LAL	F	Fifth of five
2;6	GR	M	Third of four
	AAC	F	Second of three
	MMG	F	Only child
2;9	AL	M	Second of two
	SYW	F	Only child
	MGG	F	First of two
3;0	RG	M	Eighth of eight
	RoG	M	Second of two
	LAT	F	Second of three
3;3	RF	M	Fifth of five
	RM	M	Second of three
	ALM	F	Fourth of six
3;6	MRV	M	First of two
	MDG	F	Only child
	LEP	F	Only child
4;0	OJM	M	Only child
	MC	F	Second of three
	PB	F	Second of three
4;6	JHC	M	First of three
	PG	F	Third of three
	CS	F	No data available
5;0	AL	M	First of two
	JH	M	First of two
	LLG	F	No data available

Bibliography

In the following we have attempted to include as comprehensive a listing as possible of articles, books, and theses dealing specifically with the speech of Chicanos. Additionally, we have included a number of works concerning the influence of the Spanish language on American English as well as works concerning the speech of other Spanish-speaking groups in the United States such as that of Puerto Ricans and Jews. There exists a large number of works which emphasize the educational aspects of language education. Education is certainly an important field, but we have chosen to limit the following bibliography to works of a more linguistic nature.

Adams, R. F. *Cowboy lingo*. Boston, 1936.

———. *Western words: a dictionary of the range, cow, camp and trail.* University of Oklahoma, 1945.

Adkins, Patricia G. "Reverse borrowing of English corruptions of Spanish," *Speech Teacher,* Nov. 1968. pp. 331-33.

Agard, Frederick B. "Present-day Judaeo-Spanish in the United States," *Hispania* 33, 1950. pp. 203-10.

Ajubita, María Luisa. Language in social relations with special references to the Mexican-American problem. MA thesis, Tulane University, 1943.

Alvarez, George K. "Caló: the 'other' Spanish," *ETC.: A Journal of General Semantics* 24, 1967. pp. 7-11.

Anonymous. "Authentic Pachuco," *Time,* July 10, 1944. p. 72.

Anastasi, Anne and Fernando A. Córdova. "Some effects of bilingualism upon the intelligence test performance of Puerto Rican children in New York City," *The Journal of Educational Psychology* 44, Jan. 1953. pp. 1-19.

Anderson, John Q. "Texas stream names," in M. C. Boatwright, W. M. Hudson and A. Maxwell, eds., *A Good Tale and a Bonny Tune.* (Publications of the Texas Folklore Society 32) Southern Methodist University Press, Dallas, 1964.

Anderson, Mary. A comparative study of the English-speaking and Spanish-speaking beginners in the public schools. MA thesis, University of Texas, 1951.

Andersson, Theodore. "The bilingual in the Southwest," *Florida Foreign Language Reporter* 3, Spring, 1967.

Arispe Galvan, Robert. El dialecto español de San Antonio, Texas. Ph.D. dissertation, Tulane University, 1954.

Atwood, E. Bagby. *The regional vocabulary of Texas.* University of Texas Press, Austin, 1962.

Austin, M. "New Mexican Spanish," *Saturday Review,* 7, June 1931, p. 930.

Baker, Pauline. *Español para los hispanos.* B. Upshaw, Dallas, 1953.

Barber, Carrol. Trilingualism in Pascua: social functions of language in an Arizona Yaqui village. MA thesis, University of Arizona, 1952.

Barker, George C. "Growing Up in a Bilingual Community," *The Kiva* 17, 1951. pp. 17-32.

_____. "Pachuco: an American-Spanish argot and its social function in Tucson, Arizona." University of Arizona Social Science Bulletin 18, 1950.

_____. "Social functions of language in a Mexican-American community." *Acta Americana* 5, 1947. pp. 185-202.

_____. Social functions of language in a Mexican-American community. Ph.D. dissertation, University of Chicago, 1947.

Barker, S. Omar, "Sagebrush Spanish," *New Mexico Magazine* 20, Dec., 1942. pp. 18-19, 32-33.

Bar-Lewaw, Itzhak. "Aspectos del judeo-español de las comunidades sefardies de Atlanta (Georgia) y Montgomery (Alabama) USA," in *XI⁰ Congreso Internacional de Linguistica y Filologia Romanicas,* Madrid, 1965.

Barnes, W. C. *Arizona place names.* Tucson, 1935.

Baugh, Lila. A study of pre-school vocabulary of Spanish-speaking children. MA thesis, University of Texas, 1933.

Beberfall, Lester. "Some linguistic problems of the Spanish-speaking people of Texas," *Modern Language Journal* 42, 1958. pp. 87-90.

Beebe, Ronald. *Spanish influence in the American tradition: a selected bibliography.* Library of Congress, Legislative Reference Service, Washington, D.C., 1964.

Beltramo, Anthony F. Lexical and morphological aspects of linguistic acculturation by Mexican-Americans in San Jose, California. Ph.D. dissertation, Stanford University, 1972.

Bentley, Harold W. A dictionary of Spanish terms in English with special reference to the American Southwest. (Columbia University Studies in English and Comparative Literature) Columbia University Press, New York, 1932.

Berney, Tomi D., Robert L. Cooper, and Joshua A. Fishman. "Semantic independence and degree of bilingualism in two Puerto Rican communities," *Revista Interamericana de Psicología* 2, 1968. pp. 289-94.

Besso, Henry V. "Judeo-Spanish in the United States," *Hispania* 34, 1951. pp. 89-90.

Bierschwale, Margaret. English of the Texas range. MA thesis, Columbia University, 1920.

Blackman, Robert D. The language handicap of Spanish-American children. MA thesis, University of Arizona, 1940.

Boggs, R. S. "Phonetics of words borrowed from English by New Mexican Spanish," in *Homenaje a Fritz Kruger* 2, Mendoza: Universidad Nacional de Cuyo, 1954. pp. 305-32.

Bourke, J. G. "Notes on the language and folk usage of the Rio Grande Valley," *Journal of American Folklore* 9, 1896. pp. 81-116.

Bowen, J. Donald. "Local standards and Spanish in the southwest," in Ewton and Ornstein (1972). pp. 153-64.

_____. The Spanish of San Antoñito, New Mexico. Ph.D. dissertation, University of New Mexico, 1952.

Boyer, Mildred V. "Texas squanders non-English resources," *Texas Foreign Language*

Association Bulletin 5, Oct. 1963. pp. 1-8.

Braddy, Haldeen. "Narcotic argot along the Mexican border," *American Speech* 30, May, 1953. pp. 84-90

———. "The Pachucos and their argot," *Southern Folklore Quarterly* 24, 1965. pp. 255-71.

———. "Smugglers argot in the Southwest, " *American Speech* 21, May, 1956. pp. 96-101.

Bright, William. "Animals of acculturation in the California Indian languages," *University of California Publications in Linguistics* 4, 1960. pp. 215-46.

——— and Elizabeth Bright. "Spanish words in Patwin," *Romance Philology* 13, 1959. pp. 161-64.

Brisk, María Estela. The Spanish syntax of the pre-school Spanish-American: the case of new Mexican five-year-old children. Ph.D. dissertation, University of New Mexico, 1972.

Brown, Dolores. "A two-syllable affective affirmation in spoken Spanish," in Ewton and Ornstein (1970), 33-43.

Brüch, Josef. "Ein spanisches Wort im amerikanischen Englisch: bronco," (Anglo-Americana: Leo Hibler-Lebmannsport zum siebzigsten Geburtstag) *Wiener Beiträge zur englischen Philologie* 62, 1955. pp. 5-26.

Cabaza, Berta. The Spanish language in Texas: Cameron and Willacy counties, District 10A. MA thesis, University of Texas, 1950.

Calderón, Carlos I. "Put the accent on speech errors," *Texas Outlook,* Feb. 1959. pp. 26-28.

Callicut, Laurie T. Word difficulties of Mexican and non-Mexican children. MA thesis, University of Texas, 1934.

Campa, Arthur L. "Sayings and riddles in New Mexico," *University of New Mexico Bulletin,* (Language Series, 6:2), Sept. 1937.

Canfield, Delos Lincoln. "Diphthongization in the Spanish of the Anglo-North American," *Hispania* 24, 1940. p. 211.

———. "Tampa Spanish: three characters in search of a pronunciation," *Modern Language Journal* 35, 1951. pp. 42-44.

Cárdenas, Daniel N. "Compound and coordinate bilingualism-biculturalism in the Southwest," in Ewton and Ornstein (1972). pp. 165-80.

———. *Dominant Spanish dialects spoken in the United States.* ERIC Clearinghouse for Linguistics, Washington, D.C., 1970.

Carlisle, Rose Jeanne. A southwestern dictionary. MA thesis, University of New Mexico, 1939.

Carrow, Mary A. "Linguistic functioning of bilingual and monolingual children," *Journal of Speech and Hearing Disorders,* 22, 1957. pp. 371-80.

Cerda, Gilberto, Berta Cabaza, and Julieta Farias. Vocabulario español de Texas. (University of Texas Hispanic Studies 5) University of Texas Press, Austin, 1953.

Chacón, Estelle. "Pochismos," *El Grito* 3, Fall 1969. pp. 34-35.

Chapin, F. A. *Spanish words that have become Westernisms.* New York, 1925.

Chávez, Fray Angélico. "New names in New Mexico," *El Palacio* 64, 1956. pp. 367-80.

Cherry, Adrian. *Tampa Spanish slang with English translation.* Lamplight Press, Tampa,

Florida, 1966.

Christian, Chester C., Jr. "Language functions in the maintenance of socio-economic hierarchies," in Ewton and Ornstein (1972). pp. 181-92.

Christian, Jane M. and Chester C. Christian, Jr. "Spanish language and culture in the Southwest," in Joshua A. Fishman, et al. *Language loyalty in the U.S.: the maintenance and perpetuation of the non-English mother tongue by American ethnic and religious groups.* Mouton, The Hague, 1966. pp. 280-317.

Clark Moreno, Joseph. *Sources of information and materials concerning bilingualism, Mexican American studies and migrant education.* Bilingual Office, Barstow, California, Unified School District, 1972.

Clegg, Joseph H. Fonética y fonología del español de Texas. Ph.D. dissertation, University of Texas, 1969.

Coan, Mary Wright. The language difficulty in measuring the intelligence of Spanish-American students. MA thesis, University of New Mexico, 1927.

Cohen, Andrew D. A sociolinguistic approach to bilingual education: the measurement of language use and attitudes toward language in school and community, with special reference to the Mexican American community of Redwood City, California. 1970. [ERIC ED 043-007]

Coltharp, Mary Lurline. The influence of English on the "language" of the *Tirilones.* Ph.D. dissertation, University of Texas, 1964.

_____. The tongue of the Tirilones: a linguistic study of a criminal argot. (Alabama Linguistic and Philological Series 7.) University of Alabama Press, 1965.

_____. "Invitation to the dance: Spanish in the El Paso underworld," in *Texas Studies in Bilingualism,* G. Gilbert, ed., Gruyter, Berlin, 1970.

_____. "Some additions, lexicon of the tongue of the Tirilones," in *Studies in Language and Literature 1969-70,* Texas Western Press, El Paso. pp. 67-78.

Compeán, Ignacio and John Reyes. Caló: language of the Pachuco. Unpublished manuscript, Mini-Corps, Fresno, California, 1969.

Condit, Eleanor Daly. An appraisal of certain methods of treating bi-lingualism in the Claremont Elementary School. MA thesis, University of Southern California, 1946.

Contreras, Heles W. The phonological system of a bilingual child. Ph.D. dissertation, University of Indiana, 1962.

Conway, T. F. "The bilingual problem in the schools of New Mexico," *Alianza* 36, Feb. 1942. pp. 13, 17.

Coon, Mary W. The language difficulty in measuring the intelligence of Spanish-American students. MA thesis, University of New Mexico, 1927.

Cornejo, Richard J. Bilingualism: study of the lexicon of the five-year-old Spanish-speaking children of Texas. Ph.D. dissertation, University of Texas, 1969.

Craddock, Jerry R. *Lexical analysis of sociolinguistic studies on Southwest bilingualism (SSSB) bilingual corpuses: dialectal traits and chief interference patterns.* UTEP Cross-Cultural Southwest Ethnic Study Center, El Paso, 1972.

_____. "Spanish in North America," in Thomas A. Sebeok, ed., *Current Trends in Linguistics X,* Mouton, The Hague, 1972. pp. 305-39.

Crowley, Cornelius J. "Some remarks on the etymology of the southwestern words for *cat,*" *International Journal of American Linguistics* 28, 1962. pp. 149-51.

Darcy, Natalie T. "The performance of bilingual Puerto Rican children on verbal and nonlanguage tests of intelligence," *Journal of Educational Research* 45, March 1952. pp. 499-506.

Delmet, Don T. "A study of the mental and scholastic abilities of Mexican children in the elementary school." *Journal of Juvenile Research* 14, 1930. pp. 267-79.

Demarest, R. Differences in results on five standard tests administered to Anglo-American and Spanish-American seventh-grade boys. *American Psychologist* 1, 1946. (Abstract p. 244.)

Días, Rosario S. A vocabulary of California Spanish words of English origin used by first generation Spaniards of California. Ph.D. dissertation, Stanford University, 1942.

Dockstader, Frederick J. "Spanish loanwords in Hopi: a preliminary check-list," *International Journal of American Linguistics* 21, 1955. pp. 157-59.

Dozier, Edward P. "Two examples of linguistic acculturation: the Yaqui of Sonora and the Tewa of New Mexico," *Language* 32, 1956. pp. 146-57.

Duran, Felix L. A Compilation of Anglicisms in the Penasco area. MA thesis, New Mexico Highland University, 1939.

Eccles, Leonie Seabrook, A summary of the preparation in Spanish of the elementary grade teachers in New Mexico. MA thesis, University of New Mexico, 1939.

Eichorn, Dorothy H. and Harold E. Jones. "Bilingualism," in "Development of mental functions," *Review of Educational Research,* 22:5.425, Chapter II, Dec. 1952.

Elías Olivares, Lucía E. Study of the oral vocabulary of ten high school Mexican-American students in Austin, Texas. MA thesis, University of Texas, Austin, 1970.

Espinosa, Aurelio M. "Apuntaciones para un diccionario de nuevo mejicanismos," in *Estudios Dedicados a Adolfo Bonilla y San Martín* vol. 2, Madrid, 1928.

———. "El desarrollo de la palabra 'Castilla' entre los indios queres de Nuevo Méjico," *Revista de Filología Española* 19, 1932. pp. 261-77.

———. "El desarrollo fonético de las dos palabras 'todo' 'y' en la frase 'con todo y' + sustantivo en el español de Nuevo México," *Investigaciones Lingüísticas* 2, 1934. pp. 195-99.

———. *Estudios sobre el español de Nuevo Méjico, con nueve estudios complementarios de Amado Alonso.* Translated and edited by Amado Alonso and Angel Rosenblat. Part 2, "Morfología" translated and reviewed by Angel Rosenblat with "Notas de morfología dialectal." (Biblioteca de Dialectología Hispanoamerican 1-2.) Universidad de Buenos Aires, 1930-46.

———. "The language of the cuentos populares españoles," *Language* 3, 1927. pp. 188-98 and 4, 1928. pp. 18-27, 111-19.

———. "Nombres de bautismo nuevomejicanos," *Revue de Dialectologie Romane* 5, 1913. pp. 356-76.

———. "La palabra 'Castilla' en la lengua de los indios hopis de Arizona," *Revista de Filología Española* 22, 1935. pp. 298-300.

———. *The Spanish language: New Mexico and southern Colorado.* (Historical Society of New Mexico Publications.) New Mexican Printing Co., Santa Fe, 1911.

———. "Spanish tradition among the Pueblo Indians," in *Estudios Hispánicos: Homenaje a Archer M. Huntington.* Wellesley College Spanish Department, Wellesley, Massachusets, 1952. pp. 131-41.

_____. "Speech mixture in New Mexico: the influence of the English language on New Mexican Spanish," in *The Pacific Ocean in History,* H. Morse Stephens and Herbert E. Bolton, eds., New York, 1917. pp. 408-28.

_____. Studies in New Mexican Spanish. In *Revue de Dialectologie Romane.* Part 1: Phonology, 1.57-239, 269-300 (also in University of New Mexico Bulletin Language Series 1:2); Part 2: Morphology, 3.241-56, 4.251-86, 5.142-72; Part 3: The English Elements, 6.241-317. 1909-1915.

_____. "Syllabic consonants in New Mexican Spanish," *Language* 1:4, December, 1925. pp. 1.109-18.

Espinosa, Aurelio M., Jr. "Problemas lexicográficos del español del sudoeste," *Hispania* 40, 1957. pp. 139-43.

Ewton, Ralph W., Jr. and Jacob Ornstein, eds. *Studies in language and linguistics, 1969-70.* Texas Western Press, El Paso, 1970.

_____. *Studies in language and linguistics, 1972-73.* Texas Western Press, El Paso, 1972.

Fickinger, Paul L. A study of certain phases of the language problem of Spanish-American children. MA thesis, University of New Mexico, 1930.

Fishman, Joshua A. "A sociolinguistic census of a bilingual neighborhood," *American Journal of Sociology* 75, 1969. pp. 323-39.

_____ and Heriberto Casiano. "Puerto Ricans in our press," *The Modern Language Journal* 53:3, March 1969. pp. 157-62.

_____, Robert L. Cooper, Roxana Ma, et al. Bilingualism in the barrio. (Indiana University Publications, Language Science Monographs.) Mouton, The Hague, 1971.

_____ and Eleanor Herasimchuk. "The multiple prediction of phonological variables in a bilingual speech community," *American Anthropologist* 71, 1969. pp. 648-57.

_____ and C. Terry. "The validity of census data on bilingualism in a Puerto Rican neighborhood," *American Sociological Review* 34, 1969. pp. 636-50.

_____ et al. "Bilingualism in the barrio," *The Modern Language Journal,* 53:3, March 1969. Special issue on bilingualism.

Fitch, Michael J. Verbal and performance test scores in bilingual children. Ph.D. dissertation, Colorado State College, 1966.

Flores, Zella K. Jordan. The relation of language difficulty to intelligence and school retardation in a group of Spanish-speaking children. MA thesis, University of Chicago, 1926.

Fody, Michael, III. A glossary of non-standard Spanish words and idioms found in selected newspapers of South Texas during 1968. MA thesis, University of Southern Illinois, 1969.

Fortier, Alcee. "Los isleños of Louisiana," in Alcee Fortier, *Louisiana Studies,* New Orleans, 1894.

Friedman, Lillian. "Minorcan dialect words in St. Augustine, Florida," *Publications of the American Dialect Society* 14, 1950.

Frausto, Manuel. Vocabulario español de San Marcos, Texas. MA thesis, Southwest Texas State University, 1969.

Gaarder, A. Bruce. "Notes on some Spanish terms in the Southwest," *Hispania* 27, 1944.

_____. "Language maintenance or language shift: the prospect for Spanish in the United States," paper presented at the Child Language Conference, Chicago, Nov. 22-24, 1971.

Galvan, Mary and Rudolph Troike. "The East Texas dialect project: a pattern for education," in Aarons, Gordon, and Stewart, *Florida Foreign Language Reporter* (Special Anthology Issue) 1969.

Galván, Roberto A. "'Chichecano': neologismo jergal," *Hispania* 53:1, March 1970. pp. 86-88.

_____. El dialecto español de San Antonio, Texas. Ph.D. dissertation, Tulane University, 1955.

_____. Un estudio geográfico de algunos vocablos usados por los habitantes de habla española de San Antonio, Texas. MA thesis, University of Texas, Austin, 1949.

_____. "More on 'frito' as an English loan-word in Mexican Spanish." *Hispania* 54, 1971. pp. 511-12.

García, Ernest. "Chicano Spanish dialects and education," *Aztlán: Chicano Journal of the Social Sciences and the Arts* 2:1, Spring, 1971.

García, Lucy. Vocabulario selecto del español de Brownsville, Texas. MA thesis, Southwest Texas State University, 1972.

Garth, Thomas R., T. H. Elson and M. N. Morton. "The administration of non-language intelligence tests to Mexicans," *Journal of Abnormal Psychology* 31, 1936. pp. 53-58.

Galbraith, Clare Kearney. "Spanish-speaking children communicate," *Childhood Education,* October, 1965. pp. 70-74.

Gerritsen, William D. *An English-Spanish glossary of basic medical terminology in the dialect of northern New Mexico.* Santa Fe County Health Department, Santa Fe, 1964.

González, Gustavo. The acquisition of Spanish grammar by native Spanish speakers. Ph.D. dissertation, University of Texas, Austin, 1970.

_____. The English of Spanish-speaking migrant children: preliminary report. Southwest Educational Development Laboratory, Austin, 1969.

_____. A linguistic profile of the Spanish speaking first-grader in Corpus Christi. MA thesis, University of Texas, Austin, 1968.

_____. *The phonology of Corpus Christi Spanish.* Southwest Educational Development Laboratory, Austin, 1969.

González, Eugene. "Mexican-American parents respond to bilingual questionnaires," *California Education* 3, Sept. 1965. pp. 10-12.

González, R. J. "Pachuco: the birth of a creole," *Arizona Quarterly* 23, 1967. pp. 343-56.

Graham, Robert Somerville. "Spanish language radio in northern Colorado," *American Speech* 37:3, Oct. 1962. pp. 207-11.

Granger, Byrd H. Revised edition of Will C. Barnes, *Arizona Place Names,* 1935. University of Arizona Press, 1960.

Grant, R. V. "The localized vocabulary of California verse," *California Folklore Quarterly* 1, 1942. pp. 253-90.

Gray, Edward D. McQueen. "The Spanish language in New Mexico: a national resource," *University of New Mexico Bulletin Sociological Series* 1:2, 1912.

Gray, Hollis et al. "Gringoisms in Arizona," *American Speech,* Oct. 1949. pp. 234-36.

Griffith, Beatrice W. "The pachuco patois," *Common Ground* 7, Summer 1947. pp. 77-84.

Grinevald-Craig, Colette. La situation linguistique de la communité porto-ricaine de Cambridge, Massachusetts. Thèse, Faculté des Lettres de Paris-Nanterre, Department d'espagnol. 1968-1969.

Gross, Stuart M. A vocabulary of New Mexican Spanish. MA thesis, Stanford University, Stanford, 1935.

Gudde, Erwin G. *California place names: the origin and etymology of current geographical names*. 3rd edition. University of California Press, Berkeley, 1969. (1st edition, 1949).

Guerra, Manuel. "Psycholinguistic and sociolinguistic problems and talents of Mexican-Americans," Federal Hearings Position Paper, El Paso, Oct. 27, 1967. Published in condensed form in the Congressional Record, Feb. 7, 1968 by Hon. Edward R. Roybal.

Guerrero de la Rosa, Roberto "El slang y la jerga mexicana," *Revista Ibero-americana* 1:2, 1939. pp. 365-74.

Gumperz, John and Eduardo Hernández-Ch. "Cognitive aspects of bilingual communication," in H. Whitely, ed., *Language Use and Social Change*, Oxford University Press, London, 1970. pp. 111-25.

Hale, E. E. "Geographical terms in the Far West," *Dialect Notes* 6, 1932, part 4. pp. 217-34.

Hanson, Edith Josephine. A study of intelligence test results for Mexican children based on English and Mexican test forms. MA thesis, University of Southern California, 1931.

Hardman, Martha James. The phonology of the Spanish of El Prado, New Mexico. MA thesis, University of New Mexico, 1956.

Haught, B. F. "The language difficulty of Spanish-American children," *Journal of Applied Psychology* 15, Feb. 1931. pp. 92-95.

Hayes, Frances C. "Anglo-Spanish speech in Tampa, Florida," *Hispania* 32, 1949. pp. 48-52.

Heard, Betty R. A phonological analysis of the speech of Hays County, Texas. Ph.D. dissertation, Louisiana State University, 1969.

Heiler-Saayedra, Barbara. An investigation of the causes of primary stress mislocation in the English speech of bilingual Americans. MA thesis, University of Texas, El Paso, 1966.

Henríquez, Ureña, Pedro. "Bibliografía del sudoeste hispánico de los Estados Unidos," *Biblioteca de Dialectología Hispanoamericana* 4, 1938. pp. 41-45.

_____. "El espanol en México, Los Estados Unidos, y la América Central." *Biblioteca de Dialectología Hispanoamericana* 61, Buenos Aires, 1938.

_____. "Observaciones sobre el español en America," *Revista de Filología Española* 8, 1921. pp. 357-90.

Hernández, José González. *Chicano dictionary*. Published by the author, 1970. No location.

Herriman, G. W. An investigation concerning the effect of language handicap on mental development and educational progress. MA thesis, University of Southern California, 1932.

Hills, Elijah C. "New words in California," *Modern Language Notes* 38:3, 1923. pp. 187-88.

_____. "New Mexican Spanish," *PMLA* 21:3, 1906. (Reprinted in Elijah C. Hills, *Hispanic Studies*, American Association of Teachers of Spanish, Stanford University Press, 1929. pp. 1-46.)

Hirsch, Ruth. A study of some aspects of a Judeo-Spanish dialect as spoken by a New York Sephardic family. Ph.D. dissertation, University of Michigan, 1951.

Hoben, N. and J. T. Hood. "Help the language handicapped," *Texas Outlook* 21, June, 1937. pp. 38-39.

Hoffman, Howardine G. Bi-lingualism and oral and written expression of fifth grade children. MA thesis, University of Southern California, 1938.

Holland, W. E. "Language barrier as an education problem of Spanish-speaking children," *Exceptional Children,* Sept, 1960. (Reprinted in Staten W. Webster, ed. *The Disadvantaged Learner: knowing, understanding, educating children.* Chandler Publishing Co., San Francisco, 1966. pp. 338-49.)

Horner, Vivian M. and Vera John. "Bilingualism and the Spanish-speaking child," in Frederick Williams, ed., *Language and Poverty,* Markham Publishing Co., Chicago, 1970. pp. 140-52.

Hughes, Marie Morrison. The English language facility of Mexican-American children living and attending school in a segregated community. Ph.D. dissertation, Stanford University, 1952.

Hustvedt, S. B. " Spanish elements in the style of the *Los Angeles Star,*" *Western Folklore* 7, 1948. pp. 1-20.

Ibarra, Herbert. "Teaching in Spanish to the Spanish speaking" *Foreign Language Annals* 2, 1969. pp. 310-15.

Jackson, Lucille Prim. An analysis of the language difficulties of the Spanish-speaking children of the Bowie High School, El Paso, Texas. MA thesis, University of Texas, 1938.

Jameson, Gloria R. The development of a phonemic analysis for an oral English proficiency test for Spanish-speaking school beginners. Ph.D. dissertation, University of Texas, 1967.

January, William Spence. The Chicano dialect of the Mexican-American communities of Dallas and Fort Worth. MA thesis, Texas Christian University, 1971.

Jarvis, Gertrude O. A study of the relation of achievement in Spanish to achievement in English. MA thesis, University of Texas, 1953.

Johnson, Bruce Edward. Ability, achievement and bilingualism: a comparative study involving Spanish-speaking and English-speaking children at the sixth-grade level. Ph.D. dissertation, University of Maryland, 1962.

Johnson, Granville B., Jr. "The relationship existing between bilingualism and racial attitude," *Journal of Educational Psychology* 42:6, Oct. 1951. pp. 357-65.

Johnson, Loaz W. "A comparison of the vocabularies of Anglo-American and Spanish-American high school pupils," *Journal of Educational Psychology* 29, Feb. 1938. pp. 135-44.

Kelley, Rex Robert. Vocabulary as used on the Mexican border. MA thesis, Baylor University, 1938.

Kelly, Victor H. "The reading ability of Spanish and English speaking pupils." *Journal of Educational Research* 29, 1935. pp. 209-11.

Keniston, Hayward. "Notes on research in the Spanish spoken in the United States," *Bulletin of the American Council of Learned Societies* 34, 1942. pp. 64-67.

———. "The Spanish in the United States," in *Conference on non-English speech in the United States, Ann Arbor, Michigan, August 2-3, 1940.* American Council of Learned Societies. Bulletin No. 34, Washington, D.C., March 1942.

Kercheville, F. M. "A preliminary glossary of New Mexican Spanish," *University of New Mexico Bulletin,* (Language Series 5) 1934. pp. 1-69.

_____. *A preliminary glossary of southwestern and Rio Grande Spanish.* Kingsville, Texas, 1969.

_____. "Spanish and English in the American Southwest," *New Mexico School Review* (Santa Fe) Sept. 1936. pp. 24-25.

Keston, Morton J. and Carmina A. Jiménez. "A study of the performance on English and Spanish edition of the Stanford-Binet intelligence test by Spanish-American children," *Journal of Genetic Psychology* 85, Dec. 1954. pp. 263-69.

Kiddle, Lawrence B. "American Indian reflexes of two Spanish words for 'cat'," *International Journal of American Linguistics* 30, 1964. pp. 299-305.

_____. "Los nombres del pavo en el dialecto nuevomejicano," *Hispania* 24, 1941. pp. 213-16.

_____. "Spanish loan words in American Indian languages," *Hispania* 35, 1952. pp. 179-84.

_____. "'Turkey' in New Mexican Spanish," *Romance Philology* 5, 1952. pp. 190-97.

Kindig, Maita M. A phonological study of the English speech of selected speakers of Puerto Rican Spanish in Honolulu. MA thesis, University of Hawaii, 1960.

Kreidler, Charles. A study of the influence of English on the Spanish of Puerto Ricans in Jersey City, New Jersey. Ph.D. dissertation, University of Michigan, 1957.

Labov, W., P. Cohen and C. Robins. A preliminary study of the structure of English used by Negro and Puerto Rican speakers in New York City. Cooperative Research Project No. 3091, Columbia University, New York, 1965.

_____, P. Cohen, C. Robbins and J. Lewis. A study of the non-standard English of Negro and Puerto Rican speakers in New York City. Comparative Research Project no. 3288. 2 vols. Columbia University, New York, 1968.

Lance, Donald M. et al. A brief study of Spanish-English bilingualism: final report research project, ORR-Liberal Arts 15504. Texas A&M University, College Station, Texas, 1969.

_____. "The codes of the Spanish-English bilingual," *TESOL Quarterly* 4, 1970, 342-51.

Landman, Robert S. "Sociolinguistic deficiencies in social action programs: some personal observations," in Ewton and Ornstein (1972). pp. 193-200.

Lastra, Yolanda. "El habla y la educación de los niños de origen mexicano en Los Angeles," paper presented at the 5° Simposio del Programa Interamericano de Lingüística y Enseñanza de Idiomas, São Paulo, Jan. 9-14, 1969.

Levine, Harry, "Bilingualism: its effect on emotional and social development," *Journal of Secondary Education,* Feb. 1969. pp. 69-73.

Levy, Denah. "La pronunciación del sefardí esmirniano de Nueva York," *Nueva Revista de Filología Hispánica* 6, 1952. pp. 277-81.

_____. *El sefardí esmirniano de Nueva York. Mexico, 1952.*

Lewis, Hilda P. and Edward R. Lewis. "Written language performance of sixth-grade children of low socio-economic status from bi-lingual and from monolingual backgrounds," *Journal of Experimental Education* 33, Spring, 1965. pp. 337-42.

Linn, George Byron. A study of several linguistic functions of Mexican-American children in a two-language environment. Ph.D. dissertation, University of Southern California, 1965.

Loar, Robert L. Bilingualism and verbal comprehension. MA thesis, New Mexico State University, 1964.

Lozano, Anthony G. "Intercambio de español e inglés en San Antonio, Texas," *Archivum*

(Oviedo), 11, 1961. pp. 111-38.

Lummis, Charles F. *The land of poco tiempo.* New York, 1893. (On pages 217-250 are popular songs of New Mexico with linguistic notes.)

Luria, Max G. "Judeo-Spanish dialects in New York City," in *Todd Memorial Volumes: Philological Studies,* J. D. Fitz-Gerald and P. Taylor, eds., 2 vols. Columbia University Press, New York. Vol. 2, 1930. pp. 7-16.

Lynn, Klonda. "Bilingualism in the Southwest," *Quarterly Journal of Speech* 31, 1945. pp. 175-80.

_____. "Gringoisms in Arizona," *American Speech* 24, 1949. pp. 234-36.

MacCurdy, Raymond R., Jr. "Louisiana-French loan words for 'water-fowl' in the Spanish of St. Bernard Parish, Louisiana," in U. T. Holmes et al., eds., *Romance Studies Presented to W. M. Dey,* University of North Carolina Studies in the romance Languages and Literatures XII, Chapel Hill, 1950. pp. 139-42.

_____. The Spanish dialect in St. Bernard Parish, Louisiana. (University of New Mexico Publication 6) University of New Mexico Press, Albuquerque, 1950.

_____. "Spanish folklore from St. Bernard Parish, Louisiana," *Southern Folklore Quarterly* 13, 1949. pp. 180-91.

_____. "Spanish riddles from St. Bernard Parish, Louisiana," *Southern Folklore Quarterly* 12, 1948. pp. 129-35.

_____. "A Spanish word-list of the 'Brulis' dwellers of Louisiana," *Hispania* 42, 1959. pp. 547-54.

Mahikian, Charles. "Measuring the intelligence and reading capacity of Spanish-speaking children," *Elementary School Journal* 39, June 1939. pp. 760-68.

Mahoney, Mary Katherine. Spanish and English language usage by rural and urban Spanish-American families in two south Texas counties. MS thesis, Texas A&M University, 1967.

Mallo, Jerónimo. "La invasión del anglicismo en la lengua española de América," *Cuadernos Americanos* 18:4, 1959. pp. 115-23.

Mallory, Gloria Griffin. Sociolinguistic considerations for bilingual education in an Albuquerque community undergoing language shift. Ph.D. dissertation, University of New Mexico, 1971.

Manuel, Herschel T. "Comparison of Spanish-speaking and English-speaking children in reading and arithmetic," *Journal of Applied Psychology* 19, April 1935. pp. 189-202.

_____. *Development of Inter-American test materials.* University of Texas, Austin, 1966.

_____ and Carrie E. Wright. "The language difficulty of Mexican children," *Pedagogical Seminary and Journal of Genetic Psychology* (now *Journal of General Psychology*) Sept. 1929. pp. 458-68.

_____. "The problem of language," in H. T. Manuel, *Spanish-Speaking Children of the Southwest,* University of Texas Press, Austin, 1965. pp. 110-29.

_____. *Spanish and English editions of Stanford-Binet in relation to the abilities of Mexican children.* University of Texas, Austin, 1935.

_____. *Tests of general ability and reading.* (Inter-American series.) University of Texas, Austin, 1963.

Marcoux, Fred Wesley. Handicaps of bi-lingual Mexican children. MA thesis, University of Southern California, 1961.

Markley, James Gerald. The verbal categories of substandard Spanish. Ph.D. Dissertation, University of Illinois, 1954.

Marx, Meyer. The problem of bi-lingualism among Spanish speaking groups in the United States – a review of the literature. Project Report, University of Southern California, August, 1953.

Mason, Julian. "The etymology of *buckaroo,*" *American Speech* 35, 1960. pp. 51-55.

May, Darlene Rae. "Notas sobre el tex-mex." *Noticias culturales del Instituto Caro y Cuervo* 70, 1966. pp. 17-19.

Mazeika, Edward John. A descriptive analysis of the language of a bilingual child. Ph.D. dissertation, University of Rochester, 1971.

McClendon, Juliette Jane Canfield. Spanish-speaking children of Big Springs: an educational challenge. Ph.D. dissertation, University of Texas, 1964. (Especially Chapter 6 and the appendix on 'Variants used by Big Springs Spanish speaking children with central Mexican equivalents.')

McClendon, Sally. "Spanish words in Eastern Pomo," *Romance Philology* 23, 1969. pp. 39-53.

McKee, Okla M. Five hundred non-dictionary words found in the El Paso-Juarez Press. MA thesis, Texas Western College, 1955.

McSpadden, George F. "Some semantic and philological facts of the Spanish spoken in Chilili, New Mexico." *University of New Mexico Bulletin, Language Series* 5:3, Albuquerque, 1934. pp. 71-102.

Meriam, Junius L. Learning English incidentally: a study of bilingual children. *United States Office of Education Bulletin* No. 15, 1937.

Metcalf, Allan A. *Riverside English: the spoken language of a Southern California community.* English Department, University of California, Riverside, 1971. (Contains a section on Mexican American English on pp. 35-37.)

Mexican American Affairs Unit. *Language, culture, education, articles, books, unpublished materials, 1962-68.* U.S. Office of Education, Washington, D.C., n.d.

Michel, Joseph, "A pilot project for recording the speech of the five-year-old Texas Spanish-English pre-school bilingual child," in Aarons, Gordon, and Stewart, *Florida Foreign Language Reporter* (Special Anthology Issue), 1969.

Miller, Wick R. "Spanish loanwords in Acoma," *International Journal of American Linguistics* 25, 1959. pp. 147-53; 26, 1960. pp. 41-49.

Montemayor, Elsa Diana. A study of the Spanish spoken by certain bilingual students of Laredo, Texas. MA thesis, Texas Woman's University, 1966.

Montoya, Atanasio. "Removing the language difficulty," *American Childhood* 17, March 1932. pp. 12-15.

Moore, Joan W. and Alfred Cuellar. "Language and culture," in Joan W. Moore, *Mexican Americans,* Prentice Hall, Englewood-Cliffs, N. J., 1970. pp. 119-36.

Moran, Mattie Belle. A study of the oral and reading vocabularies of beginning Spanish-speaking children. MA thesis, University of Texas, 1940.

Moreno, H. M. *Dictionary of Spanish-named California cities and towns.* San Luis Obispo, 1916.

Morrill, D. B. "The Spanish language problem," *New Mexico Journal of Education* 14, May 1918. pp. 6-7.

Morrison, Charlotte Amos. A comparison of the achievement of Mexican pupils learning English in a segregated school and in a non-segregated school, 1952. MA thesis, University of Oregon, 1952.

Mullins, Martha Mersman. The personality differences between unilingual and bi-lingual ninth grade students in depressed areas. MA thesis, University of New Mexico, 1961.

Murphy, Raymond Paul. Integration of English lexicon in Albuquerque Spanish. Ph.D. dissertation, University of New Mexico, 1972.

Murphy, Spencer L., Jr. "Notes on *anglicismos* in American Spanish," *Hispania* 37:4, 1954. pp. 457-59.

Nall, Frank C. "Role expectations: a cross-cultural study," *Rural Sociology* 27, Mar. 1962. pp. 28-41.

Natalicio, Eleanor Diana Siedhoff. Formation of the plural in English: a study of native speakers of English and native speakers of Spanish. Ph.D. dissertation, University of Texas, 1969.

Nathan, Jerome M. The relationship of English language deficiency to intelligence test scores of mentally retarded Mexican-American children. MA thesis, University of California at Los Angeles, 1955.

Navarro Tomás, Tomás. "The linguistic atlas of Spain and the Spanish in the Americas," in *American Council of Learned Societies Bulletin No. 34: Conference on Non-English Speech in the United States, Ann Arbor, Michigan, August 2-3, 1940,* Washington, D.C., 1942.

New York City Board of Education. *Interviewing parents and teachers in Spanish: a guide for school personnel.* New York, 1954.

Nichols, Madaline. *A bibliographical guide to materials on American Spanish.* Harvard University Press, Cambridge, 1941.

O'Brien, Mary Ross. A comparison of the reading ability of Spanish-speaking with non-Spanish-speaking pupils in grade 6A of the Denver Public Schools. MA thesis, University of Denver, 1937.

Ornstein, Jacob. "The archaic and the modern in the Spanish of New Mexico," *Hispania* 34, 1951. pp. 137-42.

_____. "Language varieties along the US-Mexican border," paper read at the 2nd International Congress of Applied Linguistics, Cambridge, England. 1972.

_____. "Mexican-American sociolinguistics: a well kept scholarly and public secret," paper presented at the 4th Triennial Conference of Symbolic Processes, Washington, D.C. April, 1972.

_____. "Sociolinguistic research on language diversity in the American Southwest and its educational implications," *Modern Language Journal* 55, 1971. pp. 223-29.

_____. "Sociolinguistics and new perspectives in the study of Southwest Spanish," in R. W. Ewton, Jr. and Jacob Ornstein, eds., *Studies in Language and Linguistics 1969-70.* pp. 127-84.

_____. Sociolinguistics and the study of Spanish and English language varieties and their use in the U.S. Southwest with a proposed plan for research: a state of the art paper. Southwest Cooperative Educational Laboratory, Albuquerque, New Mexico, 1971.

——. "Toward a classification of Southwest Spanish nonstandard variants," paper presented at the 32nd Summer Meeting of the Linguistic Society of America, 1970.

Ortiz, Carmelita Louise. English influences on the Spanish of Tampa. MA thesis, University of Florida, 1947.

——. "English influences on the Spanish of Tampa," *Hispania* 32, 1949. pp. 300-04.

Ott, Elizabeth. A study of levels of fluency and proficiency in oral English of Spanish-speaking school beginners. Ph.D. dissertation, University of Texas, Austin, 1967.

Page, Dorothy. Performance of Spanish-American children on verbal and non-verbal intelligence tests. MA thesis, University of New Mexico, 1931.

Palomares, Uvaldo and Laverne C. Johnson. "Evaluation of Mexican-American pupils for EMR classes," *California Education* 3, April 1955. pp. 27-29.

Paredes, Américo. "Folk medicine and the intercultural jest." In June Helm, ed., *Spanish-speaking People in the United States. Proceedings of the 1968 Annual Spring Meeting of the American Ethnological Society.* University of Washington Press, Seattle, 1968. pp. 104-19.

Patella, Victoria M. and William P. Kuvlesky. "Language patterns of Mexican Americans: are the ambitious un-Mexican?" paper presented at the Rural Sociological Society Meeting, Washington, D.C., August, 1970.

Patterson, Maurine. Some dialectical tendencies in popular Spanish in San Antonio [Texas]. MA thesis, Texas Woman's University, 1946.

Pearce, Thomas M. "The New Mexico place name dictionary," *Names* 6, 1958. pp. 217-55.

——. *New Mexico place names.* University of New Mexico Press, Albuquerque, 1965.

——. "Trader terms in southwestern English," *American Speech* 16, 1941. pp. 179-86.

Peña, Albar A. *A comparative study of selected syntactical structures of the oral language status in Spanish and English of disadvantaged first grade Spanish-speaking children.* University of Texas, Austin, 1967.

Peñalosa, Fernando. "Chicano multilingualism and multiglossia." ERIC Ed 056 590, n.d.

Penuelas, Marcelino C. *Lo español en el suroeste de los Estados Unidos.* Ediciones Cultura Hispánica, Madrid, 1964.

Phillips, Robert Nelson, Jr. "The influence of English on the /v/ in Los Angeles Spanish," in Ewton and Ornstein (1972). pp. 201-12.

——. Los Angeles Spanish: a descriptive analysis. Ph.D. dissertation, University of Wisconsin, 1967.

Porges, Ana E. The influence of English on the Spanish of New York. MA thesis, University of Florida, 1949.

Post, Anita. "Some aspects of Arizona Spanish," *Hispania* 16, 1933. pp. 35-42.

——. *Southern Arizona Spanish phonology.* (University of Arizona Bulletin 5, Humanities Bulletin 1.) University of Arizona, Tucson, 1934.

Poulter, Virgil L. "Comparison of voiceless stops in the English and Spanish of bilingual natives of Fort Worth-Dallas." In *Texas Studies in Bilingualism,* ed. Glenn G. Gilbert, Walter de Gruyter Co., Berlin, 1969. pp. 42-49.

Protheroe, Donald Wesley. The language used by children of constrasting socio-economic groups in tasks related to concept formation. Ph.D. dissertation, Wayne State University, 1967.

Rael, Juan B. "Associative interference in New Mexican Spanish," *Hispanic Review* 7, 1939. pp. 324-36.

_____. "Associative interference in Spanish," *Hispanic Review* 8, 1940. pp. 346-49.

_____. *"Cosa nada* en el español nuevomejicano," *Modern Language Notes* 49, 1934. pp. 31-32.

_____. A study of the phonology and morphology of New Mexican Spanish based on a collection of 410 folk tales. Ph.D. dissertation, Stanford University, 1937.

Ramírez, Carina. Lexical usage of and attitude toward Southwest Spanish in the Ysleta, Texas area. MA thesis, University of Texas-El Paso, 1971.

Ramírez, Manuel D. "Some semantic and linguistic notes on the Spanish spoken in Tampa, Florida," *Revista Inter-Americana* 1:1, 1939. pp. 25-33.

Ranson, Helen M. "'Manitos' and their language," *Hispania* 36, Aug. 1953. p. 310.

_____. "Viles Pochismos," *Hispania* 37, Sept. 1954, pp. 285-87.

Rapier, Jacqueline L. "Effects of verbal mediation upon the learning of Mexican-American children," *California Journal of Educational Research* 18:1, Jan. 1967. pp. 40-48.

Reynolds, Selma Fay. Some aspects of Spanish as spoken and written by Spanish speaking students of a junior high school in Texas. MA thesis, Texas State College for Women, 1945.

Richie, Eleanor L. "Spanish place names in Colorado," *American Speech* 10, 1935. pp. 88-92.

Richthofen, E. von. *The Spanish toponyms of the British Columbia coast, with sideglances at those of the States of Washington, Oregon and Alaska.* Ukranian Free Academy of Sciences, (Series Onomastica 26) 1963.

Rivera de Velásquez, M. Contrastive analysis of phonological systems of English and Puerto Rican Spanish with implications for second language teaching. Ph.D. dissertation, University of Indiana, 1964.

Rizzo, Gino L. "Lingua e costumi spagnoli in California ad un secolo dall' occupazione statunitense," *Quaderni Iberoamericani* 17, 1955. pp. 24-30.

Rodríguez, Darío E. "Some physiological and educational aspects of bilingualism," *Aztlán: Chicano Journal of the Social Sciences and the Arts* 2:1, Spring 1971. pp. 79-106.

Rogde, M. "Learning to speak English in the first grade," *Texas Outlook* 22, Sept. 1938. pp. 40-41.

Rosaldo, Renato. "El léxico como reflejo de la psicología del mexicano," *Hispania* 36, 1953. pp. 67-70.

Rosenberg, S. L. Millard. "Huellas de Espana en el estado de California," *Boletín de la Real Academia Española* 20, 1933. pp. 333-48.

_____. "Spain in modern California," *The Spanish Review* (New York) 1, 1934. pp. 195-99.

Rubel, Arthur J. "Some cultural aspects of learning English in Mexican American communities," in Kazamias, A. M. and E. H. Epstein, eds., *Schools in Transition: essays in comparative education.* Allyn and Bacon, Boston, 1968. pp. 370-82.

Sáez, Mercedes de los Angeles. Puerto Rican English phonotactics. Ph.D. dissertation, University of Texas, 1962.

Salado Alvarez, Victoriano. "Méjico peregrino: mejicanismos supervivientes en el inglés de Norte America," *Anales del Museo Nacional de Arqueología, Historia y Etnografía* 19, México, 1924. pp. 111-79.

Samora, Julian, Lyle Saunders and Richard Larson. "Medical vocabulary knowledge among hospital patients," *Journal of Health and Human Behavior* 2, Summer 1961. pp. 83-92.

Sánchez, A. M. "The Spanish-speaking child and the English language," *New Mexico Educational Association Journal and Proceedings,* 22nd Annual Meeting, 1947.

Sánchez, George I. "Bilingualism and mental measurement," *Journal of Applied Psychology* 18, Dec. 1934. pp. 765-72.

_____. "The implications of a basal vocabulary to the measurement of the abilities of bilingual children," *Journal of Social Psychology* 5, Aug. 1934. pp. 395-402.

_____. "Spanish in the Southwest," in *Summary of the Proceedings of the Southwest Conference on Social and Educational Problems of Rural and Urban Mexican-American Youth.* Occidental College, April 6, 1963.

_____. A study of the scores of Spanish-speaking children on repeated tests. MA thesis, University of Texas, 1931.

_____. and Charles L. Eastlack. *Say it the Spanish way.* The Good Neighbor Commission of Texas, Austin, 1960.

Sánchez, Nellie. *Spanish and Indian place names of California—their meaning and their romance.* A. M. Robertson Co., San Francisco, 1930.

Sawyer, Janet Beck Moseley. A dialect study of San Antonio, Texas: a bilingual community. Ph.D. dissertation, University of Texas, 1958.

_____. "Aloofness from Spanish influence in Texas English," *Word* 15, 1959. pp. 270-81.

_____. "Social aspects of bilingualism in San Antonio, Texas," *Publications of the American Dialect Society* 41, 1964. pp. 7-15.

_____. "The Speech of San Antonio, Texas," in Juanita V. Williamson and Virginia M. Burke (eds.): *A Various Language: Perspectives on American Dialects*, Holt, Rinehart and Winston, New York, 1971. pp. 570-82.

Sawyer, Jesse O. "The implications of Spanish /r/ and /rr/ in Wappo history," *Romance Philology* 18, 1964. pp. 165-77.

_____. "Wappo words from Spanish," *University of California Publications in Linguistics* 34, 1964. pp. 163-69.

Schaer, Bertha A. "A new language for Jose," *Texas Outlook*, Dec. 1966. pp. 32-33.

Scott, Carmen C. Spanish language maintenance and loyalty in El Paso-Juarez: a sociolinguistic study of the contact situation in a highly bilingual area. MA thesis, University of Texas, El Paso, 1969.

Sebeok, Thomas A., ed. *Current trends in linguistics IV: Ibero-American and Caribbean linguistics.* Mouton, The Hague, 1968.

Seris, Homero. Bibliografía de la lingüística española. *Publications del Instituto Caro y Cuervo* 19, 1964.

Shafer, Robert. "The pronunciation of Spanish place names in California," *American Speech* 17, 1942. pp. 239-46.

Sharp, John M. "The origin of some non-standard lexical items in the Spanish of El Paso," in R. W. Ewton, Jr. and Jacob Ornstein, eds., *Studies in Language and Linguistics 1969-1970.* Texas Western Press, El Paso, 1970. pp. 207-32.

Shipley, William. "Spanish elements in the indigenous languages of Central California," *Romance Philology* 16, 1962. pp. 1-21.

Shulman, David. "Some California contributions to the American vocabulary," *American Speech* 24, 1949. pp. 264-67.

Sinclair, John L. "Vaquero lingo," *New Mexico Magazine* 15, Dec. 1937. pp. 20-21, 38-39.

Smith, Alva Louis. A comparative study of facts and factors affecting and effecting the retardation of bi-lingual children. MA thesis, University of Texas, 1952.

Socrates, Hyacinth. "Southwestern slang," *The Overland Monthly* (San Francisco), 3, 1869.

Sola Pool, David de. "The use of Portuguese and Spanish in the historic Shearith Israel Congregation in New York," in *Studies in Honor of M. J. Benardete*. Las Américas, New York, 1965. pp. 359-62.

Solé, Carlos. *Bibliografía sobre el español en América, 1920-1967*. Georgetown University Press, Washington, D.C., 1970.

Sorvig, Ralph W. "Southern plant names from Spanish," *American Speech* 28, 1953. pp. 97-105.

_____. A topical analysis of Spanish loanwords in written American English of the American Southwest. Ph.D. dissertation, University of Denver, 1952.

Southwest Council of Foreign Language Teachers. *Our bilinguals: social and psychological barriers, linguistic and pedagogical barriers.* (Reports of the Second Annual Conference.) El Paso, 1965.

Spencer, Robert F. "Spanish loan words in Keresan," *Southwest Journal of Anthropology* 3, 1947. pp. 130-46.

Sprinkle, Eunice Caroline. A comparative study of the reading interests of Mexican and white children. MA thesis, University of Southern California, 1941.

Stewart, George R. "Two Spanish word lists from California," *American Speech* 16, 1941. pp. 260-69.

Stockwell, Robert P. and J. Donald Bowen. *The sounds of English and Spanish.* University of Chicago Press, Chicago and London, 1965.

_____, J. Donald Bowen, and John W. Martin. *The grammatical structures of English and Spanish.* University of Chicago Press, Chicago and London, 1965.

Taylor, Allan R. "Spanish *manteca* in Alaskan Eskimo," *Romance Philology* 16, 1962. pp. 30-32.

Teschner, Richard V. Anglicisms in Spanish: a cross-referenced guide to previous findings, together with English lexical influence on Chicago Mexican Spanish. Ph.D. dissertation, University of Wisconsin-Madison, 1972.

Tireman, Lloyd Spencer. *Spanish vocabulary of four Spanish-speaking pre-first-grade children.* University of New Mexico Press, Albuquerque, 1948.

_____and V. E. Woods. Aural and visual comprehension of English by Spanish-speaking children. *Elementary School Journal* 40, Sept.-June 1939-40. pp. 204-11.

Trager, George L. "The days of the week in the language of Taos Pueblo," *Language* 15, 1939. pp. 51-55.

_____. "Some Spanish place names in Colorado," *American Speech* 10, 1935, pp. 203-07.

———. "Spanish and English loanwords in Taos," *International Journal of American Linguistics* 10, 1944. pp. 144-58.

——— and Genevieve Valdez. "English loans in Colorado Spanish," *American Speech* 12, 1937. pp. 34-44.

Trejo, Arnulfo D. Vocablos y modismos del español de Arizona. Ph.D. dissertation, Mexico City College, 1951.

Trujillo, Luis M. Diccionario de español del Valle de San Luis de Colorado y del norte de Nuevo México. MA thesis, Adams State College, 1961.

Tsuzaki, Stanley Mamoru. English influences in the phonology and morphology of the Spanish spoken in the Mexican colony in Detroit, Michigan. Ph.D. dissertation, University of Michigan, 1963.

Ulibarrí, Horatio. "Language acquisition patterns," in *Interpretive Studies on Bilingual Education.* University of New Mexico, College of Education. U.S. Department of Health, Education and Welfare, March 1969.

Umphrey, G. W. and Emma Adetto. "Linguistic archaisms of the Seattle Sephardim," *Hispania* 19, 1936. pp. 255-264.

U.S. Bureau of the Census. *Mother tongue of the foreign-born White population.* (Fifteenth Census of the United States, vol. 2, chapter 7.) U.S. Government Printing Office, Washington, D.C. 1932.

———. *Nativity and parentage of the White population: mother tongue by nativity, parentage, country of origin, and age for States and large cities.* (Sixteenth census of the United States.) U.S. Government Printing Office, Washington, D.C., 1943.

———. *Population of Spanish monther tongue.* (Sixteenth census of the United States: 1940 population.) U.S. Government Printing Office, Washington, D.C., 1942.

U.S. Commission on Civil Rights. Congressional 'si' on bilingualism. *Civil Rights Digest*, Spring 1968, pp. 17-18.

Valdez, R. F. "The fallacy of the Spanish surname survey," *Journal of the California Teachers' Association* 65:3, May 1969. pp. 29-32.

Van de Grift Sanchez, N. *Spanish and Indian place names of California, their meaning and their romance.* San Francisco, 1914.

Vásquez-Arjona, Carlos. "Spanish and Spanish-American influences on Bret Harte," *Revue Hispanique* 76, 1929, pp. 573-621. (Vocabulary, pp. 617-21.)

Vincent, Henrietta H. A study of performance of Spanish-speaking pupils on Spanish tests. MA thesis, New Mexico State Teachers College, 1933.

Wagner, Henry R. *The Spanish Southwest, 1542-1794: an annotated bibliography.* Berkeley, California, 1924.

Wagner, Max Leopold. "Ein mexicanish-amerikanischer argot: das pachuco," *Romanistiches Jahrbuch* 6, 1953. pp. 237-66.

Ward, Hortense Warner. "Ear marks," *Texas Folklore Society Publications* 19, 1944. pp. 106-116.

Wolf, N. Standardization of a Spanish translation of the Davis-Eells Games (Elementary A) on Mexican-American children in the elementary schools in Los Angeles County. MA thesis, University of California at Los Angeles, 1955.

Wolff, H. "Partial comparison of the sound systems of English and Puerto Rican Spanish,"

Language Learning 3, 1950. pp. 38-40

Woodbridge, Hensley C. "Spanish in the American South and Southwest: a bibliographical survey for 1940-1953," *Orbis* 3, 1954. pp. 236-44.

Wooton, Elmer O. and Paul Carpenter Standley. *Flora of New Mexico.* Washington, 1915.